D1090318

Universal Jurisdiction

Pennsylvania Studies in Human Rights

Bert B. Lockwood, Jr., Series Editor

A complete list of books in the series is available from the publisher.

Universal Jurisdiction

National Courts and the Prosecution of
Serious Crimes under International Law

Edited by Stephen Macedo

PENN

University of Pennsylvania Press

Philadelphia

10   9   8   7   6   5   4   3   2   1

Published by

University of Pennsylvania Press
Philadelphia, Pennsylvania 19104-4011

Library of Congress Cataloging-in-Publication Data

Universal jurisdiction : national courts and the prosecution of serious crimes
under international law / edited by Stephen Macedo.
     p. cm.—(Pennsylvania studies in human rights)
   Includes bibliographical references and index.
   ISBN 0-8122-3736-6 (cloth : acid-free paper)
     1. Criminal jurisdiction. 2. International offenses. 3. Criminal courts.
I. Macedo, Stephen, 1957– II. Series.

K5036.U55 2003
345′.01—dc22

                                                          2003053378

Contents

Introduction

Stephen Macedo

When former Chilean dictator Augusto Pinochet was detained in London based on an extradition request from Spain, the world's attention was focused for the first time on the idea of universal jurisdiction. Holding former heads of state accountable for heinous acts committed while in office was not altogether new. The victors in armed conflicts have often initiated war crimes trials.[1] Likewise, nations emerging from dictatorships and civil wars have sometimes decided to put local oppressors on trial. But Pinochet fought on the winning side of the cold war. The government of Chile had enacted, moreover, an amnesty for all serious crimes committed during the harshest years of Pinochet's dictatorship. Upon his surrender of power, the former general and president had also been given immunity from prosecution as "Senator for Life."[2] Perhaps, in spite of all this, Pinochet deserved to stand trial. His immunity could be said to have been granted under duress: as a condition for handing over power. So maybe Pinochet should have been held accountable for his crimes. But what business was it of courts in Spain and Britain to decide these questions? How could Spanish and British judges—Judge Baltasar Garzón in Spain and a specially constituted Appellate Committee of the British House of Lords (which considered the Spanish extradition request)—presume to hold Pinochet legally accountable?

Equally sensational are recent efforts to hold Henry Kissinger legally accountable for actions he took while serving as national security advisor and secretary of state of the United States. Kissinger has in fact been sued in a U.S. court in connection with the assassination of Rene Schneider in Chile.[3] The popular American news program *60 Minutes* aired a program describing some of the charges against Kissinger. The journalist Christopher Hitchens argued for a much broader investigation of possible criminal responsibility on Kissinger's part: for various assassinations, the Cambodia bombing, and other matters. The suit that has been initiated against Kissinger is not based on universal jurisdiction, though future legal actions could be. If American prosecutors will not investigate, Hitchens argues that legal proceedings should be initiated in any competent national court based on universal jurisdiction.[4]

The envelope has been pushed still further by Belgium's highest court, which ruled on February 12, 2003, that Ariel Sharon, prime minister of Israel, could be tried for war crimes based on universal jurisdiction because of his alleged responsibility for atrocities committed against unarmed Palestinians by Lebanese Phalangists while he was minister of defense in the 1980s.[5] In 2001, survivors of massacres during 1982 at the Sabra and Shatilla refugee camps in Beirut filed criminal complaints in Belgium against Sharon and Amos Yaron, who were, respectively, defense minister and army chief of staff in 1982. Sharon was found indirectly responsible by an investigative commission in Israel, and he was forced to resign as defense minister as a result, but criminal charges were never filed. The new complaints are based on Belgium's 1993 law providing for universal jurisdiction over crimes against humanity and war crimes wherever they occur. In its February 2003 ruling, the Belgian high court said that the case against Sharon could not go forward so long as he enjoys the immunity that attaches to his office as prime minister (this is consistent with international law), but he could be subject to prosecution once out of office. Other cases in Belgium have been filed against Iraqi President Saddam Hussein, Palestinian Authority President Yassir Arafat, Rwandan President Paul Kigame, former Rwandan President Hissene Habre, and many others.[6]

When should national courts in Europe or elsewhere undertake legal proceedings based on the principle of universal jurisdiction? When if ever is this a legitimate and proper form of jurisdiction? It is, critics charge, one thing for courts in Cambodia or the U.S. or Israel or a Palestinian state (should one come into existence) to contemplate such prosecutions, but is it the business of courts in "third-party" states to take responsibility for these criminal prosecutions when others have failed to act?

Sensational cases—real and speculative—have helped put universal jurisdiction in the headlines. The glare of these cases could distort our view of what universal jurisdiction really amounts to in practice. In fact, while the legal proceedings against Pinochet in London provoked much discussion of universal jurisdiction, the Spanish courts could claim a direct connection with the alleged crimes due to the fact that Spaniards were among the victims of the Chilean dictatorship. A clear reliance on universal jurisdiction came to fruition in June 2001 when two Rwandan nuns were convicted by a Belgian jury for crimes committed in Rwanda against Rwandans. This first jury trial based on universal jurisdiction was partly a response to the frustrating paucity of resources and consequent limited capacities of the UN-sponsored International Criminal Tribunal for Rwanda. The prosecution and the verdict were widely hailed, even by such normally skeptical observers as the editorial page writers of the *Wall Street Journal*.[7]

Officials in Rwanda also applauded the verdict in Belgium. "It is highly positive that Belgium, a foreign country, pursues and punishes crimes against humanity committed in Rwanda," Rwandan justice minister Jean de Dieu Mucyo told the Reuters news agency, "[o]ther countries should follow this example."[8]

There is reason to worry that universal jurisdiction may, when not guided by proper standards and exercised wisely, be used to settle political scores and to interfere with matters properly within the sphere of legitimate self-governance. It would be wrong, however, to suggest that universal jurisdiction prosecutions will always or even typically be regarded as outside meddling. Rwandans welcomed the Belgian trial. After Pinochet was returned to Chile, for reasons of ill health, the "self-amnesty" that he had extracted as a condition of relinquishing power was rescinded. The legal proceedings against Pinochet in Spain and London provided Chileans with what turned out to be a welcome opportunity to revisit the crimes of the dictatorship (see, in particular, the essays below by Richard Falk and Pablo De Greiff). I will say a bit more about these worries later in this introduction.

As the following essays make clear, universal jurisdiction is not new. It has been provided for in a number of international conventions and in much national legislation. Universal jurisdiction is playing a growing role in the emerging regime of international accountability for serious crimes. The challenge is to define that role and to clarify when and how universal jurisdiction can be exercised responsibly.

Jurisdictional issues may seem at first to be legalistic and arcane, but they are of enormous political importance. To insist that certain acts should be regarded as serious crimes under international law is only the first step in bringing the accused to justice. The actual enforcement of violations of international criminal law presents enormous challenges. Who may legitimately decide to prosecute allegations of torture, war crimes, crimes against humanity, and other serious crimes under international law? These are often crimes of state: crimes committed by public officials claiming to be acting in an official capacity, to protect and preserve national security, or to punish enemies of the nation or the state. Persons accused of serious crimes under international law may try to evade arrest and prosecution by fleeing the jurisdiction where the crime was committed. The states in which heinous mass crimes occur are often subject to ongoing instability. Despots charged with crimes may hand power to compliant cronies or extort promises of immunity as the price of ceding authority. There are genuine questions, of course, about the compatibility and relative importance of accountability for political crimes in times of transition. For any number of reasons, therefore, the jurisdiction in which heinous crimes have been committed may be unable or unwilling to prosecute. If the courts of the nation in which the crimes were committed cannot or will not act, and if there is no effective international tribunal with competence to hear the relevant charges, when and under what conditions should the courts of some other state get involved?

Universal jurisdiction is the principle that certain crimes are so heinous, and so universally recognized and abhorred, that a state is entitled or even obliged to undertake legal proceedings without regard to where the crime was committed or the nationality of the perpetrators or the victims.[9] It applies to the most serious crimes under international law: slavery, war crimes, crimes against humanity, torture, and some others. Universal jurisdiction appears as a potent weapon: it would cast all the world's courts as a net to catch alleged perpetrators of serious crimes under international law. It holds the promise of a system of global accountability—justice without borders—administered by the competent courts of all nations on behalf of humankind.

In spite of its growing importance, and its even greater potential as a tool of accountability, universal jurisdiction is not widely understood. There are, moreover, no clear principles of international law to help guide the use of universal jurisdiction and to help thoughtful observers decide when its use is justified. This volume and the larger project of which it is a part are designed to help dissipate some of the mystery: the essays gathered here aim to clarify the origins of the principle of universal jurisdiction, its role in famous and not-so-famous cases, the legal arrangements being put in place to support it, and the problems and issues surrounding its future role in the international legal order. This volume is one product of the Princeton Project on Universal Jurisdiction, an international collaboration among scholars and jurists that has been under way at Princeton University since January 2000. These essays are exercises in "engaged" scholarship: they attempt not simply to clarify universal jurisdiction but also to establish its appropriate place in an emerging regime of international legal accountability.

The essays that make up the bulk of the volume are one part of the Princeton Project. Equally important, if considerably shorter, are the Princeton Principles on Universal Jurisdiction, which immediately follow this introduction. A distinguished group of jurists and scholars from around the world gathered in Princeton in January 2001 to formulate these consensus principles in the hope of helping to guide the future development of international law. That distinguished group of participants—listed at the end of this volume—debated, refined, and in due course endorsed the Principles (with one dissent).

The Princeton Principles, and the essays gathered here, attempt to address some of the basic questions—both political and legal—that surround universal jurisdiction: when and how may national courts, in states with no direct connection with the victims or the perpetrators of serious crimes under international law, properly take responsibility for holding accused persons accountable? Against which crimes should it be exercised, and according to what legal standards? When, if ever, should criminal prosecution be deferred out of respect for the immunities that traditionally attach to office, or based on amnesties that have been granted as part of a peace settlement, or in order to negotiate a transition toward democratic rule? When should extradition requests based on universal jurisdiction be honored? Can common standards be articulated, in our complex world, to help guide these decisions and others? Our aim is to examine universal jurisdiction as a legal concept and as part of a wider set of political and legal movements to expand legal accountability and the global rule of law, and thereby to end impunity for serious crimes under international law.

The Principles are a set of guidelines or standards for the development and use of universal jurisdiction. They were announced on July 23, 2001, and have since received attention and support. We reprint, in the section following this introduction, the Principles and supporting materials in their original form. These materials have been translated into five languages and distributed as a document of the General Assembly of the United Nations, as *The Princeton Principles on Universal Jurisdiction.*[10] The following essays offer intellectual foundations for the principled guidelines embodied in the Princeton Principles. Whether or not they attract a consensus, we hope that these essays and the Principles contribute to a better understanding of universal jurisdiction's role in international justice.

Universal jurisdiction and the questions that surround it are of growing importance. There is, for one thing, a growing determination that grave international crimes must not go unaddressed, much less unpunished. Dramatic evidence of this determination includes the establishment of ad hoc international tribunals to prosecute crimes committed in Rwanda and the former Yugoslavia. The world's attention has been riveted by the spectacle of Slobodan Milosovic in the criminal dock in The Hague. In addition, and to the surprise of many, the decades-long effort to create an International Criminal Court (ICC) came to fruition on July 1, 2002. The existence of an International Criminal Court might seem to obviate the need for universal jurisdiction, but the opposite is true. The jurisdiction of the ICC is complementary to national courts.[11] As former UN high commissioner for human rights Mary Robinson argues in the preface to the Princeton Principles, prosecutions in international courts "will never be sufficient to achieve justice." For the foreseeable future, international courts—like the tribunals dealing with crimes in the former Yugoslavia and Rwanda—face daunting challenges with very limited resources. The resources of the ICC will always be limited. The successful trial of the Rwandan nuns in Belgium is but one proof that ordinary national courts will play a crucial role in the emerging system of international accountability. As A. Hays Butler explains in his essay, below, in the process of ratifying the statute to create an International Criminal Court, increasing numbers of legislatures around the world have provided for the exercise of universal jurisdiction as a complementary alternative for the prosecution of serious crimes under international law. In an ideal world, it would often be preferable to prosecute crimes under international law in an international tribunal established by the UN Security Council or, better still, in the International Criminal Court. The ICC provides elaborate procedural protections worked out on the basis of a broad international consensus. We are, however, a long way from a world in which the ICC has the resources and support (notably from the US) that it needs to function effectively as an antidote to impunity.

The Principles are quite brief. They seek to clarify universal jurisdiction and specify some of the serious crimes to which it applies (including piracy, slavery, war crimes, crimes against humanity, genocide, and torture—the list is not exhaustive). The Principles affirm that states have an obligation to prosecute or extradite those accused of committing such serious crimes. There should be no statute of limitations on the prosecution of these crimes, according to the Principles, and blanket amnesties generally are inconsistent with a nation's obligation to hold individuals accountable for the crimes.[12]

In the lively debates at Princeton University in January 2001, questions were raised about whether the Principles go too far, or not far enough, in providing for criminal accountability. At the end of the day, one of the participants—and only one—decided not to endorse the Princeton Principles. Nicolas Browne-Wilkinson, a member of the House of Lords of the United Kingdom and the senior law lord who wrote the lead opinion for the House of Lords allowing for Pinochet's extradition to Spain, filed the following dissent from the views he believed were expressed in the Princeton Principles:

I am strongly in favour of universal jurisdiction over serious international crimes if, by those words, one means the exercise by an international court or by the courts of one state of jurisdiction over the nationals of another state with the prior consent of that latter state, i.e. in cases such as the ICC and Torture Convention. But the Princeton Principles propose that individual national courts should exercise such jurisdiction against nationals of a state which has not agreed to such jurisdiction. Moreover the Principles do not recognize any form of sovereign immunity: Principle 5(1). If the law were to be so established, states antipathetic to Western powers would be likely to seize both active and retired officials and military personnel of such Western powers and stage a show trial for alleged international crimes. Conversely, zealots in Western States might launch prosecutions against, for example, Islamic extremists for their terrorist activities. It is naïve to think that, in such cases, the national state of the accused would stand by and watch the trial proceed: resort to force would be more probable. In any event the fear of such legal actions would inhibit the use of peacekeeping forces when it is otherwise desirable and also the free interchange of diplomatic personnel. I believe that the adoption of such universal jurisdiction without preserving the existing concepts of immunity would be more likely to damage than to advance chances of international peace.[13]

The Principles do acknowledge, however, the possible danger of abusive and disruptive prosecutions. If it is important to extend accountability for serious crimes under international law, it is equally important to ensure that accused persons are held accountable according to the rule of law. The Principles insist on international norms of due process and assert the importance of various legal safeguards for the accused, including the prohibition on double jeopardy. The rights of the accused must be protected, proceedings must be fair, and the independence and impartiality of the judiciary must be respected. The Principles assert that states should refuse to extradite accused persons who are liable to be subject to sham proceedings with no assurance of due process, or torture, or "any other cruel, degrading, or inhuman punishment," or the death penalty.[14]

The Principles do not take a stand on particular cases: they are general guidelines and standards. Having already mentioned the anxieties that have arisen with respect to the possible prosecution of the prime minister of Israel and in light of the aforementioned reservations of Lord Browne-Wilkinson, I should emphasize that the Principles acknowledge that under current international law, sitting heads of state, other public officials, and accredited diplomats cannot be prosecuted while in office for acts committed in their official capacity: the language of the Princeton Principles is such as to acknowledge the existence of these temporary (or "procedural") immunities under international law as it currently stands (see Principle 5 and the following commentary to the Principles). Once out of office, however, former heads of state or other officials are not immune from prosecution for the most serious crimes under international law, such as genocide, torture, war crimes, and crimes against humanity. On this difficult question of who should be prosecuted and when, the Principles in effect acknowledge the existence of temporary immunities in current international law but do not affirm them as a matter of basic principle.

The issue of immunities from prosecution for heads of state, accredited diplomats, and other office holders, is a vexed area of international law where there is room for further reflection and growth. The contending opinions that accompany the decision by the International Court of Justice in *Democratic Republic of Congo v Belgium* amply illustrate the difficult questions raised by the problem of immunities.[15]

The brief commentary, which follows the Principles, should help clarify some questions.

A clear view of the origins, nature, and promise of universal jurisdiction could easily be obscured by the intense glare surrounding famous cases; therefore, the scope of the essays that compose the bulk of this volume is quite broad.

The first two essays describe the history and growing acceptance of universal jurisdiction as a tool of international law. M. Cherif Bassiouni traces the origins of universal jurisdiction: its place in the writings of early modern jurists, its early role as a response to piracy, and its affirmation in various treaties, conventions, and statutes. Bassiouni acknowledges that the Princeton Principles are a progressive gloss on practice: universal jurisdiction is not as well established in international law as some human rights organizations and others have claimed. Bassiouni supports the cautious approach of the Princeton Principles: states should do far more than they have done to support accountability in national courts, but for the time being, universal jurisdiction should be reserved for the most heinous crimes. Stephen A. Oxman adds a brief comment emphasizing the importance of clarity with respect to the core meaning of universal jurisdiction in the absence of other jurisdictional bases for prosecuting. A. Hays Butler describes the growing trend toward national legislation in support of universal jurisdiction. The surprising culmination of the ratification process of the Rome Statute establishing an International Criminal Court has encouraged increasing numbers of states to provide their national courts with universal jurisdiction so these courts may be effective complements to the ICC.

The next three essays explore the limited but significant role of universal jurisdiction in two famous cases and one abortive attempt to prosecute. The trial of Adolph Eichman and the legal proceedings against Augusto Pinochet raise questions that are relevant to the wider project of expanding accountability under international law, though neither exemplified a prosecution based squarely on universal jurisdiction.

Gary J. Bass argues that the trial of Eichmann in Israel reveals certain tensions inherent in the exercise of universal jurisdiction: especially the interplay of universal and more particular interests in the prosecution of crimes. At Nuremberg, Nazis stood trial for crimes against humanity, whereas in Jerusalem, Eichmann was tried under an Israeli statute making "crimes against the Jewish people" a capital offense. Very often, Bass insists, states are liable to want some particular interest in, or connection with, a given set of crimes in order to undertake the politically costly process of prosecution. Nevertheless, Bass insists that the universal horror and outrage of the Nazi acts played a crucial role in the Israeli prosecution: Eichmann was convicted for crimes against the Jewish people and for crimes against humanity. Lori F. Damrosch adds a comment on Bass that raises the question of which crimes should be covered by universal jurisdiction: she suggests reasons for a flexible conception of the serious crimes that should be covered. She also questions the permissibility of abductions, such as occurred as a prelude to the Eichmann case.

Richard A. Falk argues, similarly, that even if universal jurisdiction did not form a part of the narrow legal ground on which the House of Lords held that Pinochet could be extradited to Spain, universal jurisdiction nevertheless played an important role in helping to legitimize the proceedings against Pinochet. The Pinochet litigation also raised important questions relevant to future exercises of universal jurisdiction: did the legal proceedings in Britain and Spain flaunt Chilean sovereignty, or manifest inadequate respect for constitutional democracy in Chile? How should foreign governments and courts contemplating such prosecutions take account of the purported threats to peace or democratic stability if an agreed policy of impunity is overturned? Did the rejection of Pinochet's immunity from prosecution damage the political and legal climate in Chile? Pablo De Greiff's comment discusses the tradeoff between amnesties and criminal prosecutions in eras of transition to democracy. He emphasizes that the Chilean Truth and Reconciliation Commission operated under some severe restraints, including a constitution shaped by Pinochet. An Amnesty Law delayed the chance for Chilean democracy to come fully to grips with the horrors of the dictatorship, but De Greiff emphasizes that difficult circumstances can force at least temporary compromises with respect to the pursuit of justice.

Stephen P. Marks describes the abortive attempt to bring Chadian dictator Hissène Habré to justice in Senegal on the basis of universal jurisdiction. Marks's wide-ranging essay considers the legal grounds for proceeding against Habré, in what was hailed as the first case based on "the Pinochet precedent." He recounts the long campaign to build a case against Habré and to bring him to justice, including the role of human rights groups, other non-governmental organizations (NGOs), and victims' organizations. Marks argues that Habré's prosecution in Senegal based on universality was clearly justified: it could have provided "a degree of retributive and corrective justice for the voiceless victims of mass atrocities" in Chad. The failure to prosecute reinforced impunity for ex-heads of state who have committed heinous acts.

Our next three essays provide valuable analytic perspectives. Universal jurisdiction gives all states with competent judiciaries the power to prosecute heinous crimes: the presence of the accused is enough; the prosecuting state no longer needs any particular connection to the alleged perpetrators or victims. Anne-Marie Slaughter considers the question of how domestic court judges will in practice define and limit universal jurisdiction. Echoing a distinction made in Bassiouni's essay, Slaughter describes two different accounts of the reasons for universal jurisdiction. One emphasizes the heinous nature of the crimes and the fact of universal abhorrence; the other emphasizes the pragmatic or practical need to allow any nation to prosecute certain crimes that may or may not be especially heinous. Piracy, for example, is not an especially heinous crime, but pirates are a nuisance to all and their offenses occur on the high seas. The first rationale for universal jurisdiction—international morality—tends to trace the sources of universal jurisdiction to international law. The second rationale—international convenience—tends to trace universal jurisdiction to sources in domestic or national law. Slaughter describes the distinct problems to which each account gives rise, and she provides a more satisfactory hybrid account, one that emphasizes the interactions between domestic and international law, and communication among domestic courts and international legal institutions and experts.

Leila Nadya Sadat considers the relationship between criminal prosecutions on the basis of universal jurisdiction and various alternatives to prosecution, including amnesties and truth commissions. If legal prosecution of those alleged to have committed serious crimes serves the cause of justice, must the pursuit of justice nevertheless sometimes give way to measures designed to dampen, and leave behind the horrors of past civil conflict? Sadat argues that, in general, truth commissions, lustration laws, and reparations should be seen as complements to, not substitutes for, legal accountability for those accused of serious crimes under international law. Truth commissions have often functioned as precursors to individualized criminal accountability, and that is proper. Blanket amnesties for past criminal deeds are most often self-serving government declarations that undermine the authority of the law itself and should not be honored. If beneficiaries of an amnesty travel abroad, they may properly forfeit the impunity they were granted at home.

Diane F. Orentlicher analyzes the relationship between the recent expansion of universal jurisdiction and the growth of other mechanisms to enforce accountability, including the move to establish an International Criminal Court, the establishment of various ad hoc tribunals, and tribunals that contain a mix of national and international elements (such as those in Sierra Leone and being planned for Cambodia). Like Slaughter, in her use of the term "transjudicial communication," Orentlicher emphasizes the importance of "transjurisdictional communication" and also the role of NGOs in facilitating this communication. She describes the dynamic interactions among national and international courts and reflects on the problems that may attend future efforts to balance competing jurisdictional claims among these various courts.

Michael Kirby, justice of the High Court of Australia, examines the novelty of universal jurisdiction from the point of view of a common law judge. Kirby describes and analyzes the many factors that encourage common law judges to react cautiously to legal novelty in general and to universal jurisdiction in particular. He warns of the dangers of legal formalism and conservatism but also asserts that typical judges are likely to resist allowing their own jurisdictions to become safe havens for persons accused of gross offenses. Kirby approvingly cites examples of ways in which international covenants on human rights have helped shape domestic law in Australia and elsewhere, even, recently, the United States. Drawing on many of the essays that precede his in this volume, Kirby argues that common law judges may find grounds for asserting universal jurisdiction over some crimes under international law. Kirby's essay might be read as, at least in part, an extended reflection on the dissenting remarks by Nicolas Brown-Wilkinson, quoted in full above.

Finally, Lloyd Axworthy, former foreign minister of Canada, offers a unique perspective on the political struggles behind Canadian efforts to prosecute suspected World War II–era criminals and that nation's leading role in helping to establish the International Criminal Court. Reaffirming an observation also made in the essay by Butler, Axworthy emphasizes that the act of ratifying the Rome Statute to create the ICC gave Canadians the chance to reexamine domestic law in order to provide a clearer and more comprehensive basis for universal jurisdiction. He argues that the complementarity principle of the International Criminal Court helped reassure Canadians that their national sovereignty would be preserved by giving Canadian national courts the first opportunity to try any Canadian accused of crimes within the ICC's jurisdiction. He concludes by suggesting that the horrible events of September 11 make the extension of international criminal accountability even more imperative, so that there should be no safe harbor for terrorists.

Universal jurisdiction is one instrument that can be used to hold individuals accountable for the most serious crimes under international law. As things stand, universal jurisdiction is understood poorly and liable to being exercised haphazardly. Of course, responsible observers must acknowledge the possibility of abuse. Rogue states might use it to harass political opponents from abroad. Powerful states might invoke it to prosecute foreign tyrants while treating homegrown war criminals with impunity. There is a danger even when well-meaning states, intent on justice, deploy universal jurisdiction based on idiosyncratic standards rather than common norms. Conflicting standards and competing jurisdictional claims could lead to real conflict. The development of an international rule of law could be delayed or at least temporarily derailed by the absence of widely understood and accepted legal standards. The currently incoherent jurisprudence of universal jurisdiction is likely to result in confusion and, at best, uneven justice—hence the need for widely accepted norms such as the Princeton Principles.

Universal jurisdiction encourages every competent court to represent the world community and to be prepared to prosecute those accused of perpetrating the most heinous crimes, wherever those crimes were committed and whoever was the victim. This could be a progressive development of vast importance in international justice. But for that aspiration to be realized, we must begin to generate shared legal standards to support and give practical structure to our principled political aspirations to greater justice. The Princeton Project on Universal Jurisdiction and the supporting papers gathered here are meant to be a contribution toward the promotion of accountability and justice under the rule of law. These Principles and papers will not, and are not intended to, end the many controversies that surround universal jurisdiction. I do hope that they clarify what universal jurisdiction is and how its reasonable and responsible exercise by national courts can promote greater justice for victims of serious crimes under international law.

Part I
The Princeton Principles

Preface

Mary Robinson, United Nations High
Commissioner for Human Rights (1997–2002)

The subject of universal jurisdiction is of great relevance to all who work for
human rights. I regard the search for ways to end impunity in the case of gross
violations of human rights as an essential part of the work of my Office, and
an essential instrument in the struggle to defend human rights. I welcome
the initiative of the Princeton Project and trust that the wide dissemination
of these Principles will play a positive role in developing and clarifying the
principle of universal jurisdiction.

In my daily work as high commissioner for human rights I see many situations involving gross, and sometimes widespread, human rights abuses
for which the perpetrators often go unpunished. Torture, war crimes—
including abuses involving gender-based violence—and enforced disappearances are but a few of these crimes. The recent increase in transnational criminal activity, encouraged by globalization and open borders, has
added to the challenges we face in fighting against impunity for such
abuses. Trafficking of persons, and of women and children specifically, is an
issue of particular concern to my Office. These disturbing trends have given
me cause to reflect on the possibilities for alternative means of securing
justice and accountability.

Two important and complementary means currently exist for the implementation of international criminal jurisdiction: prosecution by international criminal tribunals and the domestic application of the principle of
universal jurisdiction. As far as the former is concerned, I am encouraged
by the increasing number of states that are signing and ratifying the Statute of the International Criminal Court, and I hope that this permanent
Court will soon be a reality. Even before the Court's establishment, the ICC
Statute has proved an invaluable tool in the struggle against impunity. The
Statute codifies crimes against humanity for the first time in a multilateral
treaty, and it enumerates certain acts as war crimes when committed in non-
international armed conflicts.

Through its cornerstone principle of complementarity, the ICC Statute highlights the fact that international prosecutions alone will never be sufficient to achieve justice and emphasizes the crucial role of national legal systems in bringing an end to impunity. The sad reality is that territorial states often fail to investigate and prosecute serious human rights abuses. The application of universal jurisdiction is therefore a crucial means of justice.

The principle of universal jurisdiction is based on the notion that certain crimes are so harmful to international interests that states are entitled— and even obliged—to bring proceedings against the perpetrator, regardless of the location of the crime or the nationality of the perpetrator or the victim. Human rights abuses widely considered to be subject to universal jurisdiction include genocide, crimes against humanity, war crimes, and torture. While the principle of universal jurisdiction has long existed for these crimes, however, it is rapidly evolving as a result of significant recent developments. I applaud the fact that the Princeton Principles acknowledge that this doctrine continues to develop in law and in practice.

One aspect which might be mentioned is the application of universal jurisdiction to other offenses in international law, since this has been raised recently in various fora. The UN Declaration on the Protection of all Persons from Enforced Disappearances, for example, provides for the exercise of universal jurisdiction for alleged acts of forced disappearances, a vision already contained at the regional level in the Inter-American Convention on Forced Disappearance of Persons. The international community is currently also considering a draft international convention on the protection of all persons from enforced disappearance.

Universal jurisdiction was discussed recently at the symposium on the challenge of borderless cyber-crime to international efforts to combat transnational organized crime, held in conjunction with the signing conference for the UN Convention against Transnational Organized Crime in Palermo, Italy. Discussions in treaty negotiations have raised the question of allowing civil jurisdiction for conduct which constitutes an international crime, in the context of the draft Hague Conference on Jurisdiction and Foreign Judgments in Civil and Commercial Matters. These negotiations are of concern to my Office, as they may have important implications regarding the access to courts for victims seeking remedies for human rights violations. The International Court of Justice is also considering issues related to universal jurisdiction in the ongoing case concerning the arrest warrant against the former Minister for Foreign Affairs of the Democratic Republic of Congo by a Belgian investigating judge, who was seeking his provisional detention for alleged serious violations of international humanitarian law.

These developments suggest that new ground is being broken with regard to the application of the principle of universal jurisdiction. This is not to say, however, that the exercise of universal jurisdiction is an easy matter. There are significant practical and legal challenges regarding the application of this principle. The obstacles faced by universal jurisdiction were recently elaborated by the International Law Association in its very informative report on the subject.

Obstacles to the exercise of universal jurisdiction include the question of the application of sovereign immunity defenses. In this regard, the decision of the British House of Lords in the Pinochet case confirming that former heads of state do not enjoy immunity for the crime of torture under UK law was refreshing and, along with other recent cases, has seriously challenged the notion of immunity from criminal liability for crimes under international law committed in an official capacity.

An additional area that I am particularly concerned about is the issue of amnesty laws. I stress that certain gross violations of human rights and international humanitarian law should not be subject to amnesties. When the United Nations faced the question of signing the Sierra Leone Peace Agreement to end atrocities in that country, the UN specified that the amnesty and pardon provisions in Article IX of the agreement would not apply to international crimes of genocide, crimes against humanity, war crimes, and other serious violations of international humanitarian law. We must be cautious not to send the wrong message regarding amnesties for serious violations of human rights and international humanitarian law, and I believe that the Princeton Principles correctly express the position that certain crimes are too heinous to go unpunished.

The exercise of universal jurisdiction holds the promise for greater justice for the victims of serious human rights violations around the world. My Office will continue to monitor developments in this rapidly evolving area, including the ongoing efforts of the Princeton Project to strengthen universal jurisdiction as a tool to end impunity. I encourage the wide dissemination of the Princeton Principles on Universal Jurisdiction.

The Princeton Principles on Universal Jurisdiction

The Challenge

During the last century, millions of human beings perished as a result of genocide, crimes against humanity, war crimes, and other serious crimes under international law. Perpetrators deserving of prosecution have only rarely been held accountable. To stop this cycle of violence and to promote justice, impunity for the commission of serious crimes must yield to accountability. But how can this be done, and what will be the respective roles of national courts and international tribunals?

National courts administer systems of criminal law designed to provide justice for victims and due process for accused persons. A nation's courts exercise jurisdiction over crimes committed in its territory and proceed against those crimes committed abroad by its nationals, or against its nationals, or against its national interests. When these and other connections are absent, national courts may nevertheless exercise jurisdiction under international law over crimes of such exceptional gravity that they affect the fundamental interests of the international community as a whole. This is universal jurisdiction: it is jurisdiction based solely on the nature of the crime. National courts can exercise universal jurisdiction to prosecute and punish, and thereby deter, heinous acts recognized as serious crimes under international law. When national courts exercise universal jurisdiction appropriately, in accordance with internationally recognized standards of due process, they act to vindicate not merely their own interests and values but the basic interests and values common to the international community.

Universal jurisdiction holds out the promise of greater justice, but the jurisprudence of universal jurisdiction is disparate, disjointed, and poorly understood. So long as that is so, this weapon against impunity is potentially beset by incoherence, confusion, and, at times, uneven justice.

International criminal tribunals also have a vital role to play in combating impunity as a complement to national courts. In the wake of mass atrocities and of oppressive rule, national judicial systems have often been unable or unwilling to prosecute serious crimes under international law, so international criminal tribunals have been established. Treaties entered into in the aftermath of World War II have strengthened international institutions, and have given greater clarity and force to international criminal law. A signal achievement of this long historic process occurred at a United Nations Conference in July 1998 when the Rome Statute of the International Criminal Court was adopted. When this permanent court becomes effective, the international community will acquire an unprecedented opportunity to hold accountable some of those accused of serious crimes under international law. The jurisdiction of the International Criminal Court will, however, be available only if justice cannot be done at the national level. The primary burden of prosecuting the alleged perpetrators of these crimes will continue to reside with national legal systems.

Enhancing the proper exercise of universal jurisdiction by national courts will help close the gap in law enforcement that has favored perpetrators of serious crimes under international law. Fashioning clearer and sounder principles to guide the exercise of universal jurisdiction by national courts should help to punish, and thereby to deter and prevent, the commission of these heinous crimes. Nevertheless, the aim of sound principles cannot be simply to facilitate the speediest exercise of criminal jurisdiction, always and everywhere, and irrespective of circumstances. Improper exercises of criminal jurisdiction, including universal jurisdiction, may be used merely to harass political opponents, or for aims extraneous to criminal justice. Moreover, the imprudent or untimely exercise of universal jurisdiction could disrupt the quest for peace and national reconciliation in nations struggling to recover from violent conflict or political oppression. Prudence and good judgment are required here, as elsewhere in politics and law.

What is needed are principles to guide, as well as to give greater coherence and legitimacy to, the exercise of universal jurisdiction. These principles should promote greater accountability for perpetrators of serious crimes under international law, in ways consistent with a prudent concern for the abuse of power and a reasonable solicitude for the quest for peace.

The Princeton Project

The Princeton Project on Universal Jurisdiction has been formed to contribute to the ongoing development of universal jurisdiction. The Project is sponsored by Princeton University's Program in Law and Public Affairs and the Woodrow Wilson School of Public and International Affairs, the International Commission of Jurists, the American Association for the International Commission of Jurists, the Urban Morgan Institute for Human Rights, and the Netherlands Institute of Human Rights. The Project convened at Princeton University in January 2001 an assembly of scholars and jurists from around the world, serving in their personal capacities, to develop consensus principles on universal jurisdiction.[1]

This assembly of scholars and jurists represented a diversity of viewpoints and a variety of legal systems. They are, however, united in their desire to promote greater legal accountability for those accused of committing serious crimes under international law.

The Project benefited from the indispensable efforts of leading scholars whom it had commissioned to write working papers on various aspects of universal jurisdiction and who gathered in Princeton in November 2000 to discuss these papers and an early draft of these Principles.

On January 27, 2001, those assembled at Princeton University to participate in the Princeton Project on Universal Jurisdiction, after considerable and thoughtful debate, arrived at a final text. Each participant might have chosen different words to restate existing international law and to identify the aspirations implicit in international law, but in the end the Principles were adopted.[2]

The development and adoption of these Principles is part of an ongoing process taking place in different countries and involving scholars, researchers, government experts, international organizations, and other members of international civil society. Those involved in these efforts share the goals of advancing international criminal justice and human rights.

These Principles on Universal Jurisdiction are intended to be useful to legislators seeking to ensure that national laws conform to international law, to judges called upon to interpret and apply international law and to consider whether national law conforms to their state's international legal obligations, to government officials of all kinds exercising their powers under both national and international law, to nongovernmental organizations and members of civil society active in the promotion of international criminal justice and human rights, and to citizens who wish to better understand what international law is and what the international legal order might become.

The assembly is as mindful of the importance of universal jurisdiction as it is of the potential dangers of the abusive or vexatious exercise of criminal jurisdiction, including universal jurisdiction. It has therefore reaffirmed throughout the Principles legal and judicial safeguards to help deter potential abuses. These safeguards established in international due process norms to protect persons accused of crimes are especially important in the case of a person facing prosecution, based solely on universal jurisdiction, in a state that is not that person's state of nationality or residence.

Furthermore, the assembly recognizes that a scarcity of resources, time, and attention may impose practical limitations on the quest for perfect justice, and that societies emerging from conflict must sometimes allocate priorities among initiatives that contribute to a just and lasting peace, including accountability for international crimes. Moreover, the assembly acknowledges that a range of reasonable disagreement sometimes exists within societies and among societies about the culpability of alleged criminals, the good faith of prosecutions, and the wisdom and practicality of pursuing alleged perpetrators. For these reasons, universal jurisdiction should be exercised with prudence and in a way that ensures the application of the highest standards of prosecutorial fairness and of judicial independence, impartiality, and fairness.

The assembly commends these Principles to states in the belief that their implementation will promote justice, reinforce the rule of law, and advance the other values and goals described above.

The Princeton Principles on Universal Jurisdiction

The participants in the Princeton Project on Universal Jurisdiction propose the following principles for the purposes of advancing the continued evolution of international law and the application of international law in national legal systems:

PRINCIPLE 1 — FUNDAMENTALS OF UNIVERSAL JURISDICTION

1. For purposes of these Principles, universal jurisdiction is criminal jurisdiction based solely on the nature of the crime, without regard to where the crime was committed, the nationality of the alleged or convicted perpetrator, the nationality of the victim, or any other connection to the state exercising such jurisdiction.
2. Universal jurisdiction may be exercised by a competent and ordinary judicial body of any state in order to try a person duly accused of committing serious crimes under international law as specified in Principle 2(1), provided the person is present before such judicial body.
3. A state may rely on universal jurisdiction as a basis for seeking the extradition of a person accused or convicted of committing a serious crime under international law as specified in Principle 2(1), provided that it has established a prima facie case of the person's guilt and that the person sought to be extradited will be tried or the punishment carried out in accordance with international norms and standards on the protection of human rights in the context of criminal proceedings.
4. In exercising universal jurisdiction or in relying upon universal jurisdiction as a basis for seeking extradition, a state and its judicial organs shall observe international due process norms including but not limited to those involving the rights of the accused and victims, the fairness of the proceedings, and the independence and impartiality of the judiciary (hereinafter referred to as "international due process norms").
5. A state shall exercise universal jurisdiction in good faith and in accordance with its rights and obligations under international law.

PRINCIPLE 2—SERIOUS CRIMES UNDER INTERNATIONAL LAW

1. For purposes of these Principles, serious crimes under international law include: (1) piracy; (2) slavery; (3) war crimes; (4) crimes against peace; (5) crimes against humanity; (6) genocide; and (7) torture.
2. The application of universal jurisdiction to the crimes listed in paragraph 1 is without prejudice to the application of universal jurisdiction to other crimes under international law.

PRINCIPLE 3—RELIANCE ON UNIVERSAL JURISDICTION IN THE ABSENCE OF NATIONAL LEGISLATION

With respect to serious crimes under international law as specified in Principle 2(1), national judicial organs may rely on universal jurisdiction even if their national legislation does not specifically provide for it.

PRINCIPLE 4—OBLIGATION TO SUPPORT ACCOUNTABILITY

1. A state shall comply with all international obligations that are applicable to: prosecuting or extraditing persons accused or convicted of crimes under international law in accordance with a legal process that complies with international due process norms, providing other states investigating or prosecuting such crimes with all available means of administrative and judicial assistance, and undertaking such other necessary and appropriate measures as are consistent with international norms and standards.
2. A state, in the exercise of universal jurisdiction, may, for purposes of prosecution, seek judicial assistance to obtain evidence from another state, provided that the requesting state has a good faith basis and that the evidence sought will be used in accordance with international due process norms.

PRINCIPLE 5—IMMUNITIES

With respect to serious crimes under international law as specified in Principle 2(1), the official position of any accused person, whether as head of state or government or as a responsible government official, shall not relieve such person of criminal responsibility nor mitigate punishment.

PRINCIPLE 6—STATUTES OF LIMITATIONS

Statutes of limitations or other forms of prescription shall not apply to serious crimes under international law as specified in Principle 2(1).

PRINCIPLE 7—AMNESTIES

1. Amnesties are generally inconsistent with the obligation of states to provide accountability for serious crimes under international law as specified in Principle 2(1).

2. The exercise of universal jurisdiction with respect to serious crimes under international law as specified in Principle 2(1) shall not be precluded by amnesties which are incompatible with the international legal obligations of the granting state.

PRINCIPLE 8 — RESOLUTION OF COMPETING NATIONAL JURISDICTIONS
Where more than one state has or may assert jurisdiction over a person and where the state that has custody of the person has no basis for jurisdiction other than the principle of universality, that state or its judicial organs shall, in deciding whether to prosecute or extradite, base their decision on an aggregate balance of the following criteria:
  (a) multilateral or bilateral treaty obligations;
  (b) the place of commission of the crime;
  (c) the nationality connection of the alleged perpetrator to the requesting state;
  (d) the nationality connection of the victim to the requesting state;
  (e) any other connection between the requesting state and the alleged perpetrator, the crime, or the victim;
  (f) the likelihood, good faith, and effectiveness of the prosecution in the requesting state;
  (g) the fairness and impartiality of the proceedings in the requesting state;
  (h) convenience to the parties and witnesses, as well as the availability of evidence in the requesting state; and
  (i) the interests of justice.

PRINCIPLE 9 — *NON BIS IN IDEM*/DOUBLE JEOPARDY
  1. In the exercise of universal jurisdiction, a state or its judicial organs shall ensure that a person who is subject to criminal proceedings shall not be exposed to multiple prosecutions or punishment for the same criminal conduct where the prior criminal proceedings or other accountability proceedings have been conducted in good faith and in accordance with international norms and standards. Sham prosecutions or derisory punishment resulting from a conviction or other accountability proceedings shall not be recognized as falling within the scope of this Principle.
  2. A state shall recognize the validity of a proper exercise of universal jurisdiction by another state and shall recognize the final judgment of a competent and ordinary national judicial body or a competent international judicial body exercising such jurisdiction in accordance with international due process norms.
  3. Any person tried or convicted by a state exercising universal jurisdiction for serious crimes under international law as specified in Principle 2(1) shall have the right and legal standing to raise before any

national or international judicial body the claim of *non bis in idem* in opposition to any further criminal proceedings.

PRINCIPLE 10—GROUNDS FOR REFUSAL OF EXTRADITION

1. A state or its judicial organs shall refuse to entertain a request for extradition based on universal jurisdiction if the person sought is likely to face a death penalty sentence or to be subjected to torture or any other cruel, degrading, or inhuman punishment or treatment, or if it is likely that the person sought will be subjected to sham proceedings in which international due process norms will be violated and no satisfactory assurances to the contrary are provided.

2. A state which refuses to extradite on the basis of this Principle shall, when permitted by international law, prosecute the individual accused of a serious crime under international law as specified in Principle 2(1) or extradite such person to another state where this can be done without exposing him or her to the risks referred to in paragraph 1.

PRINCIPLE 11—ADOPTION OF NATIONAL LEGISLATION

A state shall, where necessary, enact national legislation to enable the exercise of universal jurisdiction and the enforcement of these Principles.

PRINCIPLE 12—INCLUSION OF UNIVERSAL JURISDICTION IN FUTURE TREATIES

In all future treaties, and in protocols to existing treaties, concerned with serious crimes under international law as specified in Principle 2(1), states shall include provisions for universal jurisdiction.

PRINCIPLE 13—STRENGTHENING ACCOUNTABILITY AND UNIVERSAL JURISDICTION

1. National judicial organs shall construe national law in a manner that is consistent with these Principles.

2. Nothing in these Principles shall be construed to limit the rights and obligations of a state to prevent or punish, by lawful means recognized under international law, the commission of crimes under international law.

3. These Principles shall not be construed as limiting the continued development of universal jurisdiction in international law.

PRINCIPLE 14—SETTLEMENT OF DISPUTES

1. Consistent with international law and the Charter of the United Nations states should settle their disputes arising out of the exercise of universal jurisdiction by all available means of peaceful settlement of disputes and in particular by submitting the dispute to the International Court of Justice.

2. Pending the determination of the issue in dispute, a state seeking to exercise universal jurisdiction shall not detain the accused person nor seek to have that person detained by another state unless there is a reasonable risk of flight and no other reasonable means can be found to ensure that person's eventual appearance before the judicial organs of the state seeking to exercise its jurisdiction.

Commentary

Why Principles? Why Now?

The Princeton Principles on Universal Jurisdiction (Principles) are a progressive restatement of international law on the subject of universal jurisdiction. Leading scholars and jurists gathered twice at Princeton University to help clarify this important area of law.[1] The Principles contain elements of both *lex lata* (the law as it is) and *de lege ferenda* (the law as it ought to be), but they should not be understood to limit the future evolution of universal jurisdiction. The Principles are intended to help guide national legislative bodies seeking to enact implementing legislation; judges who may be required to construe universal jurisdiction in applying domestic law or in making extradition decisions; governments that must decide whether to prosecute or extradite, or otherwise to assist in promoting international criminal accountability; and all those in civil society concerned with bringing to justice perpetrators of serious international crimes.

Participants in the Princeton Project discussed several difficult threshold questions concerning universal jurisdiction. How firmly is universal jurisdiction established in international law? It is of course recognized in treaties, national legislation, judicial opinions, and the writings of scholars, but not everyone draws the same conclusions from these sources. Commentators even disagree on how to ascertain whether universal jurisdiction is well established in customary international law: for some, the acceptance by states that a practice is obligatory (*opinio juris*) is enough; for others, the consistent practice of states is required.

When it is agreed that an obligation has been created in a treaty, legal systems differ in how they incorporate international obligations into domestic law. In many legal systems, the national judiciary cannot apply universal jurisdiction in the absence of national legislation. In other systems it is possible for the judiciary to rely directly on treaties and customary international law without waiting for implementing legislation. (These and other complexities will be explored in a collection of essays being published

under the auspices of the Princeton Project). Accordingly, Principle 3 encourages courts to rely on universal jurisdiction in the absence of national
legislation, so long as their legal systems permit them to do so. Principle
11 calls upon legislatures to enact laws enabling the exercise of universal
jurisdiction. Principle 12 calls for states to provide for universal jurisdiction
in future treaties and protocols to existing treaties.

Participants in the Princeton Project also carefully considered whether
the time is ripe to bring greater clarity to universal jurisdiction. While it has
been with us for centuries, universal jurisdiction seems only now to be coming into its own as a systematic means for promoting legal accountability.
Universal jurisdiction was given great prominence by the proceedings in
London involving former Chilean leader General Augusto Pinochet, and
now courts around the world are seriously considering indictments involving universal jurisdiction.[2]

In light of current dynamics in international criminal law, some supporters of universal jurisdiction question whether now is the time to clarify
the principles that should guide its exercise. Might it not be better to wait
to allow for unpredictable, and perhaps surprisingly progressive, developments? Is there a danger of stunting the development of universal jurisdiction by articulating guiding principles prematurely?

Everyone connected with the Princeton Project took this problem seriously. It commonly arises when codification is undertaken. Nevertheless,
these concerns seem especially significant in the case of universal jurisdiction, given the wide gulf between what the law of universal jurisdiction is
and what advocates of greater justice would like it to be.

After considerable discussion, those who gathered in Princeton in January 2001 favored our effort to bring greater clarity and order to the use
of universal jurisdiction. Our aim is to help guide those who believe that
national courts have a vital role to play in combating impunity even when
traditional jurisdictional connections are absent. These Principles should
help clarify the legal bases for the responsible and reasoned exercise of universal jurisdiction. Insofar as universal jurisdiction is exercised, and seen
to be exercised, in a reasoned, lawful, and orderly manner, it will gain wider
acceptance. Mindful of the need to encourage continued progress in international law, these Principles have been drafted so as to invite rather than
hinder the continued development of universal jurisdiction.

The Principles are written so as to both clarify the current law of universal jurisdiction and encourage its further development. As already noted,
the Principles are addressed sometimes to the legislative, executive, or judicial branches of government, and sometimes to a combination of these.[3]
The Principles are intended for a variety of actors in divergent legal systems who will properly draw on them in different ways. We acknowledge, for
example, that in some legal systems, and according to some legal theories,
judges are constrained in their ability to interpret existing law in light of

aspirations to greater justice, or other principled aims.[4] Nevertheless, judges on international and regional tribunals, and judges on national constitutional and supreme courts, often have greater interpretive latitude.

Our hope is that these Principles might inform and shape the practice of those judges and other officials who can act to promote greater justice and legal accountability consistent with the constraints of their offices. We also offer these Principles to help guide and inform citizens, leaders of organizations in civil society, and public officials of all sorts: all of these different actors could benefit from a clearer common understanding of what universal jurisdiction is and when and how it may reasonably be exercised.

When and How to Prosecute Based on Universality?

In defining universal jurisdiction, participants focused on the case of "pure" universal jurisdiction, namely, where the nature of the crime is the sole basis for subject matter jurisdiction. There has been some scholarly confusion on the role of universal jurisdiction in famous prosecutions, such as the trial in Jerusalem of Adolph Eichmann.[5] In addition, it is important to recall that simply because certain offenses are universally condemned does not mean that a state may exercise universal jurisdiction over them.

Participants in the Princeton Project debated whether states should in general be encouraged to exercise universal jurisdiction based solely on the seriousness of the alleged crime, without traditional connecting links to the victims or perpetrators of serious crimes under international law. On the one hand, the whole point of universal jurisdiction would seem to be to permit or even encourage prosecution when states find within their territory a non-citizen accused of serious crimes under international law.

In this way, universal jurisdiction maximizes accountability and minimizes impunity. The very essence of universal jurisdiction would seem, therefore, to be that national courts should prosecute alleged criminals absent any connecting factors (for example, even if the crimes were not committed against the enforcing states' citizens, or by its citizens).

There is, nevertheless, great concern that particular states will abuse universal jurisdiction to pursue politically motivated prosecutions. Mercenary governments and rogue prosecutors could seek to indict the heads of state or other senior public officials in countries with which they have political disagreements. Powerful states may try to exempt their own leaders from accountability while seeking to prosecute others, defying the basic proposition that equals should be treated equally. Members of peacekeeping forces might be harassed with unjustified prosecutions, and this might deter peacekeeping operations.

Should the Principles insist at least that the accused is physically present in the territory of the enforcing state? Should other connecting links also be required? Participants decided not to include an explicit requirement of a territorial link in Principle 1(1)'s definition. This was done partly to allow for further discussion, partly to avoid stifling the evolution of universal jurisdiction, and partly out of deference to pending litigation in the International Court of Justice.[6] Nevertheless, subsection (2) of Principle 1 holds that a "competent and ordinary" judicial body may try accused persons on the basis of universal jurisdiction "provided the person is present before such judicial body."

The language of Principle 1(2) does not prevent a state from initiating the criminal process, conducting an investigation, issuing an indictment, or requesting extradition, when the accused is not present.

The Principles contain a number of provisions describing the standards that legal systems and particular prosecutions would have to meet in order to exercise universal jurisdiction responsibly and legitimately. Subsections (3) and (4) of Principle 1 insist that a state may seek to extradite persons accused or convicted on the basis of universal jurisdiction "provided that it has established a prima facie case of the person's guilt" and provided that trials and punishments will take place in accordance with "international due process norms," relevant human rights standards, and the independence and impartiality of the judiciary. Later Principles contain additional safeguards against prosecutorial abuses: Principle 9, for example, guards against repeated prosecutions for the same crime in violation of the principle of *non bis in idem*, or the prohibition on double jeopardy.[7] Principle 10 allows states to refuse requests for extradition if the person sought "is likely to face a death penalty sentence or to be subjected to torture" or cruel or inhuman treatment or sham proceedings in violation of international due process norms. The Principles reinforce proper legal standards for courts and should help guide executive officers considering extradition requests.

Of course, effective legal processes require the active cooperation of different government agencies, including courts and prosecutors. The establishment of international networks of cooperation will be especially important to the effective development of universal jurisdiction. Therefore, Principle 4 calls upon states to comply with their international obligations to either prosecute or extradite those accused or convicted of crimes under international law, so long as these legal processes comply with "international due process norms." Universal jurisdiction can only work if different states provide each other with active judicial and prosecutorial assistance, and all participating states will need to insure that due process norms are being complied with.

All legal powers can be abused by willfully malicious individuals. The Princeton Principles do all that principles can do to guard against such abuses: they specify the considerations that conscientious international actors can and should act upon.

Which Crimes Are Covered?

The choice of which crimes to include as "serious crimes under international law" was discussed at length in Princeton.[8] The ordering of the list of "serious crimes" was settled by historical progression rather than an attempt to rank crimes based upon their gravity.

- "Piracy" is a crime that paradigmatically is subject to prosecution by any nation based on principles of universality, and it is crucial to the origins of universal jurisdiction, so it comes first.[9]
- "Slavery" was included in part because its historical ties to piracy reach back to the Declaration of the Congress of Vienna in 1815. There are but a few conventional provisions, however, authorizing the exercise of universal jurisdiction for slavery and slave-related practices.[10] The phrase "slavery and slave-related practices" was considered but rejected by the Princeton Assembly as being too technical in nature. However, it was agreed that the term "slavery" was intended to include those practices prohibited in the Supplementary Convention on the Abolition of Slavery, the Slave Trade, and Institutions and Practices Similar to Slavery.[11]
- "War crimes" were initially restricted to "serious war crimes," namely, "grave breaches" of the 1949 Geneva Conventions and Protocol I, in order to avoid the potential for numerous prosecutions based upon less serious violations.[12] The participants, however, did not want to give the impression that some war crimes are not serious, and thus opted not to include the word "serious." The assembly agreed, though, that it would be inappropriate to invoke universal jurisdiction for the prosecution of minor transgressions of the 1949 Geneva Conventions and Protocol I.
- "Crimes against peace" were also discussed at length. While many argue that aggression constitutes the most serious international crime, others contend that defining the crime of "aggression" is in practice extremely difficult and divisive. In the end, "crimes against peace" were included, despite some disagreement, in part in order to recall the wording of Article 6(a) of the Nuremberg Charter.[13]
- "Crimes against humanity" were included without objection, and these crimes have now been authoritatively defined by Article 7 of the Rome Statute of the International Criminal Court.[14] There is not presently any conventional law that provides for the exercise of universal jurisdiction over crimes against humanity.
- "Genocide" was included without objection. Article 6 of the Genocide Convention provides that a person accused of genocide shall be tried in a court of "the State in the territory of which the act was committed."[15] However, Article 6 does not preclude the use of universal jurisdiction by an international penal tribunal, in the event that such a tribunal is established.

- "Torture" was included without objection though some noted that there are some disagreements as to what constitutes torture. "Torture" is intended to include the "other cruel, inhuman, or degrading treatment or punishment" as defined in the Convention against Torture and Other Cruel, Inhuman, or Degrading Treatment or Punishment.[16] Moreover, the Torture Convention implicitly provides for the exercise of universal jurisdiction over prohibited conduct.[17]

Apartheid, terrorism, and drug crimes were raised as candidates for inclusion. It should be carefully noted that the list of serious crimes is explicitly illustrative, not exhaustive. Principle 2(1) leaves open the possibility that, in the future, other crimes may be deemed of such a heinous nature as to warrant the application of universal jurisdiction.

When and Against Whom Should Universal Jurisdiction Be Exercised?

Among the most difficult questions discussed in the Princeton Project was the enforcement of universal jurisdiction, and the question of when if ever to honor immunities and amnesties with respect to the commission of serious crimes under international law.

Especially difficult moral, political, and legal issues surround immunities for former or current heads of state, diplomats, and other officials (see Principle 5). Immunity from international criminal prosecution for sitting heads of state is established by customary international law, and immunity for diplomats is established by treaty. There is an extremely important distinction, however, between "substantive" and "procedural" immunity. A substantive immunity from prosecution would provide heads of state, diplomats, and other officials with exoneration from criminal responsibility for the commission of serious crimes under international law when these crimes are committed in an official capacity. Principle 5 rejects this substantive immunity ("the official position of any accused person, whether as head of state or government or as a responsible government official, shall not relieve such person of criminal responsibility nor mitigate punishment"). Nevertheless, in proceedings before national tribunals, procedural immunity remains in effect during a head of state's or other official's tenure in office, or during the period in which a diplomat is accredited to a host state. Under international law as it exists, sitting heads of state, accredited diplomats, and other officials cannot be prosecuted while in office for acts committed in their official capacities.[18]

The Princeton Principles' rejection of substantive immunity keeps faith with the Nuremberg Charter, which proclaims: "The official position of defendants, whether as Heads of State or responsible officials in Government Departments, shall not be considered as freeing them from responsibility or mitigating punishment."[19] More recently, the Statutes of the International Criminal Tribunal for the Former Yugoslavia (ICTY) and that of the International Criminal Tribunal for Rwanda (ICTR) removed substantive immunity for war crimes, genocide, and crimes against humanity.[20] Principle 5 in fact tracks the language of these statutes, which, in turn, were fashioned from Article 7 of the Nuremberg Charter.[21]

None of these statutes addresses the issue of procedural immunity. Customary international law, however, is quite clear on the subject: heads of state enjoy unqualified "act of state" immunity during their term of office. Similarly, diplomats accredited to a host state enjoy unqualified ex officio immunity during the performance of their official duties.[22] A head of state, diplomat, or other official may, therefore, be immune from prosecution while in office, but once they step down any claim of immunity becomes ineffective, and they are then subject to the possibility of prosecution.

The Principles do not purport to revoke the protections afforded by procedural immunity, but neither do they affirm procedural immunities as a matter of principle. In the future, procedural immunities for sitting heads of state, diplomats, and other officials may be called increasingly into question, a possibility prefigured by the ICTY's indictment of Slobodan Milosevic while still a sitting head of state.[23] Whether this unprecedented action will become the source of a new regime in international law remains to be seen. Participants in the Princeton Project opted not to try and settle on principles governing procedural immunity in order to leave space for future developments.

Another possible limit on the prosecution of "serious crimes under international law" are statutes of limitations.[24] Principle 6 reaffirms that statutes of limitations do not apply to crimes covered by universal jurisdiction. Conventional international law supports this position, at least as concerns war crimes and crimes against humanity.[25] Admittedly, the practice of states leaves something to be desired, here as elsewhere. Subsection (1) of Principle 13 provides that national judicial organs shall construe their own law in a manner "consistent with these Principles." If a nation's law is silent as to a limitations period with respect to a certain serious crime under international law, for example genocide, a local judge could draw on this subsection and legitimately refuse to apply by analogy another statute of limitations for a crime that was codified, e.g., murder. Because the laws of many nations include limitations periods, a number of participants suggested that the Principles should exhort states to eliminate statutes of limitations for serious crimes under international law; Principle 11 does this.

Another significant discussion took place on the topics of amnesties and other pardons that might be granted by a state or by virtue of a treaty to individuals or categories of individuals. Some participants were very strongly against the inclusion of any principle that recognized an amnesty for "serious crimes under international law." Others felt that certain types of amnesties, coupled with accountability mechanisms other than criminal prosecution, were acceptable in some cases: at least in difficult periods of political transition, as a second best alternative to criminal prosecution. Much controversy surrounds accountability mechanisms such as South Africa's Truth and Reconciliation Commission. We considered trying to specify the minimum prerequisites that should have to be satisfied in order for accountability mechanisms to be deemed legitimate (including such features as individualized accountability), but in the end those assembled at Princeton decided not to try and provide general criteria. Accordingly, Principle 7 expresses only a presumption that amnesties are inconsistent with a state's obligations to prevent impunity.[26] Subsection (2) recognizes that if a state grants amnesties that are inconsistent with obligations to hold perpetrators of serious international crimes accountable, other states may still seek to exercise universal jurisdiction.

Who Should Prosecute?

Principle 8 seeks to specify factors that should be considered when making judgments about whether to prosecute or extradite in the face of competing national claims. The list of factors is not intended to be exhaustive.[27] This Principle is designed to provide states with guidelines for the resolution of conflicts in situations in which the state with custody over a person accused of serious international crimes can base its jurisdiction solely on universality, and one or more other states have asserted or are in a position to exercise jurisdiction.

Originally, the drafters expressed a preference for ranking the different bases of jurisdiction so as to indicate which should receive priority in the case of a conflict. Almost without exception, the territorial principle was thought to deserve precedence. This was in part because of the longstanding conviction that a criminal defendant should be tried by his "natural judge." Many participants expressed the view that societies that have been victimized by political crimes should have the opportunity to bring the perpetrators to justice, provided their judiciaries are able and willing to do so.

Although it was decided not to rank jurisdictional claims, the Principles do not deny that some traditional jurisdictional claims will often be especially weighty. For example, the exercise of territorial jurisdiction will often also satisfy several of the other factors enumerated in Principle 8, such as the convenience to the parties and witnesses, as well as the availability of evidence.

What Protections for the Accused?

If universal jurisdiction is to be a tool for promoting greater justice, the rights of the accused must be protected. Principle 9 protects accused persons against multiple prosecutions for the same crime. There was no objection among the participants as to desirability of such safeguards. Several of the participants, however, questioned whether the prohibition on double jeopardy—*non bis in idem*—was a recognized principle of international law. Under regional human rights agreements, *non bis in idem* has been interpreted to apply within a state, but not between states. It was noted, however, that the importance of the doctrine of *non bis in idem* is recognized in almost all legal systems: it qualifies as a general principle of law and, as such, could be said to apply under international law.[28] Subsection (3) specifically grants an accused the right "and legal standing" to invoke the claim of *non bis in idem* as a defense to further criminal proceedings. This provision is designed to allow a defendant to independently raise this defense in jurisdictions that would otherwise only permit the requested state, in its discretion, to invoke the double jeopardy principle on an accused person's behalf.

Subsection (1) of Principle 10 requires that an extradition request predicated upon universality be refused if the accused is likely to face the death penalty, torture, or "other cruel, degrading, or inhuman punishment or treatment." This latter phraseology should be construed in accord with its usage as described in the Torture Convention.[29]

There was also some discussion about whether to include a provision on trials *in absentia* in the Principles. Although generally considered anathema in common law countries, such trials are traditional in certain civil law nations, such as France, and serve a valuable function with respect to the preservation of evidence. In the end it was decided not to refer to such trials in the Principles.

Conclusion: Promoting Accountability through International Law

Several of the remaining principles have already been mentioned, and their import should be clear. Principles 11 and 12 call upon states both to adopt legislation to enable the exercise of universal jurisdiction and to include provisions for universal jurisdiction in all future treaties. The first sentence of Principle 13 was included by the drafters to memorialize their intention that nothing in the Principles should be construed as altering the existing obligations of any state under terrorism conventions.

Subsection (1) of Principle 14 calls for states to peacefully settle disputes arising out of the application of universal jurisdiction. An example of the appropriate resolution sought by this subsection is the case of *Democratic Republic the Congo v Belgium,* which is pending before the International Court of Justice as these Principles go to press.[30] The case involves a dispute regarding Belgium's assertion of universal jurisdiction over the Congo's Minister of Foreign Affairs.

Universal jurisdiction is one means to achieve accountability and to deny impunity to those accused of serious international crimes. It reflects the maxim embedded in so many treaties: *aut dedere aut judicare,* the duty to extradite or prosecute. All of the participants in the Princeton Project felt it important that the Principles not be construed to limit the development of universal jurisdiction or to constrain the evolution of accountability for crimes under international law, and this conviction is made explicit in Principle 13.

National courts exercising universal jurisdiction have a vital role to play in bringing perpetrators of international crimes to justice: they form part of the web of legal instruments which can and should be deployed to combat impunity. The Princeton Principles do not purport to define the proper use of universal jurisdiction in any final way. Our hope is that these Principles can bring greater clarity and order to the exercise of universal jurisdiction, and thereby encourage its reasonable and responsible use.

Part II
Essays and Comments

Chapter 1
The History of Universal Jurisdiction and Its Place in International Law

M. Cherif Bassiouni

Introduction

This article explores the history and evolution of universal jurisdiction by tracing it through its conventional and customary international law, as well as the practice of states. Within that context, it also addresses the legal and policy issues relating to the desirability and applicability of universal jurisdiction.

The exercise of universal jurisdiction may fill a jurisdictional gap, and in this case, it is necessary to ensure accountability for international crimes. But it can also be exercised in competition with other valid theories of jurisdiction. In that respect, it is important to have rules and guidelines for the exercise of conflicting jurisdictional efforts by states and between states and international judicial bodies.

Aside from these legal and policy considerations, it is necessary to separate, on the one hand, the expectations of international criminal justice advocates for universal jurisdiction to be expanded as a way of preventing impunity and enhancing accountability and, on the other hand, the status of international law. Quite frequently, the proponents of expanded universal jurisdiction seek to rely on customary international law, as well as on specific treaties dealing with certain historic crimes, such as piracy, slavery and slave-related practices, and war crimes. Frequently, however, that reliance is either misplaced or misrepresented.

Universal jurisdiction has become the preferred technique by those seeking to prevent impunity for international crimes. While there is no doubt that it is a useful and, at times, necessary instrument of international criminal justice, it is also attended by various dangers. If used in a politically motivated manner or simply to vex and harass leaders of other states, universal jurisdiction could disrupt world order and deprive individuals of their basic rights. Even with the best of intentions, universal jurisdiction could be used imprudently, creating unnecessary frictions between states and abuses of legal processes. For these reasons and more, the exercise of universal jurisdiction ought generally to be reserved for the most serious international crimes, such as genocide, crimes against humanity, and war crimes, though there may be other international crimes for which universal jurisdiction is provided for by an applicable treaty, as in the case of terrorism.

This essay assesses the status of universal jurisdiction as a recognized international theory and the extent to which it is embodied in national laws and applied in national judicial decisions. What we will find is that while universal jurisdiction is attaining an important place in international law, it is not as well established in conventional and customary international law as its ardent proponents, including major human rights organizations, profess it to be. These organizations have listed countries, which they claim rely on universal jurisdiction; in fact, the legal provisions they cite do not stand for that proposition, or at least not as unequivocally as represented.[1]

Jurisdiction and Territoriality

The term *jurisdiction,* whether it applies to civil or criminal matters, includes the power to prescribe or make laws, the power to decide legal disputes, and the power to enforce legal decisions or verdicts. It also includes the means by which the exercise of jurisdiction is obtained over a person. These powers have historically been reserved to sovereign states.

The powers to enforce and prescribe law are not always coextensive. This means that a sovereign state, or an entity exercising some of the attributes of sovereignty, can exercise either power without exercising the other. Thus a sovereign state or a legal entity that has some sovereign attributes can enforce the prescription of another state, or of international law, even though the enforcing power may not have prescribed what it enforces.[2] The powers to prescribe and enforce laws derive from sovereignty; thus, national criminal jurisdiction has historically been linked, if not limited, to the territory of a state. Throughout the course of legal history, jurisdictional powers have primarily been exercised in accordance with the principle of territorial jurisdiction.[3]

Sovereignty, jurisdiction, and territory have traditionally been closely linked. This is due to the recognized importance of avoiding jurisdictional conflicts between states and providing legal consistency and predictability. Such consistency protects against the potential denial of rights and abuses of judicial processes by exposing persons to multiple prosecutions for the same conduct. Linking jurisdiction to territoriality, while allowing it to extend extraterritorially when a valid legal nexus to the enforcing state exists, is the most effective way to achieve these results. That is why private international law provides rules for the resolution of jurisdictional conflicts between states.[4]

With respect to criminal jurisdiction, sovereignty is not necessarily limited to singular states but also extends to multistate alliances and international organizations. Examples include the WW II Allies' establishment of the International Military Tribunal (IMT) sitting at Nuremberg[5] in 1945 and of the International Military Tribunal for the Far East (IMTFE) sitting at Tokyo[6] in 1946. The power that the Allies exercised collectively derived from the power they had to act singularly as the IMT judgment expressly states it: "The Signatory Powers created this Tribunal, defined the law it was to administer, and made regulations for the proper conduct of the Trial. In doing so, they have done together what any one of them might have done singly; for it is not to be doubted that any nation has the right thus to set up special courts to administer law."[7] In both of these tribunals, the victorious states exercised their powers to enforce international criminal law because they exercised sovereign prerogatives in fact over the occupied territories where these tribunals were established.

Nearly fifty years later, in 1993 and in 1994, the Security Council established pursuant to its powers under Chapter VII of the United Nations Charter,[8] the International Criminal Tribunal for the former Yugoslavia[9] (ICTY) and the International Criminal Tribunal for Rwanda[10] (ICTR) respectively. In these two instances, the Security Council assumed a quasi-sovereign prerogative over two war-torn territories.[11] The council enunciated substantive legal norms, which are extant in international criminal law, and provided for their territorial enforcement through these two ad hoc tribunals.[12]

Furthermore, until the 1920s, the practice of states was to preserve the connection between territorial state sovereignty and the exercise of national criminal jurisdiction. Neither the legislation nor the practice of states, save for few exceptions, included extraterritorial criminal jurisdiction except with respect to the conduct of their citizens when abroad under the theory of "active personality."[13] Under this theory, a state may exercise its sovereign power by prescribing conduct for its nationals, even where they are abroad.[14]

After the 1920s, states developed national legislation applicable extraterritorially. Such legislation was to be applied whenever a territorial link existed between the proscribed conduct and its harmful impact within the prescribing state. This included the occurrence of harmful conduct against a state's citizens abroad. This form of extraterritorial jurisdiction is identified in various ways: "protected interest," "objective territoriality,"[15] or "passive personality."[16] After the end of World War II, states asserted wider forms of extraterritorial jurisdiction, particularly in economic areas, when extraterritorial conduct has a territorial impact and also as a means to protect their citizens abroad. But this expansion of jurisdiction was still premised on a territorial connection or a connection between the prescribing and enforcing powers of a state and its nationals.

The reach of a state may, therefore, be universal with respect to the forms of extraterritorial jurisdictional described above, but in all of them there is a connection or legal nexus between sovereignty and the territoriality of the enforcing state, or the nationality of the perpetrator or victim, or the territorial impact of the extraterritorially proscribed conduct.

The universal reach of extraterritorial national jurisdiction is not the same thing as universal jurisdiction. Nor does the fact that certain conduct is universally condemned mean that universal jurisdiction applies to it. The term *universal* has caused confusion that is apparent in some judicial opinions[17] and in the writings of many jurists on the theory of universal jurisdiction. Universal jurisdiction, according to Principle 1 of the Princeton Principles on Universal Jurisdiction, is "criminal jurisdiction based solely on the nature of the crime, without regard to where the crime was committed, the nationality of the alleged or convicted perpetrator, the nationality of the victim, or any other connection to the state exercising such jurisdiction." Major scholarly international organizations, like the International Association of Penal Law and the International Law Association, have long urged states to exercise universal jurisdiction over certain international crimes.[18]

The Theory of Universal Jurisdiction

The theory of universal jurisdiction transcends national sovereignty, which is the historical basis for national criminal jurisdiction. Two positions can be identified to justify this. The first is the normative universalist position, which recognizes the existence of certain core values that are shared by the international community. These values are deemed important enough to justify overriding the usual territorial limitations on the exercise of jurisdiction. The second position is a pragmatic policy-oriented one, which recognizes that occasionally there exist certain shared international interests that require an enforcement mechanism not limited to national sovereignty. These two positions share common elements. First, they both require the existence of common values and/or interests shared by the international community. Second, there must be a need to collectively prosecute the more serious transgressions of these values/interests. Third, there must exist an assumption that expanded jurisdiction will deter and prevent crime, and ultimately enhance world order, justice, and peace. Under both positions, the goal is to give each and all sovereignties, as well as international organs, the power to individually or collectively enforce certain international proscriptions. Universal jurisdiction applies when the proscription does not originate with the enforcing state and the conduct does not occur within the territory of that state. When universal jurisdiction can be asserted, there is no need for a link or nexus between the enforcing power, be it national or international, and the conduct in question, or the perpetrator or victim's nationality. Universal jurisdiction is, as already noted, based solely on the nature of the crime.

However, these two positions differ in fundamental ways. They vary in the way they describe the nature and sources of the values/interests that give rise to an international or supranational proscription. They also differ in their definition of international community and the nature and extent of the legal rights and obligations incumbent upon states.[19]

The universalist normative position can be traced to metaphysical and philosophical conceptions arising in different cultures and at different times. For example, in the three monotheistic faiths of Judaism, Christianity, and Islam, full sovereignty rests with the Creator. Transgressions of the Creator's norms confer the power to enforce religious laws by the religious community, irrespective of any limitations in space or time.[20]

Early modern Western jurists and philosophers developed the normative universalist position based partly on Christian concepts of natural law. But contrary to some contemporary authors who refer to them, the early jurists and philosophers did not extend their universalist views of certain wrongs to include universal criminal jurisdiction.[21] Cesare Beccaria in his pamphlet, *On Crimes and Punishments,*[22] expressed the universalist view that there exists a community of nations that share common values. These values bind all members of the international community and commit them to the enforcement of the values. But he did not propound universal criminal jurisdiction. He expressed his views as follows: "There are also those who think that an act of cruelty committed, for example, at Constantinople may be punished at Paris for this abstract reason, that he who offends humanity should have enemies in all mankind, and be the object of universal execration, as if judges were to be the knights errant of human nature in general, rather than guardians of particular conventions between men."[23]

Earlier, Hugo Grotius, in his two-volume *The Law of War and Peace,* first published in 1625, had argued from the same philosophical premise but relied on a pragmatic policy-oriented approach of pursuing "enemies of the human race" on the high seas. Grotius's premise was a posited right to freedom of navigation on the high seas. Because the right of freedom of navigation on the high seas was applicable universally, it followed that an infringement upon that right by pirates would be universally punished. This doctrine became the foundation of the modern theory of universal jurisdiction for certain international crimes.

Many legal scholars since the nineteenth century have advocated the theory of universal jurisdiction without clarifying the philosophical foundation of that theory or its legal elements. Instead they argue, much like the early universalists, that certain international crimes imply that all states, irrespective of any existing national legislation, and even contrary to national legislation, have the power to prosecute, irrespective of any territorial connection to the crime, or any connection to the nationality of the perpetrator or the victim.[24]

Universal jurisdiction has received increasing support among legal scholars, and increasing numbers of states are enacting laws that provide for universal jurisdiction, but it has not yet been supported by the practice of states. In fact, there are only a few cases known to scholars in which pure universal jurisdiction—in other words, without any link to the sovereignty or territoriality of the enforcing state—has been applied.[25]

A 1990 Report of the Council of Europe aptly summarizes the contemporary law and practice of states with respect to universal jurisdiction:[26]

There are considerable differences of opinion among member states concerning the purpose of the principle of universality, according to which criminal jurisdiction is exercised over offences committed abroad, without the requirements underlying the previously mentioned principles of jurisdiction necessarily being present.

Some states are only prepared to apply the principles to certain offences if they are authorised or obliged to do so under international law. Some conventions authorise the assertion of universal jurisdiction, others require such jurisdictional action so as not to leave certain offences unpunished. The majority of states have felt at liberty to introduce the principle in their national legislation without any such authorisation or obligation. Nevertheless, many of the latter group have evidently tried to keep in line with existing international agreements when establishing universal jurisdiction. However, there are also a number of states which have reserved a considerable degree of universal jurisdiction over offences not covered by any agreement. They assume that any conflict of competence with other states which may arise from their extensive claims can be avoided in practice by a broad application of the principle of discretionary jurisdiction, or by imposing conditions for prosecution, such as the requirement to authorisation from a central body or for the presence of the suspect. The latter requirement is, for that matter, imposed by all states on the exercise of jurisdiction based on this principle, at least in practice.

Some convention would seem to permit the asserting of universal jurisdiction in relation to offences covered therein. The Red Cross Conventions of 1949 would be examples, though not all states party to these conventions have asserted universal jurisdiction under these instruments. The 1961 Single Convention on Narcotic Drugs and the amending Protocol of 1972, and the 1971 Convention of Psychotropic Substances are also examples. Some states have established jurisdiction based on universality in respect of offences covered by these treaties.

Other conventions clearly envisage or require the taking of universal jurisdiction: treaties on counterfeiting, piracy, hijacking and actions endangering the safety of civil aviation afford examples. Virtually all states have established universal jurisdiction over such offences. Comparable conventions envisaging the taking of universal jurisdiction are those relating to the combat against terrorism, the prevention of torture, the protection of diplomatic staff, the physical protection of nuclear material and the taking of hostages.

The maxim *aut dedere aut judicare* (either extradite or prosecute) is reflected in an increasing number of conventions, although the way it is translated into national legislation and its effect differ from state to state and even from category to category of offence within a single country.

There is sometimes no clear distinction between the principle of universality and other principles on which extraterritorial jurisdiction is based, such as the "representation" principle or the principle of protection. There are often differences of opinion as to which principle should form the basis of a particular term of extraterritorial jurisdiction. It has also been shown that, under special circumstances, forms of jurisdiction have been established which cannot be classified under any of the traditional principles of jurisdiction described above. These can be found, for example, in military law, in certain emergency laws and in legislation regarding taxes and customs duties.

The difficulty of categorising these different forms of extraterritorial legislative criminal jurisdiction can perhaps be explained by the fact that they do not always have a sound theoretical basis. The committee considered it its task to study the theoretical basis for such jurisdiction and, where possible, to describe it or develop it further.[27]

Universal jurisdiction, it should now be evident, has frequently been confused with other theories of extraterritorial criminal jurisdiction. As we have seen, however, with few exceptions the legislation and practice of states allows for criminal jurisdiction when there is a connection between the crime and the enforcing state based on the crime's territorial impact or based on the nationality of the perpetrator or of the victim. As discussed below, explicit or implicit recognition of the theory of universal jurisdiction in conventional international law has been limited to certain international crimes.

Scholars, including this writer, support the proposition that an independent theory of universal jurisdiction exists with respect to serious international crimes. The grounds for such a theory are both the normative universalist position and the pragmatic policy position mentioned above. It is necessary to have guidelines for the application of this theory in order to avoid jurisdictional conflicts, disruptions of world order, abuse and denial of justice, and to enhance the predictability of international criminal law. Supplying such guidelines has been the purpose of the Princeton Project on Universal Jurisdiction.

Universal Jurisdiction in International Criminal Law

The sources of substantive international criminal law are essentially conventions and customs that embody general principles of law and the writings of scholars that interpret those conventions and customs.[28] Conventional international criminal law is the better source of international criminal law insofar as it is more apt to satisfy the basic principles of legality, namely, no crime without a law, no punishment without a law.

Gauging the degree of support for universal jurisdiction requires two inquiries.[29] First, it must be determined to what extent it is supported by national legislation in all or in most national legal systems.[30] Second, conventional and customary international criminal law must be referenced to determine the existence of international legal norms that provide for the application of universal jurisdiction by national criminal justice systems and by internationally established adjudicating bodies.[31]

Until recently, very few states had legislative provisions allowing their legal systems to prosecute crimes based solely on universal jurisdiction. As demonstrated in Hays Butler's essay in this volume, "The Growing Support for Universal Jurisdiction in National Legislation," increasing numbers of states are enacting legislation to enable the exercise of universal jurisdiction. To the knowledge of this writer, no state practice presently exists whereby states have resorted to universal jurisdiction without the existence of national legislation, even when international treaties provide for such a jurisdictional basis.

Since the end of World War I, the international community has established five international investigating commissions and four international ad hoc criminal tribunals; none of them has been based on the theory of universal jurisdiction.[32] The Statute of the International Criminal Court (ICC) also does not establish universal jurisdiction for "situations" referred to it by states; rather, it has only a universal scope as to the crimes within the court's jurisdiction.[33] These crimes are genocide, crimes against humanity, and war crimes.[34] Because "referrals"[35] to the ICC are made by a state party[36] or by a nonstate party,[37] it is difficult to argue that the ICC's jurisdiction flows from the theory of universal jurisdiction. However, "referrals" by the Security Council for the crimes within the jurisdiction of the court do constitute universal jurisdiction.[38]

International criminal law includes 28 crime categories.[39] These 28 categories are evidenced by 281 conventions concluded between 1815 and 1999.[40] These international crimes are aggression, genocide, crimes against humanity, war crimes, unlawful possession and/or use of weapons, theft of nuclear materials, mercenarism, apartheid, slavery and slave-related practices, torture, unlawful human experimentation, piracy, aircraft hijacking, unlawful acts against civil maritime navigation, unlawful use of force against internationally protected persons, crimes against UN and associated personnel, taking of civilian hostages, unlawful use of the mail, attacks with explosives, financing of terrorism, unlawful traffic in drugs and related drug offenses, organized crime, destruction and/or theft of national treasures and cultural heritage, unlawful acts against the environment, international traffic in obscene materials, falsification and counterfeiting, unlawful interference with submarine cables, and bribery of foreign public officials.[41] Among the penal provisions contained in these conventions there are provisions on criminal jurisdiction, and, of these, only 32 conventions contain a reference to a jurisdictional theory[42] and among them a few, discussed below, can be construed explicitly or implicitly as reflecting universal jurisdiction. Conversely, 93 provisions reflect the obligation to prosecute or extradite, evidencing the legislative choice of this enforcement technique over that of conferring universal jurisdiction to any and all states.[43]

Because conventional and customary international criminal law overlap with respect to certain crimes, it is useful to examine whether universal jurisdiction vis-à-vis serious international crimes arises under any of the sources of international criminal law. What follows is an assessment of the evolution of universal jurisdiction with respect to serious international crimes based on conventional and customary international law sources. These serious international crimes are piracy, slavery and slave-related practices, war crimes, crimes against humanity, genocide, apartheid, and torture.[44] They are discussed below in the order of the emergence in international criminal law.

Piracy

Piracy is deemed the basis of universal criminal jurisdiction for *jus cogens* international crimes, but that was not always the case. (*Jus cogens* is a peremptory norm of international law. The concept originated in Roman law, and meant the law applicable to one and all.) The term *piracy* has its origins in Greek literature as *peiretes* and is reported in Homer's *Iliad*[45] and *The Odyssey*,[46] as well as in Thucydides, *History of the Peleponnesian War*.[47] It then appeared in Roman literature, notably in the writings of Cicero, who referred to pirates as *pirata* and *praedones* (land-based predators, later referred to as brigands and bandits).[48] Cicero is also credited with the notion that *pirata* and *praedones* are "enemies of the human race."[49] Grotius, relying on Aristotle and Cicero, elaborated on the theory of "enemies of the human race" and its application in wartime, which was the context in which piracy was viewed at that time.[50]

Early modern thinking about piracy was not, however, linked to universal jurisdiction as it would be in the nineteenth and twentieth centuries.[51] Alberigo Gentili[52] and Balthasar de Ayala[53] adopted the universalist view of piracy and its universal condemnation by all states because it was dictated by the customary law of nations. But they understood piracy essentially in the context of war. However, Grotius, whose approach was more pragmatic, saw the problem of dealing with pirates as part of his view of a certain order on the high seas. From a jurisdictional perspective, Grotius, an advocate of the openness of the high seas, *mare liberum*, posited the principle that ships on the high seas were an extension of the flag state's territoriality. Thus, the flag state should be able to exercise its jurisdiction over nonnational ships and persons for acts of piracy. It was not, therefore, an application of universal jurisdiction whereby any and all states could exercise their jurisdiction over any and all pirates. Instead it was the recognition of the universal application of the flag state's right to defend itself against pirates and eventually to pursue them as both a preventive and punitive measure.

The early law of piracy developed in the national laws and practices of the major seafaring nations between the 1600s and 1800s. Though they developed along separate lines, they had parallel outcomes. This is probably due to nations' commonality of interests in securing themselves from the perils of piracy. These developments were based on the recognition that the flag state had the power to seize and punish piracy as it was defined by national law.[54] Piracy has been widely recognized in customary international law as the international crime par excellence to which universality applies. Chief Justice John Marshall recognized the universal reach of United States law whenever the acts of piracy were against a U.S. vessel and U.S. nationals. Chief Justice Marshall, writing in *United States v Klintock*, in 1818, said of pirates:

Persons of this description are proper objects for the penal code of all nations [emphasis added]; and we think that the general words of the Act of Congress applying to all persons whatsoever, though they ought to not be so construed as to extend to persons under the acknowledged authority of a foreign state, ought to be so construed as to comprehend those who acknowledge the authority of no state. Those general terms ought not to be applied to offences committed against the particular sovereignty of a foreign power; *but we think they ought to be applied to offences committed against all nations, including the United States, by persons who by common consent are equally amenable to the laws of all nations* [emphasis added].

The certificate issued by the Supreme Court concludes "[t]hat the act of the 30 of April, 1790, does extend *to all persons on board all vessels which throw off their national character by cruising piratically and committing piracy on other vessels*" [emphasis added].[55]

Positive international law in the twentieth century has clearly established universal jurisdiction for piracy.[56] The 1958 Geneva Convention on the Law of the High Seas[57] includes two provisions on jurisdiction over piracy. Article 18 states:

"A ship or aircraft may retain its nationality, although it has become a pirate ship or aircraft. The retention or loss of nationality is determined by the law of the state from which such nationality was derived."

Article 19 states: "On the high seas, or in any other place outside the jurisdiction of any state, every state may seize a pirate ship or aircraft, or a ship taken by piracy and under the control of pirates, and arrest the persons and seize the property on board. The courts of the state which carried out the seizure may decide upon the penalties to be imposed and may also determine the action to be taken with regard to the property, subject to the rights of third states acting in good faith." This article clearly establishes universal jurisdiction.

Then, in 1982, the Montego Bay Convention on the Law of the Sea[58] reiterated a provision in the 1958 Geneva Convention and provided the same text, namely: "On the high seas, or in any other place outside the jurisdiction of any State, every State may seize a pirate ship or aircraft, or a ship or aircraft taken by piracy and under the control of pirates, and arrest the person and seize the property on board. The courts of the State which carried out the seizure may decide upon the penalties to be imposed, and may also determine the action to be taken with regard to the ships, aircraft or property, subject to the rights of third parties acting in good faith." Thus universal jurisdiction for the crime of piracy is firmly established in positive international law.

Slavery

Slavery has been associated with piracy since 1815, when the Vienna Declaration of the Congress of Vienna equated traffic in slavery to piracy. Since then, there has been a gradual development to include slavery and slave-related practices in positive international law relying on the same type of universal condemnation that exists with respect to piracy. Nevertheless, universal condemnation, which is evident in twenty-seven conventions on the subject of slavery and slave-related practices from 1815 to 1982, did not always produce the resulting universality of jurisdiction.[59] There are also forty-seven other conventions elaborated between 1874 and 1996 applicable to this category of crimes,[60] which, like piracy, is deemed part of the "compelling law."[61]

An analysis of the treaty provisions contained in these conventions reveals that only a few establish universal jurisdiction or allow a state to exercise it.[62] Conventions concerning the suppression of the traffic in women and children and "white slave traffic"[63] and other slave-related practices do not contain specific provisions on universal jurisdiction nor does the Forced Labor Convention.[64]

Universal jurisdiction is evident in treaty provisions for slave trafficking on the high seas, which has been equated with piracy. Universal jurisdiction arises from the use of the high seas, and it is the most effective way to combat such traffic in persons. However, with respect to sexual exploitation of persons, it seems that the conventions have left it to the states to decide what jurisdictional theories they would rely upon. This may be explained in part by the fact that such practices rely on transiting people through state territory and that the ultimate stage of such trafficking is exploitation on the territory of a state. As a result, a state could exercise territorial criminal jurisdiction to combat this international crime without the need for universal jurisdiction. This neutral position on universal jurisdiction is expressed in the 1950 Convention for the Suppression of the Traffic in Persons and of the Exploitation of the Prostitution[65] of Others, which in Article 11 states, "Nothing in the present Convention shall be interpreted as determining the attitude of a Party towards the general question of the limits of criminal jurisdiction under international law."

Whenever slavery and slave-related practices are committed during an armed conflict, they are subject to international humanitarian law and become a war crime. However, even though the crime is international and is classified as serious, the jurisdictional theory relied upon in such cases is usually territoriality.

The provisions contained in all the treaties relevant to slavery and slave-related practices require the signatory states to take effective measures to prevent and suppress such practices. They also provide specific state obligations regarding criminalization and punishment, extradition, and mutual legal assistance. All of these provisions can best be characterized as reflecting the concept of "either extradite or prosecute." This is even true with respect to the more recent treaty provisions that link slavery to piracy. For example, the 1958 Geneva Convention on the Law of the High Seas provides that "every state shall adopt effective measures to prevent and punish the transport of slaves in ships authorized to fly its flag, and to prevent the unlawful use of its flag for that purpose. Any slave taking refuge on board any ship, whatever its flag, shall *ipso facto* be free."[66]

The 1982 Montego Bay Convention on the Law of the Sea also adopted the identical provision in Article 99.

Slavery, like piracy, has greatly diminished in the last two centuries, and that may well have made it possible for states to recognize the application of the theory of universal jurisdiction to what has heretofore been essentially universally condemned. While customary international law and the writings of scholars recognize slavery and slave-related practices as a serious crime under international law, state practice does not yet support universal criminal jurisdiction for all forms and manifestations of slavery and slave-related practices.[67]

Furthermore, the dramatic increase in the last two decades of trafficking in women and children for sexual exploitation has not yet been the subject of a specialized convention.[68] With respect to this category of serious international crimes, it is essentially the writings of scholars that drive the notion that universal criminal jurisdiction should extend to all manifestations of this category of international crimes.

War Crimes

Of all the international crime categories, war crimes are the most elaborately defined and regulated in law.[69] The four Geneva Conventions of 1949[70] and their two Additional Protocols[71] are the most comprehensive codifications of applicable rules and regulations, with the most specific and wide-ranging penal characteristics, of any other category of international crime.[72] The so-called Law of Geneva overlaps with the so-called Law of The Hague,[73] much of the latter having been incorporated into the former. The Law of Geneva has become custom.[74] War crimes are considered serious international crimes.

There are no provisions in these conventions that specifically refer to universal jurisdiction. One can assume that the penal duty to enforce implicitly includes the right of the state parties to exercise universal jurisdiction under their national laws. This arises out of the obligation to prevent and repress "grave breaches" and also out of the provisions of Articles 1 and 2, which are common to the four Geneva Conventions, to wit:

Article 1
    The High Contracting Parties undertake to respect and to ensure respect for the present Convention in all circumstances.
Article 2
    In addition to the provisions which shall be implemented in peacetime, the present Convention shall apply to all cases of declared war or of any other armed conflict which may arise between two or more of the High Contracting Parties, even if the state of war is not recognized by one of them.
    The Convention shall also apply to all cases of partial or total occupation of the territory of a High Contracting Party, even if the said occupation meets with no armed resistance.
    Although one of the Powers in conflict may not be a party to the present Convention, the Powers who are parties thereto shall remain bound by it in their mutual relations. They shall furthermore be bound by the Convention in relation to the said Power, if the latter accepts and applies the provisions thereof.[75]

No convention dealing with the law of armed conflict contains a specific provision on universal jurisdiction. While the Geneva Conventions did provide for universality prior to 1949, it was only then that the term came to require that the accused be physically present on the enforcing state's territory. It requires that there be a nexus to the enforcing state by means of a physical presence, unless the enforcing state has some other nexus via either the nationality of the perpetrator or the victim or has control over the territory over which the crime was committed. It is nevertheless valid to assume that the 1949 Geneva Conventions and Protocol I provide a sufficient basis for states to apply universality of jurisdiction to prevent and repress the "grave breaches" of the conventions.

Customary international law as reflected by the practice of states does not, in the judgment of this writer, mean that universal jurisdiction has been applied in national prosecutions. There are a few cases that are relied upon by some scholars to assert the opposite, but such cases are so few and far between that it would be incorrect to conclude that they constitute customary law practice.

The recognition of universal jurisdiction for war crimes is essentially driven by academics and experts' writings. These confuse the universal reach of war crimes with the universality of jurisdiction over such crimes. There is also confusion arising out of collective enforcement mechanisms, such as the International Military Tribunals established after World War II in Nuremberg and Tokyo (IMT and IMTFE), and the international tribunals established more recently for the former Yugoslavia and Rwanda (ICTY and ICTR). The post–WW II tribunals were collective actions based on the inherent powers of the states as participants in armed conflicts and also on the basis of territoriality. The Yugoslavia and Rwanda tribunals are a form of collective enforcement deriving from the power of the Security Council, but their judicial jurisdiction is territorial. In all of these situations criminal jurisdiction is based on territoriality. With respect to the tribunals at Nuremberg and Tokyo, jurisdiction could be said to have also relied on "passive personality." As stated above, the International Criminal Court (ICC) does not have universal jurisdiction though its reach is universal, except insofar as "referrals" from the Security Council to the ICC, which are based on the theory of universality.[76]

Notwithstanding the above, there is nothing in the Law of Armed Conflict that prohibits national criminal jurisdiction from applying the theory of universality. It can even be argued that the general obligations to enforce, which include the specific obligations to prevent and repress "grave breaches" of the 1949 Geneva Conventions and Protocol I, allow states to expand their jurisdiction to include the theory of universality.

Crimes against Humanity

Crimes against humanity were first defined in positive international criminal law in Article 6(c) of the Nuremberg Charter as "murder, extermination, enslavement, deportation, and other inhumane acts committed against any civilian population, before or during the war; or persecutions on political, racial or religious grounds in execution of or in connection with any crime within the jurisdiction of the Tribunal whether or not in violation of the domestic law of the country where perpetrated.[77]

Similarly, the IMTFE Charter[78] and the Allied Control Council for Germany Law No. 10[79] provided for the prosecution of "crimes against humanity." In prosecutions under all three instruments, however, jurisdiction was territorial in nature, though it can also be argued that it extended to "passive personality." Jurisdiction over crimes against humanity as provided for in the statutes establishing tribunals for former Yugoslavia and Rwanda, and the ICC, jurisdiction[80] is likewise territorial except in the case of "referrals" to the ICC by the Security Council, in which case the jurisdiction is universal.[81] It is also important to note that there is no specialized convention for crimes against humanity.[82] As a result, one cannot say that there is conventional law providing for universal jurisdiction for "crimes against humanity."

With respect to the practice of states, nations such as Canada,[83] Israel,[84] Germany,[85] France,[86] Belgium,[87] and Switzerland[88] have national law provisions for prosecutions of crimes against humanity. But the jurisprudence arising out of these laws does not reflect the theory of universality. The cases prosecuted in these states have been based on the territorial, passive personality, or active personality theories of jurisdiction.

As the Canadian supreme court noted in *Regina v Finta:*

Canadian courts have jurisdiction to try individuals living in Canada for crimes which they allegedly committed on foreign soil *only when the conditions specified in s. 7(3.71) are satisfied.* The most important of those requirements, for the purposes of the present case, is that the alleged crime must constitute a war crime or a crime against humanity. It is thus the *nature* of the act committed that is of crucial importance in the determination of jurisdiction. Canadian courts may not prosecute an ordinary offence that has occurred in a foreign jurisdiction. The only reason Canadian courts can prosecute individuals such as *In re Finta* is because the acts he is alleged to have committed are viewed as being war crimes or crimes against humanity. As Cherif Bassiouni has very properly observed, a war crime or a crime against humanity is not the same as a domestic offence.[89] [emphasis added]

Genocide

The serious international crime of genocide did not exist before the 1948 Convention on the Prevention and Punishment of the Crime of Genocide.[90] Article 6 of the convention states: "Persons charged with genocide or any of the other acts enumerated in article III shall be tried by a competent tribunal of *the State in the territory of which the act was committed,* or by such international penal tribunal as may have jurisdiction with respect to those Contracting Parties which shall have accepted its jurisdiction"[91] [emphasis added]. It is clear from the plain meaning and language of this provision that jurisdiction is territorial and that only if an "international penal tribunal" is established and only if state parties to the Genocide Convention are also state parties to the convention establishing an "international penal tribunal" can the latter court have universal jurisdiction. However, such universal jurisdiction will be dependent upon the statute of that "international penal tribunal," if or when it is established.

Since the adoption of the Genocide Convention, two international ad hoc criminal tribunals were established, namely, the International Criminal Tribunal for the former Yugoslavia (ICTY)[92] and the International Criminal Tribunal for Rwanda (ICTR),[93] in 1993 and 1994, respectively. On July 1, 2002, the treaty for the International Criminal Court came into force.[94] All three statutes contain a provision making genocide a crime within the jurisdiction of the court. But that, in itself, does not give these tribunals universal jurisdiction.

Article 4 of the ICTY defines genocide.[95] Article 2 of the ICTR also defines genocide.[96] However, the jurisdiction of both tribunals is territorial; their competence extends only to crimes committed within the territory of the former Republic of Yugoslavia and Rwanda, respectively. As for the ICC, Article 6 defines genocide in almost the same terms as Article 2 of the Genocide Convention.[97] The jurisdiction of the ICC, as stated above, is essentially territorial as to the parties; the parties can refer cases to the

ICC for crimes that did not occur on their territory and are obligated to surrender persons who are on their territory, whether nationals or non-nationals. Thus, while the reach of the ICC is universal as to "referral" by state parties under Article 14 and non–state parties under Article 12(3), "referrals" by the Security Council have a universal scope and also represent a theory of universal jurisdiction.

Notwithstanding the fact that Article 6 of the Genocide Convention hardly justifies the contention that it reflects the theory of the universality of jurisdiction,[98] commentators argue consistently that customary international law has recognized universality of jurisdiction for crimes of genocide. Nevertheless, state practice has ignored that argument. As Theodor Meron states, "[I]t is increasingly recognized by leading commentators that the crime of genocide (despite the absence of a provision on universal jurisdiction in the Genocide Convention) may also be cause for prosecution by any state."[99]

Notwithstanding this absence of support in conventional international law and in the practice of states, the ICTY's Appeals Chamber, when addressing genocide in the *Tadic* case, stated that "universal jurisdiction [is] nowadays acknowledged in the case of international crimes."[100] Similarly, the ICTR held in the case of *Prosecutor v Ntuyahaga* that universal jurisdiction exists for the crime of genocide.[101]

A number of states have enacted national legislation of a universal reach (see the essay by A. Hays Butler, this volume).

Apartheid

The crime of apartheid did not officially exist until 1973, when the United Nations adopted the Convention on the Suppression and Punishment of the Crime of Apartheid.[102] The convention provides in Article VI, in pertinent part, as follows:

The States Parties to the present Convention undertake:
(b) To adopt legislative, judicial and administrative measures to prosecute, bring to trial and punish in accordance with their jurisdiction persons responsible for, or accused of, the acts defined in article II of the present Convention, whether or not such persons reside in the territory of the State in which the acts are committed or are nationals of that State or of some other State or are stateless persons.[103]

Article VI of the convention states: "Persons charged with the acts enumerated in article II of the present Convention may be tried by a competent tribunal of any State Party to the Convention which may acquire jurisdiction over the person of the accused or by an international penal tribunal having jurisdiction with respect to those State Parties which shall have accepted its jurisdiction."[104]

There is clearly a departure in the text of these two articles from the jurisdictional provision contained in the Genocide Convention, as Articles VI and V of the Apartheid Convention provide unambiguously for universal jurisdiction.[105]

Torture

Torture was established as a crime in conventional international law in the 1984 Convention against Torture and Other Cruel, Inhuman, or Degrading Treatment or Punishment.[106] Article 5 of the convention provides:

1. Each State Party shall take such measures as may be necessary to establish its jurisdiction over the offences referred to in article 4 in the following cases:
   (a) When the offences are committed in any territory under its jurisdiction or on board a ship or aircraft registered in that State;
   (b) When the alleged offender is a national of that State;
   (c) When the victim is a national of that State if that State considers it appropriate.
2. Each State Party shall likewise take such measures as may be necessary to establish its jurisdiction over such offences in cases where the alleged offender is present in any territory under its jurisdiction and it does not extradite him pursuant to article 8 to any of the States mentioned in paragraph 1 of this article.
3. This Convention does not exclude any criminal jurisdiction exercised in accordance with internal law.[107]

The premise of the enforcement scheme in this convention is the concept of "extradite or prosecute."[108] Throughout the convention there are several references to the jurisdiction of the enforcing state, and Article 7(1) of the convention states: "The State Party in the territory under whose jurisdiction a person alleged to have committed any offence referred to in article 4 is found shall in the cases contemplated in article 5, if it does not extradite him, submit the case to its competent authorities for the purpose of prosecution."[109]

But Article 7(1) is more a reflection of "extradite or prosecute" than it is of universal jurisdiction. It establishes the duty to extradite and only in the event that a person is not extradited is a state obligated to prosecute, by implication, in reliance on universal jurisdiction.

In the famous case, *In re Pinochet*, which reached the House of Lords, there was indeed reference to genocide and other international crimes. In the rehearing there was also a reference to universal jurisdiction as a concomitant to international crimes:

That international law crimes should be tried before international tribunals or in the perpetrator's own state is one thing; that they should be impleaded without regard to a long-established customary international law rule in the Courts of other states is another. It is significant that in respect of serious breaches of 'intransgress- ible principles of international customary law' when tribunals have been set up it is with carefully defined powers and jurisdiction as accorded by the states involved; that the Genocide convention provides only for jurisdiction before an international tribunal of the Courts of the state where the crime is committed, that the Rome Statute of the International Criminal Court lays down jurisdiction for crimes in very specific terms but limits its jurisdiction to future acts.[110]

Notwithstanding this *dicta,* the issue was whether the United Kingdom's courts were competent to decide Spain's extradition request for the crimi- nal charge of torture. The other issue was whether extradition should be granted in accordance with the United Kingdom's treaty obligation toward Spain and in accordance with United Kingdom law. The United Kingdom is bound by the United Nations' Torture Convention and is obligated there- under to prosecute or extradite. Spain, also a state party to the convention, sought extradition because its nationals were the victims of the alleged crimes of torture. Thus the *Pinochet* case, in the opinion of this writer, does not stand for the proposition of universal jurisdiction, nor for that matter is the extradition request from Spain for torture based on universal jurisdiction. The Torture Convention, however, implicitly allows universal jurisdiction.

Other Sources of International Criminal Law

There are several international crimes that have not yet risen to the level of serious international crimes but that may explicitly, or implicitly, pro- vide for the theory of universality. For example, the 1963 Tokyo Hijack- ing Convention provides in Article 3(3): "This Convention does not exclude any criminal jurisdiction exercised in accordance with national law."[111] Similarly, the 1970 Hague Hijacking Convention states in Article 4(3): "This Convention does not exclude any criminal jurisdiction exercised in accordance with national law."[112] Article 7 further provides: "The Contract- ing State in the territory of which the alleged offender is found shall, if it does not extradite him, be obliged, without exception whatsoever and whether or not the offence was committed in its territory, to submit the case to its competent authorities for the purpose of prosecution. Those author- ities shall take their decision in the same manner as in the case of any ordi- nary offence of a serious nature under the law of that State."[113]

The 1971 Montreal Hijacking Convention states in Article 5(3): "This Convention does not exclude any criminal jurisdiction exercised in accor- dance with national law."[114] In addition, the 1988 Montreal Convention on Hijacking provides in Article 3: "In Article 5 of the Convention, the follow- ing shall be added as paragraph 2 *bis:* A2 *bis.* Each Contracting State shall likewise take such measures as may be necessary to establish its jurisdiction over the offences mentioned in Article 1, paragraph 1 *bis,* and in Article 1, paragraph 2, in so far as that paragraph relates to those offences, in the case where the alleged offender is present in its territory and it does not extradite him pursuant to Article 8 to the State mentioned in paragraph 1(a) of this Article."[115]

The 1988 Convention on the Suppression of Unlawful Acts against the Safety of Maritime Navigation states in Article 7(4, 5):

4. The rights referred to in paragraph 3 shall be exercised in conformity with the laws and regulations of the State in the territory of which the offender or the alleged offender is present, subject to the proviso that the said laws and regulations must enable full effect to be given to the purposes for which the rights accorded under paragraph 3 are intended.
5. When a State Party, pursuant to this article, has taken a person into custody, it shall immediately notify the States which have established jurisdiction in accordance with article 6, paragraph 1 and, if it considers it advisable, any other interested States, of the fact that such person is in custody and of the circumstances which warrant his detention. The State which makes the preliminary enquiry contemplated in paragraph 2 of this article shall promptly report its findings to the said States and shall indicate whether it intends to exercise jurisdiction.[116]

Article 10(1) of this convention further provides as follows:

1. The State Party in the territory of which the offender or the alleged offender is found shall, in cases to which article 6 applies, if it does not extradite him be obliged, without exception whatsoever and whether or not the offence was committed in its territory, to submit the case without delay to its competent authorities for the purpose of prosecution, through proceedings in accordance with the laws of that State. Those authorities shall take their decision in the same manner as in the case of any other offence of a grave nature under the law of that State.[117]

The Protocol for the Suppression of Unlawful Acts against the Safety of Fixed Platforms Located on the Continental Shelf provides in Article 3:

1. Each State Party shall take such measures as may be necessary to establish its jurisdiction over the offences set forth in article 2 when the offence is committed:
   (a) against or on board a fixed platform while it is located on the continental shelf of that State; or
   (b) by a national of that State.

2. A State Party may also establish its jurisdiction over any such offence when:
   (a) it is committed by a stateless person whose habitual residence is in that State;
   (b) during its commission a national of that State is seized, threatened, injured or killed; or
   (c) it is committed in an attempt to compel that State to do or abstain from doing any act.
3. Any State Party which has established jurisdiction mentioned in paragraph 2 shall notify the Secretary-General of the International Maritime Organization (hereinafter referred to as "the Secretary-General"). If such State Party subsequently rescinds that jurisdiction, it shall notify the Secretary-General.
4. Each State Party shall take such measures as may be necessary to establish its jurisdiction over the offences set forth in article 2 in cases where the alleged offender is present in its territory and it does not extradite him to any of the States Parties which have established their jurisdiction in accordance with paragraphs 1 and 2 of this article.
5. This Protocol does not exclude any criminal jurisdiction exercised in accordance with national law.[118]

The Convention on the Prevention and Punishment of Crimes against Internationally Protected Persons, Including Diplomatic Agents states in Article 3:

1. Each State Party shall take such measures as may be necessary to establish its jurisdiction over the crimes set forth in article 2 in the following cases:
   (a) when the crime is committed in the territory of that State or on board a ship or aircraft registered in that State;
   (b) when the alleged offender is a national of that State;
   (c) when the crime is committed against an internationally protected person as defined in article 1 who enjoys his status as such by virtue of functions which he exercises on behalf of that State.
2. Each State Party shall likewise take such measures as may be necessary to establish its jurisdiction over these crimes in cases where the alleged offender is present in its territory and it does not extradite him pursuant to article 8 to any of the states mentioned in paragraph 1 of this article.
3. This Convention does not exclude any criminal jurisdiction exercised in accordance with internal law.[119]

Similarly, the Convention on the Safety of United Nations and Associated Personnel provides in Article 10:

1. Each State Party shall take such measures as may be necessary to establish its jurisdiction over the crimes set out in article 9 in the following cases:
   (a) When the crime is committed in the territory of that State or on board a ship or aircraft registered in that State;
   (b) When the alleged offender is a national of that State.
2. A State Party may also establish its jurisdiction over any such crime when it is committed:
   (a) By a stateless person whose habitual residence is in that State;
   (b) With respect to a national of that State; or
   (c) In an attempt to compel that State to do or abstain from doing any act.
3. Any State Party which has established jurisdiction as mentioned in paragraph 2 shall notify the Secretary-General of the United Nations. If such State Party subsequently rescinds that jurisdiction, it shall notify the Secretary-General of the United Nations.
4. Each State Party shall take such measures as may be necessary to establish its jurisdiction over the crimes set out in article 9 in cases where the alleged offender is present in its territory and it does not extradite such person pursuant to article 15 to any of the States Parties which have established their jurisdiction in accordance with paragraph 1 or 2.
5. This Convention does not exclude any criminal jurisdiction exercised in accordance with national law.[120]

The 1979 Convention against the Taking of Hostages states in Article 6:

1. Each State Party shall take such measures as may be necessary to establish its jurisdiction over any of the offences set forth in article 1 which are committed:
   (a) in its territory or on board a ship or aircraft registered in that State;
   (b) by any of its nationals or, if that State considers it appropriate, by those stateless persons who have their habitual residence in its territory;
   (c) in order to compel that State to do or abstain from doing any act; or with respect to a hostage who is a national of that State, if that State considers it appropriate.
2. Each State Party shall likewise take such measures as may be necessary to establish its jurisdiction over the offences set forth in article 1 in cases where the alleged offender is present in its territory and it does not extradite him to any of the States mentioned in paragraph 1 of this article.

3. This Convention does not exclude any criminal jurisdiction exercised in accordance with internal law.[121]

The 1961 Single Convention on Narcotic Drugs provides in Article 36(4) that "[n]othing contained in this article shall affect the principle that the offences to which it refers shall be defined, prosecuted and punished in conformity with the domestic law of a Party."[122] Article 22(5) of the 1971 Convention on Psychotropic Substances employs identical language to the 1961 Single Convention.[123]

The 1954 Hague Convention for the Protection of Cultural Property explicitly provides for universality in Article 28: "The High Contracting Parties undertake to take, within the framework of their ordinary criminal jurisdiction, all necessary steps to prosecute and impose penal or disciplinary sanctions upon those persons, of whatever nationality, who commit or order to be committed a breach of the present Convention."[124] The 1970 UNESCO Cultural Convention states in Article 12: "The States Parties to this Convention shall respect the cultural heritage within the territories for the international relations of which they are responsible and shall take all appropriate measures to prohibit and prevent the illicit import, export and transfer of ownership of cultural property in such territories."[125]

The 1923 Convention on Obscene Materials provides in Article 2:
Persons who have committed an offence falling under Article 1 shall be amenable to the Courts of the Contracting Party in whose territories the offence, or any of the constitutive elements of the offence, was committed. They shall also be amenable, when the laws of the country shall permit it, to the Courts of the Contracting Party whose nationals they are, if they are found in its territories, even if the constitutive elements of the offence were committed outside such territories.

Each Contracting Party shall, however, have the right to apply the maxim *non bis in idem* [no double jeopardy] in accordance with the rules laid down in its legislation.[126]

The 1929 Convention on the Suppression of Counterfeiting states in Article 17: "The participation of a High Contracting Party in the present Convention shall not be interpreted as affecting that Party's attitude on the general question of criminal jurisdiction as a question of international law."[127]

The 1884 Submarine Cables Convention provides in Articles 1, 8, and 9 as follows:

Article 1
The present Convention shall be applicable, outside of the territorial waters, to all legally established submarine cables landed in the territories, colonies or possessions of one or more of the High Contracting Parties.
Article 8
The court competent to take cognizance of infractions of this Convention shall

be those of the country to which the vessel on board of which the infraction has been committed belongs.

It is, moreover, understood that, in cases in which the provision contained in the foregoing paragraph cannot be carried out, the repression of violations of this Convention shall take place, in each of the contracting States, in the case of its subjects or citizens, in accordance with the general rules of penal competence established by the special laws of those States, or by international treaties.
Article 9

Prosecutions on account of the infractions contemplated in articles 2, 5 and 6 of this Convention, shall be instituted by the State or in its name.[128]

Lastly, the Mercenaries Convention states in Article 9(2, 3):

2. Each State Party shall likewise take such measures as may be necessary to establish its jurisdiction over the offences set forth in articles 2, 3, and 4 of the present Convention in cases where the alleged offender is present in its territory and it does not extradite him to any of the States mentioned in paragraph 1 of this article.
3. The present Convention does not exclude any criminal jurisdiction exercised in accordance with national law.[129]

As can be seen, these conventions relate mostly to what is commonly "terrorism" and narcotics. These activities involve individuals and small groups who are usually not state sponsored. Consequently, it is easier for states to recognize and apply the theory of universality and other enforcement modalities to these types of actors than to those who carry out state policy. This explains why, notwithstanding the extensive harm caused by genocide and crimes against humanity (and to a lesser extent apartheid and torture), states have been reluctant to use the same enforcement modalities in these later crimes. In other words, conventions on international crimes involving state policy or state action contain less effective enforcement mechanisms than other international conventions.[130]

Conclusion

The historical evolution of serious crimes under international law (from their recognition as being offensive to certain values to their universal condemnation and finally to their universal proscription) developed in different ways. The distinctive historical evolution of each of these serious international crimes resembles that of other categories of international crimes.[131] Their emergence, growth, and inclusion in positive international criminal law went through different stages that were in some respect similar, but the gestational periods within each of these stages differed.[132]

The practices of piracy, slavery, torture, and what is now contained in international humanitarian law have existed as far back as human history is recorded. And while piracy, slavery, and war crimes have evolved over centuries through declarative prescriptions and later in enforcement proscriptions,[133] some crimes like genocide, apartheid, and torture did not. Each became international crimes by virtue of their respective embodiment in single conventions adopted in 1948, 1973, and 1984. Crimes against humanity, however, had a short gestational period between 1919 (when it was first proposed and almost adopted) and 1945 (when it was embodied in positive international criminal law in the Nuremberg Charter.)[134] And while it has been included in the statutes of the ICTY, ICTR, and ICC, crimes against humanity have still not been the subject of a specialized convention, as have genocide, torture, and apartheid.[135]

Universal jurisdiction, as discussed above, resembles a checkerboard. Some conventions recognize it, and some customary practices of states demonstrate its existence, although uneven and inconsistent. The tendency of state practice has been to not apply it. Great confusion has resulted from the fact that the "universality" has at least five meanings:

(1) universality of condemnation for certain crimes;
(2) universal reach of national jurisdiction, which could be for the international crime for which there is universal condemnation, as well as others;
(3) extraterritorial reach of national jurisdiction (which may also merge with universal reach of national legislation);
(4) universal reach of international adjudicative bodies that may or may not rely on the theory of universal jurisdiction; and
(5) universal jurisdiction of national legal systems without any connection to the enforcing state other than the presence of the accused.

The writings of scholars have driven the recognition of the theory of universal jurisdiction for serious international crimes and have offered new interpretations of customary international law, albeit without much support in the law and practice of states (although national legislation providing for universal jurisdiction is growing, as Hays Butler makes clear). These scholarly writings reflect universalistic normative views as well as pragmatic policy perspectives. Over time the combination of these sources of law produced a cumulative effect: many have been persuaded that universal jurisdiction is an effective method to deter and prevent serious crimes by increasing the likelihood of prosecution and punishment of the perpetrators, and reducing impunity for these crimes.[136] In conclusion, the policy-based assumptions and goals of those who promote universal jurisdiction are that a broader jurisdictional mechanism can prevent, deter, punish, provide accountability, and reduce impunity, and also enhance the prospects of justice and peace.

Irrespective of the checkered nature of the recognition and application of the theory of universal jurisdiction in international law and national practice, there are favorable policy arguments that support its application. But universal jurisdiction must not be allowed to become a wildfire, uncontrolled in its application and destructive of orderly legal processes. If that were to happen, it would produce jurisdictional conflicts between states that could threaten world order, subject individuals to abuses of judicial processes and to politically motivated harassment. Universal jurisdiction exercised without the guidance of responsible consensus principles such as those embodied in the Princeton Principles on Universal Jurisdiction could lead to increased conflict and the denial of justice.

To avoid these negative outcomes and enhance the responsible use of universal jurisdiction, it is necessary to create norms that bind states and international adjudicating bodies.[137] It is hoped that the Princeton Principles, or perhaps a set of revised and refined principles, will in time garner consensus among scholars and, ultimately, among governments. Then an international convention should be convened so that guidelines on universal jurisdiction can become positive international law.

The history of contemporary international law is replete with examples of scholarly and NGO initiatives that have set in motion a process that ripened into conventional international law. The Princeton initiative is one of these instances, and this writer hopes that it will result in an international convention on universal jurisdiction for serious international crimes that includes jurisdictional priorities, provides rules for resolving conflicts of jurisdiction, and minimizes the exposure of individuals to multiple prosecutions, abuses of process, and denial of justice.[138] Many of these issues are taken up in the essays that follow.

Chapter 2
Comment: The Quest for Clarity

Stephen A. Oxman

M. Cherif Bassiouni's impressive treatment of the historical development of universal jurisdiction certainly supports his conclusion that universal jurisdiction resembles a "checkerboard" and is replete with unevenness and inconsistency.[1] Indeed, as I read this fascinating history I began to have images of the old Chinese proverb, "We're in a muddy river that leads to a muddy lake." Our hope, of course, in the Princeton Project on Universal Jurisdiction is to understand that river as best we can and to help purify the water so that in due course the lake is as clear as possible, or at least clearer than it would be without our efforts.

Toward that end it is essential to ask with respect to universal jurisdiction: is there a way to simplify the complexity, to reduce the concept to the bare essentials, and to make it more understandable to nonexperts? I came to the view that the best way to do this is to focus mainly on the case of "pure" universal jurisdiction and to construct guiding principles that, if they work well when applied to the pure case, can be adapted as necessary to take account of less pure cases and other refinements.

As Bassiouni points out, some confusion arises because the universality principle has at least five meanings.[2] I submit it is the fifth meaning he lists that should be our focus in the Princeton Project, namely "universal jurisdiction of national legal systems without any connection to the enforcing state other than the presence of the accused."[3] Is this not the pure case—in other words, a case where none of the traditional jurisdictional nexuses exists and where the *only* nexus, other than the presence of the accused, is the universally recognized heinousness of the alleged crime itself? That is, there is jurisdiction "without regard to where the crime was committed, the nationality of the alleged or convicted perpetrator, the nationality of the victim, or any other connection to the state exercising such jurisdiction."[4] (There is, of course, the "super pure" case in which jurisdiction would exist even without the presence of the accused, a position taken recently by Belgium; but I believe clear analysis will be most facilitated if we focus in the first instance on the pure case, leaving the super pure case for subsequent consideration in light of the results of the main analysis.)

In focusing on that pure case, there is a certain humbling effect, on me at least, for it would appear from Bassiouni's essay, as well as the other essays that follow, that as a matter of actual historical and current custom and practice, there have been many fewer instances than one might expect of the pure case of universal jurisdiction.

An example of how confusion has arisen concerning the prevalence of universal jurisdiction is, as Bassiouni has observed elsewhere,[5] the treatment of the Genocide Convention. Some commentators assert that a country embraces universal jurisdiction because it has a provision in its law concerning genocide—the assumption being that genocide includes universal jurisdiction, and therefore through incorporation by reference, a country that has a norm on genocide also has endorsed universal jurisdiction. But even assuming the validity of such incorporation by reference, is the central premise not erroneous because the Genocide Convention, as Bassiouni has pointed out, does not in fact provide for universal jurisdiction except where a special international tribunal is established for that purpose—and we are here focusing on national, not international, tribunals?[6] Confusion can also arise because, to say the least, there is not always a bright line delineating what is or is not part of customary international law.

That there have been fewer pure cases than one might expect is perhaps not surprising because nations and their courts seem predisposed, for understandable reasons, to avoid the less familiar, somewhat scary waters of universal jurisdiction when instead they can find, or fictionalize, a traditional jurisdictional nexus—or can extradite the defendant to a forum where such a traditional nexus exists. Just as a U.S. court will avoid deciding a case on constitutional grounds if it can be decided on statutory grounds, so do national courts seem to avoid embracing the universality principle when a less extraordinary jurisdictional basis exists.

Given the relative paucity of pure universal jurisdiction cases—and given what Bassiouni calls "the checkered nature of the recognition and application of the theory of universal jurisdiction in international law and national practice"[7]—is there not a particularly inviting opportunity for the formulation of consensus principles to guide practice in this area? And should not the principles focus on the pure case? Moreover, should not the principles reflect both what the law is and what it should be? In that way we may build on, yet also move beyond, such inconsistencies, ambiguities, and undue complexities as exist in current law and articulate a compelling, more easily understood, and workable conceptual framework, a framework for what Bassiouni calls "a broader jurisdictional mechanism" that can—provided it does not become a "wildfire"—"prevent, deter, punish, provide accountability, and reduce impunity, and also enhance the prospects of justice and peace."[8]

Let me make the same point in a somewhat different way. The great sweep of Bassiouni's essay reminds us implicitly that universal jurisdiction is and should be mainly about a body of law—not about "getting" the perpetrators of heinous crimes. If the main object were to "get" people, lawless summary executions (preceded if necessary by lawless abductions) would no doubt suffice, and there would be no real need for a body of law except as a fig leaf.

The problem is that the existing body of law on universal jurisdiction is imperfect in a variety of ways made apparent in Bassiouni's treatment. These deficiencies can and should be corrected. In that way we may achieve an outcome where, increasingly over time, alleged perpetrators of these heinous crimes will have to face credible charges in some legitimate court of law, will have a full and fair opportunity to defend themselves, and will face appropriate punishment if found guilty. That outcome will also have the salutary effect of strongly deterring would-be perpetrators. Let us hope that these objectives will be materially advanced by the work of the Princeton Project on Universal Jurisdiction

Two final comments. First, as part of an effort to reduce complexity and add clarity, may I suggest another way of looking at the issue, a conceptual framework perhaps not rooted in the historical evolution of universal jurisdiction but rooted rather in the present-day fact that there is growing acceptance around the world of the notion that there should be accountability for heinous crimes of the type we are discussing. That is, no one seems to be seriously arguing that people credibly alleged to have perpetrated such crimes should escape scot-free. If we suppose that everyone agrees that there must be accountability in some forum for such crimes, then does not the analysis boil down conceptually to determining what is the most appropriate forum? Are we not then involved in addressing reasonably straightforward questions concerning what legal forums are available and what interests in prosecution these different forums might assert? (Lawyers will be familiar with the weighing of traditional factors and interests under the rubrics of *forum non conveniens* and conflicts of law.) Is this a useful way to conceptualize the issue, or is it too simplistic? A helpful discussion of some of these matters can be found in Leila Nadya Sadat's contribution to this volume.

Second, Bassiouni's essay would seem to indicate that the development of universal jurisdiction over time has not explicitly included much attention to the need for flexibility, much less possible mechanisms for flexibility such as truth commissions. As Richard Falk observes in his essay in this volume on the Pinochet case, flexibility may well be needed during the fragile early period of a transition lest the transition be killed in its cradle.[9] Bassiouni's fine essay leaves the reader eager to know much more about how the need for flexibility fits into, or onto, the historical development of universal jurisdiction. Fortunately, some of the essays that follow cast additional light on this problem.

Chapter 3
The Growing Support for Universal Jurisdiction in National Legislation

A. Hays Butler

Introduction

Many countries that signed the Rome Statute of the International Criminal Court have either enacted or are in the process of enacting legislation authorizing the Statute.[1] At a minimum, in adopting such statutes, states must enact legislation permitting the surrender of accused persons to the court and requiring authorities to cooperate with the court. However, some states, in an effort to assure that their national courts can be an effective complement to the International Criminal Court (ICC), have gone much further and have provided their courts with universal jurisdiction[2] over crimes subject to ICC jurisdiction.[3] While such enabling statutes have become particularly important since the adoption of the Rome Statute, similar laws have existed for many years and were adopted primarily in response to international obligations to implement various conventions adopted since World War II, such as the Geneva Conventions. The purpose of this essay is to survey such statutes and to compare differing national approaches to universal jurisdiction. The essay also shows that in recent years there has been remarkable progress in many countries in broadening the scope of the universal jurisdiction that domestic courts are authorized to exercise. Whereas in 1999 Belgium was virtually alone in authorizing its courts to exercise universal jurisdiction over genocide, crimes against humanity, and war crimes in internal armed conflicts, as of this writing, numerous other countries, such as the United Kingdom and Germany, have adopted similar legislation.

For purposes of analyzing such legislation, it is useful to divide the statutes into three categories. The first category generally includes legislation that has been recently enacted, primarily in response to the Rome Statute. These statutes, particularly those adopted in Canada, the United Kingdom, and Belgium, demonstrate how the Rome Statute has led some jurisdictions to comprehensively revise earlier legislation on universal juris-diction in an effort to create domestic enforcement systems that effectively complement the international enforcement system established by the Rome Statute. Such legislation includes unique and unconventional features, pro-viding, for example, national courts with universal jurisdiction over inter-national crimes, such as crimes against humanity, even when not required to do so by international treaty obligations.

The second category generally includes legislation enacted prior to the Rome Statute. The purpose of such legislation has been to implement a state's obligations under international conventions establishing an exten-sive body of rules and principles for dealing with crimes under inter-national law. These conventions frequently require states (1) to recognize certain conduct as constituting an international crime, (2) to criminalize the conduct in their domestic law, (3) to prosecute or extradite alleged offenders, and (4) to establish criminal jurisdiction in their court systems over such conduct.[4] Prominent examples of this type of legislation include the Geneva Conventions Act in the United Kingdom and Article 23 of the Organic Law of the Judicial Branch in Spain upon which the Audiencia Nacional based its assertion of universal jurisdiction over the crimes com-mitted in Chile by General Pinochet.[5]

The third category includes legislation on universal jurisdiction that places significant chronological and/or geographical restrictions on the exercise of universal jurisdiction (for example, by limiting prosecutions to crimes committed in Europe during World War II, or to crimes committed in one particular state, such as Rwanda or the former Yugoslavia). While the statutes in both the second and third categories involve the implemen-tation of treaty obligations, these restrictions on the exercise of universal jurisdiction justify placing these enabling statutes in a separate category.

This essay will survey and compare these differing national approaches to universal jurisdiction. Examples have been chosen generally from com-mon law and European jurisdictions, both because the statutory material from these states is readily available (generally in English) and because the jurisdictions provide outstanding illustrations of different national approaches to providing their national courts with universal jurisdiction.[6]

Universal Jurisdiction Legislation Enacted after the Rome Statute

One of the most significant consequences of the Rome Statute has been its impact on domestic statutes concerning prosecutions for international crimes based on universal jurisdiction. The statutes enacted in Belgium, Canada, and the United Kingdom, in particular, demonstrate this remark-able trend. In adopting legislation implementing the Rome Statute, these states have adopted comprehensive legislation providing their courts with universal jurisdiction over genocide, war crimes, and crimes against humanity (the crimes covered by the Rome Statute).

Belgium

Belgium's statute represents one of the most extensive assertions of universal jurisdiction over genocide, crimes against humanity, and war crimes by any state as well as one of the best examples of a statute that, to a significant extent, reflects the vision underlying the Princeton Principles on Universal Jurisdiction (the Principles). In 1993 Belgium adopted a statute implementing the 1949 Geneva Conventions and the two protocols. The statute prohibited as "crimes under international law" twenty acts that constitute "grave breaches" under the conventions. In 1999 the Belgium legislature added the crimes of genocide and crimes against humanity.[7] The new legislation also provided the Belgian courts with comprehensive and unconditional universal jurisdiction over these crimes: "The Belgian courts shall be competent to deal with breaches provided for in the present Act, irrespective of where such breaches have been committed."[8] By criminalizing the same conduct prohibited by the Rome Statute and asserting universal jurisdiction over such crimes, the statute demonstrates an intention to create a domestic enforcement system that will complement the ICC's jurisdiction.

The act contains a number of striking features that assure that the Belgian courts effectively complement the ICC. The typical universal jurisdiction enabling statute enacted prior to the adoption of the Rome Statute implements a state's obligation under an international treaty (such as the Geneva Conventions). The universal jurisdiction provided for in the Belgian statute significantly exceeds, however, Belgium's international treaty obligations. No international convention requires Belgium to prosecute crimes against humanity or to assert universal jurisdiction over genocide offenses.[9] In addition, Belgium has exceeded its treaty obligations under the Geneva Conventions by including violations occurring in both international and noninternational armed conflicts.[10] The comprehensive scope of serious international crimes covered by the statute covers the majority of the crimes that are defined in the Principles as appropriate for universal jurisdiction, including piracy, slavery, war crimes, crimes against peace, crimes against humanity, genocide, and torture. See Principle 2.[11]

Second, the scope and design of the universal jurisdiction conferred by the statute also assures that the Belgian courts will effectively complement the International Criminal Court. The restrictions on the exercise of such jurisdiction that appear in the statutes of many jurisdictions, including double criminality and extradition requirements,[12] are notably absent.[13] Even more significant, the statute permits Belgian courts to exercise universal jurisdiction even if the accused is not present in Belgium.[14] As Human Rights Watch has described the legislation: "Belgium has probably provided for the most extensive exercise of universal jurisdiction over human rights of any country. Belgian courts can try cases of war crimes (internal or international), crimes against humanity, and genocide committed by non-Belgians outside of Belgium against non-Belgians, without even the presence of the accused in Belgium."[15]

Canada

One of the positive results of the Rome Statute has been the stimulus given to many states to improve their existing legislation on universal jurisdiction. The Crimes against Humanity and War Crimes Act, a recently enacted Canadian statute, is a good example of this phenomenon.[16] Canada took advantage of the implementation of the Rome Statute to simplify and improve its existing statutes on universal jurisdiction. In 1987 Canada had adopted legislation providing that any person who commits a war crime or a crime against humanity outside Canada "shall be deemed to [have] commit[ted] that [crime] in Canada" at the time of the act or omission, if the crime, "committed in Canada, would constitute an offense against the laws of Canada in force at [that time]."[17] The statute thus established extraterritorial jurisdiction over crimes against humanity and war crimes by creating the fiction that the crimes were committed in Canada.[18]

The Supreme Court of Canada's decision in *R. v Finta* [1994] 1 S.C.R. 701, the first and only case brought under this legislation, established a number of serious obstacles to effective universal jurisdiction prosecutions under this statute. Finta was acquitted, and the case was appealed to the Supreme Court of Canada. While affirming the statute's constitutionality, the court interpreted the legislation in a manner that made prosecution so difficult that the government shifted its emphasis to citizenship revocation and deportation proceedings.[19]

The new Canadian statute attempts to eliminate the obstacles created by the *Finta* decision. The legislation replaces the earlier provisions with actual offenses of genocide, crimes against humanity, and war crimes and makes it an offense to commit such crimes either inside or outside Canada. Unlike the earlier statute, prosecutions can be brought directly for these international crimes, rather than having to rely on domestic crimes, such as murder. This removes the burden on the prosecution of proving the elements of both the international crime and the underlying domestic offense.[20]

The statute's definition of offenses is designed to reflect both the corresponding offenses in the Rome Statute and the evolving standards of international law. For example, a war crime is defined as an "act or omission committed during an armed conflict that, at the time and in the place of its commission, constitutes a war crime *according to customary international law or conventional international law* [emphasis added] applicable to armed conflicts, whether or not it constitutes a contravention or the law in force at the time and in the place of its commission."[21] The definition of each offense, however, is also directly linked to the definitions in the Rome Statute. Section 4(4) stipulates that the definitions of genocide, crimes against humanity, and war crimes set forth in the Rome Statute reflect the state of customary international law as of the date of the adoption of the Rome Statute.[22]

There is one significant difference between the Belgian statute and the Canadian statute. Unlike the Belgian statute, a defendant over whom the court has jurisdiction may not be prosecuted for an offense unless he is present in Canada. This difference between the Belgian and Canadian legislation reflects the common law emphasis on the right of confrontation and the difficulty of conducting trials in absentia consistent with due process standards.[23]

United Kingdom

As with Canada and Belgium, the United Kingdom, in legislation implementing the Rome Statute, has significantly expanded the scope of universal jurisdiction provided to British courts under earlier statutes. The United Kingdom originally implemented its obligations under the Geneva Conventions and the Torture Convention in two separate statutes. When the United Kingdom became a party to the UN Convention against Torture, it provided its courts with universal jurisdiction in Section 134(1) of the Criminal Justice Act of 1988. The Geneva Conventions Act of 1957 provides that any person, "whether in or outside the United Kingdom," who commits "graves breaches" of the four Geneva Conventions of 1949 is guilty of a felony and subject to the criminal jurisdiction of the British courts.[24] These are crimes committed during international armed conflicts and include offenses such as "willful killing, torture, or inhuman treatment."[25] States are required to adopt legislation permitting prosecution for such acts regardless of the location of the crime.[26]

The International Criminal Court Act, recently enacted by the Parliament, substantially expands the universal jurisdiction provided by these earlier statutes.[27] In addition to providing various forms of assistance to the ICC, the legislation makes crimes that are offenses under the Rome Statute (for example, genocide, crimes against humanity, and war crimes)[28] offenses under British domestic law.[29] Under the legislation, British courts have jurisdiction over such offenses whether committed by a United Kingdom national or by anyone residing in the United Kingdom, irrespective of the suspected offender's nationality or the country in which the crime was committed.[30] This provision, in a manner similar to that of the Canadian and Belgian statutes, effectively provides the British courts with universal jurisdiction over crimes covered by the Rome Statute. The purpose of the legislation is both to permit universal jurisdiction prosecutions and to assure that British citizens accused of committing serious international crimes the right to be tried in British courts. As Robin Cook, the foreign secretary, explained in the House of Commons on April 3, 2001: "[This] provision removes any concern that the absence of such a provision could leave Britain a safe haven for war criminals who have not yet been indicted by the International Criminal Court. . . . [In addition, this section] means that in all circumstances Britain will be able to pursue any bona fide allegation of an offense by United Kingdom citizens through our domestic courts rather than allowing procedures to take their course through the International Criminal Court.[31]

While the new legislation expands jurisdiction over international crimes, "official position" immunity may still constitute a defense, as the law lords held in the *Pinochet* decision:

The House of Lords decided in essence that, as far as civil and criminal liability is concerned, a head of state enjoys absolute and complete immunity while he remains in office (*immunity ratione personae*). At common law, heads of state forfeit personal immunity on ceasing to serve in that capacity, but still cannot be sued for acts performed in their official capacity while they were heads of state (*immunity ratione materiae*).
. . . It is clear . . . that following the entry in force of the Torture Convention for a particular state, the head of state cannot claim *immunity ratione materiae* for acts that fall within the criminal prescription of the Convention.[32]

While the International Criminal Court Act provides that any immunity based on official capacity will not prevent surrender of any person to the ICC,[33] it does not appear to remove the immunity for sitting heads of state from prosecution recognized in the *Pinochet* decision. It is important to distinguish between the immunity rules applicable in proceedings determining whether to surrender accused persons to the ICC for trial and immunity rules applicable in domestic prosecutions. On the one hand, where the proceeding involves surrender to the ICC, the new statute applies the immunity principles contained in the Rome Statute. On the other hand, where the proceeding involves a domestic prosecution, the statute does not appear to alter the immunity principles enunciated in the *Pinochet* decision.

The immunity recognized by the *Pinochet* decision is consistent with the position of the Principles. The topic of immunity for serious international crimes was extensively discussed in the Princeton Project. Principle 5 rejects substantive immunity: "The official position of any accused person, whether as head of state or government or as a responsible government official, shall not relieve such person of criminal responsibility nor mitigate punishment." However, the comment on the Principles also recognizes that, under customary international law, "[p]rocedural immunity remains in effect during a head of state's or other official's tenure in office, or during the period in which the diplomat is accredited to a host state."[34]

Universal Jurisdiction Statutes Implementing International Treaty Obligations

Legislation providing for universal jurisdiction adopted before the Rome Statute was primarily limited to implementing international treaty obligations. Spain's approach to universal jurisdiction is an example of this type of statute. As the Audiencia held in the *Pinochet* proceeding, Article 23(4) of the Organic Law of the Judicial Branch "provides for Spanish jurisdiction over acts committed by Spaniards or foreigners outside the national territory that can be defined, under the criminal law of Spain, as any of the offenses that it lists, beginning with genocide . . . and followed by terrorism . . . including lastly, any other offense which 'under international treaties or conventions, should be prosecuted in Spain.'"[35]

Article 23 merely provides the jurisdictional authority of the Spanish courts: "Article 23(4) is not a substantive provision of criminal law but a procedural rule. It does not define or criminalize any act or omission, and it is limited to proclaiming Spain's jurisdiction for trying offenses defined and punished in other laws."[36]

Thus, Spanish courts have universal jurisdiction for international crimes so long as the obligation to prosecute such crimes is included in an international treaty to which Spain is a party and the particular conduct in question is defined as a crime under Spanish law. For example, under Article 23, Spanish courts have universal jurisdiction over the crime of torture since torture is a crime under Spanish law and Spain ratified the Torture Convention in 1987, which requires Spain to exercise jurisdiction over torture, wherever the crime is committed.

Article 23 also provides Spanish courts with universal jurisdiction over genocide and terrorism. Since there is no obligation for any state to exercise universal jurisdiction under the Genocide Convention, Spanish courts would not have such jurisdiction under the general treaty obligation clause. Indeed, it was argued to the Audiencia that the Genocide Convention implicitly rejected universal jurisdiction by providing only for either territorial jurisdiction or jurisdiction before an international tribunal. The court rejected this argument in the *Pinochet* proceeding and held that the convention did not bar the exercise of universal jurisdiction pursuant to the language of Article 23.

A final important feature of the Spanish legislation concerns its double jeopardy provisions and their impact on amnesty defenses. Article 23(2)(c) limits the extraterritorial jurisdiction of Spanish courts to cases in which the defendant has not been "pardoned, acquitted, or punished."[37] The prosecutor argued in the *Pinochet* proceeding that the case should be dismissed because of Chile's amnesty law. The Audiencia rejected this claim and held that the amnesty law should not be construed as a true pardon since it decriminalized "criminal conduct for reasons of political convenience."

Since Pinochet's guilt or innocence was never determined in Chile, the "pardon" requirement was not satisfied.[38]

Although Germany has adopted a universal jurisdiction statute similar to Belgium's, an analysis of the older German legislation demonstrates the extensive legislative reform stimulated in many states by the Rome Statute. Section 6 of the German Criminal Code established universal jurisdiction over genocide or where Germany was subject to an international treaty obligation.[39] Unlike the Belgian and Canadian statutes, war crimes and crimes against humanity were not specifically defined as crimes in the German Criminal Code. Therefore, if German jurisdiction were established pursuant to the above provisions, German law, not international law, provided the basis for any prosecution.[40] This legal framework has now been almost entirely replaced by a new International Criminal Code that essentially incorporates the crimes covered by the Rome Statute into the German Criminal Code in a manner similar to the legislation adopted by Belgium and the United Kingdom.[41]

Universal Jurisdiction Statutes Limited to Prosecuting War Criminals in Specific Conflicts

Several jurisdictions have limited the universal jurisdiction that can be exercised by their courts to certain times and certain places. Because of these extreme limitations, these statutes contribute very little to the international effort to deter and prosecute international crimes. For example, France represents a state where universal jurisdiction over genocide and crimes against humanity appears, in general, to be geographically limited. Articles 211(1) and 212(1) of the French Penal Code of 1994 prohibit genocide and crimes against humanity. However, neither provision provides for universal jurisdiction over these crimes.[42] Jurisdiction over offenses committed outside France is governed by Article 113 of the code. Article 113 provides for extraterritorial jurisdiction based on active and passive personality principles. In addition, this article provides for extraterritorial jurisdiction for offenses committed outside France on ships flying the French flag or on aircraft registered in France. However, no provision in Article 113 provides universal jurisdiction over genocide or crimes against humanity.[43] The only international crime for which France has explicitly provided universal jurisdiction is torture.[44]

While universal jurisdiction does not generally exist over genocide and crimes against humanity under French law, it appears that such jurisdiction exists if the crimes were committed in Rwanda or the former Yugoslavia. In 1995 an investigation was commenced against Wenceslas Munyeshyaka for his role in the 1994 massacres against the Tutsis in Kigali. He was to be investigated for genocide and crimes against humanity under Articles 211 and 212 of the French Penal Code and Article 689 of the Criminal

Procedure Code. The Nimes Appeal Court held that only the crime of genocide was applicable and that there was no basis in French law for universal jurisdiction over the crime. The Cour de Cassation reversed this decision, finding that jurisdiction existed, citing the French legislation implementing the Security Council Resolution establishing the International Criminal Tribunal for Rwanda, Article 211 (Genocide), and Article 689 (Torture).[45]

While statutes appear close to passage in Australia similar to other statutes enacted after adoption of the Rome Statute, the Australian War Crimes Amendment Act 1988 is an example of universal jurisdiction legislation adopted in some countries designed exclusively to prosecute World War II war criminals. In 1987 the Australian government, in response to a report that a number of people who committed serious war crimes in World War II were residing in Australia, introduced legislation that eventually became the War Crimes Amendment Act 1988.[46] The statute permits the prosecution of war criminals whose crimes were committed between September 1, 1939, and May 8, 1945. Since the legislation applies to crimes committed outside Australia by individuals with whom Australia had no connection at the time of the crime, the jurisdiction conferred by the statute can be characterized as universal. However, this type of jurisdiction does nothing to deter future war crimes or crimes against humanity and represents a very limited legislative response to the narrow problem of war criminals from the World War II residing in Australia.[47]

Conclusion

One of the most important conclusions of the Princeton Project is the recognition of the need for legislative reform in many countries to address the significant limits imposed on the exercise of universal jurisdiction by almost all states.[48] While statutes enacted prior to adoption of the Rome Statute are very diverse, the scope of their universal jurisdiction provisions is often quite limited and subject to many restrictions. However, since the Princeton Project on Universal Jurisdiction began several years ago, there has been remarkable progress in many countries in broadening the scope of the universal jurisdiction that domestic courts are authorized to exercise. As recently as 1999, Belgium was one of the few states that authorized its courts to exercise universal jurisdiction over genocide, crimes against humanity, and war crimes in internal armed conflicts. Legislation in other jurisdictions covered one or more of these crimes but not all three. Since that time, numerous other countries, such as the United Kingdom and Germany, have adopted similar legislation.

The enactment of such legislation will enable national and international criminal standards to evolve in a complementary and mutually supportive fashion. The limited universal jurisdiction provisions in many statutes enacted prior to the Rome Statute, such as those of Spain and Germany, had been hampered by the failure of such states to directly incorporate international crimes in their criminal codes and their reliance on domestic crimes, such as homicide, as the source of substantive criminal liability. Most statutes adopted in recent years (for example, those of Canada, New Zealand, and Australia) generally incorporate international crimes covered by the Rome Statute into their criminal codes, thus permitting the state's domestic law to reflect more accurately the evolving standards of international law.

The traditional immunity for senior government officials under customary international law continues to pose a significant obstacle to domestic prosecutions for international crimes. However, there is growing recognition that such immunity is primarily procedural in nature, rather than substantive, and exists only so long as the suspected offender holds office. As the concurring opinion in the International Court of Justice's recent decision in *Democratic Republic of Congo v Belgium* noted:

> The increasing recognition of the importance of ensuring that the perpetrators of serious international crimes do not go unpunished has had its impact on the immunities which high state dignitaries enjoyed under traditional customary law. Now it is generally recognized that in the case of such crimes, which are often committed by high officials who make use of the power invested in the State, immunity is never substantive and thus cannot exculpate the offender from personal criminal responsibility. It has also given rise to a tendency, in the case of international crimes, to grant personal immunity from jurisdiction only for as long as the suspected state official is in office.[49]

As nations have gradually broadened the scope of domestic jurisdiction over international crimes and limited immunities from prosecution, a system of international criminal justice has begun to emerge in which both international criminal tribunals and national courts have an important and mutually reinforcing role to play in the enforcement of international criminal norms. The emergence of this system surely increases the likelihood that the recently established International Criminal Court will achieve its central mission, as eloquently articulated by Kofi Annan, United Nations Secretary General: "In the prospect of an International Criminal Court lies the promise of universal justice. That is the simple and soaring hope of this vision. We are close to its realization. We will do our part to see it through to the end. We ask . . . you to do yours in our struggle to ensure that no ruler, no state, no Junta, and no army anywhere in the world can abuse human rights with impunity. Only then will the innocents of distant wars and conflicts know that they, too, may sleep under the cover of justice; that they, too, have rights and that those who violate those rights will be punished."[50]

Chapter 4
The Adolf Eichmann Case:
Universal and National Jurisdiction

Gary J. Bass

> And with lightning speed my tanks turn and thunder eastward. . . .
> With furious wrath they hound all the bands of the butchers of the
> Jews: Poles, Lithuanians, Ukrainians. . . . And I see Moshe Dayan, in
> his dusty battle dress, standing awesome and gaunt, as he receives in
> grim silence the surrender of the governor general of Kishinev.
> —Amos Oz, *A Late Love*

The capture of Adolf Eichmann in Buenos Aires by Israeli agents in April
1960, and his trial in Jerusalem about a year later, was so spectacularly dramatic that it almost seems wrong to look to it as precedent. Louis Henkin,
for instance, an international law specialist, warily wrote: "For the law of
jurisdiction . . . the Eichmann case may be too extraordinary to serve as
precedent. Unpunished Nazi criminals will not long be with us. The possibility of new genocides cannot, alas, be totally discounted; but it is far from
clear that their perpetrators will be brought to judicial trial, and the coin-
cidence of factors impelling exercise of jurisdiction solely on the 'universal'
principle would in any event be rare. . . . The Eichmann case reminds us of
an area of the law that has not yet been shaken by the new winds."[1]

Since Henkin wrote, the news has been largely gloomy. True, there are
fewer and fewer Nazi war criminals who have eluded the ravages of age (if
not justice), but there is a fresh crop of Cambodians, Serbians, Croatians,
and Rwandans to take their sorry place. And the judicial punishment of perpetrators is still hardly something to take for granted—it is still, as it was
in 1961, something rare and astonishing.

There is no point in pretending that the Eichmann case is a perfectly
apposite precedent for current efforts at universal jurisdiction for war
crimes. It is, however, one of the few precedents of any kind at hand, and as
such even the most dubious aspects of the trial are receiving new attention.

For instance, prosecutors at the United Nations war crimes tribunal for the former Yugoslavia have found themselves poring over Israeli arguments for abducting Eichmann from Argentina to justify the arrests of two suspects who claim they were caught in Serbia proper.[2]

In one sense, the Israeli abduction of Adolf Eichmann and his subsequent trial before an Israeli court is an important precursor to current notions of universal jurisdiction. After all, here was a sovereign state invoking its jurisdiction over a war criminal hiding out in Argentina, and on that basis trying him. But in another sense, this was a case of distinctly nonuniversal jurisdiction: the Jewish state trying a man for the extermination of the Jews. The Eichmann case is as much about Jewish justice as universal justice.[3]

Both of these brands of justice—the national and the universal—are important for future prosecutions under universal jurisdiction. Although the legal duty of universal jurisdiction may seem to weigh equally on all states, in practice, the exercise of universal jurisdiction is politically costly for a state. It means embroiling one's diplomatic apparatus in an imbroglio and, quite likely, a confrontation with one or more states; it means setting a precedent that undermines one's own national sovereignty, something which states are not exactly in a hurry to do; it means burdening one's court system with what will probably be an incredibly complex and problematic case; and it almost certainly means a great deal of domestic turmoil and controversy. Why would a country bother? The Eichmann case gives one clear answer: because the country feels itself to have been victimized.

The problem here is that countries that feel victimized may be less likely to be able to deliver impartial justice. To be sure, the victims can always claim that those countries who stood by during a mass slaughter are not impartial but simply heartless—a kind of bias in itself and certainly one that disqualifies the bystanders from becoming judges.[4] Still, when countries undertake to punish those who persecuted their own, there is at least a risk that this will undermine the impartiality that distinguishes true justice: that the roles of victim and judge should not be blurred. This is anything but an abstract concern. During World War II, Winston Churchill became so enraged at Nazi Germany that he ended up calling for the execution of the top Nazi leadership. Bosnian and Rwandan courts are trying to prosecute enemy war criminals today. The paradox is that noninvolved countries are more likely to deliver impartial justice if there is ever a fair trial, but they are at the same time less likely to want to have such a trial in the first place.

Compared to cases that may arise in the future, Israel's trial of Eichmann is relatively free of some key political dilemmas that often bedevil universal jurisdiction. The trial could not delegitimize a leader who might otherwise have been able to negotiate a peace treaty (like Radovan Karadzic, Slobodan Milosevic, or Franjo Tudjman) or a democratization pact (like Augusto Pinochet); Eichmann was a fugitive whose genocidal power had existed only in a state that had been destroyed by Allied arms. Nor could the trial prolong a war; the war had been over since 1945. And nobody could have accused Israel of using the trial primarily to carry on a vendetta against a strategic enemy by legal means (although the prosecution did emphasize Arab links with Nazism when it could); Israel was primarily focused on punishing an architect of the Holocaust, which rises above accusations of moral equivalence, partisanship, or *tu quoque*.

Instead, the controversy around the Eichmann trial mostly revolved around the question of whether Israel had the right to try the Nazi leader. The tension between international or Israeli jurisdiction is well captured in the different crimes on trial in Nuremberg and in Jerusalem. At Nuremberg, the Nazis were accused of—among other things—crimes against humanity. That is the category that leads to the idea of universal jurisdiction; if the crimes are against humanity, then humanity is entitled to judge them. In contrast, in Jerusalem, Eichmann stood his trial under a 1950 Israeli statute—the Nazis and Nazi Collaborators (Punishment) Law—which makes "crimes against the Jewish people" a capital offense. As Walter Laqueur put it, it was a difference between being *hostis generis humani* (the enemy of all humanity) or being *hostis Judaeorum* (the enemy of the Jews).[5]

Israel was criticized by some at the time for taking justice into its own hands. The issue was whether Israel had the right to try Eichmann, as Israeli premier David Ben-Gurion argued, or whether a more impartial court should have been found, as Hannah Arendt and Telford Taylor thought. In this essay I will consider these kinds of arguments in turn. I will then make two arguments, both of which are aimed not just at the Eichmann case but also at possible future exercises of universal jurisdiction. First, I will argue that the difference between Israeli and universal jurisdiction was not actually so stark. There was a noteworthy tone of universalism to Israel's actions, even though the instrument of universal justice was Israel's own court system. Second, I will argue that much of our evaluation of the Eichmann abduction must turn on the quality of the trial he received—that the real question was not whether he was on trial for murdering humans or Jews, but whether he got a fair day in court. There are many legitimate concerns about universal jurisdiction, which, like all political trials, open the door to all manner of politicking; but as a minimum precondition for the future exercise of universal jurisdiction, a genuinely fair trial is a baseline.

Crimes against Humanity

There was a strong sense in some of the Western democracies that Israel had gone too far by seizing Eichmann. Some Israelis, too, thought that Ben-Gurion had overreached. Martin Buber, the distinguished Hebrew University philosopher, thought that victims should not become judges. Nahum Goldmann, president of the World Zionist Organization, preferred a mixed international court in Israel with an Israeli chief judge but including judges from other countries whose citizens had been killed by Eichmann's agents.[6]

Telford Taylor, the American chief prosecutor for the second round of trials at Nuremberg, was probably the most prominent Western skeptic. Taylor wrote in the *New York Times* in 1961 that Israel's action was "emotionally understandable" and had no doubt that Ben-Gurion "voices the deepest feelings of his countrymen when he proclaims that it is 'historic justice' for Eichmann to be tried in a Jewish state."[7] But Taylor argued that the "essence of law is that a crime is not committed only against the victim, but primarily against the community whose law is violated." A racially motivated lynching in the American South, Taylor wrote, "is as much a crime against whites as blacks." Israel's law, to Taylor's mind, implied that crimes against Jews were not crimes against non-Jews. To the contrary, Taylor wrote, "Nuremberg was based on the proposition that atrocities against Jews and non-Jews are equally crimes against world law."[8]

I will return to these arguments below. Before doing so, though, some of Taylor's other complaints are more easily answered. Taylor also objected to the fact that Eichmann did not face justice where he committed his crimes: "[A]s a model for the shaping of international law, there is little to be said for trying a man at a place far distant from the scene of his actions, in a land to which he had been brought by clandestine force and which was not yet a nation at the time of the alleged crimes."[9] Israel's invocations of its sovereign prerogatives, Taylor wrote, was "absolute nationalism," which put him in mind of Hitler's similar invocations[10]—a gratuitously harsh charge, since Taylor could equally well have remembered such invocations from pretty much any sovereign state (and usually not for reasons as "emotionally understandable" as Israel's when it came to Eichmann).

Taylor then argued that instead of an Israeli trial, Israel should draw up charges and ask that West Germany or the United Nations hold a trial. This, Taylor thought, would help complete the pedagogical task started at Nuremberg.[11] But, as Ben-Gurion had already pointed out, West Germany had not criticized Israel, let alone asked that Eichmann be turned over to Bonn's authority for trial. Indeed, the Federal Republic had been moving slowly on the prosecution of Nazi war criminals at home but was galvanized by the arrest of Eichmann. (It was actually a West German official—Fritz Bauer, a German Jew who had escaped the Nazis and was in 1960 serving as chief prosecutor of Hessen—who gave Israel the information that Eichmann was in Buenos Aires, because Bauer feared that if he told the Federal Republic, someone would tip off Eichmann or prevent his extradition.)[12] Soon after the Buenos Aires arrest, West German authorities finally moved against a score of Nazis—most notably Richard Baer, commandant of Auschwitz, as well as many of Eichmann's aides.[13] By not taking Taylor's advice, Israel nevertheless got some of the result he wanted: a more serious West German effort at prosecuting the Nazis.

Crimes against Nationals

Still, Taylor's criticism of the idea of "crimes against the Jewish people" is harder to dismiss. His basic argument—that crimes against humanity are, by definition, the concern of the whole human community—is still current today. In Taylor's tradition, Martha Minow, a distinguished Harvard law professor, argues that it is not just the victims who have been wronged by the gross transgression of legal norms but society as a whole.[14]

The first problem with Taylor's argument is that it holds the Israelis to a standard that the Allies themselves did not meet. This is not to say that that standard is not a desirable one in and of itself. But one should not forget that Allied justice after World War II (and World War I) rested largely on the principle that countries dealt with the crimes committed against them.

In pursuing Eichmann, Israel was merely following a trend that dates back at least to World War I. In pursuing German war crimes trials, the victorious Allied democracies showed few compunctions about holding themselves up as both victim and judge. As David Lloyd George, Britain's prime minister, told the Imperial War Cabinet: "every judge tried an offence against the society of which he was a member."[15] Georges Clemenceau, France's president, was, if anything, more emphatic, demanding to the Allies in 1918 that

[t]here would be no neutrals on the Tribunal. They had no right to it, they had not intervened in the war, and had undergone no sacrifices. The Allies had secured this right by their immense losses in men and sacrifices of all kinds.

Mr. Balfour asked if this course would not take away all appearance of impartiality? If the Allies set up the Court themselves, where would be the moral effect before the world?

M. Clemenceau said that all justice was relative, and that the impartiality of all judges was liable to be questioned. It was a misfortune which could not be helped. But when a crime took place on a scale so unprecedented in history, he thought that France, Great Britain, Italy, and the United States must place themselves high enough to take the responsibility for dealing with it.[16]

In the subsequent botched war crimes trials at Leipzig in 1921, the British, French, and Belgian charges were all based respectively on the suffering of British, French, and Belgian citizens at German hands.[17]

During World War II, the first serious Allied policy on the prosecution of war crimes rested squarely on the principle of national jurisdiction. The Moscow Declaration—written by Winston Churchill and issued in 1943 in his name and those of Franklin Delano Roosevelt and Joseph Stalin—stipulated that once an armistice was concluded with a post-Hitler German government, "those German officers and men and members of the Nazi Party who have been responsible for, or have taken a consenting part in the above atrocities, massacres, and executions, will be sent back to the countries in which their abominable deeds were done in order that they may be judged and punished according to the laws of these liberated countries and of the free governments that will be created therein."[18]

Churchill thought that the suffering of the occupied countries gave them a moral right to mete out punishment. By the same token, he also clearly thought that British suffering—although not comparable to that of the occupied and invaded countries on the Continent—also carried with it a right to punish the Nazis responsible for the bombardment of London and Coventry. For Churchill, this formula also had the advantage that it would allow Britain to distance itself from the paroxysms of vengeance that would presumably erupt once the occupied countries could settle scores with the Nazis. After getting the Moscow Declaration approved, Churchill wrote to the War Cabinet,

By this means an enormous amount of responsibility for administering retribution will pass from our hands to the many sovereign States who have been outraged and subjugated and who have every right to be the judges of the treatment administered to those who have so horribly mistreated them. I consider this dividing up of the responsibility and retribution work to be one of the most wise and just steps which we in this country or in the United States could possibly take, for I am certain that the British nation at any rate would be incapable of carrying out mass executions for any length of time, especially as we have not suffered like subjugated countries.[19]

Here, the focus was not on crimes against humanity but on atrocities committed against soldiers and civilians by the faltering German army. The Holocaust was mentioned only in passing and then as "the slaughters inflicted on the people of Poland,"[20] without explicit reference to the Jews. But the main principle of the Moscow Declaration was of national jurisdiction. The Germans were to be "judged on the spot by the peoples whom they outraged."[21]

Of course, some crimes could not be pinpointed to any one location. Nazi aggression, to take the obvious example, had been committed against Poland, the Netherlands, Yugoslavia, the Soviet Union, and so on. And the murder of the Jews was a global project to be carried out wherever Germany could find and deport Jews. So the Moscow Declaration put some crimes by top Nazi leaders in a special category: "The above declaration is without prejudice to the case of the major criminals, whose offences have no particular geographical localisation and who will be punished by the joint decision of the Governments of the Allies."[22]

Although the Moscow Declaration was largely eclipsed by the great trial for the top Nazi leaders at Nuremberg, it by no means became a dead letter. The Moscow Declaration was enshrined as a cornerstone of the Allied occupation law that governed the other war crimes trials that followed the trial of the major Nazi leaders, a law known as Control Council Law no. 10. In these trials, the Americans took particular care to prosecute those Germans who had committed war crimes against American soldiers in the course of World War II.

As the liberal political theorist Judith Shklar has pointed out, the focus of the Nuremberg prosecution of top Nazi leaders was aggressive war.[23] (It is only now, almost fifty years since Nuremberg, that such reminders have become necessary; it was quite clear at the time.) From Franklin Roosevelt and Harry Truman on down, the Americans—the prime movers behind the great trials—saw their project as outlawing war.[24] This was a global concern, but it also grew out of the American sense of fury at having been brought into World War II. Nuremberg itself was a trial, of course, by the victors.

On this account Israel in 1961 was not doing something particularly surprising. The occupied countries of Europe had run their own trials for the crimes committed on their soil and against their nationals, to general world approval.[25] Israel was a special case in that it spoke for a nation that had not possessed a state during World War II and in that its claim to speak for the entire Jewish people struck some as problematic.[26] But to focus too much on this point would seem to miss much of the humanitarian intentions in the postwar establishment of the Israeli state. One did not have to be a particularly dedicated Zionist to see why Israel took a particular interest. The connection between Israel and the remnants of European Jewry was anything but theoretical; there were few Israelis of European descent who had not lost relatives to Eichmann and his minions. Even Hannah Arendt, a tough critic of Ben-Gurion, allowed that the Israelis had a point in wanting to see Eichmann in Jerusalem. She noted that Israel "was doing no more than what all the countries which had been occupied by Germany had long since done. . . ."[27] At another point in her book on Eichmann's trial, Arendt wrote, "The Eichmann trial, then, was in actual fact no more, but also no less, than the last of the numerous Successor trials which followed the Nuremberg Trials."[28]

Certainly, to Ben-Gurion, there was no question that an Israeli court should have jurisdiction over Eichmann. Such a demonstration of Jewish sovereignty, he thought, would be a counterpoint to the Jewish powerlessness that had come before the establishment of Israel. Ben-Gurion's only moment of hesitation throughout the abduction of Eichmann was evidently not over whether it was the right thing to do but over whether the Mossad had indeed got the right man.[29] "Eichmann is accused of murdering millions of Jews, as Jews," the Israeli prime minister told the *New York Times*. "He [Hitler] never intended to murder an entire people, except the Jews. It is a unique case. Eichmann is accused of being Hitler's main instrument in this. Therefore, it is historic justice that he be tried by a Jewish state. Only a Jewish state can try him, from a moral point of view."[30] Germany, Ben-Gurion said, had shown no interest in trying Eichmann, and none of the Security Council members except Argentina had questioned Israel's right to try Eichmann. As for an international court, Ben-Gurion emphatically ruled that out: "Why should he not be tried before an international court? Because Israel does not need the moral protection of an international court. Only anti-Semites or Jews with an inferiority complex could suggest that it does. America does not need that kind of protection, nor does England or any other country. I feel very strongly about that. In any case, Eichmann's victims were not murdered because they were international people but only because they were Jews."[31]

On this point, it seems clear that most Israelis felt more or less the same way as their prime minister.[32] Arendt wrote of "the almost universal hostility in Israel to the mere mention of an international court which would have indicted Eichmann, not for crimes 'against the Jewish people,' but for crimes against mankind committed on the body of the Jewish people."[33] Natan Alterman, the great Israeli poet, wrote: "Putting Eichmann on trial before a Jewish court in Israel will compensate for the inhuman and chaotic emptiness that has marked Jewish existence from the day the Jews went into Exile until now."[34] In the Israeli press, from the highbrow *Ha'aretz* to the mass-market *Yediot Ahronot*, there was unanimity that the abduction was a triumph. Popular enthusiasm was so great that it became difficult to keep the press and Knesset from calling for Eichmann's immediate execution.[35]

This is not to say that Ben-Gurion's calculations were all simply about justice. He thought it important that Israel's Sephardic Jewish citizens learn about the catastrophe that had befallen the Ashkenazi Jews, that Israel's youth be steeped in Zionist pride, and that the world be reminded of the inadequacy of its response to the Holocaust. In Ben-Gurion's mind, national security was still an enormous problem for his new and besieged state, and national solidarity could bolster Israel's chances of survival. He made no secret of his Zionist take on the trial. In an Israeli Independence Day speech during the trial, Ben-Gurion said, "For the first time Israel is judging the murderers of the Jewish people. . . . And let us bear in mind that only the independence of Israel could create the necessary conditions for this historic act of justice."[36] Finally, Ben-Gurion had come under withering criticism from Menachem Begin and other rightists for accepting reparations and arms from West Germany, and the Eichmann trial offered an opportunity for Ben-Gurion to demonstrate that his government's willingness to deal with the Federal Republic implied no meekness about Nazism itself.[37] The courts of the Jewish state would dispense justice to the mastermind of the murder of the Jews.

A Real Dichotomy?

Is there no middle ground between universal justice and national justice? If the Eichmann case is any example, it is important not to draw the distinction too starkly. After all, Israeli law in 1961 included a number of principles of universal jurisdiction—ways in which Israel was conducting the trial *both* on behalf of the Jews and of humanity. Some of these extraterritorial principles were not Zionist at all, inherited from legislation under the old

British mandate: a standard 1936 provision for prosecuting international pirates as *hostis humani generis* and a 1936 law against dangerous drugs that evidently did not limit itself to the borders of Britain's Palestine mandate.[38]

Of course, opium and piracy have precious little in common with Nazism. But there were other acts that were more relevant. In 1950 Israel had also signed onto the UN's 1948 Genocide Convention. In the act which gave force to the Genocide Convention, Israel explicitly embraced the principle that "a person who has committed outside Israel an act which is an offence under this Law may be prosecuted and punished in Israel as if he had committed the act in Israel."[39] Israel's forward-looking ban on genocide in general was evidently meant as a complement to its backward-looking law against Nazi genocide.[40] As law professor Theodor Meron (currently serving as president of the UN war crimes tribunal for the former Yugoslavia) has noted, the law under which Eichmann was prosecuted—the Nazis and Nazi Collaborators (Punishment) Law of 1950—has something of the flavor of universal jurisdiction, but with certain important limits. Anyone who has committed crimes against humanity or crimes against the Jewish people during the Nazi regime, or committed war crimes during World War II, can—in fact, must—be brought to book by any state that has the opportunity to do so. The limitation, of course, is that this Israeli law—unlike today's broader view of universal jurisdiction for any crimes against humanity—covers only Axis states and their conquests, and war crimes in World War II.[41] The law provides for the punishment of crimes against the Jewish people, but only as a specific instance of crimes against humanity.[42]

Even Ben-Gurion made some nods to universalism. He wrote that it was Israel's duty "to recount this episode in its full magnitude and horror, without ignoring the Nazi regime's other crimes against humanity—but not as one of those crimes, rather as the only crime that has no parallel in human history."[43]

In the event, Eichmann was convicted both of crimes against the Jewish people and of crimes against humanity—for instance, the deportation of Poles, Slovenes, and Roma (Gypsies) from Lidice, Czechoslovakia.[44] In his May 1962 Supreme Court opinion denying Eichmann's appeal of his conviction by the Jerusalem district court, Justice Simon Agranat—who was American born and educated—carefully tried to conflate the two kinds of crime. He argued that the four categories in Eichmann's indictment shared a "special universalistic characteristic" and that "the category of 'crimes against the Jewish people' is nothing but . . . 'the gravest crime against humanity.' It is true that there are certain differences between them . . . but these are not differences material to our case." The whole indictment, Agranat concluded, could be collapsed into "the inclusive category of 'crimes against humanity.'"[45] Agranat, using reasoning that could just as easily come from a Human Rights Watch press release about Pinochet's detention in London, argued that gross atrocities should not go unpunished simply because of the "primitive" state of international law: "for the time being, international law surmounts these difficulties . . . by authorizing the countries of the world to mete out punishment for the violation of its provisions. This they do . . . either directly or by virtue of the municipal legislation which has adopted and integrated them."[46]

As law professor Pnina Lahav has pointed out, on Agranat's account, Israel was doing nothing more—and nothing less—than shouldering its international responsibility to prosecute crimes that shocked the world community. When the charge was crimes against humanity, any state could exercise jurisdiction; Israel had merely *done* what the international community recognized was the theoretical prerogative of any state.[47] If the other states could not be bothered, that was a fact that could hardly be held against Israel.

The Problem of Abduction

Of all the things about the Eichmann case that gave Hannah Arendt pause, she singled out the extraterritorial abduction as "the only almost unprecedented feature in the whole Eichmann trial, and certainly . . . the least entitled ever to become a valid precedent. . . . What are we going to say if tomorrow it occurs to some African state to send its agents into Mississippi and to kidnap one of the leaders of the segregationist movement there? And what are we going to reply if a court in Ghana or the Congo quotes the Eichmann case as a precedent? . . ."[48] Today, international lawyers generally frown on the abduction.

The Israelis knew, of course, that they were playing with fire. Isser Harel, who as Mossad chief ran the abduction of Eichmann, later wrote that the operation "caused us a great deal of inner conflict. My mind was by no means easy about the need to carry out a clandestine action in the sovereign territory of a friendly country, and the question of whether it was permissible to do so—from both the ethical and political points of view—had to be faced in all its gravity."[49] After the capture of Eichmann, the Israelis remained mum about where they had caught him, and the Foreign Ministry said that the raid had been conducted by independent volunteers; it was left to *Time* magazine to print that it had been Israeli agents in Buenos Aires. Argentina rejected a clumsy Israeli apology and demanded the return of Eichmann, and the UN Security Council condemned the Israeli operation as an infringement on Argentine sovereignty.[50]

Ben-Gurion did not deny that Israel had violated Argentine sovereignty but apologized and asked the Argentine government to consider the wider moral context.[51] Harel's argument for abduction, similar to what many Israelis said, was that the more proper options were unworkable. An Israeli request to Argentina for extradition might tip Eichmann off, and Harel feared that Europe had lost its zeal for war crimes prosecutions.[52] (Harel did claim that he checked in with two eminent jurists, who said the operation was legal. He never explained what precedents they were relying on.)[53] Argentina was also a haven to a number of other Nazi war criminals, including Josef Mengele, who had run the sickening human experiments at Auschwitz, who lived in Buenos Aires under his own name until 1959. When West Germany requested Mengele's extradition in 1959, Mengele—possibly tipped off somehow—vanished, resurfacing later in Paraguay.[54]

The same general problem that the Israelis faced has come up again and again: a war criminal at large, with no reasonable prospect for extradition. This has been pretty much the pattern for many accused Serbian and Croatian nationals, sheltered for years by the regimes of Slobodan Milosevic and Franjo Tudjman, before Milosevic's fall and Tudjman's death. So long as Milosevic was in power, scores of indicted war crimes suspects could shelter under his wing, despite the fact that Yugoslavia is a signatory to the Dayton accords (signed, ironically enough, by Milosevic himself), which mandate compliance with the UN war crimes tribunal. This meant that many key war crimes suspects presumed to be within Yugoslavia—including some senior Yugoslav army officers and Ratko Mladic, the former Bosnian Serb army chief who personally oversaw the Srebrenica massacre—remained at large. Even within Bosnia, which is for all purposes a NATO protectorate, NATO has been terribly reluctant to risk its own troops for the sake of making arrests. From the arrival of NATO troops in January 1996 until July 1997 there was not a single arrest. The victims, after all, are Bosnians, not Americans or Western Europeans.

Conversely, when a great power feels its citizens to have been the victims, then solicitude about sovereignty has sometimes melted away. Consider, for instance, America's "war on drugs." In June 1989 the Justice Department issued a legal opinion that the president could legally have the FBI abduct a foreigner abroad for breaking American laws. On that basis, President George H. W. Bush approved a daring operation to abduct Pablo Escobar Gaviria, the Colombian drug lord running the notorious Medellin cartel, although the Bush administration thought they could have also targeted Panamanian dictator Manuel Noriega. Dick Cheney, then Bush's defense secretary, wanted to offer substantial military assistance. The raid never happened, but only because of concerns about the reliability of U.S. intelligence.[55] In November 1989, another Justice Department memorandum held that the U.S. military could make arrests overseas.[56] As the invasion of Panama started, the elder Bush went to the Oval Office to sign an order that authorized the American military to arrest Noriega and others indicted in the United States for drug charges.[57] Noriega, who had thought he would be treated like a head of state or a prisoner of war, was instead whisked off to an American air force base and arrested on drug charges.[58] In 1992 the U.S. Supreme Court controversially held that a Mexican citizen who was abducted for the murder of a U.S. drug enforcement agent could be put on trial for the crime in an American court, despite a prior U.S.-Mexican extradition treaty.[59]

The disadvantage of abductions is that they are threatening to the international order; the advantage of abductions is that sometimes the abductees are people who deserve to be on trial. The abduction of Eichmann must disturb the sleep of many fugitives. It is a classic tug between sovereignty and universalism. And there is a logical consistency—albeit extreme—to the Israeli position: if sovereignty is no reason to ignore crimes against humanity, then why should sovereignty be allowed to become a bar to the *prosecution* of those who have committed crimes against humanity?

In the end, the best response to those who desperately want to carry out an abduction, as the Israelis did, is not to leave them with that kind of stark choice between abduction or impunity. Better to strengthen intermediate solutions: by entrenching a norm of extradition, by regularizing such transfers, by punishing those states that will not extradite, by stigmatizing those states that harbor war criminals, by strengthening international tribunals, and by legitimizing international law. Otherwise, the temptation for the victims may simply be too much.

Legalism

Taylor concluded his argument thus: "In whatever forum Eichmann is tried, the important thing is that the trial and judgment shall not only be but appear to be just and fair, and shall contribute to the growth of law among nations."[60] This is exactly right, but it is not necessarily a reason for skepticism about Israel trying Eichmann. There is one crucial precondition for the legitimate exercise of universal jurisdiction: the state holding the trial must have a stable and fair legal tradition. To my mind, this would mean that only liberal states—which respect civil liberties and due process at home—would be properly entitled to exercise universal jurisdiction. After all, an illiberal state cannot even afford its own citizens the benefit of a fair trial; it is in no position to start doing likewise to foreigners.

Of course, this distinction between liberal and illiberal states has to be taken seriously. It can all too easily collapse into a distinction between states we like and states we do not like. But it seems quite clear that Israel in 1960 would qualify as a liberal state, albeit an imperfect one. To be sure, Ben-Gurion's obsession with national security took its toll on civil liberties, first and foremost for the Israeli Arabs. But the Israeli judiciary was developing itself into an increasingly powerful check on executive excesses, championing free speech and individual rights. In a breakthrough opinion written by Justice Simon Agranat for a unanimous Supreme Court, Agranat defended the pro-Stalin Israeli Communist Party organ's right to publish, citing a pantheon of progressive American legal authorities: Thomas Jefferson, Louis Brandeis, Learned Hand, and Oliver Wendell Holmes.[61] As Lahav has documented in her remarkable biography of Agranat, Agranat took the lead as Israel's Supreme Court pushed for judicial review and the rights of the mentally ill in criminal trials.[62]

So when Eichmann was snatched from Buenos Aires, he would get a substantially fair trial before the district court in Jerusalem. Taylor complained that Ben-Gurion had already declared Eichmann guilty, which is a fair enough objection but misses the point: guilt or innocence was not Ben-Gurion's to declare, but the bench's. The international consensus was that Eichmann had a proper day in court. Even Arendt, famously suspicious of Ben-Gurion, admired the judges:

There is no doubt that it is Judge Landau who sets the tone, and that he is doing his best, his very best, to prevent this trial from becoming a show trial under the influence of the prosecutor's love of showmanship. . . . And Ben-Gurion, rightly called the "architect of the state," remains the invisible stage manager of the proceedings. Not once does he attend a session; in the court room he speaks with the voice of Gideon Hausner, the Attorney General, who, representing the government, does his best, his very best, to obey his master. And if, fortunately, his best often turns out not to be good enough, the reason is that the trial is presided over by someone who serves Justice as faithfully as Mr. Hausner serves the State of Israel. Justice demands that the accused be prosecuted, defended, and judged, and that all the other questions of seemingly greater import—of "How could it happen?" and "Why did it happen?," of "Why the Jews?" and "Why the Germans?," of "What was the role of other nations?" and "What was the extent of co-responsibility on the side of the Allies?," of "How could the Jews through their own leaders cooperate in their own destruction?" and "Why did they go to their deaths like lambs to the slaughter?"—be left in abeyance. Justice insists on the importance of Adolf Eichmann. . . . On trial are his deeds, not the sufferings of the Jews, not the German people or mankind, not even anti-Semitism and racism.[63]

Israel, for all its revulsion at Eichmann, nevertheless went out of its way to ensure a trial that would satisfy the world's expectations. Over and over, Israel showed a respect for due process. Eichmann got to choose his own defense counsel—Robert Servatius, a lawyer from Cologne who had defended Nazis at Nuremberg—even when the Nazi leader's wishes required special legislation allowing a non-Israeli citizen to take part in an Israeli court. Israel offered to foot Servatius's bill, eventually paying some thirty thousand dollars. The Jerusalem district court's president, who had called his objectivity into question by comparing Eichmann to the devil, was therefore jockeyed out of presiding over the case. Servatius was given free rein, even when he packed the first week—when press coverage would presumably be most intensive—with legal wrangles about jurisdiction and impartiality. The judges kept a watchful eye on the prosecutor and were not shy about voicing their annoyance with him when he strayed from the essentials of the case. The verdict, when it came, rested mostly on documentary evidence and not on the emotional impact of the testimony of Holocaust survivors. And Eichmann was able to appeal his case before the Supreme Court.[64]

This is particularly remarkable since Israel could simply have killed Eichmann in Buenos Aires, rather than going to the trouble of holding a full-fledged trial. Even Ben-Gurion's critics noted approvingly that this alternative had not been raised. Taylor was pleased that in 1961 there were no echoes of the 1944 debate in Washington and London over whether the leading Nazi war criminals should have been shot without trial.[65] Arendt noted that Israel had not followed the example of Soghoman Tehlirian, the Armenian who assassinated Talaat Pasha as a reprisal for Talaat's role as mastermind of the 1915 Armenian genocide.[66] Throughout its encounter with Eichmann, Israel demonstrated a kind of restraint.

The likes of the Eichmann trial are a rare occurrence. It is not often that a state will want to go out of its way to prosecute war criminals, and it is not so often that that state will then do so with due process. This, in short, is another way in which the Eichmann trial was a spectactularly unusual affair.

Taylor's objections seem to fall short. While one might have reservations about the dominance of national jurisdiction and prefer to see international law developing as a defender of humanity itself, it is probably more realistic in the near term to see international law piggybacking on national idealism. The cumulative effect of a number of respectably executed universal jurisdiction cases could be considerable, and it seems a trifle pure to turn one's nose up at them because the state's nationals had itself suffered at the hands of the war criminal. If there was an established international institution that would reliably do the job, then Taylor's brief would be vastly more powerful. But that seems a distant prospect even in 2003, as it must have in 1961. Until that day, then states will remain the primary actors, and they may not be prepared to wait. If so, then one can at best hope that they will use fair legal means.

In world politics, impunity and crude vengeance are the rule. Israel's relatively responsible exercise of universal jurisdiction is not something so common that one can afford to write it off.

Chapter 5
Comment: Connecting the Threads in the Fabric of International Law

Lori F. Damrosch

The *Eichmann* episode and the proposed principles of international law both raise the problem of connecting universal jurisdiction with other threads in the fabric of international law. The *Eichmann* case is of special interest not just because of the jurisdictional questions addressed and resolved in the Israeli judicial proceedings but especially because of the questions of international law raised by the manner in which Israeli authorities forcibly obtained custody of the defendant. Even on the assumption that *Eichmann* presented a proper case for the exercise of jurisdiction on a universal theory (irrespective of the place the crime was committed or the nationality of those involved), it set a problematic precedent by decoupling questions of judicial jurisdiction from those concerning state compliance with fundamental norms of international law.

The Princeton Principles on Universal Jurisdiction encourage us to make connections between universal jurisdiction and other aspects of international law, as in Principle 1(5) (a state shall exercise universal jurisdiction "in accordance with its rights and obligations under international law"), Principle 2(2) ("other crimes under international law"), Principle 7 (effect of "amnesties which are incompatible with the international legal obligations of the granting state"), and Principle 9(2) (effect of final judgments of a judicial body "exercising such jurisdiction in accordance with international due process norms").

The legitimacy of the effort to codify principles of universal jurisdiction could well depend on whether those principles are understood as integrally connected with and supportive of other equally valid principles of international law.[1] That legitimacy could be undermined if assertion of universal jurisdiction is perceived to be correlated with other actions violative of international law, especially of norms fundamental to interstate relations such as respect for territorial boundaries and prohibition of the use of force in international relations.

As to Eichmann, Argentina claimed, quite plausibly, that the "illicit and clandestine transfer of Eichmann from Argentine territory constitutes a flagrant violation of the Argentine State's right of sovereignty" and that even the understandable considerations of bringing Eichmann to justice could not justify "taking the law into one's own hands and the subjecting of international order to unilateral acts which, if repeated, would involve undeniable dangers for the preservation of peace."[2] The Security Council debated Argentina's complaint and adopted a resolution declaring that such acts could endanger international peace and requesting Israel "to make appropriate reparation in accordance with the Charter of the United Nations and the rules of international law."[3] The matter was resolved as between Argentina and Israel by the issuance of a joint communiqué in which Israel acknowledged that the incident "infringed fundamental rights of the State of Argentina."[4] It was disposed of as between Eichmann and Israel by virtue of the Israeli courts' application of the *male captus bene detentus* rule, under which irregularities in the manner in which the defendant came within the territory of the forum would not affect the forum's authority to exercise an otherwise permissible criminal jurisdiction.[5]

The dispositions of the objections to Israeli actions in the *Eichmann* case have not laid all concerns to rest. Indeed, when abduction in aid of criminal jurisdiction became a prominent technique in the U.S. government's counterterrorist and counternarcotics policies of the 1980s and 1990s, international legal scholarship devoted renewed attention to the *Eichmann* problem. Much of that literature endorsed Hannah Arendt's view that the abduction was the aspect "least entitled ever to become a valid precedent"[6] If there are proponents of universal jurisdiction who favor abduction (rather than merely tolerate it as the lesser among evils), those sentiments are kept private rather than held up for public justification and critique.[7]

Abductions come in more than one variety. In Eichmann's case, the salient feature from the point of view of international law was the fact of Israeli law enforcement action in another state's territory without consent; the human element includes the dramatic circumstances of the capture by Mossad agents and the ensuing custody and transfer to Israel for incarceration, trial, and execution.[8] In Andreas Lowenfeld's remarkable series of articles on extraterritorial kidnapping as a technique of U.S. law enforcement, a vivid description of the facts of the cases bears out his conclusion that kidnapping is never pretty: "In the five days between his seizure aboard the yacht and his arrival at Andrews [Air Force Base], Yunis had been knocked to the deck of the yacht, causing both of his wrists to be fractured; strip searched, handcuffed, and shackled with leg irons; kept for four days in a small room aboard the *Butte* without a window or air conditioning; . . . and interrogated in nine sessions over the four days. . . ."[9] Yet perhaps in the eyes of international law, the circumstances of apprehending a suspect such as Fawaz Yunis are less problematic than those in the *Eichmann* case, as Yunis was seized on the high seas rather than on another state's territory.

Another controversial instance in U.S. practice is the diversion from Egypt to Italy of the Italian aircraft carrying the hijackers of the cruise ship *Achille Lauro*. Although criminal prosecution went forward in Italy (not on a universal jurisdiction basis but because the *Achille Lauro* was an Italian-flag vessel), serious questions were raised about the international law aspects of the interception of the aircraft by U.S. fighter jets.[10] The link to the present concerns is that as in the *Eichmann* case, criminal proceedings took place after apprehension of the suspects outside the framework of normal legal procedures for rendition.

In the most notorious U.S. case on abduction in aid of criminal jurisdiction, *United States v. Alvarez-Machain*,[11] the Supreme Court assumed for purposes of the issue at hand that the kidnapping of the defendant in Mexico by bounty hunters did violate customary international law but found that it was not prohibited by the U.S.-Mexican extradition treaty. Mexico disagreed, as did other states with which the United States has comparable extradition arrangements. The U.S. action has been resoundingly condemned as a violation of international law. Nor can one find any great gains for U.S. drug enforcement efforts: the trial judge eventually dismissed the prosecution for insufficient evidence, and Alvarez-Machain has been seeking vindication through a civil suit against those responsible for his abduction. I mention *Alvarez-Machain* here not because of universal jurisdiction (indeed, it was not a universality case)—in this fairly typical drug trafficking case the asserted basis for jurisdiction was activity in Mexico with effects in the United States—but rather because the *Eichmann* episode figured so prominently in arguments made to the U.S. Supreme Court. The Court did not find it necessary to confront the *Eichmann* problem directly, however; the opinion was confined to an interpretation of the U.S.-Mexican extradition treaty as not prohibiting abduction.

Criminal cases in the counternarcotics sphere do not fall within the ambit of universal jurisdiction as understood for purposes of the Princeton Project. In the sense of the Principles, these are not "serious crimes under international law" nor likely to be considered such in the foreseeable future. The counterterrorism instances are closer to our problem, since the international law-making process has moved fairly far down a trajectory under which many (perhaps most or even all) forms of terrorism now entail prosecute-or-extradite obligations.[12] Even though the Principles would focus on universal jurisdiction as applied to a small subset of serious crimes, many commentators understand the category of universal jurisdiction crimes as more or less congruent with those entailing prosecute-or-extradite obligations. And that category grows larger with every passing year, with adoption of new multilateral treaties to address the apparently inexhaustible ingenuity of the human mind in devising methods of perpetrating evil.[13]

My own position is that there should be no implication of a limitation of universal jurisdiction to *jus cogens* crimes and that at a minimum all the prosecute-or-extradite crimes are ones as to which there is an *option* to exercise jurisdiction without any link to the crime other than custody of the offender.

Jus Cogens International Crimes

The *Eichmann* prosecution is paradigmatic of a *jus cogens* crime: commentators are unanimous that whatever may be the proper scope of *jus cogens* (also known as "peremptory norms") genocide falls within it. The International Law Commission's Report on the Vienna Convention on the Law of Treaties (a foundational text in the evolution of legal thinking on *jus cogens*) suggested a set of examples—unlawful uses of force, or "acts, such as trade in slaves, piracy or genocide, in the suppression of which every State is called upon to cooperate"—but also indicated that some legal scholars had favored extending the concept to human rights more generally, or to the principle of self-determination.[14] The commentary to the Restatement of the Foreign Relations Law of the United States says that *jus cogens* norms "might include rules prohibiting genocide, slave trade and slavery, apartheid and other gross violations of human rights, and perhaps attacks on diplomats."[15] Various authorities have suggested other candidates.[16] In the long-running effort by the International Law Commission to codify rules of state responsibility, the notion of "state crimes" has withered away, and no definitive list of *jus cogens* norms has emerged.[17]

The Principles do not limit universal jurisdiction to "*jus cogens* international crimes" but take a possibly more flexible approach to "serious crimes under international law" (Principle 2[2]). This flexibility is desirable because it is far from obvious that we should exclude from coverage "piracy-like practices" (such as air terrorism) or crimes such as attacks on diplomats that have long been thought to partake of *erga omnes* character.[18] If the dispute between the United States and Iran over the hostage crisis of 1979–81 had not been settled diplomatically, would it not have been quite consistent with the spirit of the Principles for any third country to prosecute a hostage taker on a universal jurisdiction theory? Many authorities see connections between principles of *jus cogens* and obligations owed *erga omnes* (to the international community as a whole).[19] Our collective effort would benefit if we could connect the proposed enumeration of universal jurisdiction crimes to other concepts of general international law that reflect the same commitment to universality.

Apart from *jus cogens*, as long ago as the mid-1980s the Restatement of the Foreign Relations Law of the United States had already endorsed universal jurisdiction with respect to "attacks on or hijacking of aircraft" and had suggested that "perhaps certain acts of terrorism" would also be covered by universal jurisdiction.[20] The exclusion of terrorist crimes from the 1998 Rome Statute for the International Criminal Court is not relevant to the competence of national courts to prosecute perpetrators of such crimes on a universal theory: the concerns motivating that exclusion stemmed from the drafters' preference that a consent-based court would attract more support if it focused on a handful of "core crimes."

The process for adding crimes to the category of universal jurisdiction offenses is not the same as the process for adding to the set of *jus cogens* norms. Although there are many uncertainties about both processes, it is clear that a much more restrictive standard applies to qualify a norm as *jus cogens*. One reason for maintaining a higher threshold with respect to *jus cogens* is that peremptory norms are a ground for invalidating treaties and thus pose a certain risk to stability of treaty relations. States and international tribunals have therefore been exceedingly cautious about acknowledging the existence of new peremptory norms. By contrast, accretions to the category of universal jurisdiction crimes can come about through the ordinary processes of multilateral treaty making, which is probably the principal (though not exclusive) method by which a crime is accepted as entailing the universal interest of all states.

Should the Principles on Universal Jurisdiction Deal with Irregularities in Obtaining Custody?

The Principles are not explicit on the abduction aspect of the *Eichmann* problem, namely whether a state that prosecutes wholly or partly on a universal jurisdiction theory may do so irrespective of the manner in which custody of the defendant is procured. Perhaps the drafters thought the issue was implicitly settled through the incorporation by reference of "rights and obligations under international law" (Principle 1[5]), but this indirect approach does not clarify what the legal consequence (if any) would be of violations of such obligations.

Perhaps the reason for not dealing with nonconsensual or forcible rendition is that the present project is not itself addressed to the separate and currently contested questions of whether the international law on use of force is evolving to permit certain kinds of interventions into territorial sovereignty that might have been previously considered violations of the UN Charter. There may well be room for fair debate about the legality of uses of military power to apprehend suspects accused of certain kinds of international crimes (General Mohammed Farah Aideed for the ambush of Pakistani peacekeepers in Somalia);[21] indictees of the International Criminal Tribunal for the former Yugoslavia, if the state on whose territory they are found is not willing or able to carry out the international legal obligation to cooperate with the tribunal;[22] or perhaps individuals (such as Osama bin-Laden) who elude the reach of effective law enforcement by taking shelter in the territory of a state that lacks capacity to carry out prosecute-or-extradite obligations. More broadly, this is not the place to attempt to formulate new criteria for military intervention to prevent or interrupt genocidal atrocities.[23]

Conclusion

As Gary Bass has observed in his estimable book, *Stay the Hand of Vengeance: The Politics of War Crimes Tribunals*,[24] the politics of such tribunals will always restrict their jurisdiction to the narrowest category of crimes. Universal jurisdiction of national courts need not be so limited: a wider compass can be accepted for national courts to enforce the international law in which the entire community is interested.

In general, states exercising universal jurisdiction should do so with respect to suspects who arrive in the territory by their own volition or by regular transfer from a state with custody of the suspect. Abduction from another state's territory is not a proper means of achieving jurisdiction and should find no support in the Principles. Any exception, even in the case of *jus cogens* crimes as to which the perpetrator had eluded ordinary processes of rendition, would undermine the legitimacy of the effort to articulate legal principles on universal jurisdiction. The rationale for condoning abduction—in Arendt's sense of a "desperate, unprecedented and no-precedent-setting act, necessitated by the unsatisfactory condition of international law"[25]—could conceivably be overcome if a progressive widening of the scope of universal jurisdiction opens up more alternatives for prosecution and leaves fewer havens for perpetrators.

Chapter 6
Assessing the Pinochet Litigation: Whither Universal Jurisdiction?

Richard A. Falk

> Tricky matters like easing dictators out of power should be left to politicians, diplomats, and generals, not lawyers.
> —Max Boot, "When 'Justice' and 'Peace' Don't Mix"

A Jurisprudential Bombshell

The drama associated with the attempt to hold Gen. Augusto Pinochet, the notorious former Chilean head of state (1973–90), legally accountable for crimes of state was widely shared around the world. Typical of the comments on this legal pursuit of Pinochet were the following: "pathbreaking,"[1] "breathtaking,"[2] "a decision without precedent . . . [a] beginning for what can and should be justice without borders,"[3] and a course of litigation that has "already revolutionized international law."[4]

Whatever else, then, the Pinochet legal proceedings that stretched out over a period of several years fueled the moral, political, and legal imagination relating to accountability of political leaders to an extraordinary extent and for somewhat divergent reasons. For many it was a step forward in the struggle against impunity with respect to severe crimes of state. For others it was the related breakthrough associated with piercing the veil of sovereignty that had insulated dictators and tyrants from criminal responsibility for their criminal deeds. For still others it was the fruition of a long enduring effort to gain some redress of grievances in relation to the specific ordeal of Pinochet's oppressive rule in Chile, a simple matter of historical reckoning by a particular people. For still others it was the moment when the technical lawyers' concern with "universal jurisdiction" made headlines, moved international criminal law to a new level of seriousness, and demonstrated the vitality of national courts as potential enforcement agents for several of the most crucial norms in the area of international law, thereby making the prospect of a genuine international criminal law a meaningful global project. Of course, the Pinochet litigation was an assemblage of all these things, and for many close observers their fascination with the case arose because it has so many dimensions and contains so many intriguing loose ends.

To some extent, the media response to the Pinochet drama was an instance of hype and spin as well as a display of the absence of much historical consciousness. Very little was made of the fact that a series of domestic courts had over the years imposed standards of criminal responsibility or cooperated with extradition requests for Nazi perpetrators of atrocities wherever they were to be found. The *Eichmann* and *Barbie* (French prosecution of Klaus Barbie, head of Gestapo in Lyons, for crimes against humanity and other crimes during the Nazi occupation of France) cases had certainly laid the groundwork for proceeding against Pinochet, although there were significant differences. To begin with, there was an intense moral and political consensus about the Nazi regime that was much less clearly established in relation to the Pinochet dictatorship. This consensus had been authenticated by the outcome of World War II, being vividly confirmed at the war crimes trials of surviving German leaders held at Nuremberg. In contrast, Pinochet was an anti-Communist ruler who came to and remained in power with Washington's blessings, and continued until the present to have support from a substantial minority in Chile who believed that he had rescued the country from its slide toward Communism, chaos, and economic collapse by overthrowing the Allende government of the left. Beyond this, Pinochet was the leader, the symbol of ultimate authority, and not a loyal lieutenant as in most of the other prominent cases, and this represented the first time that such a notable head of state was being directly challenged in a domestic court.[5] Even Nuremberg never had the opportunity to prosecute Hitler, and although the Tokyo Tribunal came closer to prosecuting a head of state by prosecuting several top wartime leaders, it exempted the Japanese emperor from indictment out of respect for his eminence as well as the reverential relationship of the emperor system to the Japanese people. Thus it can be said that the proceeding against Pinochet, even with the qualifications of historical recollection, does represent a watershed. Here, for the first time, a leader who was on the winning side in the cold war, who voluntarily gave up power to enable a return to constitutionalism in Chile, was being criminally charged for crimes of state committed during his period of leadership. The Pinochet case did seem to emerge in a global setting in which adherence to minimum human rights standards by governments were becoming obligatory for even the head of state. In this regard the case against Pinochet seemed at the time to be symbolic of a transition to a period of more cosmopolitan values as the underpinning for the Rule of Law.[6] The 1999 indictment and later prosecution in

The Hague before the International Criminal Tribunal for the former Yugoslavia of Slobodan Milosevic for serious international crimes while he was a sitting head of state is further evidence of what seemed in the late 1990s to be a trend toward accountability of leaders. Unlike Pinochet, the *Milosevic* proceeding is under the auspices of an international tribunal, the International Criminal Tribunal for the Former Yugoslavia, and as with Pinochet, health considerations cast doubt on whether the lengthy legal proceedings will lead to conviction and punishment. This doubt, of course, was also a continuing feature of the Pinochet case almost from the first moment of his London detention until his eventual release in Chile on grounds of mental and physical inability to stand trial.[7]

At this point the legal fate of the old and infirm Chilean former leader now several years back in Santiago after his eighteen months of detention in Britain has finally been clarified after extensive litigation in Chilean courts. As of June 2002 the supreme court of Chile has ruled that Pinochet is suffering from such a severe form of dementia that he is unable to stand trial for human rights abuses charged against him during his time in power. To lend credibility to this assessment and to meet the criticisms of Pinochet's opponents who argued that if he was too ill to stand trial, he was unfit to remain in the senate, the eighty-six-year-old former dictator resigned his lifetime seat. These developments bring the legal soap opera to an apparent end, which brings neither full satisfaction nor complete disappointment to either side.

There is little doubt that the Pinochet legal proceedings will be long studied as a momentous case. Indeed, it may serve as a defining, if ambiguous, precedent for an expanding activist role for domestic courts with respect to challenging those forms of international criminality done under color of authority by the state and its maximal leader. Perceived more critically, the Pinochet litigation, with its numerous sites of legal articulation (multiple judicial decisions in at least six countries—Spain, France, Belgium, Switzerland, Britain, and Chile—as well as formal legal proceedings and inquiries in several others) also illuminates the weaknesses and limitations of a strictly juridical approach to the underlying quest for an *effective* and *fair* regime of universal jurisdiction. Such a regime in relation to such serious crimes as genocide, crimes against humanity, torture, gross violations of human rights and of international humanitarian law is beset, to begin with, by the divergencies associated with a decentralized world order of distinct sovereign states exhibiting dramatically uneven records of adherence to the rule of law as well as highly subjective political appreciations of alleged criminality. Despite these concerns, given the current outlook of several major countries, including the United States, the path of universal jurisdiction may be more promising than the main alternative, the institution-building path of an International Criminal Court (ICC). More optimistically, building on the Pinochet experience could emphasize the complementary roles of domestic courts in a global setting in which the International Criminal Court has become an institutional reality of uncertain impact.

In the background of this view is the current realization that the International Criminal Court, despite its formal existence as of July 2002, is unlikely in the foreseeable future to provide an effective and sufficient enforcement framework for many of the most serious crimes of state. It will take years, possibly decades or more, for many important states to make a firm commitment via ratification. Some key states are likely to remain outside, and opposed, indefinitely. As the ICC attempts to operate, it is likely to be severely constrained in its applicability by the primary authorizing role entrusted to the UN Security Council and due to the constraints on prosecutorial initiative.[8] As of now, even adequate funding is far from assured.

Under these circumstances, national courts will, whatever happens, continue to have a dominant role for the foreseeable future. Yet this vital role could be easily beset by a sense of chaos, arbitrariness, and partisanship unless the present disarray left behind by the Pinochet precedent is not mitigated in the near future. Justice Richard Goldstone suggests most hopefully that the Pinochet detention and litigation both provides "a new urgency" for the ICC and may well have served as "the catalyst" for "more frequent use of the civil and criminal courts against alleged war criminals."[9]

Above all, the Pinochet experience underscores the importance of establishing a more coherent regime for administering claims associated with universal jurisdiction over behavior that qualifies as international or global crimes. In other words, those who seek to close loopholes of impunity would be well advised to do more than celebrate the impressive chase of Pinochet and welcome jurisprudential scrutiny given by various courts to such statist staple notions as "immunity," "double criminality," "extradition," and "amnesty." The weaknesses of the current decentralized international legal order were exhibited as well as its capacity for evolution in response to growing support around the world for the "globalization" of accountability for crimes of state, or, put differently, a backlash against earlier tendencies toward impunity. The strength of the human rights discourse as the foundation of normative unity also supports judicial initiatives that impose enhanced standards of individual accountability.[10] In effect, those responsible for extreme violations of human rights should be held accountable to the extent possible, or else the regime of human rights will not seem to represent much of a challenge to state power where and when it is most needed—that is, in relation to a government and its leadership, which deliberately embarks on a path of brutal oppressive rule. Ideally, of course, the prospect of accountability would be sufficiently robust to appear a consistent prospect that might be expected to exert a deterrent impact upon would-be oppressors.

This essay examines the successive stages of the Pinochet litigation from the perspective of generating an effective and fair regime of universal jurisdiction, suggesting both the relevance of what was achieved, a realization of the insufficiency of the scope and methodology of judicial inquiry as it was delimited, and a concern about the inconsistent pattern of disposition at the level of judicial practice. As such, the inquiry here will not dwell on the detailed legal argumentation pertaining to such doctrinal matters as extradition, amnesty, and immunity but will rather explore in a general way how the Pinochet case helps us identify the contours of an appropriate role for national courts. This exploration is inseparable from some view of the preferred relationship among the criminal legal systems of territorial states and the link between states and the wider international community, given the current condition of global politics, morality, and law. In the background, as well, is the degree to which the international challenge to Chilean embrace of impunity with respect to the Pinochet era was itself seemingly influential, along with such other developments as the emergence of a new generation of military leaders in Chile and the assumption of the Chilean presidency by Ricardo Lagos, who was known to be in strong sympathy with the victims of the Pinochet dictatorship, in helping to lead Chilean courts to back away from their earlier embrace of impunity in relation to Pinochet, although this effort was partially nullified by the Chilean supreme court disposition of claims against Pinochet due to its finding of his unfitness. Also of great importance for this Chilean process was the political impact of the British detention and legal proceedings in foreign courts and attendant publicity. The denial of immunity to Pinochet was apparently a crucial influence on the willingness of Chilean courts to consider complaints that sought to deny Pinochet the immunity associated with his status as "senator for life."[11]

The Chilean Backdrop

As is generally known, General Pinochet, while leader of the Chilean armed forces, organized a violent coup that successfully wrested control of the government in Santiago from the democratically elected president, Salvador Allende, on September 11, 1973. Pinochet led a military junta that thereafter initially ran the country and some months later proclaimed himself as president of Chile, and continued in that role until 1990 when he relinquished power under growing domestic pressure and with the assurances of a self-amnesty decree on the basis of a negotiated series of arrangements with opposition leaders that included leaving him in charge of the military and a permanent position in the Chilean senate. It had become clear through the results of a crucial plebiscite in 1988 that Pinochet had lost the confidence of the majority of the Chilean populace. It also became evident that important sectors of elite opinion, including much of the business community that had initially welcomed his takeover, now wanted a return to civilian government and the rule of law. According to the Human Rights

Watch, "[t]he military regime he headed dismantled Chile's long-established democratic institutions, privatized its economy, and tried to eradicate left-wing parties and organizations in a reign of terror that claimed more than 3,000 lives, involved the torture of tens of thousands more, and forced over a quarter million Chileans into exile."[12] Despite Pinochet's departure from the presidency in 1990, he remained head of the armed forces for eight more years and then, by virtue of a constitutional provision, became a senator for life with full parliamentary immunity. Pinochet's level of support in Chilean society as measured by referenda and elections remained in the vicinity of 40 percent; the armed forces continued to be a potent political force, and Pinochet himself exerted enormous influence on the military and, behind the scenes, on the exercise of authority by the elected civilian government.[13] The military remained unrepentant for the policies pursued in the 1970s, which they credited with saving the country from left extremism. In such an atmosphere it is hardly surprising that a general acceptance of impunity would emerge in Chile with respect to past offenses that might be attributed to the Pinochet period of rule. That is, the early years of transition to democracy were fragile and uncertain, and definitely did not include a mandate to apply constitutional standards retrospectively to the Pinochet period. At the same time, there were continuous urgings from human rights groups, activists, and representatives of the victims to inquire into the past, to tell the story, and to determine what had actually happened.

Responding to this welter of contradictory pressures, while treading a tightrope between reconciliation and disclosure, the Aylwin government in Chile did establish a National Commission of Truth and Reconciliation in 1991, known as the Rettig Commission. There was also a second official inquiry known as the National Corporation of Reparation and Reconciliation. Together these two bodies established an extensive record narrating the experiences of those political adversaries who were killed during the Pinochet regime. These extensive reports detailed the loss of life on the part of 3,197 individuals who were in this form officially recognized for the first time as victims of human rights abuse. These inquiries operated within strict limits and did not have the authority to consider torture or abuses other than killings or to give names of the perpetrators of abuse. The military leadership and its numerous political allies menacingly rejected even these findings along with the recommendations of the Rettig Commission to take various steps to strengthen human rights. At the same time, such findings confirmed the suspicions of many Chilean citizens and strengthened civic demands that justice be done in relation to past wrongs.

It was not until the late 1990s that the issue of the "disappeared" entered into the mainstream political debate in Chile, becoming a strong moral challenge to the democratically elected government, although human rights groups associated with the families of victims had kept the issue alive all along. By 1998, in a more secure democratizing atmosphere, even some military leaders were beginning to cooperate with political parties and human rights groups, and agreed to provide information about the disappeared. It had become clear to all parts of Chilean society that reconciliation would not be possible without addressing this set of concerns that remained open wounds for many families in Chile. The defense minister, Pèrez Yoma, in late 1999 took the rather amazing step of arranging meetings under his auspices between members of the armed forces and relatives of the disappeared and other victims. This initiative was itself controversial, as some of the human rights lawyers and organizations in Chile thought that such events might interfere with the increasingly assertive approach being taken by Chilean judges in the new atmosphere of enhanced constitutionalism that included more openness to human rights and issues of governmental accountability.

The Pinochet government had done its best to prevent its criminality from ever being legally challenged. By virtue of a government act proclaiming the end of a state of siege in April 1978, Decree 2, 191, amnesty was granted for all serious crimes committed between September 11, 1973, and March 10, 1978. This "amnesty law" was described by the government as a reconciliation initiative at the time, and its coverage was extended to opponents of the Pinochet regime, resulting in the release of several hundred political prisoners with leftist orientations from Chilean jails. There has been continuous controversy about this amnesty initiative, with both the Aylwin and Frei at various points proposing in their electoral campaigns annulment of the decree and then backing away from such a commitment under pressure from the military, and refusing to support legislative efforts aimed at annulment.

In the 1980s and into the 1990s, courts in Chile, dominated by Pinochet appointees, generally applied the amnesty law to block investigations into the alleged criminality of the dictatorship. But increasingly in relation to unresolved "disappearances" some Chilean judges started to view the absence of the body of the victim as creating a continuing crime and hence its occurrence as not covered by the amnesty decree even if the original event occurred in the 1973–78 period.

The atmosphere in Chile changed dramatically in the late 1990s, especially after the start of the Spanish criminal investigations. In this period numerous Chilean legal initiatives were instituted in relation to the alleged crimes of Pinochet and important military figures. The main investigation was being conducted by Judge Juan Guzmán Tapia as to the merits of a series of criminal complaints by individuals and organizations, including more than forty against Pinochet himself. This investigation was encouraged by a unanimous ruling of the supreme court of Chile in July 1999 that Guzmán was correct to exempt from the amnesty law all cases in which the fact of death could not be authenticated, with the result that the victim of abduction was treated as still missing. In this new atmosphere even such notorious incidents from the past as the "Caravan of Death" came under review, and the fifth chamber of the Santiago appeals court applied what came to be known as the Guzmán doctrine, removing disappearances from the amnesty law but refusing to extend scrutiny to allegations of torture and murder.

It is against this background that it is necessary to understand Chile's response to the Spanish proceedings against Pinochet as well as his subsequent detention in Britain pending the outcome of an inquiry as to whether the extradition request from Spain should be honored. The Frei government in Chile refused to cooperate with Judge Balthasar Garzón in Spain, regarding the Spanish proceedings as "an illegitimate invasion of the jurisdiction of the Chilean courts."[14] Chile also formally objected to the British detention of Pinochet as a violation of his immune status as a "special envoy" of the Chilean state. It is difficult to assess the real motives for this Chilean stand, especially whether it primarily reflected concerns that any proceedings against Pinochet abroad would result in intense agitation in Chile. It may also have expressed the sentiment that in the new atmosphere in Chile it was possible to deal with charges against Pinochet within the Chilean legal system, that it was entitled to do so as the territory where the supposed crimes took place, and that it would consolidate the transition to democracy through a clear repudiation of criminality associated with Pinochet and his years of rule. As such, questions of sovereignty and nationalist prerogatives were engaged as well as respect for a former Chilean head of state who continued to hold an official title and office, but also issues about the comparative merit of competing claims to assert criminal jurisdiction.

This interplay between Chile and Britain and Spain does raise issues of importance. To what extent should the representations of the territorial government, particularly if it is currently operating as a constitutional democracy, be entitled to respect and deference by foreign governments and their judicial bodies? Specifically, with respect to issues of status and primacy of jurisdiction? And should foreign governments take some sort of notice of purported dangers to the stability of a democratic regime if there is a failure to respect an agreed policy of impunity in relation to past crimes? Should the primacy of Chilean jurisdictional claims be respected if prospects for prosecution and conviction seem strong and the atmosphere is conducive to judicial independence? Or disregarded, if such prospects seem dubious?

The evolving Chilean withdrawal of impunity from Pinochet and his regime underscores both the importance of a more authoritative international law approach to these issues and its difficulties. Arguably, in the fragile early period of the transition it was prudent to avoid challenging amnesty and the ethos of impunity, acknowledging the wisdom of President

Aylwin's pledge to pursue justice in relation to the past "to the extent possible" (*en la medida de lo posible*).[15] A more directive approach based on canons of universal jurisdiction would have placed the Chilean political leadership and judiciary in an untenable position of either provoking renewed military interference or repudiating the framework of inquiry and accountability embodied in international law.

This complex Chilean experience during these years of restored democracy is suggestive of both the need for flexibility and the importance of initiatives taken in foreign national courts with respect to past official criminality. There seems little doubt that the Spanish proceedings, reinforced by those in several other countries, to impose criminal accountability, strengthened the Chilean resolve to seek a higher standard of justice within its own legal system. The passing into history of the cold war, a gradually more secure democratic order in Chile, a displacement of the earlier Pinochet generation of leaders in the armed forces, the ascendancy of post-Pinochet judges, the persisting activism of human rights groups, and the pressures of international public opinion have together facilitated a greater use of Chilean courts to address unresolved grievances of past victims. At the same time, counterpressures have also been mobilized, particularly in the armed forces, generating doubts about the degree of autonomy that can be expected in relation to the Chilean judicial process.[16] These changes of circumstances in Chile lent weight to the Chilean request for Pinochet's return and weakened somewhat the foundation underlying foreign criminal prosecution, but not entirely due to the uncertainties of the Chilean situation. There remained ample room for assessment and debate. Should a jurisdictional challenge be resolved in favor of a foreign court that has ample grounds in law for determining criminal allegations against such a defendant as Pinochet, or does his special relationship with Chile give that country priority in determining his degree of accountability? And should such a determination be made on strictly legal grounds by judicial institutions, or should it be decided, or at least shaped, by the views of the political branch of government? For instance, in American practice, the state department's legal advisor has the authority to communicate to the court its views on granting or withholding immunity or diplomatic recognition. Similarly, challenges based on international law directed at American foreign policy have been habitually disallowed by U.S. courts, which have either invoked the doctrine of "political questions" or denied that the initiating plaintiffs possessed the legal standing to pursue such an allegation. A more robust role for national courts would suggest greater judicial autonomy in resolving jurisdictional challenges but not necessarily unlimited autonomy.[17] A nuanced approach would clarify the considerations that would justify departing from normal expectations of deference by political branches of government to the autonomy of domestic courts.

The Spanish Request and Inquiry

These issues of jurisdictional propriety were all present in relation to the approach taken by various non-Chilean legal authorities in deciding how to respond to the interplay between the attempted initiation of criminal proceeding against Pinochet and the objections raised by the government of Chile. The Spanish proceedings, although complex, seemed to treat the controversy surrounding jurisdiction in a legalistic manner—that is, giving no overt attention to the political context.

The Spanish legal process had been initiated in 1996 by the Progressive Union of Prosecutors of Spain in the form of criminal complaints against the military leadership of Argentina and Chile for their role in disappearances of Spanish citizens in both countries. Subsequently, the charges were expanded to include torture, terrorism, and genocide. The prosecutors, in accordance with Spanish law, were joined by private complainants acting on the basis of *actio popularis,* which allows individuals and citizen organizations to bring criminal charges without any demonstration of a connection to the events. In the Chilean initiative the actions in Spain were brought by the Salvador Allende Foundation and by the Chilean Group of Relatives of Detained and Disappeared Persons (*Agrupación de Familares de Detenidos y Desaparecidos de Chile*). The allegations were initially made before two quasi-judicial bodies, so-called Investigating Courts No. 5 and No. 6, subordinate units of the Spanish National Court, which was known as *Audiencia Nacional.* Both of these courts issued orders confirming their jurisdiction to investigate genocide and terrorism, which were in turn unanimously upheld on appeal by the Criminal Division of the National Court in a plenary session in which eleven magistrates participated. All along, the Spanish public prosecutor, acting not on behalf of the government but given the role of enacting legal conscience as pertaining to both sides, raised a series of objections relating to jurisdiction, in effect, arguing the case for and against those accused on the basis of both procedural and substantive considerations.[18]

These cases were initiated before there was any prospect of obtaining the physical presence of Pinochet but included the investigation of Operation Condor, which had been organized by the Chilean National Intelligence Directorate (DINA) acting under a mandate from Pinochet to work toward "the elimination of communism" and for the sake of "Western-Christian society." Judge Garzón, presiding over Investigating Court No. 5 and acting in accordance with a decision by the Spanish supreme court, issued orders confirming jurisdiction based on the principle of universality associated with the crimes charged. These orders also stressed that the Spanish identity of victims of these policies in both Chile and Argentina, which, while not jurisdictionally necessary, added what was described as "a legitimate interest" to the Spanish proceedings.[19] After learning of Pinochet's presence in

Britain, extradition was formally requested by Garzón on the basis of both the Spanish Criminal Procedure Act and the 1957 European Convention on Extradition. The Spanish government was instructed to proceed diplomatically to request extradition of Pinochet to face charges relating to genocide, terrorism, and torture specifically associated with the activities of Operation Condor. On November 6, 1998, the Spanish Council of Ministers sent the extradition request to London, and a month later Judge Garzón formally initiated the prosecution of Pinochet in relation to the crimes alleged.

Several features here are worth highlighting. First of all, the grounding of criminal jurisdiction on Spanish legislation that affirms the universality of the alleged crimes, regardless of the time and place of their occurrence. Second, the reinforcement of jurisdictional claims based on universality with the idea of a distinct "legitimate interest" based on the national identity of some of the victims. Third, a procedural framework in which the absent accused's legal interests are protected by the assigned role of the prosecutor to serve the law with impartiality. Fourth, the availability of procedural access to any concerned party without any particular showing of a relationship to a victim; in effect, civil society and its representatives are given legal standing. Fifth, and most radical, the extension of the crime of genocide to encompass a deliberate plan to eliminate a political group, rather than being confined to ethnic, racial, and religious attributes.[20]

Other Response by Foreign Domestic Courts

It is notable that several other criminal complaints were lodged in domestic courts in Europe upon learning of Pinochet's detention in Britain.[21] It is also relevant to recall that in 1994 during a private visit to the Netherlands the public prosecutor dismissed a criminal complaint against Pinochet that had been filed under the UN Torture Convention. The grounds for dismissal given were the absence of an extradition request, lack of jurisdiction, head of state immunity, lack of Dutch public interest, and difficulties of proof.[22] It seems natural to wonder whether the response in 1998, a mere four years later, given changes in the global climate of opinion on such matters, would have been the same.[23] In any event, although there were legal proceedings of some sort in several more European countries in 1998, responding to the British detention and the Spanish request, only those in France and Belgium appeared to have reached some degree of resolution. It appears that given the priority of the Spanish request, the others were not formally presented to the British courts. If correct, this raises the question as to whether in the presence of multiple requests for extradition, a response should be based purely on priority in time. It is arguable that other factors should be taken into account, such as their relative degree of interest in prosecution, availability of evidence, and the varying strength of their jurisdictional claims. For instance, if a claim based on universal jurisdiction is reinforced by the nationality of the victim(s) of the alleged crimes, then a presumption of validity might be attached to a jurisdiction claim, with timeliness being taken into secondary account. Arranging a hierarchy of jurisdictional claims might deserve inclusion in any articulation of a principled approach to universal jurisdiction.

In France several French citizens who claimed to be victims of Pinochet crimes filed complaints requesting the prosecutor to initiate criminal proceeding against Pinochet for crimes against humanity, torture, and disappearances.[24] In French practice the prosecutor decides whether the facts deserve investigation and, if so, issues an *instruction,* which in effect declares that the complaint should be evaluated by an examining magistrate, *juge d'instrucion.* At the end of this procedure Judge Roger Leloire, *juge d'instrucion du Tribunal de instance,* of Paris issued international arrest warrants in two of the five cases presented for consideration. The reasoning relied upon is of interest.

Both arrest warrants issued related to French leftist students living in Chile or associates of the government of President Salvador Allende in the 1973–77 period. They were French citizens at the time of their arrest and disappearance. The jurisdictional foundation of the case rested on the nationality of the victims, known technically as "the passive personality" principle. Universal jurisdiction is not available for crimes against humanity in France unless the accused is present in the country. Even then, there would be a problem unless the acts complained about qualified as crimes against humanity, as otherwise prosecution would be barred by "time prescription," known in the United States as the statute of limitations. It was thus necessary to examine the substantive character of the crimes. The French court refused to extend the concept of genocide in the manner done by the Spanish court, restricting genocide to deliberate undertakings to exterminate "a national, ethnic, racial or religious group." It also refused to consider such charges in relation to Pinochet, as a French law governing crimes against humanity was not passed into law until 1994, making its attempted application to the crimes alleged against Pinochet retroactive and violative of the maxim *nullum crimen sine lege.*

Such a ruling made the time prescription relevant. If the crimes were classified as murder and torture, then jurisdiction lapsed due to time. The French judicial authority refused to regard the Chilean amnesty decree as operative in French courts, and thus French citizens could otherwise have proceeded. However, in relation to the cases of disappearance, the time prescription does not begin until the person who disappeared is found, whether dead or alive. This approach is supported both by Article 17 of the United Nations General Assembly Declaration on Protection of All Persons from Enforced Disappearances and by the Inter-American Convention on Forced Disappearances. As a result Judge Leloire ruled that for the crime of "sequestration and disappearance, the time prescription does not apply."[25]

The Belgian court proceeded somewhat differently. First of all, the criminal complaint was filed by six Chilean exiles living in Belgium, charging crimes committed under international law as specified in the Belgian statute implementing the Geneva Conventions of 1949 and Additional Protocols of 1977 comprising international humanitarian law. The magistrate addressed issues of public immunity, universal jurisdiction for international crimes, and the matter of time prescription.

On the matter of immunity, the magistrate concluded that Pinochet was immune for all official acts arising from the exercise of his role as head of state. Relying on Nuremberg and the authority of legal scholars, the magistrate decided that Pinochet was not immune in relation to torture, murder, and hostage taking, which could not possibly be considered as falling within the scope of official acts. Unlike the French approach, the Belgian law was deemed to confer universal jurisdiction on the Belgian courts, allowing it to proceed even when the accused is not present in the country and the victims are not Belgian in the setting of alleged severe violations of international humanitarian law. The magistrate also overcame the objection based on retroactivity by concluding that the crimes charged to Pinochet were common crimes in Belgium at the time of their commission in Chile even though their occurrence was prior to the 1993 enactment of the Belgian implementing statute. The magistrate did finally conclude that the absence in Chile of an armed conflict as defined in the Geneva Additional Protocol II of 1977 meant that a basis of legal authority related to international humanitarian law did not apply to the facts charged.

The only remaining issue was whether an international arrest warrant could be issued on the basis of the contention that these complainants had been victims of crimes against humanity. Here, the difficulty was that Belgian criminal law statutes made no explicit reference to crimes against humanity.[26] The Belgian magistrate, nevertheless, found a legal basis to proceed: "[W]e find that, before being codified in a treaty or statute, the prohibition on crimes against humanity was part of customary international law and of international *jus cogens,* and this norm imposes itself imperatively and *erga omnes* on our domestic legal order." The magistrate added, "Customary international law is equivalent to conventional international law and is directly applicable in the Belgian legal order."[27] There were several other statements in this opinion that are relevant, in the spirit of the Spanish judicial response and far less positivistic than either the eventual outcome in the House of Lords or in the French legal system. For instance, the Belgian magistrate accepted the mission of "combating impunity" and the relevance in such circumstances of the principle of general international law, *aut dedere aut judicare.* One more assertion is worth quoting to give the flavor of the Belgian response: "The struggle against impunity of persons responsible for crimes under international law is, therefore, a responsibility of all states. National authorities have, at least, the right to take such measures as are necessary for the prosecution and punishment of crimes against humanity."[28] This leads to the conclusion that universal jurisdiction is firmly established in relation to crimes against humanity in customary international law, and exists "even more strongly as a matter of *jus cogens.*"[29] Luc Reydams notes the contrast between the Belgian and French approaches, associating, with implicit irony, the former approach with the celebrated advocacy by the great French jurist, Georges Scelle, of *dédoublement fonctionnel*—insisting that those who act for the state have a dual function of representing their particular state and acting as an agent for the international legal order.[30]

The British Response

Most of the attention given to the pursuit of Pinochet has focused on the British response to the Spanish extradition request. I believe this is somewhat misleading in relation to the underlying issues of universal jurisdiction. The legal developments in Chile, Spain, and Argentina with respect to the criminality of the Pinochet regime seems as important, or more so, in relation to the fundamental jurisdictional and substantive questions at issue. The British role was in a sense peripheral and quite accidental, revolving around its willingness to respond to an extradition request, and hence focused on the collateral issue of whether the charges against Pinochet in Spanish courts were "extradition crimes" from the perspective of British law. Part of the explanation for the disproportionate interest in the British treatment of these issues is undoubtedly the journalistic dimension relating to the sudden legal vulnerability of this former military dictator, an interest deepened by Margaret Thatcher's vigorous solicitude for Pinochet, whom she defended as a personal friend, a guest of the country, and an ally of Britain at the time of the Falklands crisis. More relevant here is the fact that the British legal system, due to his physical detention, was in a position to determine the fate of Pinochet outside of his own country and that it did so in a series of carefully argued and reasoned legal decisions.

Following the useful lead of Christine Chinkin, it seems helpful to distinguish within the British sphere three phases of litigation: *Pinochet I, Pinochet II,* and *Pinochet III.*[31] Most attention will be devoted to Pinochet III, the final determination of a judicial character taking place in the House of Lords, and followed by the determination of the home secretary (also called secretary of state) to send Pinochet back to Chile on grounds of health, concluding that he was unfit to stand trial by British standards.

Pinochet I

In response to the Spanish international arrest warrant, dated October 16, 1998, relating to a series of crimes alleged to be committed by Pinochet, a

London magistrate issued a provisional warrant the next day for Pinochet's detention at a clinic where he was undergoing medical treatment. The warrant was issued under the Extradition Act of 1989. There was a second international arrest warrant issued by Spain a few weeks later that dealt with the additional enumerated crimes of torture and conspiracy to commit torture, detention of hostages, and conspiracy to commit murder.

Pinochet responded by seeking a writ of habeas corpus and leave for judicial review of his detention. The Divisional Court of the queen's Bench Division unanimously quashed both warrants, partly by regarding Pinochet as immune during his period as head of state and partly by refusing to regard extraterritorial claims to prosecute for a murder committed in Chile as entitled to be treated as an "extradition crime." The Crown Prosecution Service was given leave to appeal, on behalf of Spain, to the House of Lords because there were issues of general importance presented relating to immunity and extradition. In the meantime Spain expanded once more its extradition request to include genocide, torture, murder, and hostage taking in Chile and elsewhere. Reflecting concern that the legal issues had not been fully addressed in the Divisional Court, the House of Lords instructed the attorney general to appoint an amicus curiae to examine the international law issues at stake. As a result, Amnesty International, Human Rights Watch, and several other organizations (including the Association of the Relatives of the Disappeared Detained) and individuals, were treated as "intervenors" and distinguished in British usage from "neutral jurists" who could only file amicus briefs. Intervenors are entitled to provide oral testimony as well as to offer independent written submissions. As well, the House of Lords panel appointed a neutral jurist to provide legal advice on the case in the form of written submissions.

By a vote of 3–2 on November 25, less than two weeks after the appeal was heard, a specially constituted Appellate Committee of the House of Lords upheld extradition on the ground that Pinochet was not immune in relation to crimes committed under international law.[32] The main argument had revolved around the issue of whether the alleged crimes could be assimilated into the official functions of a head of state so as to benefit from immunity. The narrow majority decided, in the words of Lord Nicholls, that "international law has made plain that certain types of conduct, including torture and hostage-taking, are not acceptable conduct on the part of anyone. This applies as much to heads of state, and even more so, as it does to everyone else; the contrary conclusion would make a mockery of international law." Lord Steyn added that since the criminal charges against Pinochet were "international crimes deserving of punishment," that it was "difficult to maintain that the commission of such high crimes may amount to acts performed in the functions of a Head of State."[33]

The arguments favorable to Pinochet were articulated by the two dissenting judges. Lord Slynn was unconvinced on the core issue of universal jurisdiction. In his words, "[i]t does not seem to me that it has been shown that there is any State practice or general consensus let alone a widely supported convention that all crimes against international law should be justiciable in National Courts on the basis of the universality of jurisdiction." His lordship went on to say, "Nor is there any jus cogens in respect of such breaches of international law which require that a claim of State or Head of State immunity, itself a well established principle of international law, should be overridden."[34] Although basing their decision on the availability of immunity to Pinochet as head of state, these two dissenting judges also stressed several other factors. They made reference to the eleven pending prosecutions in Chile as well as the relevance of the amnesty decree, the impact of the 1990 Commission on Truth and Reconciliation, and the ruling of the Chilean supreme court that the amnesty decree did not apply to crimes that occurred or persisted after 1978.

The home secretary, Jack Straw, days later, on December 9, authorized a magistrate to proceed with extradition for the crimes alleged in the Spanish request but deleted genocide on the grounds that it was not an extradition crime under British law. It seems that Straw did not consider whether the Spanish charge was conceptually acceptable, rather that regardless of the factual grounds, extradition was unavailable. It should be noted that it was the home secretary who possessed the authority to bring diplomatic and other extralegal considerations to bear, even to the extent of disregarding the judicial outcome, if it was found to harm national interests. In this setting the Chilean request could be considered, both with respect to whether there was any serious prospect of bringing Pinochet to justice in Chile, the repercussion for British-Chilean relations of rejecting the Chilean government's intervention in the case, and assessments of how a prosecution of Pinochet anywhere might affect the orderly transition to democracy in Chile.

Pinochet II

Pinochet's counsel filed a petition with the House of Lords contending that *Pinochet I* be set aside on the grounds of the undisclosed connections between one of the judges, Lord Hoffman, and Amnesty International.[35] Lord Browne-Wilkinson presided over a new panel of law lords that unanimously set aside the earlier determination, calling for a new hearing before a new group of judges. The reasoning was based on the idea that since Amnesty International, as an intervenor in favor of extradition, was in effect a party to the appeal, and that as a result Lord Hoffmann must be disqualified from participation. He was in effect acting simultaneously as party and judge in the same case, and this was deemed unacceptable. At the same time, the government of Chile formally entered the judicial arena, not to support Pinochet's claim of immunity, but to insist that it possessed a sovereign right and interest in having the question of Pinochet's accountability resolved in Chile where its courts were considering a series of criminal charges brought against the former leader.[36] This point had been disputed by the human rights community that expressed the view at the time that on the basis of past performance and future prospects, it was virtually inconceivable that courts in Chile would have the independence and political will to address adequately the charges against Pinochet.[37] Also, the charges against Pinochet for which extradition was being requested were again amended, being narrowed and were expressed with greater specificity in relation to time and place.[38]

Pinochet III

The original appeal to the House of Lords was reargued, but more elaborately. This time a panel of seven law lords was convened, excluding Lord Hoffmann but including the other four law lords who had participated in *Pinochet II*. The enlargement of the panel to seven was unusual in the practice of the House of Lords and apparently reflected the sense that the issues posed were of great importance and needed to be resolved as authoritatively as possible. In this setting hearings commenced on January 18, 1999, and lasted two weeks. The same intervenors as in the earlier hearings were allowed to participate but were now joined by the government of Chile, which put forward an argument in support of Pinochet's claim of state immunity as well as its claim of sovereign prerogative to prosecute alleged crimes committed on its territory. The judgment of the House of Lords on March 24 denied the claim of immunity by a 6–1 majority and held Pinochet extraditable, but only for the commission of torture subsequent to September 29, 1988, the date on which Britain enacted Section 134 of the Criminal Justice Act, making torture a crime in the United Kingdom regardless of where it was committed or the nationality of the perpetrator. In this sense the crux of the criminality associated with the Pinochet regime, even as to torture, was not accepted as a valid basis for extradition. The majority rejected the view that there was any basis for charges of criminality under international law in British domestic courts other than what was explicitly incorporated into British positive law. It was a narrow, legalistically framed judicial response to the Spanish request. The decision does at least stand substantively for the proposition that international crimes to this extent are not shielded from judicial prosecution by state immunity or by notions of the territoriality of criminal law.

The lead law lord in *Pinochet III*, Lord Browne-Wilkinson, offers an interesting comment as to both the Spanish venue of potential prosecution and the proper domain of legal inquiry in the setting of assessing an extradition request:

It may well be thought that the trial of Senator Pinochet in Spain for offences all of which related to the state of Chile and most of which occurred in Chile is not calculated to achieve the best justice. But I cannot emphasise too strongly that that is no concern of your Lordships. Although others perceive our task as being to choose between the two sides on the grounds of personal preference or political inclination, that is an entire misconception. Our job is to decide two questions of law: are there any extradition crimes and, if so, is Senator Pinochet immune from trial for committing those crimes.[39]

In effect, then, the British inquiry is whether under *national* law in all three countries it is permissible to assert universal jurisdiction for crimes essentially committed within Chile and even then, whether the crime alleged is such that its commission is not barred from prosecution because of an immunity enjoyed by this defendant who was head of state at the time. Another stage-setting conclusion was the decision to grant the Republic of Chile "leave to intervene" on the ground that the claim of immunity by Pinochet is for the benefit of the state rather than the person. The charges against Pinochet for which the Spanish warrant requested extradition had been changed several times but what was forwarded finally to the House of Lords were the following series of crimes: conspiracy to commit torture between 1972 and 1990; conspiracy to take hostages between 1973 and 1990; murder in connection with torture committed in various countries, including Italy, France, Spain, and Portugal between 1972 and 1990; torture at various times during 1973; conspiracy to murder in Spain between 1975 and 1976, and in Italy in 1975; attempted murder in Italy in 1976; torture between 1973 and 1977; and torture on June 24, 1989. Note that the home secretary omitted on his own authority presentation of the genocide charges although contained in the Spanish request and unanimously affirmed over the prosecutors objections by the highest court in Spain, presumably because of the British view that the facts alleged in relation to Operation Condor did not appear to constitute "genocide" as the crime had been generally understood. On November 5, 1998, the eleven-member Penal Chamber of the Audiencia Nacional upheld the novel idea put forward by Judge Garzón of "political genocide." In the language of its decision the following reasoning was relied upon: "It was an action of extermination, not done by chance, is an indiscriminate manner, but that responded to the will of destroying a determinate sector of the population, a very heterogeneous, but distinctive, group."[40]

It is important to appreciate the narrowness of the eventual British authorization for extradition as compared to the breadth of the Spanish request, which had received such strong judicial backing despite the legal arguments against asserting jurisdiction being fully presented on behalf of Pinochet by the chief prosecutor of the Spanish public prosecutor's office. Aside from torture, the charges against Pinochet were not extraterritorial crimes according to British law and hence could not qualify as "extradition crimes." The only other offense that seemed on its face to qualify, the allegation of hostage taking due to the extraterritorial reach of the U.K. law, Taking of Hostages Act of 1982, did not do so because the facts presented in support of the charge related to the disappeared, and that was a conception of a hostage not embraced by the British law, which regarded a hostage as a person detained with the intention to compel someone who is not a hostage to do some act or refrain from a particular course of action.[41]

The majority of the panel of law lords followed the view on extradition most carefully articulated by Lord Browne-Wilkinson, who also invoked and relied upon the legal opinions written by his colleagues on the panel. He made it plain that it was not only that the crime of torture must be currently an extradition crime under British law but also that the facts need to satisfy the double criminality rule so as to demonstrate that it was such a crime *at the time of its commission*. Since the U.K. did not incorporate the 1984 UN Convention on Torture into British internal law until September 29, 1988, only acts of torture or conspiracy to commit torture that were subsequent to that date were subject to extradition. At the same time, Lord Browne-Wilkinson affirms in strong language the evolution of international criminal law as establishing "the jus cogens nature of the international crime of torture," which "justifies states in taking universal jurisdiction over torture wherever committed."[42] Representatives of the government of Chile joined in accepting this jurisdictional analysis of legal authority as it pertained to torture.

The Torture Convention was viewed as providing a system of enforcement that would discourage an alleged torturer from moving around the world in an effort to avoid detention and prosecution. This essential idea of the convention is expressed by the Latin maxim *aut dedere aut punire* (either extradite or punish). It was also relevant that the three countries involved in the British litigation had all ratified the convention by 1988 and that if the state with the most obvious claim based on territoriality does not assert it, then the state where the individual is found must either prosecute or grant extradition. Such a view would suggest that Britain itself might have had a duty to arrest and prosecute Pinochet for the post-1988 torture had there been no extradition request, although such a possibility does not seem to have been explicitly raised.

The issue of immunity was also important. The definition of torture in the convention makes it necessary that the perpetrator be a public official. As Lord Browne-Wilkinson notes, "[I]f Senator Pinochet is not entitled to immunity in relation to the acts of torture alleged to have occurred after 29 September 1988, it will be the first time . . . when a local domestic court has refused to afford immunity to a head of state or former head of state on the grounds that there can be no immunity against prosecution for certain international crimes."[43]

Thus, in relation to reliance upon torture and conspiracy to torture by the Pinochet regime, the House of Lords decision denies the Spanish request for all but the most marginal instances, isolated incidents occurring at the end of his presidency and quite likely the most difficult to connect with prevailing government policy in the 1988–90 period. In this regard, if Spain had been given the opportunity to proceed with a criminal trial of Pinochet, it would have been, at best, a highly artificial event that might have turned out to be a fiasco from the perspective of substantive justice, especially if a Spanish court came to believe that the post-1988 allegations of torture were either not sustained by sufficient evidence or too tenuously tied to the authority of Pinochet. Beyond this, if the Spanish court had felt that Britain had unduly narrowed their request, it is possible that evidence of the whole pattern of torture from 1973 onward would have been considered so as to substantiate the post-1988 incidents of torture and thereby put Pinochet indirectly on trial for a portion of the real criminality of his regime. In turn, such an expanded inquiry might have exerted a downward pressure on a future extradition request of this nature, undermining confidence that the requesting government would not claim authority beyond what was approved.

The issue of public immunity was treated within the narrow scope afforded by the decision as to extradition crimes. Lord Browne-Wilkinson set forth in his opinion the views on immunity accepted by the majority judges, although elaborated on in various ways in their separate opinions. The major premise is that public immunity applies to both civil and criminal acts performed by officials of a state, extending both to action performed (*ratione materiae*) and to the person who acts officially (*ratione personae*). Pinochet is entitled to full immunity during his tenure as president of Chile, subject only to the exception associated with international crimes that qualify as crimes against humanity and are violations of norms with a *jus cogens* status. Lord Browne-Wilkinson accords decisive weight to the impact of the Torture Convention, advancing the view that without its existence the status of torture as an international crime would not have been of sufficient weight to compel the curtailing of immunity. In his words, "Not until there was some form of universal jurisdiction for the punishment of the crime of torture could it really be talked about as a fully constituted international crime."[44] The Torture Convention required all parties to establish torture as an international crime and to make it enforceable via domestic courts. Lord Browne-Wilkinson goes on to demonstrate that there is no way to give such a directive coherence without denying the claim of immunity to a head of state. It needs to be recalled that torture as defined is a crime that can be committed only by a public official, and thus the directive in the convention would be meaningless if immunity could be invoked, and it would be ridiculous to conclude that such immunity would be denied to lower officials of the state but accorded to the leader who authorized and oversaw the pattern of criminality. The opinion notes in contrast that there is no reason immunity should not be accorded in relation to the charges of murder and conspiracy to murder, which fail to qualify as extradition crimes, but separately are not established as "international crimes" whose enforcement is mandated by treaty.

Lord Goff provides an elaborate argument in support of the views taken in the earlier House of Lords dissent by Lord Slynn and Lord Lloyd to the effect that there is nothing in the Torture Convention that justifies the conclusion that public immunity is to be withdrawn from an accused head of state.[45] Lord Goff distinguishes those cases before *international* tribunals that impose criminal accountability on public officials for their governmental activity. His argument, in its essence, is that extending this accountability to *domestic* courts cannot be presumed, was not properly argued by the lawyers on either side, and is not implied by the logic of the Torture Convention. Although none of the law lords supported Lord Goff, his reasoning is careful and should form part of the Pinochet experience that guides future understanding of controversies concerning the unavailability of an immunity argument. A lengthy opinion by Lord Hope addresses the complexity of the immunity question, concluding narrowly that the Torture Convention does have the effect of withdrawing the immunity of a head of state charged with the international crime of torture provided its occurrence had the seriousness of impact to have a disruptive effect generally on international society, which in this instance appears to have been the case.[46]

Only Lord Millett among the law lords situates the whole judicial inquiry within the context of the post-Nuremberg evolution on an international level of criminal accountability. As a result, for Lord Millett the whole train of developments within the United Nations and especially the International Law Commission are relevant to the dispute over the availability of immunity to Pinochet. Also relevant is the experience of domestic courts, and in particular, "[t]he landmark decision" in the Eichmann case.[47] Lord Millett takes particular note of the linkage between "the scale and international character of the atrocities" and the "fully justified . . . application of the doctrine of universal jurisdiction."[48] Drawing from this past experience, Lord Millett concludes that "crimes prohibited by international law attract universal jurisdiction under customary international law if two criteria are satisfied."[49] First, the crime must be contrary to a peremptory norm, thereby infringing *jus cogens*; second, the criminal allegations "must be so serious and on such a scale that they can justly be regarded as an attack on the international legal order."[50]

A major point advanced by Lord Millett is as follows: he believes that universal jurisdiction is validly available either on the basis of statutory incorporation or via common law and that customary international law is part of the English common law. This enables Lord Millett to draw a far broader conclusion as to jurisdictional authority than that of his brethren: "In my opinion, the systematic use of torture on a large scale and as an instrument of state policy had joined piracy, war crimes and crimes against the peace as an international crime of universal jurisdiction well before 1984. I consider that it had done so by 1973. For my own part, therefore, I would hold that the courts of this country already possessed extra-territorial jurisdiction in respect to torture and conspiracy to commit torture on the scale of the charges in the present case and did not require the authority of statute to exercise it."[51]

Such a view would, of course, have enabled a far less restrictive response to the Spanish request at least as far as torture was concerned and would have placed the approach taken toward universal jurisdiction in these two countries closer to a level of parity.

Lord Millett also takes a corresponding view of the availability of immunity on behalf of Chile. He rejects the idea that Chile has the exclusive right to prosecute Pinochet but agrees that it enjoys a primary right under the Torture Convention and in customary international law. All states, whether territorial or not, have a right and obligation to proceed if the acts qualify as a *jus cogens* crime of sufficient magnitude, which torture in this instance does. In other words, Chile conceded that the statutory directive to prosecute under the Torture Convention would be a valid basis for proceeding against Pinochet absent the immunity plea, but that granting immunity in foreign courts would acknowledge and confirm the Chilean right and duty to apply the convention. Lord Millett joins the others in rejecting such reasoning.

The opinion of Lord Millett ends with an emphasis on the role of customary international law as an evolving process that is fundamental to its development in this setting of individual liability for international crimes. He believes that the disallowance of immunity to Pinochet adds to international custom by confirming that "the exalted rank of the accused can afford no defence."[52]

From the perspective of the future of universal jurisdiction, it would be useful to highlight the arguments presented on both sides of this exemplary judicial encounter on matters of fundamental principle relating to universal jurisdiction. Of particular importance is the relevance of customary international law to the exercise of universal jurisdiction absent reinforcing statutory enactment. To the extent that customary international law is accepted as a sufficient grounds for a domestic court to address the jurisdictional issue, it contributes to both a standardization of approach and a generally expanded role, although, of course, important differences as to the perceived content and authority of customary international law would be almost certain to persist. For instance, domestic courts might generally accept the *jus cogens* status of genocide in customary international law and yet disagree as to the scope of the crime as in relation to such an accusation being directed at Pinochet and his regime.

Concluding Note

Despite the narrowness of authorization for extradition, the contributions of the House of Lords 6–1 decision should still be viewed as groundbreaking. It was the first time that a former head of state was being potentially held legally accountable before a domestic court for alleged criminal activity of a political character during his period of rule.[53] The public understanding of the case was inevitably organized around either/or outcomes relating to extradition, making the British final result a smashing victory for accountability and a decisive defeat for impunity. The fact that Pinochet was made subject to extradition and potential criminal liability was virtually all that mattered in the critical arena of public opinion. Such an outcome seems also to have greatly strengthened the resolve of both the Chilean legal system to overcome their past embraces of impunity and encouraged the international community to move elsewhere against tyrants accused of massive crimes against humanity. At the same time, as indicated, counterpressures to prosecution remain strong in Chile, and the final outcome of medical unfitness for trial should not have come as a surprise. The legal proceedings of the Hague International Criminal Tribunal for the Former Yugoslavia involving Milosevic undoubtedly appeared more appropriate in light of the Pinochet case and could not be so easily criticized as nothing more than an expression of anti-Serbian geopolitics.[54]

Jurisprudentially, the Pinochet experience has opened up the issue of universal jurisdiction to an unprecedented degree. It is not only the passions aroused by the person of Pinochet and the differing views as to whether he should be held individually accountable in a judicial setting other than Chile (or possibly an international tribunal). It is also that the domestic courts of several countries were engaged in assessing whether to seek extradition and if so, on what basis, with what scope. In this regard, it is important to insist that the final House of Lords disposition was particularly caught up by the characteristically British positivistic emphasis on statutory authority. It does not seem to provide a generalized model for how domestic courts should respond to claims of universal jurisdiction. Perhaps the unevenness of the Pinochet legal outcome in various judicial bodies does strengthen the argument for agreeing upon a global framework for the application of universal jurisdiction. Such an agreement would minimize the divergencies of approach that emerged in the different countries faced with assessing criminal charges directed at Pinochet. What the House of Lords decision also suggests is that such a framework, even if widely endorsed, and ratified, by official state action would not necessarily govern the operations of domestic courts unless specifically incorporated by enabling legislation.

The health and age of Pinochet left in doubt all along the final outcome of current Chilean efforts to roll back impunity in relation to their former dictator. At the very least, the decision by the Chilean supreme court to strip away his personal immunity represents a historic move and precedent of lasting significance. What is unclear is the scope of accountability that would be available in Chilean courts for potential liability of Pinochet for crimes during his period of leadership, including the applicability of immunity for some part of the charges on the grounds that the wrongs were not established as international crimes at the time of their commission. In other words, there remain important loose ends of a conceptual nature in what has ended up being permanently unresolved (failing health or death, bringing the Chilean proceedings to a halt) with respect to the depiction of "the *Pinochet* precedent."

Beyond this ambit of uncertainty lie other concerns. When the Pinochet experience is broadened to encompass the world as a whole, issues of judicial unevenness and political outlook assume great prominence. It should be remembered that all the action in the Pinochet litigation occurred within European Union countries—that is, within legal systems with strong credentials of constitutionalism, judicial independence, shared democratic values, and a common geopolitical outlook. But what if criminal charges are brought in a state where courts lack autonomy and where the government is authoritarian and intensely anti-Western? Such factors raise a fundamental issue as to whether the world as a whole is ready for universal jurisdiction in criminal proceedings based on Pinochet-like charges. Without considering the viability of implementing universal jurisdiction on a global scale, enthusiasm for the Pinochet experience seems unwarranted or, at best, premature.

If anything, this prematurity has been accentuated by the effects of September 11, 2001, as well as by the blatant opposition of the U.S. government during the Bush presidency to all facets of legal internationalism. For now, the Pinochet litigation stands as a legal milestone, but for the time being, despite hopes having been raised a few years back, the struggle for individual accountability on the part of public officials remains stalled. Maybe the establishment of the International Criminal Court will insert new life into the struggle and even embolden domestic courts here and there to surprise the world as much as did Spanish and British legal procedures back in 1998 when General Pinochet was first detained

Chapter 7
Comment: Universal Jurisdiction and Transitions to Democracy

Pablo De Greiff

Instead of recapitulating the account of the *Pinochet* case offered in Richard Falk's contribution to this volume, I will use that account in order to establish a dialectical relationship between the case and the principles of universal jurisdiction defended in the Princeton Project. My aim is to clarify both the Principles using materials from the case and how the prior adoption of these principles could have changed the outcome of the case. I also aim to examine in some detail two issues with respect to which the exercise of universal jurisdiction, even if based on the Princeton Principles, raises serious questions. These two issues have to do with the promotion of democracy and with the recognition of accountability procedures that do not lead to penal measures for perpetrators of human rights abuses.

The Case and the Principles

The *Pinochet* case obviously provides material for reflection on the halting steps toward the assertion of jurisdiction on the basis of the principle of universality rather than on the basis of more traditional jurisdictional grounds such as territoriality or passive personality. The pure case of universal jurisdiction is one in which there is no other jurisdictional nexus than the presence in a particular state of the perpetrator of serious crimes under international law. Although Falk celebrates the movement in the direction of universality he perceives in the *Pinochet* case, perhaps the case offers more evidence of what some of the participants in the Princeton Project have called "universality plus" than of pure universal jurisdiction.[1] Only the proceedings in Belgian courts approach an instance in which universality was deemed to be a sufficient ground of jurisdiction. Proceedings in French courts, at least as far as charges of crimes against humanity were concerned, required basing jurisdiction on passive personality (French law also requires the presence of the accused in French territory).

The proceeding that advanced furthest, namely the Spanish request for extradition, although it moved in the direction of universality, started with an explicit appeal to passive personality—some of the victims of Pinochet's regime happened to be Spanish—and even when the charges were subsequently clarified and broadened and the request seemed to be grounded on universality, the nationality of some of the victims was still used as a tether that confirmed "a legitimate interest" in the proceedings on the part of Spain. The Princeton Principles endorse the exercise of universal jurisdiction even in the absence of a territorial or a national nexus. However, since universality alone might clash with the recognition of valid interests such as the proper acknowledgment of other countries' good faith efforts to complete a legitimate transition to democracy or, as Leila Nadya Sadat puts it, even with comity,[2] Principle 8 offers a variety of considerations other than universality that might help courts decide whether to exercise jurisdiction. I will return to this issue below.

The *Pinochet* case does represent a clear example of the limitations of immunity that are progressively becoming the norm in international law and practice. The case, of course, was centrally concerned with the question of immunity. It illustrates the erosion of the force of claims of immunity on the part of heads of states when the acts for which they are charged clearly violate basic principles of international humanitarian law. Despite the Divisional Court decision during the first stage of the case, the two dissents in the second stage, the sole dissent in the third stage,[3] the late support of the Chilean government for immunity, and notwithstanding the narrow temporal limitations that characterized the final decisions, the case is groundbreaking on this score.

One area in which the case provides a negative illustration of one of the principles offered here and in which, therefore, the outcome would have been different had the principles been adopted before, has to do with the relevance of customary international law for the exercise of universal jurisdiction absent reinforcing statutory enactment. Falk's paper correctly underscores the fact that the proceedings in Spain rested both on Spanish legislation that affirms the universality of the crimes in question as well as on international law. Falk also severely criticizes the House of Lords for a narrow, positivistic treatment of the case that reduced it mostly to a matter of whether international law explicitly incorporated into British positive law justified granting the Spanish request for extradition. So, rather than reading universal jurisdiction into customary or *jus cogens* law, the law lords addressed the jurisdictional question in terms of the treaty model of parallel criminalization.[4] They thus took ratification of the Torture Convention, on the part of Chile, Spain, and Britain, to settle the jurisdictional question. In doing so, the lords thereby established strict temporal limitations on the relevant charges. Only those charges that referred to crimes committed after parliamentary action that incorporated the convention into British statutory law and that occurred after Chile's ratification of the convention were deemed relevant.

It is not just that in taking this tack regarding the jurisdictional question the law lords, as one commentator put it, "dodged one of the foundational issues of international jurisprudence, namely, the ultimate source of universal jurisdiction;"[5] the adoption of the temporal limits on chargeable offenses meant that even if the extradition request had been granted, this would have likely led to an odd and difficult trial in Spain—odd, for Pinochet would not have been charged for the bulk of the offenses, which on most accounts took place long before Chile's own (ironic?) ratification of the Torture Convention in 1988, and difficult, for the evidentiary links to those late and less systematic abuses were weaker.[6] If the law lords could have been persuaded to rely on universal jurisdiction with respect to serious crimes under international law, it would have made a clear difference. Extradition might then have proceeded on the basis of a broader and more significant set of charges. Moreover, this would have represented a more meaningful step forward in the international defense of human rights.

Universal Jurisdiction and the Promotion of Democracy

The *Pinochet* case raises another important question concerning the exercise of universal jurisdiction, namely how to rank the different jurisdictional claims that different countries may raise in any given situation.

In the case of the Chilean general, different countries requested his extradition. Leaving aside purely contingent reasons like chronological priority—in other words, which country happens to file the first request— is it possible to articulate, if not fixed, determining criteria, at least relevant considerations for making decisions of this sort? Falk argues that changes in circumstances in Chile, including "a gradually more secure democratic order . . ., a displacement of the earlier Pinochet generation of leaders in the armed forces, the ascendancy of post-Pinochet judges, the persisting activism of human rights groups" among other factors, "lent weight to the Chilean request for Pinochet's return and weakened somewhat the foundation underlying foreign criminal prosecution."[7] At one point, he talks about "the special relationship" between Pinochet and Chile. But what is this "special relationship" that, by its very nature, can settle this momentous jurisdictional question? Given the difficulties that have been encountered almost without exception when trials of perpetrators have been initiated in their own countries and, moreover, given the seminal motivating notion behind the idea of universal jurisdiction—that is, the idea of the perpetrator as *hostis humanis generis* (enemy of all humanity)—it is not obvious why considerations concerning the nationality of the victims (or the perpetrator) should be sufficient for deciding the proper jurisdiction, despite the intuitive appeal of these factors.

Diane F. Orentlicher seems to be trying to articulate the same idea behind Falk's talk of "a special relationship" in her objections to what she calls the "impunity rationale" for universal jurisdiction. According to this rationale, vindicating the claims of justice of humanity is not only a sufficient reason for the exercise of universal jurisdiction but also one that overrides all other claims, including, for example, the claims of a democracy in transition or, more generally, any claim that arises from the territorial state. In place of this stringent rationale, Orentlicher defends a "balance of interests approach," which she finds both in different extradition agreements and the Rome Statute of the International Criminal Court. This method for resolving jurisdictional questions takes into consideration the diverse interests of both national and international communities. What is most relevant here is the reason she defends this approach. According to Orentlicher, this approach is likely to recognize that "there are compelling reasons to give priority to prosecutions by the territorial state, *provided there are sufficient guarantees of fair process* [her italics]." In particular, in-country justice may do more to advance a country's process of rehabilitation and reconciliation following mass atrocity than the remote proceedings of an international tribunal. In addition to being more accessible to communities directly affected by atrocious crimes, domestic prosecutions are more likely to inspire a sense of "ownership" by those societies.[8] Although this is an argument framed against the quick exercise of jurisdiction by an international tribunal, the same argument applies against such exercise by a foreign state.

I take this argument to be important for two reasons. First, it contextualizes the discussion of universal jurisdiction by putting it in something closer to its proper setting. Most occasions for the possible exercise of this type of jurisdiction are likely to arise in processes of transitions from authoritarianism. Second, the idea of ownership is perhaps more suggestive than that of a "special relationship" between victims and perpetrators. While the former has both prospective and retrospective elements that will be explored presently, the latter seems to be unduly retrospective.

However, even Orentlicher's argument is nothing more than the beginning of a fuller account of why decisions about the exercise of universal jurisdiction should be tempered by considerations that stem from the interests of national communities and, in particular, of the states where crimes were committed and of the nationality of the perpetrators. The two points underscored above can be carried further by introducing into the discussion a concept that has not received the salience in the human rights literature that it deserves, namely, the concept of democracy.[9] So it is not enough to put the discussion of universal jurisdiction in the context of transitions *from authoritarianism,* and to talk, as Orentlicher does, about rehabilitation and reconciliation. It is important to situate the discussion in the context of transitions *to democracy* and thus to talk about the considerations that are likely to promote the development and entrenchment of democratic institutions and attitudes. Doing so will also happen to be helpful in the clarification of the notion of ownership.

This is not the place for a full discussion of what democracy entails or of the relationship between this concept and the notion of human rights. The following sketch, however, will suggest the ways in which introducing this concept will enrich the discussion of the principles of universal jurisdiction. Democracy, at the most general level, is the name of a form of organizing the distribution and the exercise of state power in a way that expresses and promotes the value of self-governance. Although in the political domain this value can be operationalized by means of periodic elections—which, as long as they are free from the most obvious forms of manipulation, seem to satisfy the understanding of democracy of many foreign policy makers—this by no means exhausts the full meaning, or all the requirements, of a functioning democracy.

To see why this is so, some remarks about the justification of democracy should suffice. Again, remaining at a broad level of generality, one could say that the justification for the sort of political participation that is involved in democratic politics can be justified in terms of both epistemic and normative premises.[10] Given that in the international domain it is particularly important to be mindful of the universalizability of justifications, these premises will be thin. So part of the justification for democratic participation is epistemic in the sense that it is reasonable to say that allowing citizens to participate in the formulation and the implementation of the laws they live by increases the possibility that those laws will capture and satisfy the citizens' own interests. Just as in the domain of moral validity it is reasonable to assume that a norm that gains the rational and free assent of those who are affected by it is a valid norm, it makes sense, in the political domain, to think about the legitimacy of a law in terms of the rational and free assent that the law can gain from a citizenry that is given the opportunity to participate in processes of consultation and contestation. In both moral and political domains, this defense of participation is most persuasive when the point is put negatively: if the only way of securing support for a norm is by excluding from consideration some of those affected by it, then we have reasons to question the validity or the legitimacy of such a norm. The basic insight behind this position is that for a broad range of matters, each of us knows what is in our own best interest. Whatever doubts one may have about this claim, that it contains a kernel of truth is, once again, best seen when given a negative formulation: the claim is that others are in an even worse position than each of us is to know what is best for us.

The argument just sketched is the epistemic side of the justification of democratic participation. It rests on the premise that in general the best way to guarantee that people's perspectives are represented is to allow them to represent those interests themselves. But this cannot be the whole reason in favor of participating in either moral or political processes; the correct representation of one's views is not the only value served by participation. If it were, the argument in favor of participation would be undermined by recalling the opacity of our own impressions of what is best for us, especially concerning long-term interests and issues that require complex coordination with others. The other part of this defense of participation is more explicitly normative in spirit, and it corresponds to the conception of human worth of modernity, which sees individuals in John Rawls's terms as "self-originating sources of valid claims."[11] So the first, more epistemic part of this argument in favor of participation captures the intuition that the legitimacy of norms is not divorced from correctness (and that the rational acceptability by all who are affected by them, under conditions of free and open participation, is the relevant standard of correctness). The second and more normative part of the defense captures the intuition that in morality it matters not only that norms be correct (or valid) but also that they be our own. Similarly, in the domain of politics, at least of democratic politics, it matters a whole lot not only that we live under sound laws—in other words, under laws that promote our interests, as each group sees those interests from its own perspective—but also that we live under laws of which we can consider ourselves to be the authors.

This brief sketch of the justificatory grounds of democracy serves to clarify what I take to be the intuition behind Falk's notion that the "special relationship" between Pinochet and Chile "lent weight to the Chilean request for Pinochet´s return and weakened somewhat the foundation underlying foreign criminal prosecution."[12] The discussion also serves to clarify the core idea behind Orentlicher's claim that "trials in the territorial state are more likely than prosecutions abroad to inspire a sense of 'ownership' by societies recently scourged by atrocious crimes."[13] The crucial insight behind these claims, I believe, is that democracy is a system that requires that citizens see themselves as the authors and the executors of their own laws. So it is not just because Chileans constituted the bulk of Pinochet's victims that there are reasons to think that the general ought to be tried in Chile. This argument lends itself too easily to a retrospective, retributivist reading according to which Chileans now have the right to exact retribution from their former oppressor. Although this might be the case, it misses the fundamental point; for the reasons outlined in the brief sketch of democracy offered above, democracy is a system which requires that citizens see themselves as the authors and the executors of the laws they live by. Chilean democracy, then, is better served by proceedings that encourage a sense of self-government and authorship over Chile's destiny than by a judicial proceeding in a foreign country, which, even if it would have led to just deserts, would have done so in a paternalistic way. This understanding of the requirements of democracy is the proper context in which to place the discussion of universal jurisdiction. In particular, it serves to contextualize Principle 8 of the Princeton Project, a principle that counsels states that have custody over alleged perpetrators of crimes under international law, if they have no basis for subject matter jurisdiction other than the universality principle, to base their decisions of whether to prosecute or extradite on the basis of a variety of criteria that include the nationality connection of the alleged perpetrator to the requesting state.

Universal Jurisdiction, Amnesties, and Accountability

The final point where a useful relationship between the Principles and the *Pinochet* case can be established has to do with the issue of the recognition that other countries ought to give to the amnesties and accountability procedures adopted by a particular state. Needless to say, the point made in the previous section, that there ought to be a presumption in favor of procedures against perpetrators in their territorial states, is a defeasible presumption. In the particular case at issue here, Falk, of course, is correct in thinking that the Chilean argument in favor of Pinochet's repatriation gained force only to the extent that recent developments in Chile have made it more likely that there would be a good faith effort to hold him accountable for his crimes. This general point is duly reflected in the formulation of Principle 8.

Indeed, it should be clear that the presumption in favor of territoriality as a relevant (not overriding) criterion of jurisdiction is one that becomes operative only if there are no amnesties or other procedures that illegitimately hinder prosecutions in the territorial state. Principle 7 provides that "[a]mnesties are generally inconsistent with the obligation of states to provide accountability for serious crimes under international law. . . ."

It should be clear that neither the Chilean amnesty of 1978 nor the proceedings of the Truth and Reconciliation Commission could give Pinochet protection from efforts by other countries to exercise universal jurisdiction over him. The Amnesty Law is inconsistent with Principle 7. In addition to the fact that since the amnesty covered crimes against humanity and, arguably, genocide, and thus violated international law, it was not adopted by a democratic procedure. Indeed, the amnesty was passed by Pinochet as one of a set of measures intended to soften the image of the regime, after he won the notoriously undemocratic plebiscite of January 4, 1978.[14] The sweeping decree, enacted by the military junta on April 18, 1978, covered all crimes against persons committed in the period between September 11, 1973, and March 10, 1978. Although Pinochet himself argued that he considered it "an ethical imperative" to pass a measure that would help Chileans to "leave[] behind hatreds" and thereby promote "national re-unification," and defended an amnesty that was allegedly "impartial," for it made no distinctions between its potential beneficiaries, this is a very good example of how formal equality can sometimes lead to grossly unequal treatment; after all, it was only agents of the junta, not the opposition, that used terror during the period in question. In this sense, this is a paradigm of a self-amnesty and hence should not be taken as a bar to the exercise of universal jurisdiction on the part of other states.

The accountability mechanisms involved in the work of the Truth and Reconciliation Commission pose problems of a different sort. The commission was established by President Aylwin on April 25, 1990, by executive decree. In many senses it represented a compromise, for the Concertación—the alliance of opposition parties that defeated Pinochet in the plebiscite of 1988—had offered during the campaign to do its best to repeal the Amnesty Law.[15] This provoked the oft-quoted reaction on the part of Pinochet: "Nobody will touch me. The day one of my men is touched, the rule of law will end. I have said this once and I will not repeat it ever again. But it should be known that this is going to be like this."[16] It was, of course, not only threats such as this that made Aylwin back off from attempts at prosecutions. Successful prosecutions would have required massive constitutional reforms. The 1980 constitution (The Constitution of Liberty [!]) was the expression of a political vision that Pinochet outlined in a historic speech on July 9, 1977. He then argued that Chile needed a new form of democracy, "one that would be authoritarian, protected, integrative, technified." A democracy is authoritarian, he explained, "when it possesses strong and vigorous authority in order to defend citizens from demagoguery and violence. . . ."[17] True to the plan, the constitution is littered with "authoritarian enclaves,"[18] including designated senators, increased executive powers at the expense of the legislature, an expanded emergency legislation, insulation from dismissal for military commanders, electoral system reforms that give advantages to the right, a National Security Council that arguably provides the military with legal justification for a coup d'état, and barriers against amendment. The constitution thus provided for an authoritarian and, even more, protected form of democracy.

Against this background, not surprisingly, the work of the Truth and Reconciliation Commission is problematic. After nine months of arduous work, in early 1991 the commission presented its massive, two-volume report. It is not that the veracity of the contents of the report have been questioned—at least not by the majority of Chileans. Two fundamental problems diminished the effectiveness of the report. The first is the direct result of its mandate. The commission was charged with investigating "the most serious human rights violation," and it proceeded to define these in the following terms: "[Serious violations of human rights] are here understood as situations of those persons who disappeared after arrest, who were executed, or who were tortured to death, in which the moral responsibility of the state is compromised as a result of actions by its agents or persons in its service, as well as kidnappings and attempts on the lives of persons committed by private citizens for political purposes."[19]

In addition to the fact that this definition made victims of human rights abuses many agents of the state who may have died in the course of carrying out repressive measures, the essential problem with this way of defining the commission's mandate is that it allowed it to investigate deaths, leaving out of consideration another form of gross abuse, far more frequent than death but perhaps equally pernicious—namely, torture. While there were roughly three thousand cases of death during the seventeen years of dictatorship, the number of tortures is far greater. Precise numbers are difficult to come by, at least in part because of the victims' continued reluctance to disclose their misfortune and humiliation. But in a country of fifteen million the numbers are outrageous: the Vicariate of Solidarity, the group supported by the Catholic Church, which did so much to help and to record victims during the period, registered 104,000 cases of torture. The Chilean Human Rights Commission, headed by Jaime Castillo, twice exiled by the regime and later a member of the Truth and Reconciliation Commission, estimates that 500,000 suffered violations of human rights, and FASIC, the group supported by Christian churches deems that one million detained persons suffered mistreatment.[20] The narrow mandate of the commission has meant that these victims have remained largely in the shadows. It is not just that their bad fates are rarely mentioned in accounts of the dictatorship, and in this way their suffering remains unrecognized, but that they have been underserved by the successor administrations. While families of the disappeared have received different forms of compensation totaling ninety million dollars, it was only recently that the victims of torture have been offered somewhat rudimentary psychological counseling.[21]

The second problem that diminished the effectiveness of the report was its lack of success in finding the whereabouts of the remains of the disappeared. Although, again, this should not come as a surprise, given that the commission had no subpoena powers, this remains, in the phrase often used in Chile, "an open wound."

One more difficulty afflicted the work of the commission, but this one is wholly extrinsic to it. The military, as well as the supreme court, failed to acknowledge the report's conclusions. Despite the fact that the report assiduously abided by its decision not to name names, Pinochet called its findings "personal and precarious convictions [that] have been transformed into condemnatory sentences against many persons, outside due process, opening the way to their discredit before public opinion and exposing them to terrorist vengeance." The general categorically asserted that "the Army of Chile solemnly declares that it will not accept being placed on the dock of the accused for having saved the freedom and sovereignty of the Fatherland" and insisted that "the army certainly sees no reason to seek pardon for having taken part in a patriotic labor."[22] This reluctance to acknowledge the violation continues to this date. On the eve of his eighty-fifth birthday, on his first public address after his return to Chile from detention in London, Pinochet hypocritically accepted "responsibility for all the deeds that it is

said the Army committed [*de todos los hechos que dicen que el Ejército cometió*]."
This, of course, is not acknowledgment of responsibility, for no facts are
accepted. Facts are reduced to hearsay: "what they say."[23] Since there can be
no reconciliation without the recognition of the pain inflicted, this obsti-
nacy on the part of the leaders of the former regime has thwarted one of
the aims of the commission.

Now, given the political constraints under which the commission operated, I do not think that it can be blamed for the difficulties it encountered
or generated. Perhaps it was the best that the circumstances allowed. In the
words of President Aylwin's inaugural address, his aim always was to "reconcile the virtue of justice with the virtue of prudence."[24] But if this is so,
one may think it unacceptably harsh for Principle 7(2) to declare the work
of the commission an insufficient bar to the exercise of universal jurisdiction on the part of other states. It must be recalled, though, that this principle does not declare such efforts illegitimate *tout court*. It merely declares
that oppressors cannot gain benefits from having made the work of future
accountability mechanisms difficult, especially not the benefits of traveling
among humanity, the humanity that rightly considers them *hostis humanis
generis*.

Chapter 8
The *Hissène Habré* Case: The Law and Politics of Universal Jurisdiction

Stephen P. Marks

Introduction

When the state prosecutor brought the case against former Chadian president Hissène Habré[1] to a regional tribunal in Dakar on February 3, 2000, journalists and activists hailed it as the first case based on the *Pinochet* precedent.[2] Human rights groups hoped this case would set a pattern of prosecutions denying impunity to former heads of state for massive violations of human rights committed while they were in power. The legal basis was sought in both treaty law and customary international law for the exercise of criminal or other jurisdiction over a former head of state in the custody of a state unrelated to the perpetrator(s), victim(s), or place of the alleged crimes, that is, universal jurisdiction.

This essay will review the basic historical context of the rule of Hissène Habré in Chad from 1982 until he was overthrown in 1990 by the current head of state, Idriss Deby (Part 1), the initial efforts by the Deby government to investigate his alleged crimes (Part 2), the proceedings against Habré in Senegal from February 2000 to March 2001 (Part 3), the limits on Senegal's competence and the issue of the self-executing character of the Torture Convention (Part 4), and finally the tentative lessons of the case (Part 5).

To set the stage for the attempted exercise of universal jurisdiction by a Senegalese judge over the crimes of Hissène Habré, we begin with some brief historical reminders of postindependence Chad and Habré's rule.

Historical Context: A Legacy of Cold War Support for Dictators

The attempted exercise of universal jurisdiction over Hissène Habré is set in the context of two trends in foreign affairs, one during and the other after the cold war. The first is the trend of major powers in the 1960s through the 1980s to support dictators of newly independent countries for strategic advantages that outweighed, in their realpolitik calculation, any concern over brutal practices, even when the practices in question amounted to massive violations of human rights. Chad gained independence from French colonial rule only to fall into decades of civil war among rival ethnic groups drawing upon various foreign powers for support in the struggle to gain and hold on to power for their respective groups. Hissène Habré is one of many brutal leaders who victimized their own people with the support of major powers. The second trend is the post–cold war manifestation of the political will of a growing group of like-minded countries, prodded and encouraged by global civil society, to hold perpetrators of human rights violations accountable and for this purpose, to expand the purview of international criminal law, even with respect to former heads of state. The *Pinochet* precedent, along with the creation of the International Criminal Tribunal for the Former Yugoslavia and the International Criminal Tribunal for Rwanda, as well as the adoption of the Rome Statute of the International Criminal Court, are part of this second trend. The tension between these two trends—between power calculations based on national interest and accountability for abuse of the human interest—explains the evolution of the law and politics of universal jurisdiction.

Independence to 1982

France, having defeated the local ruler in 1900, formed the territory of Chad in 1916 and granted it independence in 1960.[3] Chad was a vast territory of five hundred thousand square miles with poor communications, few known resources, a tiny market, and an impoverished population[4] belonging to two hundred tribes with a colonial heritage of economic dependence, political rivalry, and cultural isolation.

François Tombalbaye, the country's first president, established a one-party regime, but the authority of the state declined as economic conditions deteriorated and ethnic and regional conflict worsened. Chad's government and national army were too incompetent to stop various uncoordinated and poorly organized rebel groups, one of whose leaders was Hissène Habré. Tombalbaye called in the French for military assistance, ended reform efforts, and, claiming he had put down a coup supported by Libyan rebels, severed relations with Libya, incarcerated political prisoners, and mismanaged drought-relief efforts. He was overthrown in a coup in 1975, and Col. Félix Malloum ruled by military government from 1975 to 1978. Malloum was no better than the unpopular Tombalbaye in satisfying the expectations of most urban Chadians, especially the radicalized unions, students, and city dwellers. In 1977 Malloum and Habré negotiated a formal alliance, the Fundamental Charter, the basis of the National Union

Government formed in 1978, with Malloum as president and Habré as prime minister. Civil war raged from 1979 to 1982, following the collapse of the fragile Malloum-Habré alliance. In 1979 Habré forces sent Malloum into retirement under French protection, and eventually a Transitional Government of National Unity (Gouvernement d´Union Nationale de Transition—GUNT) was set up with Goukouni Oueddei[5] as president and Habré as minister of national defense, veterans, and war victims. In 1980 Habré's army attacked one of the constituent groups of GUNT, and Chad was again plunged into a cycle of violence, with Goukouni supported militarily by Libya and Habré fleeing to Sudan. Eventually, Goukouni's relations with Libya deteriorated, and he asked the Libyan forces to leave, thus opening the way for Habré's forces, supported by Egypt, Sudan, and, reportedly, the United States, to take over the capital, N'Djamena, on June 7, 1982.

The Habré Regime

With the support of France, the United States, and other African nations, Habré consolidated his power and worked to secure international recognition for his government. He immediately gave the most influential positions to fellow Goranes, preferring his clan, the Anakaza, within that ethnic group. All decisions had to be made with their knowledge or be in their interest, according to the Commission of Inquiry set up after Habré's fall.[6] He created his personal army, called the Securité Présidentielle (SP), consisting mainly of people from his tribe. With the support of his political party, the National Union for Independence and Revolution (Union Nationale Pour l'Indépendance et la Révolution—UNIR), he established a personality cult, ascribing to himself attributes of God.[7] His principal means of controlling the population and suppressing dissident voices was the Documentation and Security Directorate (Direction de la Documentation et la Sécurité—DDS), created in 1983.[8]

All four directors of the DDS were Goranes, like Habré.[9] According to one, its agents were placed in all areas of activity, including the civil service, neighborhoods, and businesses.[10] The agency grew to 23 branches, including 584 highly armed soldiers in the Special Rapid Action Brigade (Brigade Spéciale d'Intervention Rapide), whose work, according to the Commission of Inquiry, included "all the dirty deeds such as arrest, torture, murder and large-scale massacres."[11] There was also a Terrorist Mission Branch (Service Mission Terroriste—SMT) "in charge of persecution and physical liquidation of Chadian opposition figures located abroad," which carried out "scores of assassinations and kidnappings."[12] All DDS agents were required, beginning in 1990, to swear to keep secret all DDS activities because Habré wanted to end the leaks he attributed to DDS staff that had led to the "continuous flow of correspondence from Amnesty International, demanding that he cease summary executions and other human rights violations."[13]

In December 1990 Col. Idriss Deby, former chief of staff and leader of a rebel movement, successfully attacked government forces, bringing down the Habré regime, due in part to the fact that France kept its troops out of engagements with the rebels. With the complicity of several high officials, Habré was able to retrieve over three million francs CFA from the national treasury on November 30, 1990, and another 115 million from several provincial accounts on December 1, although most of his other efforts to empty the accounts of the state failed.[14] Deby took power as Habré fled the same day and settled in Senegal, with family members and close associates as well as a sizeable portion of the national treasury. He has resided there since December 1990.

Failed Efforts to Bring Habré to Justice

African governments were well aware of Habré's record, and international human rights groups had documented his abuses. Chadian organizations acting on behalf of victims denounced his record and sought redress. Two failed attempts were made to hold Habré accountable in the 1990s. The first was a truth commission (the Commission of Inquiry), whose recommendations were not implemented. The second was a halfhearted request, eight years later, to extradite him for trial in Chad.

The Truth Commission

On assuming power, Idriss Deby called Habré "a dictator who tortured and detained those who opposed him, and a kleptomaniac who stole international aid and fled with most of the Government treasury."[15] In December 1990 the new government of Col. Idriss Deby created a Commission of Inquiry into the Crimes and Embezzlements of the Former President, His Coprincipals and/or Coconspirators (Commission d'Enquête sur les Crimes et Détournements Commis par l'ex-Président, Ses Co-auteurs et/ou Complices).[16] Its mandate covered ten items, the first of which was to investigate kidnapping, detention, murder, disappearances, torture and acts of barbarity, mistreatment, other attacks on physical or moral integrity, and all acts in violation of human rights and illicit trafficking of drugs.[17]

The commission began work on March 1, 1991, without adequate material resources to carry out its work and operating under a considerable psychological disadvantage because it had to meet in the headquarters of the DDS, where witnesses were hardly likely to feel trust toward their interviewers. The commission's report is candid about some of its members dropping out of the commission's work because they found it too dangerous and others "just reappearing at the end of the month to receive paychecks and then disappearing," and the need to replace three-quarters of the membership.[18] Its mandate had two parts, one on crimes against persons and the other on misappropriation and embezzlement of public goods. The commission's methods as described in the report are those of criminal investigation, including depositions and hearings of former political prisoners, prisoners of war, former DDS agents, and family members of victims of political killing. Usually investigators deposed witnesses alone but worked in teams when significant information was involved.[19] The commission heard 1,726 witnesses and conducted three exhumations. Complaining of the lack of time[20] and means and availability of witnesses, it could cover only 10 percent of the crimes of the "tyrant Habré"[21] and calculated that the eight years of the Habré régime resulted in 40,000 "victims" (killed and tortured), 80,000 orphans, 30,000 widows, and 200,000 people without moral or material support due to the repression.[22]

The commission recommended, inter alia, that the government create a National Human Rights Commission and "begin without delay judicial process against those responsible for this horrible genocide, guilty of crimes against humanity."[23] Apparently, no effort was made to implement this latter recommendation until 1998 when a request for extradition from Senegal was considered, to be discussed below.

Asylum

Meanwhile, Habré settled comfortably in Dakar, where he invested in real estate and other businesses, and acquired three villas where he lives with his three wives.[24] According to the High Commission for Refugees, Habré neither sought nor was granted political or territorial asylum, although some of his supporters and bodyguards were granted refugee status.[25] He appears to enjoy a special status as guest of the government rather than political asylum.

Whether he could or should have received asylum or whether he can or should be extradited to Chad for the purpose of criminal process has not been formally raised. The issues of asylum and extradition are, nevertheless, relevant to the question of universal jurisdiction insofar as they can set limits on a government's recourse to universal jurisdiction. The argument can be made that Habré's reputation and the evidence collected by the Commission of Inquiry in his country as well as numerous reports by human rights nongovernmental organizations (NGOs) and international agencies should have persuaded the Senegalese government to refuse asylum, had he sought it, in accordance with UN General Assembly pronouncements on territorial asylum.[26] Whether such pronouncements by the General Assembly—limited, it should be noted, to war crimes and crimes against humanity—establish or restate positive international law is a matter if dispute. Michael Scharf considers that the references during the drafting process to the view that the Declaration on Territorial Asylum "was not intended to propound legal norms or to change existing rules of international law" is evidence that "from the onset, the General Assembly resolutions concerning crimes against humanity were not intended to create any binding duties" and—combined with UN and state practice regarding amnesty where such crimes are involved "confirms that customary international law has not yet crystallized in this area."[27] I believe Scharf overlooks two points. First, while no single resolution can purport, under Articles 10 and 13 of the charter, to create binding law,[28] the accumulation of normative statements, especially in the form of a set of UN "Principles" or a "Declaration," with progressively greater majorities and no dissenting votes, contributes to both the material and psychological elements of emerging custom.[29]

The second point raised by Scharf concerns UN support for amnesties. In fact, UN practice has tended *not* to endorse "amnesty for peace deals in situations involving crimes against humanity" and more often does just the opposite with respect not only to crimes against humanity but also to violations of human rights in general.[30] The issue of balancing the political implications of postconflict reconciliation and stability with the requirements of justice is complex.[31] The UN has tended not to encourage amnesty or "self-amnesty," and whatever Faustian bargains have been concluded in state practice do not appear to overturn the trend to support the principle of denial of asylum to perpetrators of serious international crimes.[32] One finds a greater attraction to political expediency in the political science literature than in the more principled action of the UN.[33]

The practice of states like Panama, Saudi Arabia, France, Zambia, Zimbabwe, and Brazil has been to admit former dictators, sometimes by granting asylum and rejecting the argument that asylum should be denied to persons responsible for international crimes or that such persons should be prosecuted or extradited.[34] That Senegal accepted such an individual bringing with him $11 million of money stolen from the state in 1990 is not surprising. By 2000 the rule against granting asylum had "crystallized," and the political and moral price for harboring such a person had become higher.[35]

Extradition

Where a former dictator's record of abuse does not prevent him or her from establishing residence abroad, that record may be the basis for a request for extradition. Chadian justice minister Limane Mahamat announced in January 1998 the intention of the Chadian government to request formally the extradition of Habré under the 1960 justice cooperation convention with Senegal to face charges in Chad ranging from graft to murder.[36] In fact, the idea of such a request was discussed within the Ministry of Justice, but, presumably after discrete soundings of the Senegalese government, the Chadian authorities did not make the formal extradition request to

Senegal. The fact that at least three of Habré's ministers were kept in the Deby government and that Limane Mahamat did not last as minister of justice may also explain in part the failure to proceed with the request. Had a formal request been made, Habré might have invoked the political offense exception,[37] and the Senegalese authorities could have refused due to its assessment of the risk of persecution or of an unfair trial.

On the first point, the political offense exception does not apply to the types of crimes of which Habré is accused.[38] An ousted head of state may be presumed to be sought for political reasons when the country he fled requests extradition. However, the international crimes included in the charges made against Habré by the Commission of Inquiry should exclude the application of this exception. This exclusion of the exception is reinforced by the more recent movement against impunity, including the Set of Principles for the Protection and Promotion of Human Rights through Action to Combat Impunity.[39]

A request for extradition can legitimately be challenged if there are grounds for considering that the accused would be persecuted or not receive a fair trial for political reasons.[40] The Model Convention on Extradition enumerates seven mandatory grounds for refusing extradition, including "if the person would be subjected to torture or cruel, inhuman treatment or degrading punishment or if that person has not or would not receive the minimum guarantees in criminal proceedings as contained in the International Covenant on Civil and Political Rights, article 14."[41] This principle is reinforced by the Torture Convention, to which both Chad and Senegal are parties.[42] Moreover, the Committee against Torture considers pertinent for determining the existence of a danger that the accused will be tortured whether "there is evidence of a consistent pattern of gross, flagrant or mass violations of human rights" and whether "the author engaged in political or other activity within or outside the State concerned which would appear to make him/her particularly vulnerable to the risk of being placed in danger of torture were he/she to be expelled, returned or extradited to the State in question."[43]

Evidence is available to the Senegalese government to cast doubt on the fairness of the Chadian justice system and its propensity toward repression.[44] As an editorial in the *New York Times* put it: "Ideally Mr. Habré would be tried in Chad itself, but the government of Mr. Deby, replete with former allies of Mr. Habré and with a record of its own abuses, has made no effort to bring its former dictator to trial."[45] In 1995 Amnesty International described the interests of the Deby government as follows: "Repressive governments are especially distinguished by their tendency to turn a blind eye to past crimes and their surprising haste to grant immunity, or even promotion, to suspected perpetrators of human rights violations. This is notably the case with Chad under the presidency of Colonel Idriss Deby, who has continued the practices of his predecessor Hissein Habré, under whom he served as chief of staff and whom he himself drove from power in December 1990.[46]

Human Rights Watch, whose advocacy director, Reed Brody, worked with the Chadian plaintiffs and their Senegalese lawyers, explained that "with many ranking officials of the Deby government, including Deby himself, involved in Habré's crimes, . . . the new government did not pursue Habre's extradition from Senegal."[47]

The grave situation of human rights in Chad was summarized by another leading international human rights organization, also involved in the case: "With mass forced exile of political leaders and the intellectual elite, imprisonments, arbitrary suspension of human rights defence associations and the hounding and harassment of journalists, unwarranted recourse to the judicial apparatus by the Executive Branch for settling political scores, etc., human rights violations in Chad are grave, flagrant and systematic and can, on more than one count, be laid at the door of the Chadian authorities, who have taken no specific or effective steps to bring them to an end."[48]

More recent developments, in particular the willingness of the Chadian authorities to bring cases against members of the DDS on behalf of victims of the Habré régime,[49] might alter this rationale for barring extradition. Two days after the appellate court in Dakar rejected Senegal's competence to try Habré, the Chadian government finally spoke out, saying that should the appellate judgment be confirmed, it would "pursue other procedures to prosecute" Habré.[50]

In sum, the hypothetical duty to refuse asylum to an author of massive human rights violations or to extradite to the country where the acts were committed without accepting the political offense exception is moot in the *Habré* case because he was admitted into Senegal. If conditions for a fair trial can be met in Chad, Senegal should comply with a request for Habré's extradition; if they are not met, Senegal is barred from doing so under a peremptory norm of international law reflected in the nonrefoulement provision of Article 3 of the Torture Convention. With respect to the crime of torture, the Torture Convention makes it a requirement on all states parties to consider the offenses defined in the convention as extraditable offenses in any extradition treaty existing between them, and, for states that make extradition conditional on the existence of a treaty, the convention may be considered as the legal basis for extradition.[51] For states that do not make extradition conditional on the existence of a treaty, they must recognize such offenses as extraditable vis-à-vis another state party.[52] Finally, the acts punishable under the convention "shall be treated, for the purpose of extradition between States Parties, as if they had been committed not only in the place in which they occurred but also in the territories of the States required to establish their jurisdiction in accordance with article 5, paragraph 1."[53] Thus emerges a key provision of the Torture Convention establishing the duty to extradite or punish (*aut dedere aut judicare*) of states parties, which reads in substantial part: "Each State Party shall likewise take such measures as may be necessary to establish its jurisdiction over such offences in cases where the alleged offender is present in any territory under its jurisdiction and it does not extradite him pursuant to article 8 to any of the States mentioned in paragraph I of this article" (based on territoriality, nationality, or passive personality).[54]

Treaty-based universal jurisdiction is thus established: states parties are obliged to take necessary measures to prosecute alleged perpetrators whom they do not extradite, an obligation that Article 7(1) makes even clearer: "The State Party in the territory under whose jurisdiction a person alleged to have committed any offence referred to in article 4 is found shall in the cases contemplated in article 5, if it does not extradite him, submit the case to its competent authorities for the purpose of prosecution."

The Right or Duty to Prosecute

There is some disagreement as to whether this duty to extradite or punish under customary international law is permissive or mandatory. According to Michael Scharf, there would be no duty to prosecute, although Senegal would have the right to do so.[55] Human rights groups and other scholars tend to see the rule as a mandatory one, at least as regards crimes against humanity.[56] The editors of *International Criminal Law* usefully point to the trend of General Assembly resolutions over the past thirty years to reinforce the position that states have an obligation to arrest and extradite or put on trial and punish perpetrators of certain international crimes.[57] The accumulation of authority for a customary rule establishing an *obligation* to prosecute or extradite (beyond the *right* to do so) would be stronger were it not for the number of abstentions and even occasional negative votes (four for Resolution 2712). Nevertheless, the most significant documents are GA Resolution 44/162, endorsing the Principles on the Effective Prevention and Investigation of Extralegal, Arbitrary, and Summary Executions, and GA Resolution 47/133 containing the Declaration on the Protection of All Persons from Enforced Disappearances, which were adopted without a vote.

Therefore, if Chad, relying on its territorial jurisdiction, or any other country relying on passive personality or universal jurisdiction, were to request extradition, Senegal would have an obligation to honor the request. In considering the request it should not allow Habré to benefit from the political offense exception. However, it could reject the request if it had sufficient evidence that Habré would be subjected to persecution or not be given a fair trial in Chad. If it does not extradite him, it is bound under conventional and customary international law to try him for those offenses under international law for which universal jurisdiction is recognized and about which it has sufficient evidence to indict. This duty was invoked by the victims' organizations and rejected by the Senegalese judiciary, although in late 2002, Senegal agreed to consider extraditing Habré to Belgium.

The Proceedings against Habré in Senegal in 2000 and 2001

The case was prepared by a group of international NGOs and advisors and Chadian and Senegalese NGOs and victims' associations. The leading international partners were the New York–based Human Rights Watch (HRW), the Paris-based International Federation of Human Rights Leagues (FIDH), and the London-based Interights. The local groups consisted of three Chadian organizations—the Chadian Association for the Promotion and Defense of Human Rights (ATPDH), the Chadian Association of Victims of Political Repression and Crime (AVCRP), and the Chadian League for Human Rights (LTDH)—and several Senegalese human rights groups, including the National Organization for Human Rights (ONDH) and the Dakar-based African Assembly for the Defense of Human Rights (RADDHO). ATPDH took the original initiative of seeking HRW's assistance, and that organization brought together a coalition of Chadian, Senegalese, and international groups into what was called the International Committee for the Trial of Hissène Habré.[58] After some deliberation, the coalition decided to use the procedure of private prosecution rather than await the Senegalese prosecutor to act on his own.[59] They filed a criminal complaint supported by private parties (*"plainte avec constitution de partie civile"*) with the investigating judge of the Dakar regional court (*juge d'instruction près le Tribunal Régional hors classe de Dakar*), Demba Kandji, on January 25, 2000.[60]

The Indictment

Once the complaint was filed, the case moved, in the words of Human Rights Watch, "with stunning speed," describing the unfolding of events as follows: "The judge first forwarded the file to the prosecutor for his nonbinding advice. The prosecutor, made aware of the need to act quickly so that Habre did not flee the country as well as so the victims could be heard before returning to Chad, gave his favorable advice within two days. The next day the victims gave their closed-door testimony before the judge—something they had waited 9 years to do! The judge then called in Habre on February 3, 2000 and indicted him on charges of *complicité d'actes de torture* (accomplice to torture) and placed him under house arrest."[61]

The plaintiffs documented 97 cases of political killing, 142 cases of torture, and 100 cases of disappearances. Judge Kandji heard six ordinary

Chadian citizens, who traveled from Chad in January and May to testify as to their arrest and torture. For example, a former civil servant, Souleyman Guengueng, told of his arrest in August 1988 by the DDS and incarceration and torture for two years. His testimony was summarized in chilling terms: "Mr. Guengueng said he lost consciousness for so long on three occasions that his fellow prisoners left him for dead. Up to 10 men were kept in one cell built for a single prisoner, and their legs eventually became paralyzed. And he said three to four people died every day from malaria, flea infestation, lack of food, suffocation or sheer heat. He also recalled how 300 of their fellow prisoners had been jammed into one small cell; the guards would pour water into the cell from the ceiling, forcing the men to lick the floor or their bodies so they would not die of thirst."[62]

Another witness, Samuel Togoto, told of his arrest in 1988 and torture by tying his hands and feet together behind his back and being beaten for one or two hours until his limbs were paralyzed.[63] The judge also heard from the president of the Chadian Commission of Inquiry, who cited the number of political assassinations and cases of systematic torture under the Habré regime at 40,000.[64] Judge Kandji, with permission from the French legal authorities, heard testimony from a French doctor, Helène Jaffé, who had treated 581 victims of torture.[65]

On January 27, 2000, the state prosecutor (*procureur de la République*) agreed to a criminal investigation,[66] and the assistant state prosecutor, Abdulaye Gaye, confirmed this approval formally on January 28.[67] On February 3, he summoned Habré, indicted him for complicity in acts of torture, imposed restrictions on his movement and actions, and opened an investigation with a view to further indictments (*information judiciaire contre X . . .*) against anyone who may be responsible for disappearances, crimes against humanity, and acts of barbarity.[68]

Rejection of Jurisdiction by the Appellate Court

On February 18, 2000, Me Madické Niang, Hissène Habré's principal lawyer, filed a motion to dismiss the indictment to the indicting chamber of the appellate court of Dakar (*Chambre d'accusation de la cour d'appel de Dakar*).[69] In May, François Diouf, who had replaced Abdulaye Gaye as the assistant state prosecutor, joined this motion. The plaintiffs submitted their motion to dismiss Habré's motion and to declare that Senegal had jurisdiction based on Articles 4 through 7 of the Torture Convention, Article 79 of the Constitution, and rules of customary international law.[70] Judge Kandji sent letters rogatory (*commissions rogatoires*, or request from one court to another to examine witnesses) to Chad and France on March 20.[71] On April 12 the attorney general responded to the plaintiffs' motion, reversing the position taken in February and siding with Habré.[72] The indicting chamber initially scheduled its hearing for June 15, 2000, and postponed it first to

June 20, and finally to July 4.[73] The indicting chamber, consisting of Chiekh Tidiane Diakhate, president, and Alpha Poussey Ni Dially and Amath Diouf, judges (*conseillers*), rendered its judgment on July 4, 2000.[74] The Court, after rejecting plaintiffs' preliminary objections,[75] addressed the merits and excluded each of the three charges against Habré, although in fact he has only been charged for complicity in acts of torture. On the erroneously assumed charge of crimes against humanity, the Court said that Senegalese law does not punish such crimes and Article 4 of the Criminal Code prevents Senegalese courts from judging crimes not punishable under the law. This dictum could inhibit prosecution if the investigation (*information judiciaire*) opened by Judge Kandji were to conclude that Habré should be indicted. The Court does not address directly the charge in the investigation of complicity in acts of barbarity. It may nevertheless be implied that the Court denied jurisdiction because this term is used in Article 288 of the Criminal Code as an aggravating circumstance for homicide and that this use is therefore limited to situations covered by that article, which do not include acts by foreigners outside of Senegal against non-Senegalese victims. No mention is made of barbarous acts being either part of crimes against humanity or torture.[76]

The heart of the judgment from the perspective of universal jurisdiction is the appellate court's rejection of jurisdiction over acts of torture. It did so by interpreting Senegal's jurisdiction to prescribe and its jurisdiction to adjudicate (*compétence législative et compétence juridictionnelle*). The Court explained that jurisdiction to prescribe had been exercised by the adoption of a law in 1996[77] making torture a separate crime rather than merely an aggravating condition of crimes or offenses covered by Article 288 of the code. The 1996 law brought Senegal into compliance with the requirements of Article 4 of the Torture Convention. Jurisdiction to adjudicate is a separate matter and, although Article 5 of the Torture Convention requires states parties to establish jurisdiction, the Court considered that Article 5 did not indicate the competent tribunal, unlike the London Charter defining the mandate of the International Military Tribunal of Nuremberg and the Genocide Convention providing for submission of accused persons to an internal penal court.[78] The Court carried this hairsplitting further by distinguishing universal jurisdiction from "universal penalization" (*incrimination universelle*). While torture may be universally punishable, Senegalese courts will not have jurisdiction until and unless the legislature modifies Article 669 of the Code of Criminal Procedure to be in conformity with the Torture Convention and to recognize universal jurisdiction. A treaty provision cannot supercede the Code of Criminal Procedure, notwithstanding the constitutional rule that treaty obligations prevail over statute.[79]

The Court concluded that by indicting Habré for complicity in crimes against humanity, acts of torture, and acts of barbarity—which in fact was the case only for complicity in acts of torture—the investigating judge "manifestly violated the rules of subject-matter and territorial jurisdiction," requiring nullification of the indictment.

Another argument made by the defense is that the case was invented by the Abdou Diouf regime with the complicity of NGOs in order to set a precedent to enhance the concept of international criminal justice.[80] Indeed, human rights groups in Senegal and abroad are quite open about the strategy of using this case to make a political point. One of the NGO activists in the case, Delphine Djiraibe, president of ATPDH, who initially contacted Human Rights Watch for support in bringing the case in Senegal, for example, described the *Habré* case as sending "a message to other African leaders that nothing will be the same any longer."[81] The strategy was most clearly defined in Human Rights Watch's publication *The Pinochet Precedent: How Victims Can Pursue Human Rights Criminals Abroad.*[82] Human Rights Watch candidly states that the arrest of Pinochet was "a 'wake-up call' to tyrants everywhere . . . [giving] hope to other victims that they can bring their tormentors to justice abroad."[83] Habré's indictment was a "direct result" of the *Pinochet* case, according to Brody, which he said had "inspired victims around the world."[84]

Related to this partisan argument that the plaintiffs were part of an international campaign is the political complaint against Western advocates whose own governments supported the Habré regime. As the Senegalese intellectual Babacar Sine put it, "Hissene Habre was received and honored in Paris as a head of state and ally. . . . France never regarded him as a dictator. . . . This case is much more complex than the role of Habre. There is the role of France that supported him. There is the role of the United States that supported him. If we are to judge Hissene Habre, we have to also judge those who supported him."[85]

Both claims—that the plaintiffs' case was brought as part of an internationally orchestrated litigation strategy building on the *Pinochet* precedent and that France and the United States backed Habré while he was president—are factually correct but legally irrelevant. As a matter of law, neither argument should deter the Senegalese court from applying domestic and international law to this case. The equal application of the law is a principle of the Senegalese constitution[86] and of international human rights agreements to which Senegal is a party.[87] Neither the association of the plaintiffs with a campaign supported by international human rights organizations nor the defendant's favorable treatment by foreign governments should prevent the Senegalese courts from allowing plaintiffs to benefit from the principle of equality before the law.

Failure to apply the principle of equality before the law merely reinforces the claim that certain people are regarded as above the law. Djiraibe explained that in Chad the elite are above the law as well as certain "political opponents who make enough noise to earn some money and find some protection under the law. The rest of society cannot count on the law to protect them."[88] She described Habré as the "ultimate untouchable" in this context.[89] His untouchability appears to extend to Senegal, where it is reported that his bodyguard sued him for breach of contract in 1995 and "disappeared" before the court could render its judgment.[90] The question then is whether Habré has unduly influenced the Senegalese judicial system.

Alleged Interference with Judicial Independence

A troubling aspect of the case is the alleged interference with the independence of the judiciary. The change in government in March 2000 brought about shifts in key judicial positions that strongly suggest interference of the executive in the independence of the judiciary. Three related events undermine Senegal's reputation in this regard: new president Abdoulaye Wade's appointing Habré's lawyer as the presidential legal advisor, moving the investigating judge to the Ministry of Justice, and promoting of the president of appellate court hearing the case to the State Council (*Conseil d'état*). Although the Senegalese constitution guarantees judicial independence from the executive,[91] these events have justifiably provoked expression of concern by the Dakar bar, independent members of the legal profession, and the UN.

In March 2000, Abdoulaye Wade succeeded Abdou Diouf as president of Senegal. Wade decided, one month later, to appoint Habré's chief defense counsel, Madické Niang, as his adviser on judicial matters.[92] In order to bypass a ruling of the Dakar bar (*Conseil de l'ordre des avocats du Sénégal*) that Niang could not practice before the Senegalese courts while working for the president, Wade issued a new order making him a paid judicial consultant to the government[93] in "an obvious subterfuge purporting to allow Niang to both work with Wade and to represent Habré and other clients."[94] To add to the complexity of the situation, Niang had been vice president of the National Organization for Human Rights (ONDH), a reputable Senegalese human rights NGO.

On June 30, 2000, Wade, acting in his capacity as president of the Superior Council of the Magistracy (*Conseil supérieur de la magistrature*), promoted the president of the indicting chamber (*Chambre d'Accusation*) of the appellate court of Dakar, Cheikh Tidiane Diakhate, to the conseil d'etat while the case was before his court. The promotion of Cheikh Tidiane Diakhate while Habré's motion to dismiss was pending appears, as Human Rights Watch said in a letter to the special rapporteur on the independence of judges and lawyers, "to be an effort to manipulate the judiciary to obtain the government's desired result."[95]

At the same meeting of June 30, Wade presided over the superior council of the magistracy's decision to move Demba Kandji, the most senior investigating magistrate who indicted Habré in February, to the public prosecutor's office (*parquet général*), where he became assistant state prosecutor at the Dakar court of appeals on July 3, the day before the court heard the case, thus placing him under the authority of the justice ministry and removing him from the investigation.[96] Brody has not hesitated to consider that there "can be no doubt that his transfer was a reprisal for his handling of the Habré case."[97] According to the Constitution, judges fall under the sole authority of the law when carrying out their function.[98] The judgment of the indicting chamber of the Court of Appeals on July 4, 2000, to drop the torture charges came after what Human Rights Watch called "an intense lobbying and media campaign by Habré, who has reportedly spent lavishly in an effort to have the case dropped."[99] From the three measures mentioned above and the postponement twice before the Court finally met on July 4, it is evident that, for the moment at least, President Wade has been influenced by this campaign.

Not only the human rights groups supporting the plaintiffs but also some international figures noted the radical shift in the Senegalese position. The president of the ONDH, Me Sidiki Kaba, said on the day of the decision dismissing charges, "The state prosecutor completely reversed his position."[100] The representative of the RADDHO said, "This is the most important human rights case in Senegal's history and we are behaving like a banana republic."[101] Habré's main defense attorney called the July 4, 2000, dismissal "a victory of law and of Senegalese justice."[102] Plaintiffs' lawyers were justifiably concerned over the judge's transfer and attacks on him in the Senegalese press and denounced the "pro-Habre lobby" in Dakar as well as the "u-turn by the public prosecutor's office."[103] Alioune Tine, who runs the Dakar-based RADDHO, said, "It's an almighty slap in the face for Senegalese law."[104]

Being alerted to these facts by the NGOs involved in the case, the special rapporteur on the independence of judges and lawyers, Dato' Param Cumaraswamy, and the special rapporteur on torture, Sir Nigel Rodley, expressed concern to the government of Senegal over the conditions surrounding the July 4 judgment.[105] They issued a joint communication on July 28, 2000, noting all three suspicious actions and reminding the government of Senegal of its obligations under the Torture Convention. They also drew its attention to Commission on Human Rights Resolution 2000/43, which stresses the general responsibility of all states to investigate allegations of torture and to ensure that those who encourage, order, tolerate, or perpetrate such acts be held responsible and severely punished. They called upon Senegal to "ensure that the judiciary is able to independently and impartially investigate the allegations against Hissène Habré in accordance with Article 80 of the Constitution of Senegal and the United Nations Basic Principles on the Independence of the Judiciary."[106]

Review by the Supreme Court

The plaintiffs announced right away that they were appealing the July 4 judgment to the Supreme Court (*Cour de Cassation*).[107] In January 2001, plaintiffs' attorneys filed their appeal, and Habré's lawyers submitted a twenty-three–page detailed reply. Without warning to the plaintiffs, the Court set the date for the oral phase on February 20, 2001. Although caught a bit off guard, the plaintiffs were able to be represented by Boucounta Diallo (current president of the ONDH) and Sidiki Kaba (recently elected president of the International Federation for Human Rights), arguing against Madické Niang and Helène Cissé for Habré. The unexpected new player before the three-judge panel of the Court was a new state prosecutor, Ali Cité Bâ, who reversed the position expressed on behalf of the state in July by François Diouf and supported the exercise by Senegal of universal jurisdiction. Ali Cité Bâ told the Court that the appeal against the denial of jurisdiction under the Torture Convention and the plaintiffs' claims were well founded and that the procedural defects alleged by the defense were not valid.[108]

Following this oral phase, the Court first announced that it would render its judgment on March 6 but postponed it allegedly because of a Muslim holiday and scheduled it for March 20, 2001. On March 20, the Court handed down its decision refusing to reverse the appellate judgment of July 4, 2000. Seven of the eleven grounds for reversal were minor procedural issues, which the Court rejected one at a time. The substantive grounds relating to universal jurisdiction were the fourth, sixth, and seventh, to which the Court responded together. The Court referred to the obligation of Article 4 of the Torture Conventions to criminalize torture and repeated the position of the appellate court that this obligation had been met by a law of August 28, 1996, inserting Article 295(1) into the Criminal Code. The Court added that the appellate judges "took note that no modification had occurred to Article 669 of the Code of Criminal Procedure and concluded that Senegalese courts do not have jurisdiction over acts of torture committed by a foreigner outside of the [national] territory, whatever the nationality of the victims."[109] The Court then alluded to Senegal's duty *aut dedere aut judicare* under article 5(2) of the Torture Convention but interpreted this duty as a sign of the non–self-executing character of the convention. Thus, Article 79 of the Constitution, making international law superior to statutory law, "does not apply when the execution of the convention establishes a prior obligation on Senegal to take legislative measures."[110] The consequence of this reasoning for universal jurisdiction is in the rejection of the seventh ground for reversal, which is worded as follows:

[V]iolation of the principle of universal jurisdiction in that the indicting chamber declared that Senegalese courts lacked jurisdiction because universal jurisdiction cannot be applied unless Article 669 of the Code of Criminal Procedure is modified, whereas that article cannot prevent the application either of an international convention establishing universal jurisdiction or of the provisions of the Vienna Convention [on the Law of Treaties], applicable in Senegal, in particular, articles 27 and 53 which do not allow a state party to an international convention to rely on a gap or inadequacy of its municipal law to avoid international obligations.[111]

The Court's reply to this ground was "that no text of procedure recognizes that Senegalese courts have universal jurisdiction to prosecute and judge alleged perpetrators or accomplices, should they be on the territory of the Republic, for acts committed outside of Senegal by foreigners falling under the provisions of the law of August 28, 1996, which brings Senegalese legislation into conformity with article 4 of the [Torture] Convention. . . ."[112] The Court added that "Hissène Habré's presence in Senegal cannot by itself justify prosecution against him."[113] Thus ended the attempt to create a *Pinochet* precedent in Africa through the Senegalese criminal justice system.

The case did not end there, however. The plaintiffs sought Habré's extradition to Belgium, where they had filed a case against him under the Belgian universal jurisdiction law.[114] On April 7, 2001, Senegalese president Wade announced that he had asked Habré to leave Senegal. On April 18, 2001, Human Rights Watch filed a communication with the Committee against Torture on behalf of the victims, alleging violation of Articles 5 and 7 of the convention and requesting provisional measures, pending the committee's disposition of the case, to prevent him from leaving Senegal.[115] The Office of the High Commissioner for Human Rights responded on April 27, 2001, that the case had been registered (Communication No. 181/2001) and that Senegal "has also been requested not to expel Mr. Hissène Habré and to take all necessary measures to prevent Mr. Hissène Habré from leaving the territory of Senegal except pursuant to an extradition demand."[116]

The judgments of July 4, 2000, and March 20, 2001, raise several complex legal issues relevant to the law and politics of universal jurisdiction, the conflict between municipal and international law with respect to the self-executing character of the Torture Convention; and political interference with the independence of the judiciary.

Legal Issues Regarding Senegal's Exercise of Universal Jurisdiction

Personal, temporal, and subject-matter limitations may affect the exercise by a state of universal jurisdiction. The *Hissène Habré* case raises issues regarding all three limitations that may be instructive for future litigation based on universal jurisdiction. In the final analysis, it was the self-executing nature of the Torture Convention that was critical to Senegal's eventual rejection of universal jurisdiction.

Personal Jurisdiction

In order for Senegal to exercise jurisdiction over Hissène Habré, he would need to be personally responsible for the crimes in question and not be protected from jurisdiction because of an immunity based on his current or former status. As already mentioned,[117] evidence of the personal responsibility of Habré for complicity in the crimes alleged is set out in the Commission of Inquiry report[118] and the Complaint.[119] This evidence includes not only the direct responsibility of Habré over the DDS but also testimony from witnesses as to his giving orders and personally supervising torture.[120]

Expectations regarding criminal liability of former heads of state have been considerably heightened because of the *Pinochet* case. The House of Lords decided that former head of state immunity did not extend to universally condemned international crimes like torture committed or presided over by the accused when he was head of state. Before the *Pinochet* case, litigation against ex-heads of state was not unknown.[121] In the *Pinochet* case, the House of Lords expressed several lines of reasoning to reject the defense based on former head of state immunity. One line of reasoning held that immunity applied only to official acts, but crimes like torture are *ultra vires* (exceeding the official's authority) and are not considered official acts covered by immunity. Take, for example, Lord Steyn in the November 25, 1998, opinions: "Qualitatively, what [Pinochet] is alleged to have done is no more to be categorized as acts undertaken in the exercise of the functions of a Head of State than the examples . . . of a Head of State murdering his gardener or arranging the torture of his opponents for the sheer spectacle of it. It follows that in my view General Pinochet has no statutory immunity. . . . General Pinochet is not entitled to an immunity of any kind."[122]

In the March 24, 1999, opinions, Lord Browne-Wilkinson reached a similar conclusion, but his reasoning was based on a teleological interpretation of the Torture Convention: torture was an official act, but the convention, in creating jurisdiction to punish such official acts, trumps any claim of immunity. He wrote:

Under the Convention the international crime of torture can only be committed by an official or someone in an official capacity. They would all be entitled to immunity. It would follow that there can be no case outside Chile in which a successful prosecution for torture can be brought unless the State of Chile is prepared to waive its right to its officials immunity. Therefore the whole elaborate structure of universal jurisdiction over torture committed by officials is rendered abortive and one of the main objectives of the Torture Convention—to provide a system under which there is no safe haven for torturers—will have been frustrated. In my judgment all these factors together demonstrate that the notion of continued immunity for ex-heads of state is inconsistent with the provisions of the Torture Convention.[123]

While the temporal limitation was disputed (only acts committed while the convention was applicable law in the U.K. were extraditable), in the end the above argument against immunity prevailed. That the claim to former head of state immunity was not raised in the *Habré* case is perhaps a sign that the holding in *Pinochet* is widely accepted with respect to that aspect of the case. Sriram and Paust are categorical on this point: "[T]he reach of universal jurisdiction is . . . universal with respect to the status of perpetrators. For example, with respect to international crimes there is absolutely no head of state, diplomatic, or public official immunity under customary international law or any international criminal law treaty or instrument."[124]

In the *Democratic Republic of the Congo (DRC)* case brought against Belgium before the International Court of Justice, the DRC argued that the Belgian arrest warrant issued in absentia against Adbulay Yerodia Ndombasi, DRC minister of foreign affairs at the time the warrant was issued, for crimes covered under Belgian's universal jurisdiction legislation, was a violation of the rule of customary international law of absolute immunity from criminal process of an incumbent foreign minister. In its judgment of February 14, 2002, the Court agreed by thirteen votes to three that Belgium had failed to respect Yerodia's immunity.[125] This might suggest that a former head of state, like Hissène Habré, could not be prosecuted for international crimes in Senegal or elsewhere. However, unlike Yerodia, Habré was not an incumbent at the time of criminal proceedings alleging international crimes in Senegal or Belgium. Moreover, the Court noted that immunity did not mean impunity. Therefore, after a foreign minister, and by extension a head of state, ceases to hold public office, a state exercising universal jurisdiction may try the former official for acts committed before or after he or she held office. Some treaties (such as those relating to torture and genocide) stipulate that the crime in question is punishable even if committed by a public official acting in a public capacity. There is a strong case for exercising universal jurisdiction with respect to such crimes against a former high official for acts committed while in office but not for instituting proceeding while the official is in office. Thus the *Yerodia* case might cause Belgium to drop efforts to prosecute Sharon; it does not appear to call for it to drop the case against Habré. In fact, the *Sharon* indictment was first rejected by the indicting chamber of the Brussels appellate court but was reinstated by the Cour de Cassation on February 12, 2003, which agreed that Sharon could be tried once he no longer exercises his official functions.[126]

U.S. practice appears inconsistent as to the question of whether immunity should be granted on behalf of alleged torturers. A federal court agreed with the State Department in denying that Radovan Karadžić should be protected by immunity from civil action in his capacity as president of the self-proclaimed Republika Srpska while in the U.S. at the invitation of the United Nations.[127] However, in a more recent case the State Department decided that a Peruvian officer convicted of abuse of authority and quietly released from prison, who had been detained by the FBI in Houston for possible prosecution for torture while on his way to Washington for a meeting of the Inter-American Commission on Human Rights unrelated to this case, should be granted immunity from prosecution because he was considered a diplomatic representative of Peru, present in the U.S. for an official appearance before a body of the OAS.[128]

Neither of these examples of U.S. practice offers any basis for considering that Hissène Habré should be immune from prosecution in Senegal. Unlike Karadžić, he makes no claim to occupy any office entitling him to immunity. Unlike the Peruvian official, he was not traveling as the diplomatic representative of any country.

Temporal Jurisdiction

Other problems were raised regarding the temporal limitation on Senegal's authority to exercise universal jurisdiction. The conventional basis of universal jurisdiction requires that the acts in question be punishable under Senegalese law, either prospectively since the date of entry into force for Senegal of the treaty or retroactively if, contrary to the normal operation of criminal law, the act of ratification extends the temporal scope of Senegal's criminalization of torture. The matter is complicated by the fact that torture was not punishable as such under Senegalese law until June 16, 1996. However, acts fitting the definition of torture were punished under other charges.[129] Habré's lawyer added to the confusion by including in the motion to dismiss the misleading statement that "[r]atification [sic] by a law No. 9626 of June 16, 1996 of the Convention Against Torture and Other Degrading Treatment [sic] cannot suffice to establish jurisdiction of Senegalese courts."[130] In fact, that law related to the adoption of legislation required by the Torture Convention but not to ratification. In a press statement, Habré's lawyer referred to the June 16, 1996, date as the effective one, whereas the alleged crimes occurred between 1982 and 1990.[131] The Ministry of Justice, in its communication of November 2000 to the high commissioner of human rights, took the same position. The assumption of the defense is that ratification alone does not make torture punishable under Senegalese law and that jurisdiction cannot be asserted for acts occurring prior to the publication of the relevant implementing legislation.

Senegal signed the convention on February 4, 1985, and ratified it on August 21, 1986; it entered into force on June 26, 1987.[132] Whether because torture was already punishable under other charges or because the Constitution made the convention directly applicable under Senegalese law after the date of publication, the effective date is June 26, 1987, and not June 16, 1996.

The more complex question is whether Senegal's temporal jurisdiction includes torture or complicity attributable to Hissène Habré between June 7, 1982, and June 26, 1987. The radical position would hold that entry into force of the convention for Senegal gave its courts jurisdiction over any acts of torture regardless of when they were committed or whether those acts where punishable in Senegal or in the country where they were committed at the time they were committed. Such an argument is difficult to sustain on the basis of the convention. However, one could argue that torture and crimes against humanity were punishable under customary international law and that entry into force of the convention for Senegal merely established the legal basis for its courts to exercise universal jurisdiction over torture wherever and whenever committed. This position would be consistent with Article 15(2) of the International Covenant on Civil and Political Rights, which provides an exception to nonretroactivity for trial and punishment "for any act or and omission which, at the time when it was committed, was criminal according to the general principles of law recognized by the community of nations."

A more moderate position on the conventional basis of universal jurisdiction would limit the temporal scope to acts committed after the entry into force of the convention. A still more restrictive interpretation of universal jurisdiction would recognize universal jurisdiction after entry into force of the convention but only if the crime was punishable in Chad at the time it was committed. Chad acceded to the Torture Convention on June 9, 1995.[133] This third position is unacceptable because it would defeat the object and purpose of the convention, which is "to make more effective the struggle against torture or other cruel, inhuman or degrading treatment or punishment throughout the world."[134] Requiring the state exercising universal jurisdiction under Article 5(2) to limit its penal action to acts committed in states where they were punishable would facilitate impunity for a head of state or other official who is likely to be able to prevent torture from being punishable while in power.[135] The Court could reasonably have concluded that such contemporaneous consent is not necessary and is in fact contrary to the "no safe haven" philosophy of the convention.[136]

In considering extradition from Senegal to Belgium, the date of ratification by both the requested state and the requesting state could be important as it was in the *Pinochet* case. That precedent need not be followed, however, with respect to Senegal's independent right—and some would argue duty—to prosecute for torture, which existed at least from the date of entry into force of the convention on June 26, 1987, and before that date on the basis of customary universal jurisdiction over acts of torture and crimes against humanity.

In the case of *Hissène Habré*, the intermediary position limiting the temporal scope to acts after the entry into force would not prevent the Senegalese courts from trying him, since all eight plaintiffs referred to incidents that occurred after June 26, 1987, except one.[137] In the evidence presented by the AVCRP, 736 cases of arbitrary arrest, 142 cases of torture, 97 summary executions, 100 disappearances, and 46 deaths by starvation are listed. Those cases appear to fit the definition of torture and occurred after

June 26, 1987, and should therefore be punishable in Senegal. For the cases prior to that date, Senegal could consider them under customary international law incriminating torture and crimes against humanity, which are not subject to that temporal limitation.

In the *Habré* case, the appellate court did not need to stretch the principle of nonretroactivity to accommodate an exception to produce "some sense of accountability."[138] It erred by considering that only the law of 1996 could constitute the basis for indicting Habré and that it would not be applied retroactively and by rejecting the argument that the indictment could rely on the Torture Convention itself, which was in force for Senegal since June of 1987. Only the application of the torture charge to acts prior to that date would present a problem of retroactivity.

The second aspect of the temporal limitation on universal jurisdiction in the *Habré* case concerns Senegal's ten-year statute of limitations for serious crimes. The facts on which the indictment was based occurred during the eight years from 1982 to 1990, thus ten years before the February 3, 2000, indictment. According to the attorneys for the victims, that prescription should begin to run only "when prosecution became possible after Habre fell from power in December 1990."[139] The Senegalese Code of Criminal Procedure suspends the statute of limitations if an obstacle in law or fact prevents prosecution.[140] The issue is therefore whether there were indeed legal and practical obstacles to the exercise of jurisdiction prior to Habré's departure from office and arrival in Senegal in December 1990. In other contexts—such as post-Communist Eastern Europe—it has been argued that suspending the statute of limitations would be a dangerous political act disruptive of the continuous application of the law.[141] The Senegalese condition for suspending the statute (obstacle *de jure* or *de facto* preventing the prosecution) is not directly relevant to failure to prosecute under previous Communist regimes since it has to do with the unprecedented attempt to try a foreign individual who could not have been prosecuted because he embodied legality as head of state and enjoyed full head of state immunity. Moreover, Senegalese courts have suspended the statute of limitations in cases involving embezzlement by public officials until their acts are known.[142] Prior to the investigation by the Commission of Inquiry and given the secrecy of the DDS,[143] it could be argued that the facts were not known before Habré left power. Furthermore, head of state immunity constituted a legal obstacle applicable to Habré while he was president of Chad.

The Appellate and Supreme Courts preferred, however, to apply Article 669 of the Senegalese Code of Criminal Procedure, which enumerates the only acts for which Senegalese courts can try foreigners. Finding no legal basis there or in the convention to sustain the indictment, it did not address the statute of limitations. Had they found a legal basis to sustain the indictment, the matter of the statute of limitations would probably have been considered. Plaintiffs could have then argued that the statute began to run from 1990 and that Habré had been indicted ten months before the expiration of the statute.

Moreover, crimes against humanity (but not torture) are not subject to the statute of limitations.[144] Although Senegal is not a party to the convention on imprescribility, the principle is widely accepted, and Senegal manifested its support at least for the future by ratifying the Rome Statute of the International Criminal Court, which provides for nonapplication of the statute to crimes against humanity in Article 29.

Subject-Matter Jurisdiction

The subject-matter jurisdiction as recognized in customary international law is summarized in the Restatement: "A state may exercise jurisdiction to define and punish certain offenses recognized by the community of nations as of universal concern, such as piracy, slave trade, attacks on or hijacking of aircraft, genocide, war crimes, and perhaps terrorism, even where none of the bases of jurisdiction indicated in §402 is present."[145]

Universal jurisdiction over perpetrators of acts of torture or complicity in such acts based on customary international law is reinforced by the inclusion of torture among the violations of customary international law of human rights enumerated in §702 of the Restatement and the prohibition of that crime as one of the peremptory norms of international law. A reporter's note to this section says that "though it has not yet been authoritatively determined, violation by a state of customary law of human rights . . . may permit prosecution of individual officials responsible for such acts under the laws of any state, as an exercise of universal jurisdiction."[146] With respect to the charge of torture, the conventional basis is even stronger.

The issue on which attention should be focused is whether the evidence supports the accusation for crimes over which universal jurisdiction is recognized. The nature of the acts of which Habré was accused by NGOs and the Commission of Inquiry leave no doubt about the appropriateness of the charge of complicity in torture. His personal role in ordering the torture is supported by the documentation of his direct responsibility over the DDS.[147] The complaint stresses that "no doubt is possible, in addition to the physical torture inflicted on detainees during interrogation . . . the conditions of detention described by all the plaintiffs qualify as permanent state of physical and mental torture, corresponding to the definition in Article 1 of the Convention."[148] The Commission of Inquiry provides many more direct testimonies of specific cases, with photographs of the sequelae[149] and a description of each of the types of torture with thirteen drawings showing how they were practiced.[150]

Although the indictment did not include this charge, the case can reasonably be made that the elements of crimes against humanity, as defined, for example, in the Statute of the International Criminal Court,[151] were present. The principal issue for the court to determine would be whether the acts enumerated in the definition, many of which can be documented in the practices of the government acting under direct orders from Habré, were part of an "attack directed against any civilian population," which the Rome Statute defines as "a course of conduct involving the multiple commission of acts referred to in paragraph 1 against any civilian population, pursuant to or in furtherance of a State or organizational policy to commit such attack."[152] The mandate and scope of activity of the DDS could be evidence of such a policy.[153]

The victims' complaint also notes that torture, murder, forced disappearances, and even imprisonment or other forms of deprivation of liberty are elements of the charge of crimes against humanity. Citing an attached amicus brief by Eric David, director of the Center of International Law of the Free University of Brussels, plaintiffs call the Court's attention to the fact that "even if Senegalese domestic law does not punish crimes against humanity as such, customary international criminal law is a normal part of Senegalese penal law which Senegal can apply."[154] The principle in question goes back to the post–Word War II prosecutions and the 1973 principles of international cooperation in the detection, arrest, extradition, and punishment of persons guilty of war crimes and crimes against humanity.[155] One of these principles also prohibits states from taking "any legislative *or other measures* which may be prejudicial to the international obligation they have assumed in regard to the detection, arrest, extradition and punishment of persons guilty of war crimes and crimes against humanity."[156] The reference to "other measures" could mean judicial and failure to prosecute or extradite Habré may place Senegal in violation of these principles.

The third charge is acts of barbarity (*actes de barbarie*), which are punishable under Article 288 of the Senegalese Criminal Code insofar as such acts, as well as torture, result in homicide. Evidence was presented to the regional court in Dakar of particularly atrocious acts resulting in death and observed by surviving witnesses who testified. Universal jurisdiction over such crimes, whether resulting in death or not, would be subsumed under crimes against humanity[157] or the crime of torture under the Torture Convention.[158]

The fourth crime, alleged by the plaintiffs but also not repeated in the indictment or by the Appellate and Supreme Courts, is forced disappearances. These crimes were declared a violation of international law in the 1992 UN Declaration,[159] and the General Assembly has reminded governments of their obligation to investigate, prosecute, and punish those responsible for enforced or involuntary disappearances.[160] At the request of the Subcommission on Prevention of Discrimination and Protection of Minorities (now the Subcommission on the Promotion and Protection of Human Rights), a working group has prepared a draft international convention on the protection of all persons from enforced disappearance and sent it to the Commission on Human Rights for its consideration.[161] According to this draft text, the crime of forced disappearance is defined,[162] and provision is made for universal jurisdiction.[163] This crime was also defined in the Statute of the International Criminal Court.[164]

The victim organization AVCRP enumerated one hundred cases of disappearances.[165] Whether or not Senegal accepts the emerging customary international law qualification of these acts as international crimes for which it may exercise universal jurisdiction, these acts are part of the definition of crimes against humanity, which is better established as a basis for universal jurisdiction.

Genocide is a fifth potential charge against Habré, although it was not part of the February 3, 2000, indictment. The Commission of Inquiry seems to have considered that the number of political deaths plus the poverty of families who had lost their breadwinner constituted genocide.[166] The charge of genocide based on these facts does not fit the accepted definition, unless plaintiffs prove the "[d]eliberately inflicting on the group [of] conditions of life calculated to bring about its physical destruction in whole or in part."[167] The commission also provided documents from the archives of the DDS apparently enumerating systematic executions and destruction of villages, which would be relevant to a genocide charge.[168] The complaint cites evidence from two Hadjeraye people and two Zaghawa people showing the systematic nature of the repression against these two groups in 1987 and 1989 respectively,[169] claiming that "there is no doubt that the individual victims of these [waves of] repression were targeted as members of ethnic communities."[170]

Non–Self-Executing Character of the Torture Convention

While Senegal has ratified the Torture Convention, it has not adopted implementing legislation incorporating the provision of the convention into municipal law. Article 4 requires states parties to "ensure that all acts of torture are offenses under its criminal law"[171] and to "make these offences punishable by appropriate penalties," while Article 5 requires states parties to "take such measures as may be necessary to establish its jurisdiction over such offences in cases where the alleged offender is present in any territory under its jurisdiction and it does not extradite him pursuant to article 8." Does failure of Senegal to modify its Code of Criminal Procedure constitute a valid basis for not exercising jurisdiction?

The principal basis for the claim that Senegalese courts lacked jurisdiction was the interpretation of Article 669 of the Code of Criminal Procedure. Counsel for Habré claimed that Article 669 provided an inclusive enumeration of cases under which foreigners may be tried in Senegal, viz., felonies and offenses against state security, counterfeiting of official seals and money.

The central argument the Appellate and Supreme Courts used to reject jurisdiction based on the Torture Convention was that the treaty was non—self-executing in Senegal. The Court noted that the Torture Convention formally delegated to states parties the responsibility to take special measures to implement the convention and specifically to establish jurisdiction of their criminal courts pursuant to Article 9 of the convention.[172]

The plaintiffs countered that the Torture Convention established a basis for jurisdiction and takes precedence over the Code of Criminal Procedure. The appellate court followed Hissène Habré's argument that the indictment was based on Articles 288 and 46 of the Senegalese Criminal Code, dealing respectively with torture and complicity in torture, which are municipal law texts and its "logic" is therefore part of legislative and jurisdictional competence of the domestic legal system. The Court considered that the norms of internal law on which the prosecution was based were "distinct" from universal jurisdiction of the Torture Convention.

The appellate court cited French and Belgian implementing legislation establishing universal jurisdiction as required by the convention. As mentioned above,[173] the Court considered that the Senegalese parliament fulfilled its obligations by making torture a crime itself rather than an aggravating circumstance for other infractions covered by Article 288 of the code. Senegal has not fulfilled its obligations under Article 5 of the Torture Convention since the parliament should have—the Court conceded—modified Article 669 of the Code of Criminal Procedure by including universal jurisdiction over torture. Because it did not, "Senegalese courts do not have jurisdiction over acts of torture committed by a foreigner outside of Senegalese territory regardless of the nationality of the victims."[174] The Supreme Court repeated this conclusion. The principal problem with these judgments is that they rejected the constitutionally grounded superiority of treaty obligations over statutory ones. Since June 26, 1987, date of the entry into force of the Convention for Senegal, according to Article 79 of the Constitution, Articles 5 and 7 of the Torture Convention should prevail over Article 669 of the Code of Criminal Procedure. As plaintiffs point out, "In accordance with Article 79 of the Constitution and the jurisprudence of the Supreme Court, ratification of international texts and their publication in the *Journal Officiel* are more than adequate to allow them to be directly applicable by Senegalese courts."[175] The appellate court rejected this line of argument, noting in passing that the Supreme Court case to which plaintiffs referred related to overturning a piece of social legislation the court found contrary to an international treaty ratified and published in Senegal. The Court then developed the argument that penal law is a special branch of law that cannot be compared to other branches because it is fundamental to social order requiring a special degree of legal formalism.[176] It appears to be carving out an exception to the constitutionally mandated hierarchy of norms. Because Article 669 does not provide for universal jurisdiction for torture, as it would if implementing legislation had been adopted, the courts cannot exercise it. In other words, the Torture Convention is non–self-executing, according to the appellate court.

The difficulty with the non–self executing argument is that the doctrine is not part of the Senegalese legal system or of the French system on which it is based. As Dinh, Daillier, and Pellet affirm, the incorporation of the treaty into municipal law is "automatic and independent of any other legal steps."[177] This monist position placing treaties above domestic legislation was maintained in Article 55 of the 1958 French Constitution, which is identical to Article 79 of the Senegalese Constitution of 1967.[178]

Of course, as Article 27 of the Vienna Convention on the Law of Treaties reaffirms, a defect of municipal law cannot be invoked to excuse the failure to implement an obligation under international law.[179] The consequences of a violation of international law resulting from a defect of municipal law are in the realm of international responsibility. It is not an easy matter for foreign nationals to invoke international responsibility of Senegal for the failure to implement the convention by not establishing criminal jurisdiction to try nonnationals for complicity in torture. One solution, proposed by Quoc Dinh and others is outlined as follows: "Only national courts can contribute to an effective solution, either by granting motions based on failure to comply with this requirement through the regulatory power, or by applying an international convention as superior to municipal law, notwithstanding the lack of implementing measures. Their position will be in part dictated by their understanding of the direct applicability of the treaty in question."[180]

There is authority and logic for the proposition that treaties purporting to create rights and obligations for individuals, such as obtaining redress for acts of or complicity in torture, should be applicable before national courts, even if implementing legislation has not been adopted.[181] Although French courts tend to apply a presumption of direct application of the treaty, there is some hesitation to do so.[182]

The appellate court discussed the specifics of French criminal law and only alluded to Belgian law. The self-executing character of international human rights treaties in Belgian law is particularly relevant to the reasoning of the Dakar court. In his brief, David cited a treatise on criminal law, which explained: "International norms, even approved by the Belgian legislator, do not become part of Belgian criminal law and Belgian courts have no jurisdiction over violations of them unless and until a Belgian law provides specific punishment for the acts punishable under the convention. In the absence of such a law, *Belgian criminal courts have jurisdiction over violations of these norms if, within the arsenal of existing rules of Belgian criminal law, there are provisions that explicitly or logically include the specific acts punishable under the Convention.*"[183]

Applied to Senegalese law, this logic would mean that the existence of a provision in Senegalese criminal law (Article 295[1] of the Criminal Code) making torture a crime is an adequate basis for Senegalese courts to exercise universal criminal jurisdiction as required by Articles 5 and 7 of the Torture Convention. It would not be necessary, as the Appellate and Supreme Courts claimed, to provide explicitly for universal jurisdiction in Article 669 of the Code of Criminal Procedure.

An analogy can be made to extradition for the self-executing character of the Torture Convention in Senegalese law. Article 8 of the convention provides for the convention itself to fill the lacuna created by the absence of legal basis for extradition in the normal form of a treaty.[184] An interesting feature of the logic of Article 8 is that it anticipates the absence of the normal legal basis for extradition—namely, an extradition treaty—and allows the treaty itself to provide that legal basis. The normal legal basis for prosecution is implementing legislation. One could interpret Articles 4, 5, and 7 with the same logic as Article 8 and allow the wording of these articles to provide adequate legal basis for a court to exercise jurisdiction where legislation is lacking, due to the state party's failure to fulfill its obligation under the treaty. One could also argue the contrary, namely that absence of wording in Articles 4, 5, and 7 similar to that in Article 8 is evidence of the intent not to allow the convention to establish the legal basis for jurisdiction where there is no legislation.

The conventional basis for jurisdiction seems stronger in Article 7 of the Torture Convention, which requires Senegal to "submit the case [of a person accused of torture or complicity] to its competent authorities for the purpose of prosecution," than in Article 5(2), which requires Senegal to "take . . . measures . . . to establish jurisdiction." The Supreme Court referred only to Senegal's obligation under Article 5(2) and made no reference to Article 7.

The basic issue is whether a state is obliged to consider the rights in a human rights treaty justiciable if it has not incorporated appropriate remedies into its domestic law. The International Council on Human Rights Policy describes the problem in these terms: "While the number of states that have expressly recognized torture, genocide, crimes against humanity and war crimes in their domestic criminal law has increased exponentially in recent years, it is still the case that these provisions do not exist in all countries. Even in the many states where such domestic criminal laws do exist, not all have explicitly provided for universal jurisdiction prosecutions. This gap between international obligations, and what domestic law actually allows for, is a significant problem."[185]

Even the Joinet report fails to establish a customary basis for universal jurisdiction, mentioning only the treaty and domestic law basis in Principle 20, "Jurisdiction of Foreign Courts": "The jurisdiction of foreign courts may be exercised by virtue either of a universal jurisdiction clause contained in a treaty in force or of a provision of domestic law establishing a rule of extraterritorial jurisdiction for serious crimes under international law."[186]

One could argue that "a provision of domestic law" could include a rule incorporated into domestic law by virtue of a constitutional provision recognizing "general international law,"—in other words, customary international law—as part of the national law, thus including a customary rule of universal jurisdiction. However, the failure to mention customary international law could also be interpreted as excluding this basis of jurisdiction, at least for Joinet. The customary law basis of universal jurisdiction is therefore an unsettled area of international law, with practice lagging behind theory and policy positions. Plaintiffs clearly saw the opportunity of a county that had shown leadership in human rights adding to the practice of extending universal jurisdiction. The Senegalese government, in its "observations and comments" on the joint communication of July 28, 2000, accusing Senegal of interference in the judicial process,[187] said that only "conventional international law and the exceptions provided for in article 669 of the Code of Criminal Procedure" could allow its criminal courts to exercise extraterritorial jurisdiction but not "public international law" since "there is no reference in the [Senegalese] Constitution to the rules of public international law, as there is in France."[188] It is true that Article 79 of the Senegalese constitution, identical to Article 55 of the current French constitution, refers to conventional international law, whereas the observations of the government appear to assume that the plaintiffs intended to establish universal jurisdiction on the sole basis of customary international law.

In addition to considering the Torture Convention as non–self-executing, the appellate court also relied on its understanding of criminal law as not permitting jurisdiction to be extended by treaty rather than by legislation. This interpretation would make more legal sense in a dualist system—that is, one that regards domestic and international law as essentially different. Since Senegal's constitution establishes a monist system, which holds that domestic and international law exist within a single legal order, the appellate court could have used Article 5 or 7 of the Convention to allow the exercise of universal jurisdiction but chose not to for reasons that may be extralegal.[189]

Lessons of the Case

The *Hissène Habré* case, rather than sending "a message to other African leaders that nothing will be the same any longer,"[190] reinforced impunity. The case has implications not only for the campaign against impunity, but also for Senegal's reputation as a defender of human rights, the role of investigating magistrates, the issue of the self-executing character of the Torture Convention, Senegal's duty to treat Habré as *hostis hominis generis* (enemy of the human race), the limitations of the *Pinochet* precedent, liability of other Chadian agents, and the political uses of universal jurisdiction.

The Campaign against Impunity

The Commission on Human Rights, in its resolution on torture, reminded governments "that they should abrogate legislation leading to impunity for those responsible for grave violations of human rights such as torture and prosecute such violations, thereby providing a firm basis for the rule of law."[191] The commission expressed the conviction "that exposing violations of human rights, holding their perpetrators and their accomplices and collaborators accountable, obtaining justice for their victims, as well as preserving historical records of such violations and restoring the dignity of victims through acknowledgement and commemoration of their suffering, will guide future societies and are integral to the promotion and implementation of all human rights and fundamental freedoms and to the prevention of future violations."[192]

The study on impunity Judge Joinet prepared for the Subcommission on Prevention of Discrimination and Protection of Minorities formulated, in addition to Principle 20 already quoted,[193] the principle that states should include a clause on universal jurisdiction in "all relevant human rights instruments"[194] and the principle that in the absence of such a clause applicable to the state where the violation occurred, other states may extend their jurisdiction to punish such acts.[195]

These principles are the translation into international law of the efforts of a campaign born out of the experience with democratic transitions in Latin America and refined with that of East-Central Europe. The *Habré* case underscores their relevance to Africa's potential to avoid the injustice that impunity engenders. Articles 3 through 5 of the Princeton Principles on Universal Jurisdiction further advance the campaign against impunity.

Senegal's Good Reputation

Senegal had acquired a reputation as both having one of the most independent judiciaries of postindependence Africa and of showing leadership in being the first country to ratify the Statute of the International Criminal Court, as was recalled when Habré was first indicted.[196] Reed Brody, advocacy director at Human Rights Watch, who led that organization's efforts in both the *Pinochet* and *Habré* cases, said that the former case "reaffirmed the principles of international law that a country can judge the crime of torture no matter where the acts were committed and that not even a former head of state has immunity from prosecution," adding that the case "also showed us that there are countries where these lofty principles can actually be applied in practice. Senegal can now be counted among those countries."[197] When the Dakar court reversed its position under the presumed political manipulation described above, Human Rights Watch immediately denounced the shift, saying, "President Wade should support the victims' appeal and help put an end to the routine practice of the worst tyrants moving into comfortable exile next door."[198] Alioune Tine, head of RADDHO, was more outspoken: "My country has always been a leader in human rights. . . The shenanigans surrounding this case are hurting our reputation and betraying those who placed their faith in Senegalese justice."[199]

Senegal's lawyers had attained leading positions in international human rights, including, simultaneously, secretary general of the International Commission of Jurists, secretary general of Amnesty International, and director of the UN Centre for Human Rights.[200] This moral high ground and impressive leadership was seriously undermined by the reversal of the Senegalese position under questionable circumstances on the exercise of universal jurisdiction in the *Habré* case. Me Sidiki Kaba of the ONDH summed up the harm done by the manipulations around the July 4 judgment by saying, "Whenever politics enters the courtroom, law exits."[201]

Advantages of the System of Investigating Judge

The *Pinochet* precedent exists in large part because of the procedure of investigating magistrate in Spain allowed Judge Baltasar Garzón to carry out investigations against nationals of Argentina and Chile, leading to a request for extradition in the case of *Pinochet,* notwithstanding the objections of the Spanish public prosecutor. The ministry of foreign affairs of Spain was a reluctant agent of transmission of the extradition request.

The activity of such magistrates appeared to be increasing. A Belgian court convicted four Rwandan defendants for their role in the 1994 genocide on the basis of the 1993 Belgian law that gives local courts jurisdiction over war crimes wherever committed. Belgian investigating judges have also started proceedings against sitting high officials of government, including issuing an international arrest warrant on April 11, 2000, against Abdulaye Yerodia Ndombasi, then minister for foreign affairs of the DRC, for "serious violations of international humanitarian law," which was successfully contested by the DRC before the International Court of Justice.[202] A judge has also opened an investigation against Saddam Hussein and into alleged crimes against humanity committed in Lebanon in 1982 with the acquiescence of Ariel Sharon, then Israeli defense minister and now prime minister, who avoided Brussels on his travels in Europe in early July 2001. French judicial authorities interrupted Henry Kissinger's stay at the Ritz Hotel in Paris to issue a summons to testify on disappearances of French citizens in Pinochet's Chile, and Judge Juan Guzmán, who is handling 250 lawsuits against Pinochet in Chile, filed an international subpoena against Kissinger to appear for questioning regarding two American citizens who disappeared in Chile.

The cases against the four Rwandan defendants and Sharon, as the *Pinochet* extradition case and the attempted interrogation of Kissinger, were the work of investigating magistrates. The independence of the investigating magistrate in this continental system of criminal procedure made it possible for a judge to act in the interests of human rights rather that as a representative of the state responsible for balancing the interests of the state with the interests of criminal justice. In the case of the investigating magistrate, the interests of justice can override the *raison d'état*. Judge Kandji, sometimes referred to as the Senegalese Garzón,[203] was similarly free to act on his understanding of the extent to which Senegalese law allowed universal jurisdiction to be exercised, to hear witnesses, to send letters rogatory, to issue an indictment, and not be influenced by the fact that the public prosecutor changed position and opposed the bringing of the case. The initial intervention was by Delphone Djiraibe, president of ATPDH, and the plaintiffs for a criminal action were the private victims and their associations. They were able, as were the activists in the *Pinochet* case in most of the countries where it was pursued,[204] to find a responsive and sympathetic judge whose independence was possible in large part because of the nature and independence of an investigating magistrate. The adversarial system in common law countries is also capable of holding foreign individuals accountable, for example, under the Alien Tort Claims Act and the Torture Victim Protection Act in the United States,[205] but it was the continental system that has produced the dramatic developments in Spain, Belgium, and Senegal.

The procedure of the investigating magistrate (*juge d'instruction*) may be a necessary condition for the exercise of universal jurisdiction under the present stage of judicial temerity. As Justice Michael Kirby masterfully explains in his essay in this volume, common law judges do not appear inclined to venture in this direction for at least fourteen reasons,[206] to which one could add the political question doctrine in the United States.[207] Kirby's conclusion merits repetition: "The twenty-first century will see, in common law countries, a growing rapprochement between municipal legal systems and international law, specifically the international law of human rights. . . . The basic question is whether, in the hands of such [common law] judges, universal jurisdiction, long discussed in the texts of international law, will have a life in municipal law under conditions which the judges proclaim."[208] The same reluctance does not hamper the *juge d'instruction*, who has not only the freedom to behave in a more activist mode without instructions from the ministry of justice but also the possibility, as occurred in the *Habré* case, to act on a private action (*constitution de partie civile*).[209] The question, following the judgment of the Senegalese *Cour de Cassation*, is whether this growing challenge to the impunity of former and current high officials may finally reach Habré, for example, through extradition to Belgium. In March 2002, Judge Daniel Franse, along with a Belgian prosecutor, four police officers, and a court clerk, traveled to N'Djamena to investigate the charges filed under the 1993 Belgian universal jurisdiction law. In June 2002 a Brussels appellate court held that "for cases based on universal competence . . . it is necessary that the alleged perpetrators be in the territory of the kingdom," which would have protected Habré unless extradited. However, on February 12, 2003, the Cour de Cassation removed this requirement, thus opening the way for the Habré case to move forward.[210]

Self-Executing Character of Articles 5 and 7 of the Torture Convention

The issue on which the dismissal of the plaintiffs' case hinged—failure of a state party to the Torture Convention to provide for universal jurisdiction in domestic law—is not clear in international law. I have argued that Senegal should have exercised jurisdiction based on the convention, but it is not certain and in fact is doubtful that the United States could do so in the absence of the Torture Victim Protection Act[211] with respect to civil liability, and the recent change in U.S. criminal law,[212] with respect to criminal liability. Applying a French-based monist system, Senegal should fulfill its obligations under Articles 5 and 7 without waiting for implementing legislation in the Code of Criminal Procedure. It would be helpful to provide an authoritative interpretation of the obligation to "take such measures as may be necessary to establish its jurisdiction" under Article 5(2) and to "submit the case to its competent authorities" under Article 7, so as to make it clear that state parties are obliged to prosecute even in the absence a modification of the criminal code and the code of criminal procedure for that purpose. A general comment by the Committee against Torture would be one way of accomplishing that objective. The Princeton Principles favors this approach in affirming that "national judicial organs may rely on universal jurisdiction even if their national legislation does not specifically provide for it."[213]

Senegal's Obligations under International Law

Even if one were to accept that, in the current state of its Code of Criminal Procedure, Senegal could not prosecute Habré, this defect of its internal law cannot, per Article 27 of the Vienna Convention, absolve it of its conventional obligation to the other states parties. The Wade government and the parliament should move quickly to remedy this defect and then bring Habré to justice. After the July 4, 2000, judgment, Habré's movements were no longer restricted. However, since the Committee against Torture issued its request, the Sengalese authorities have so far ensured that he does not leave the country. If he does, all countries where he might go should be informed that there is evidence that he is responsible for acts punishable by any state under international law. He should be treated as an international outlaw (*hostis humanis generis*).

Limitations of the *Pinochet* Precedent

Ending the impunity enjoyed by Idi Amin and Milton Obote of Uganda, Mengistu Haile Mariam of Ethiopia, Alfredo Stroessner of Paraguay, and Jean-Claude "Baby Doc" Duvalier, Emmanuel "Toto" Constant, Generals Raoul Cedrás and Philippe Biamby of Haiti, and Alberto Fujimori of Peru is not likely to follow an easy pattern. The *Pinochet* precedent does not serve as a precedent except metaphorically; each legal system where action is attempted is different. As Human Rights Watch discovered, each country of exile has its reasons for protecting the impunity of its guest. Panama, where Cedrás and Biamby reside, said, "[I]t would be a dangerous precedent to grant the right of asylum to resolve a political problem in a neighboring country and later deny the right of those given asylum." Saudi Arabia, where Amin resides, cited Bedouin hospitality, which dictates that "once someone is welcomed as a guest in your tent, you do not turn him out."[214] Japan considers that Fujimori's Japanese nationality protects him from extradition, although Peru's ambassador to Japan reportedly intends to seek revocation of his Japanese citizenship "to pave the way for possible extradition and Interpol issued a wanted notice for his arrest because of the charges of murder and kidnapping in Peru."[215]

In another sense, the comparison with the *Pinochet* case provides a strong argument for the prosecution of Habré. The number of people hurt and the damage done to a country economically is on a far larger scale in Chad than in Chile, and the prosecution of Habré is therefore all the more called for in the interests of retributive justice and the deterrent effect.

Criminal Liability of Other Chadian Agents of the Habré Government

These examples are limited, as are the *Pinochet* and *Habré* cases, to former heads of state. Impunity is a much broader phenomenon. The Commission of Inquiry referred to the "culpable passivity of high officials" (*passivité coupable des hauts responsables*)[216] and named three leaders of the Special Brigade of Rapid Intervention and the Presidential Security unit who gave orders and four other agents who personally conducted massacres[217] as well as 14 agents of the DDS frequently mentioned by witnesses as torturers "without pity," known for their "cruelty, sadism and inhumanity."[218]

It is a remarkable outcome of the attempt in Senegal to exercise universal jurisdiction that the Chadian criminal justice system is finally opening up and seventeen criminal cases have been brought by torture victims before the N'djamena District Court charging the Documentation and Security Directorship (DDS). Chadian president Idriss Deby is reported to have met with the victims on September 27, 2000, and promised to support their claim "even against some of the former DDS officers still in government service in Chad."[219] Again, the Chadian Association of Victims of Political Repression and Crime, representing 792 victims, took the lead.[220]

Political Implications of Universal Jurisdiction

This case illustrates the complex policy issue of expanding application of universal jurisdiction: if states actually begin exercising jurisdiction over numerous individuals, one has to consider the political implications of officials of current and previous governments traveling abroad for health or other reasons and becoming subjected to legal process more out of a political interest of the prosecuting state than the universal abhorrence for a demonic criminal.[221] As Oscar Schachter remarked,

[A] good case can be made for extending the scope of jurisdiction for certain types of heinous crimes such as those involved in hijacking, sabotage and terrorism that have a clear international dimension. In such cases, extradition may not be possible or appropriate, and trial and punishment by the State which holds the accused is justifiable. However, these cases present special problems that bear on the fairness and propriety of the judicial proceeding in a State removed from the site of the crime and having no link of nationality to the accused. Moreover, the fact that some States do not accept the prohibition against double jeopardy enhances the possibility that a person acquitted in one State may be tried and punished in another State.[222]

The decision of the indicting chamber of the appellate court of Paris on October 20, 2000, to authorize the investigating judge to issue an arrest warrant for Colonel Qadhdhafi for his alleged role in the downing of a French airliner over Niger in 1989 that resulted in 170 deaths, is a good example of the problem. The prosecutor's office had argued that customary international law entitled Qadhdhafi to head of state immunity, and the minister of foreign affairs had announced on August 29, 2000, that normalization of relations with Libya was under way. The court considered that there was no head of state immunity for acts of terrorism. As *Le Monde* reported the situation, the judges arrest warrant "could upset this rapprochement."[223] While it may be easy to applaud this willingness to hold Qadhdhafi criminally responsible for acts constituting international crimes carried out under his authority, would the reaction be the same if a warrant were issued against Bill Clinton or Tony Blair for their responsibility in war crimes committed during the bombing of Kosovo or against Bush and Blair for similar claims vis-à-vis Iraq?[224] Moreover, the Paris case was based on the nationality of the victims (passive personality principle) rather than universal jurisdiction. "With respect to former heads of state, Peter Bass suggested in 1987 that this new trend of aggressive transnational litigation against ex-heads of state may in some cases disrupt the Executive's ability to help transitions to power abroad. . . . An offer of immunity might be a useful political lever to speed the departure of disfavored leaders—to be extended when such departure is deemed to serve the national interest of the United States."[225]

However, he is clear that "[e]x-head of state immunity should not extend to leaders whose acts violate international legal norms of human rights,"[226] anticipating for the United States the position the law lords took for Britain and efforts in several countries to prosecute Saddam Hussein, among other heads of state who commit serious international crimes.

There is a downside to the claims made by Bass and others. "Leaders whose acts violate international legal norms of human rights" can refer to a wide range of current and former officials, and the norms in question cover behavior ranging from the atrocities that can be attributed to Pinochet, Habré, and similarly ruthless leaders to innumerable acts in the wide range of state behavior covered by human rights. The Commission on Human Rights has taken note of the final report of the special rapporteur on impunity of perpetrators of violations of economic, social, and cultural rights[227] and invited "[s]tates to pay attention as appropriate to the question of impunity of violations of human rights and to take suitable measure to address this important issue."[228] Would this mean that all those involved in activities resulting in these violations should be held criminally liable under universal jurisdiction? Should judges responsible for failing to abide by every due process provision of Article 14 of the International Covenant on Civil and Political Rights in cases they have decided within their jurisdiction be subject to arrest and trial in another country seeking to end impunity for violation of any and all human rights? Should U.S. officials involved in the Cuba embargo or sanctions against Iraq be subject to such action abroad by countries who consider those measures to be violative of international human rights norms? The result would be unacceptable. However, the lesson of the *Hissène Habré* case in the wake of *Pinochet* is that there are cases where universal jurisdiction under both international treaties and customary international law are clearly necessary and appropriate for an expanding range of "heinous crimes," as Schachter suggests.[229]

The judiciary in the United Kingdom, Spain, Belgium, France, and Switzerland has demonstrated an inclination to find that middle ground between impunity of ruthless leaders and chaos in the application of international criminal law. The prosecution where appropriate under universal jurisdiction of ex-heads of state like Hissène Habré is still possible, in spite of the setback of the July 4, 2000, judgment of Senegal's *Cour de Cassation.* Through the exercise of universal jurisdiction, it is still possible to provide a degree of retributive and corrective justice for the voiceless victims of mass atrocities, and this case may provide numerous lessons to improve the application of universal jurisdiction to other cases in the slow march against impunity.

Chapter 9
Defining the Limits: Universal Jurisdiction and National Courts

Anne-Marie Slaughter

By granting the power to prosecute to all states, universal jurisdiction purports to remove the need for a particular connection to any one. It stands alone among the five generally accepted bases for exercising jurisdiction in not requiring a link between any part of the offence and the state seeking to exercise jurisdiction. Universal jurisdiction is also unique in another respect: it ultimately depends on domestic courts for its application. While domestic legislatures and executives, together with international tribunals, all contribute to the definition and scope of universal jurisdiction, its final point of application will be the courtroom. It is domestic judges who must grapple with defining the relationship between international law and national law. It is domestic judges who must consider the procedural and substantive scope of universal jurisdiction in their courts. And it is domestic judges who must tell us how, when, and why universal jurisdiction is or is not applicable in a given case.

The result is a potentially dramatic extension of judicial power and a corresponding threat to judicial legitimacy. Indeed, in the wake of the *Pinochet* case and reports of subsequent prosecutions based on universal jurisdiction in national courts, government officials, scholars, and media officials have already expressed concern over how to tame this new beast. If universal jurisdiction is to be more than an abstract category in international law treatises, what should be its proper limits?

The question may remain academic because in practice, many judges have already imposed quite severe limits. Contrary to claims of rampant judicial imperialism raised both in the media and by scholars such as Jack Goldsmith and Stephen Krasner, judges have actually been very aware of the problems raised by exercising universal jurisdiction, both in terms of the basis of their own judicial power and the potential for interfering in the affairs of other nations.[1] Indeed, as Cherif Bassiouni demonstrates so conclusively in his contribution to this volume, the exercise of pure universal jurisdiction is actually very rare.[2] Justice Michael Kirby provides a firsthand insight into the precise reasons behind this judicial reluctance, listing fourteen distinct causes for concern at least among common-law judges.[3]

National judges have responded to these problems with a number of different strategies. Many judges and legislatures have in fact insisted on a more traditional jurisdictional nexus in addition to universal jurisdiction, requiring some connection through nationality or territoriality. Some judges sidestep the more problematic questions involved in universal jurisdiction even as they apply it.[4] Those few who have been willing to take the plunge and prosecute a defendant with no traditional connection to the national polity or territory have developed elaborate accounts of the basis and nature of universal jurisdiction. Each of these accounts overcomes some problems but immediately creates others. And each of these accounts is important for what it tells us about the role of judges in international lawmaking.

The two dominant accounts diverge quite sharply in their conception of the source of the demand for universal jurisdiction: international morality versus procedural convenience. This distinction has been long recognized in international law as the difference between "crimes under international law" and the jurisdictional principle of "universality."[5] In essence, crimes under international law are acts so heinous that they strike at the "whole of mankind" and shock "the conscience of nations."[6] In response, nations have come together and criminalized these acts at the international level, thereby permitting or obliging states to exercise jurisdiction over their perpetrator.

The principle of universality, by contrast, is a procedural device by which international law grants all states jurisdiction to punish specified acts that are independently crimes under national law. It is the way in which international law has responded to the pragmatic difficulties, under certain circumstances, of prosecuting offenses recognized as illegal in domestic legal systems around the world.[7] For many international lawyers the paradigmatic example of the principle of universality is piracy, a crime committed more or less indiscriminately against citizens of different nations but committed on the high seas, making it very difficult to exercise jurisdiction based on territory or nationality.[8] As Bassiouni describes, the theoretical origins of universal jurisdiction are complex and still contested.[9] At least in British and early American practice, however, the right to prosecute flowed from international law, but the crime of piracy itself was defined by national law and was prosecuted and punished under the law of the particular nation where the prosecution took place.

The purpose here is not to evaluate the relative merits of these two accounts. The point is rather to understand how each account gives rise to a different set of practical and theoretical problems that judges have had to struggle with. The standard account highlights the notion of an international polity determining what is right. Here, tying universal jurisdiction to crimes under international law is potentially quite expansionist and subject to abuse, raising the specter of a small group of nations taking it upon themselves to prosecute officials from other nations based on their particular conception of customary international law. It also creates substantial problems of retroactivity for individual defendants and raises a host of difficult procedural questions as the prosecution goes forward. Reliance on the universality principle, by contrast, ameliorates some of these problems but then decouples universal jurisdiction from the limiting concept of extraordinary crimes so grave that they merit punishment by the community of nations and indeed humankind. This account suggests a bottom-up view of international law, stressing the domestic origins of international law. Taken to its extreme, however, it risks losing sight of the necessary role of international law in determining when a state may go beyond its traditional jurisdictional boundaries.

Judges facing these different questions have imposed their own limits on universal jurisdiction, limits that in many cases are probably more restrictive than is either necessary or desirable. The result, at least at this stage in the evolution of universal jurisdiction, is that although the basis for jurisdiction over war criminals and perpetrators of genocide and crimes against humanity has been established in many countries, the actual prosecutions have been blocked in many cases. The international community thus faces less a need for limits on universal jurisdiction than a need to overcome many of the limits already imposed.

The first part of this essay briefly summarizes the general problems posed by the exercise of universal jurisdiction and the corresponding desire of many judges to insist on "universal jurisdiction plus"—the plus provided by some element of one of the more traditional bases of jurisdiction. The second part explores the "standard account" of universal jurisdiction as based on international crimes and highlights the stringent limits that this account typically entails. The third part presents an alternative account that derives from the universality principle and appears to address many of the problems posed by the standard account, although it inevitably raises new problems of its own.

Discussion of the two dominant accounts begins by focusing on the Canadian prosecution in 1992 of Imre Finta for war crimes and crimes against humanity allegedly committed during World War II.[10] The judgments in the *Finta* case appear as the "purest" forms of the two accounts; discussion of the two leading opinions in *Finta* therefore provides a useful framework for considering other judicial opinions regarding universal jurisdiction. Other judges dealing with universal jurisdiction tend to be less explicit and less self-conscious about the account of universal jurisdiction on which their decision may be based. Indeed, judges frequently refer to elements of both accounts in the course of their judgments. Yet a clearer understanding of both accounts, and the differences between them, clarify the work of judges applying universal jurisdiction and will help in the definition of universal jurisdiction. In the second and third parts, therefore, the two accounts are separated out along with their respective strengths and weaknesses.

The fourth part offers a "revised standard account," combining international and domestic law and presuming a dynamic interrelationship between them. This account is both a more accurate account of the actual dynamic between international and national law and a more helpful tool for judges, allowing them to use each body of law to supplement the other where necessary to circumvent many of the current limits imposed on universal jurisdiction. This is not carte blanche to use domestic law to prosecute absent recognition of an international crime. Rather, it recognizes that domestic law may help clarify vague provisions of international law and vice versa. Indeed, this approach should be less frightening to those concerned about the overexpansion of universal jurisdiction, since it assumes the continued predominance of states while recognizing the relevance of each state's internal constitutional structure as well as the relevance of international law.

Finally, the fifth part proposes a process solution to the question of how limits to universal jurisdiction should be defined, arguing that although national judges must tackle universal jurisdiction within the framework of their own national legal traditions, they should also take account of the views of their fellow judges in both foreign and international tribunals. Mandating such a process of "consultation" will institutionalize transnational judicial dialogue and ensure that a healthy pluralism of approaches advances the goals of the international legal system as a whole. It is clear from all the cases discussed that domestic courts are a vital part of the development of universal jurisdiction. To this end, communication among judges will only strengthen the development of universal jurisdiction and clarify its limits.

The Princeton Principles themselves either explicitly adopt or are at least consistent with many of the suggestions advanced here and in other contributions to this volume. However, they are a composite set of guidelines designed to be of maximum use to many different constituencies: national and international judges, legislators, prosecutors, defense lawyers, international officials, and human rights activists, among others. They cannot follow any particular blueprint but must instead strike a balance between generality and specificity, between the law as it is and the law as it is becoming, and between prescription and aspiration. In this essay, I note points of convergence and congruence between the Principles and my own analysis. Finally, in the appendix to this essay I offer a few additional principles of my own, designed to guide judges in strengthening transjudicial communication in this area.

Universality "Plus"

The traditional bases for criminal jurisdiction all require a link between the exercise of the state's most potent power—the power to enforce the law and thereby deprive an individual of property, liberty, and even life—and the protection of its people or territory. Territoriality is the easiest jurisdictional principle to accept in this regard; states clearly have the power to regulate what takes place on their territory. Nationality, similarly, allows a state to create order among its citizens by regulating the acts of its citizens, even where those acts have been performed outside its territory. Passive personality is explicitly based on a state's ability to protect its citizens;[11] the protective principle is equally explicit in allowing a state to guard against vital threats to its security whether defined in terms of its territorial integrity or the safety of its citizens.

The exercise of jurisdiction without a link either to people or territory raises two major problems: one internal and one external. The internal problem concerns the legitimacy of a court in concentrating the full power of the state against an individual defendant who, by definition, cannot be said to have in any way authorized the exercise of that power through nationality or conduct within the state's territory.[12] The external problem concerns the heightened danger of interference in the affairs of fellow states. When other bases of jurisdiction conflict, the solution generally depends on asking which state has the strongest link with the offense or which state has the strongest interest in exercising its jurisdictional rights. Universal jurisdiction, by contrast, allows the exercise of jurisdiction by a state with no apparent link to prosecute even when states with more traditional bases of jurisdiction do not wish to prosecute.[13] Those states are far more likely to cry foul.

Apparently responding to these concerns, many national courts have purported to exercise universal jurisdiction while actually requiring some kind of more traditional nexus to nationality or territory.[14] Thus, for instance, French courts have held that while universal jurisdiction could be exercised for torture, this could only apply where the accused was on French territory.[15] Such a requirement amounts to a territoriality nexus for France, as the French legal system otherwise allows trials in absentia. Even so, this nexus may have proved insufficient; subsequent cases calling for prosecution of foreign nationals for crimes against humanity have been based on passive personality.[16] Interestingly, the *Eichmann* prosecution relied on both passive personality and the protective principle in addition to universality.[17]

In a German prosecution for genocide related to the events in the former Yugoslavia, *Jorgic,* the Federal Supreme Court required a special link or nexus between Germany and the offense, even though no such nexus is required by the German law.[18] In the case at bar, the court found the necessary link on the basis that the defendant had lived in Germany from 1969 to 1982 and was still registered there, and that he had been arrested on German territory. This link of subsequent residence or citizenship can also be found in war crimes legislation passed in Australia, Canada, and the United Kingdom.[19] It attempts to graft at least some connection to both territory and nationality onto the pure exercise of universal jurisdiction.

These cases and statutes suggest a general discomfort with the notion that States can prosecute anyone for international crimes regardless of any traditional nexus. Indeed, one commentator, Hari Osofsky, has argued that limits can be placed on the exercise of universal jurisdiction in the United States through an adaptation of the civil law doctrine of *forum non conveniens*.[20] He adds that "[t]he four other traditional bases for jurisdiction could help establish the comparative connectedness of various possible forums for the crime."[21] In seeking limitations on the exercise of universal jurisdiction, Osofsky has returned to the traditional bases of jurisdiction.

Universal jurisdiction "plus" essentially avoids the difficult issues embedded in universal jurisdiction. Courts using this approach are trying to avoid having to address the bare fact of exercising jurisdiction with no territorial or national nexus. They thus try to create such a nexus, however thin or after the fact. Such approaches offer judges additional comfort and can provide expedient limits to universal jurisdiction. Judges who refuse such comfort, however, must struggle with the underlying justifications for universal jurisdiction and develop limits accordingly.

The Standard Account: Crimes under International Law

Judges who accept that universal jurisdiction is itself a separate and legitimate basis of jurisdiction quickly find themselves driven to articulate an underlying rationale as a framework for addressing a number of practical and principled issues that immediately arise. The two principal rationales rest on international morality and international convenience. However, neither of these accounts is ultimately satisfactory. Somewhat paradoxically, the vigorous assertion of the imperatives of the human conscience actually makes it harder to prove the crimes alleged. On the other hand, grounding universal jurisdiction in mutual convenience is counterintuitive and reduces the role of international law to that of procedural handmaiden, missing a vital opportunity to vindicate even a relatively thin conception of our common humanity. A third approach that synthesizes some elements of the first two is more promising; it will be explored more fully in Part 4.

The first account of universal jurisdiction may be called the standard account, as it is the most intuitive and best accords with the conventional wisdom summarized in most casebooks and short treatises. It can best be explored through the majority judgment of Justice Cory in the Canadian Supreme Court case *R. v. Finta*.[22] *Finta* offers a dramatic and in many ways distressing explication of many of the most important issues underlying the exercise of universal jurisdiction. The Canadian government undertook a lengthy and commendable effort to ensure that "any . . . war criminals currently resident in Canada . . . are brought to justice." These efforts included a national commission of inquiry and the subsequent adoption of legislation amending the Canadian Criminal Code to allow for the exercise of jurisdiction over war crimes and crimes against humanity committed outside Canada by non-Canadians.

In 1992, forty-eight years after the deportation of Hungary's Jews, Imre Finta stood trial in Canada for war crimes and crimes against humanity for his role in the process of "de-jewification" of Szeged in the spring of 1944, pursuant to the Hungarian Ministry of the Interior's "Baky Order."[23] Finta was charged by the Crown with having overseen the removal of the Jews from ghettoes to a concentration center, keeping them in a brickyard where they were stripped of their valuables, loaded onto boxcars, and transported, mostly to Auschwitz-Birkenau. In keeping with the requirement under the Canadian statute that the offenses charged be crimes under *both* international law and domestic law, he was charged with two counts each of unlawful confinement, robbery, kidnapping, and manslaughter under the Canadian Criminal Code.[24] For each offence, there were alternative counts alleging that the offense committed constituted a crime against humanity and a war crime.[25]

At no stage in any of the proceedings did Finta attempt to deny his involvement in these actions or produce any evidence to counter the charges.[26] The case centered, therefore, on the mental element required for the crimes charged and whether Finta had this mental element. Did Finta have to know that the acts were inhumane? In the Supreme Court, La Forest, dissenting, argued that "[i]f an accused knowingly confines elderly people in close quarters within boxcars with little provision for a long train ride, then the fact that the accused subjectively did not consider this inhumane should be irrelevant."[27] By contrast, the majority in the Supreme Court argued that Finta must know subjectively that his acts, if viewed objectively in light of the facts and circumstances, would be considered inhumane.[28]

Despite clear and ample evidence of brutal and inhumane acts, the jury acquitted Finta. So overwhelming was the evidence against Finta that the author of the B'nai Brith amicus brief in the case, in a separate article, described the case as an example of jury nullification.[29] The case is striking as an example of how, notwithstanding the best intentions and assiduous government efforts, the exercise of universal jurisdiction can go awry. It is also significant as an example of an exhaustive and carefully reasoned analysis of the foundations of universal jurisdiction by both the majority and the dissent.

Perhaps most important, however, *Finta* stands for a more ordinary exercise of universal jurisdiction than the highly publicized and politicized cases against former leaders such as Pinochet. More ordinary also than the cases brought against alleged perpetrators of war crimes in Bosnia, in which grim media images and the existence of a special international tribunal focus both public and judicial attention on the importance of prosecution. *Finta* involved the kind of defendant who would likely become far more frequent if universal jurisdiction were genuinely institutionalized: a perpetrator of unspeakable acts living far in time and space from the place of their commission, hoping to bury his past forever. Of this kind of defendant David Matas writes: "[W]hen the accused is old, when he has been a quiet friendly neighbour for decades, when the crime was committed a long time ago and far away in another country, and when the victim is a stranger and a foreigner, there are many people . . . who have little or no interest in a prosecution."[30]

The Majority Opinion

The decision in *Finta* turned on the correct interpretation of particular sections of the Canadian Criminal Code that had been enacted to allow for extraterritorial jurisdiction in certain cases involving people who were Canadian nationals at the time of prosecution, even if not at the time of the alleged offense.[31] The majority decided that the legislation had created two new offenses, war crimes and crimes against humanity, both of which required a different *mens rea* from that required for the equivalent offenses under domestic law. These offenses, war crimes and crimes against humanity, were not only different from the crimes that could be said to underlie them, such as murder, kidnapping and robbery, but also "far more grievous."[32]

Justice Cory's majority decision demonstrates an understanding of crimes against humanity and war crimes as crimes created by international law that are essentially unrelated to the underlying domestic law crimes.[33] They are crimes created by the "community of nations" in recognition of the horror and heinousness of the acts committed. For Justice Cory, "those persons indicted for having committed crimes against humanity or war crimes stand charged with committing offences so grave that they shock the conscience of all right-thinking people."[34] Universal jurisdiction can thus be exercised in the name of universal morality as enshrined and codified in international law.

Inherent Limits

The principal advantage of this account is that it captures the common-sense intuition that universal jurisdiction is a potentially fearsome power that should only be exercised in extraordinary circumstances. The inherent limits built into this account flow from the combination of the degree of depravity or fundamental inhumanity necessary to classify certain acts as international crimes and the necessity of agreement on that classification by a considerable majority of sovereign states.

A related safeguard is the often unstated but very deep assumption that international law typically regulates only relations among states and recognizes only states as subjects. Typically, therefore, states can be held responsible for failing to prevent the commission of acts by their subjects, but how they choose to designate and regulate such acts is up to them. Only acts that require an extra measure of condemnation, by the international community as a body, merit designation as international crimes, with the accompanying specification of their perpetrators as owing independent duties under international law.

The problem of sovereign interference is thus minimal on this account. Sovereign states have all the protections that they have with respect to any other body of international law—they are free to exercise their sovereign will to constrain themselves through agreements with other states. They must agree, based on the heinous nature of certain offenses, that the state with the closest traditional link to the offense may not be the state that prosecutes it.

A further limit inherent in the international crimes account of universal jurisdiction concerns the problem of retroactivity. Assuming that the crime is defined under international law, then the prohibition on retroactive criminality requires that international law have prohibited the act at the time of its commission. This limit is even more restrictive if the requirement is read to mean that international law must have prohibited the act as committed by an individual rather than by a state. Hans Kelsen, for instance, accepted that international law recognized the crimes committed by the Nazis at the time they were committed, but argued that international law up to that point had provided only for collective rather than individual responsibility.[35]

Finally, the crimes under the international crimes account limits the exercise of universal jurisdiction based on a state's internal conception of the relationship between international and domestic law. "Monist" states are theoretically free to prosecute international crimes as soon as they are established at international law. "Dualist" states, on the other hand, must take the additional step of transposing the international law crime into domestic law. Courts in these states can only exercise universal jurisdiction if they are explicitly authorized to do so by domestic legislation. In addition, formally monist states such as the United States can transform themselves into effectively dualist states by attaching reservations to a treaty through the ratification process that require additional implementing legislation before the treaty can be actually applied.

Imposed Limits

The crimes under international law account of universal jurisdiction also raises a number of problems, many of which, notwithstanding the inherent limits just described, are related to the perception of unchecked judicial authority and hence a fear of expansion of the doctrine. The perception of these problems naturally leads to a search for additional safeguards, resulting in additional imposed limits on when and how courts can exercise universal jurisdiction. This can be a dangerous dynamic, resulting, as in the *Finta* case, in lofty rhetoric condemning the crimes while letting the accused go free.

Punishing Immorality

The first problem grows out of a particular response to the apparent limit of retroactivity.[36] As noted above, Justice Cory in *Finta* could have argued that Finta's alleged crimes were crimes under international law at the time of commission,[37] but he appears to have accepted that international law did not prohibit war crimes and crimes against humanity on an individual basis prior to the Second World War.[38] He nevertheless found that the principle of non-retroactivity was trumped by a higher principle of morality—the international morality that underlies the definition of crimes under international law.

Cory relies on an account found in the writings of Kelsen and Georg Schwarzenberger.[39] Kelsen believed that the Nuremberg and Tokyo Charters created new law, an exception to the prohibition on *ex post facto* laws. He recognized that the rule against retroactive legislation is a principle of justice but concluded that justice also required punishment of the accused, who were aware of the "immoral character" of the acts they committed. Kelsen continues: "Justice required the punishment of these men, in spite of the fact that under positive law they were not punishable with retroactive force. In case two postulates of justice are in conflict with each other, the higher one prevails; and to punish those who were morally responsible for the international crime of the second World War may certainly be considered as more important than to comply with the rather relative rule against *ex post facto* laws, open to so many exceptions."[40]

Here's the rub. The emphasis on morality as a trumping principle fits well with Cory's account of universal jurisdiction as based on the need to punish the most morally culpable offences. Yet Cory's development of this account could justify prosecution even for acts that are universally recognized as being legal at the time of their commission. It is a far-reaching and, to many, frightening proposition.

It is in this light that Cory's concern with strict procedural protections, in the form of an emphasis on jury decision making, can be better understood. He insists that the defendant can be convicted only if the jury finds that he knew subjectively that his acts were of the serious nature of war crimes and/or crimes against humanity. The defendant must be found to know "that the facts or circumstances of his or her actions were such that, viewed objectively, they would shock the conscience of all right-thinking people."[41]

Why raise the *mens rea* bar so high? Because "[t]he degree of moral turpitude that attaches to crimes against humanity and war crimes must exceed that of the domestic offences of manslaughter and robbery. It follows that the accused must be aware of the conditions which render his or her actions more blameworthy than the domestic offence."[42] If prosecution and punishment is to be based on international morality, then the defendant must have subjectively understood the precise degree to which his or her actions were immoral. The expansiveness of the jurisdictional account meets its limit in the restrictiveness of the *mens rea* requirement.

Crimes under Natural Law?

A second major problem with the crimes under international law account is that it can conflict sharply with the requirement in many nations and the deeply felt principle that crimes should be prosecuted and punished only on the basis of positive law. Customary international law is simply too indeterminate and unstable, in the eyes of many judges, to permit the exercise of universal jurisdiction and counter a charge of retroactivity.[43] This concern drives much of the third decision by the House of Lords in the Pinochet case. [44] Only one judge was willing to find that torture was a crime under British law before incorporation of the Torture Convention into British law on the basis of customary international law.[45] Further, all the law lords interpreted the double criminality principle of the Extradition Act[46] to require that the act be criminal under both domestic legal systems at the time it was committed and not at the time of extradition, an implicit nod to the principle of nonretroactivity.[47]

For other judges, the uncertainty of customary international law and concerns about retroactivity make them unwilling to override key structural provisions in their domestic constitutions. Thus, in *Nulyarimma v. Thompson*,[48] an Australian case on the question of whether genocide was a crime under Australian law by virtue of its status under international law, the majority of judges relied on the rule that only the legislature can create new crimes.[49] It is therefore impossible for the court to recognize a crime under customary international law. By contrast, the Australian High Court upheld legislation allowing for prosecution of war crimes and crimes against humanity committed in Europe during 1939 and 1945 whether or not the defendant was a national of Australia at the time of the offense, although not without a vigorous dissent by Brennan, discussed below.[50] These issues can be particularly acute for courts struggling with their own constitutional role and decisions about the powers of the separate branches of government.[51]

Courts appear no more willing to rely on customary international law as the basis of universal jurisdiction in so-called monist legal systems. In France, the Cour de Cassation has failed to recognize universal jurisdiction for genocide and crimes under the Geneva Conventions in the absence of an express provision for such jurisdiction in French law.[52] Similarly, the court in Senegal in the *Hissène Habré* case declined to recognize universal jurisdiction in the absence of express incorporation.[53]

Those few judges who are willing to accept jurisdiction based on customary international law must fall back once again on the seriousness of the offense, with the attendant need for procedural protections to ensure that any defendant potentially subject to such grave stigma be assured of every safeguard. Having determined that customary international law allows for universal jurisdiction for certain crimes under international law, Lord Millett argues that two criteria must be fulfilled before crimes prohibited by customary international law can attract universal jurisdiction.[54] The first is that the offenses be "contrary to a peremptory norm of international law." The second, more significantly, is that the offenses "be so serious and on such a scale that they can justly be regarded as an attack on the international legal order."[55] The seriousness of the offense allows its prosecution. Without this level of seriousness, such prosecution would not be possible. It seems that where customary international law is relied on for the creation of universal jurisdiction, the prosecution will face significant hurdles before it can prove that the crimes reach the seriousness required as a result.[57]

*   *   *

The standard account of universal jurisdiction links such jurisdiction to the definition of crimes under international law. This category of crimes merits special definition in international law due to their especially heinous nature. Conviction of a war crime or a crime against humanity is qualitatively different from a conviction for murder or rape or kidnapping, however grave those acts may be. Accordingly, however, defendants in danger of a conviction carrying such moral opprobrium must be granted every possible procedural safeguard, over and above those granted under domestic law. Further, any defendant facing such a charge should be granted the protection of a law that is as clear and determinate as possible. This concern leads courts to focus on treaties over customary law and domestic statutes over treaties.

The standard account thus appears to breed its own limits. In turn, however, setting the bar too high for prosecutions may result in no prosecutions, a position that counters the aim of international law to prosecute these offenses. Since 1995, as a result of the *Finta* decision, the Canadian Department of Justice has taken a policy decision not to prosecute under universal jurisdiction and to confine Canadian efforts to expulsion of foreign war criminals.[58] Similarly, some judges have chosen simply to recognize international law only when it has been expressly incorporated into domestic law, but not otherwise. This cuts off the potential for over-expansion, but may again result in a lack of prosecutions. In both instances, the limits imposed will strike many observers as simply too stringent.

An Alternative Account: Domestic Crimes with an International Jurisdictional Link

A second account of universal jurisdiction evident in a number of judicial opinions relies not on international law as the source of the crimes, but on domestic law. The offenses underlying crimes against humanity and war crimes—offenses such as murder, kidnapping, confinement, and robbery— are prohibited by the domestic laws of virtually all nations. Defendants charged with such crimes are thus charged and prosecuted under domestic law. Such prosecutions cannot take place, however, for crimes committed outside the territory of the prosecuting state unless international law authorizes extraterritorial jurisdiction. International law thus provides the procedural trigger for such prosecutions; domestic law defines the substance.[59]

This account of universal jurisdiction is broadly consistent with the distinction between the universality principle in international jurisdiction and the substantive concept of crimes against international law. However, the actual relationship between domestic and international law in this account is more complex. It is exhaustively explicated in Judge La Forest's dissenting opinion in *Finta*, which directly seeks to circumvent the problems raised by the standard account as developed in Judge Cory's majority opinion. La Forest's analysis merits some attention here, in order fully to understand both its strengths and weaknesses.

La Forest begins from the proposition that the Canadian legislation simply extends Canadian jurisdiction for crimes already recognized in Canadian law, creating the legal fiction that the crimes were committed in Canada.[60] The legislation thus "remove[s] . . . the obstacle of extraterritoriality and . . . [enables] Canada to serve as a *forum* for the domestic prosecution of these offenders."[61] When, however, may this "obstacle of extraterritoriality" be overcome? When the acts are committed under "conditions [that tie] them to international norms."[62] For instance, crimes against humanity "are aimed at giving protection to the basic human rights of all individuals throughout the world, and notably against transgressions by states against these rights."[63] In the Canadian definition, they include as part of the offense an "act or omission that is committed against any civilian population or any identifiable group of persons. . . ."[64] This definition, itself borrowed from international law and embedded in the Canadian statute, is the "jurisdictional link grounding prosecution for the underlying Canadian offence."[65]

This is a "bottom-up" view of universal jurisdiction, in which it can be exercised for acts or omissions prohibited under national law around the world, as long as such acts or omissions have an "international aspect" sufficient to overcome the normal presumption of territorial jurisdiction and thus to provide a jurisdictional link to a non-territorial court.[66] But La Forest complicates matters still further by combining this account with a different "top-down" account from that adopted by the majority. He also recognizes that war crimes and crimes against humanity "are crimes under international law. They are designed to enforce the prescriptions of international law for the protection of the lives and the basic human rights of the individual, particularly . . . against the actions of states."[67] They fall into a particular category of international crimes, however, in which pragmatic considerations dictate overcoming the normal presumption that such crimes will be prosecuted by the territorial state.[68]

Where the offenses occur in situations where prosecution is unlikely or impossible, this account argues, universal jurisdiction is made available to states. La Forest continues:

It would be pointless to rely [for prosecution] solely on the state where [a war crime or crime against humanity] has been committed, since that state will often be implicated in the crime, particularly crimes against humanity . . . Extraterritorial prosecution is thus a practical necessity in the case of war crimes and crimes against humanity. Not only is the state where the crime took place unlikely to prosecute; following the cessation of hostilities or other conditions that fostered their commission, the individuals who perpetrated them tend to scatter to the four corners of the earth. Thus, war criminals would be able to elude punishment simply by fleeing the jurisdiction where the crime was committed. The international community has rightly rejected this prospect.[69]

For a Canadian court to prosecute war crimes and crimes against humanity under the Canadian legislation, therefore, a determination must be made as to whether the acts alleged constitute war crimes or crimes against humanity under international law. This determination must be made by the judge, however, not the jury, as a jurisdictional determination.[70] It is then up to the jury to make the substantive determination whether the defendant has committed the offenses charged under the Canadian Criminal Code.

Inherent Limits

The La Forest account has a number of advantages. First, it overcomes the retroactivity problem without relying on international morality. The defendant cannot claim retroactivity because the crimes with which he is charged were already illegal under domestic law in every legal system and were therefore already illegal at the time of their commission.[71] In the Belgian proceedings regarding an extradition request for Pinochet, Judge Vandermeersch similarly refers to domestic law when discussing the claim of retroactivity.[72] While he fully accepts that crimes against humanity are part of Belgian law by virtue of incorporation of customary international law, he reinforces this argument with reference to the existence of the criminal elements of crimes against humanity in both Belgian and Chilean law.[73] These approaches to claims of retroactivity may not be convincing to everyone.[74] However, the acceptance of the idea that these acts were criminal in domestic systems throughout the world, particularly in the systems of the territory where the offense was committed and the territory where the prosecution is being held, tends to reduce unease about the application of these laws, even if they are, technically, retroactive.[75]

A second major advantage of the La Forest approach is that it facilitates actual prosecutions by avoiding the imposition of a very high *mens rea* requirement. Judge Vandermeersch's comments are particularly interesting in this regard: "The judicial authorities of several states have often given the impression that as far as crimes against humanity are concerned, they looked more for motives and juridical pretexts so as not to prosecute such crimes rather than check to what extent international law and internal law would allow them to institute such prosecutions."[76] La Forest is similarly distressed at the paradox of the majority opinion in *Finta*, whereby the effective result was to make prosecutions extremely difficult if not impossible. From his perspective, the defendant is entitled to all the procedural safeguards built into any domestic criminal prosecution, but no more.[77]

A third advantage of the La Forest approach is that it ensures that the "judge and especially the jury are able to function largely pursuant to a system of law which, being our own, is more familiar to us and more precise."[78] Only the judge is required to navigate the complexities of international law as part of a preliminary jurisdictional determination.

In a larger sense, these advantages all flow from the built-in constraints of the La Forest approach—inherent limits so strong that they avoid the need for additional imposed limits. On this account, the offense charged must be a violation of both domestic and international law at the time committed. It must further be a violation of a type of international crime that, in the eyes of the international community, may warrant the exercise of the universality principle, largely on pragmatic grounds. Yet even here, La Forest notes that under international law the exercise of this principle of jurisdiction is permissive rather than mandatory.[79] He thus concludes that "it is not self-evident that these crimes could be prosecuted in Canada in the absence of legislation."[80] Thus at least in many states, this account would allow prosecutions to go forward only based on a domestic statute.

Problems

Notwithstanding these apparent advantages, the La Forest account is problematic on a number of grounds and may also be too restrictive, albeit for different reasons than the standard account. First, his distinctions between substance/procedure and morality/pragmatism become increasingly artificial. The ultimate effect is one of complexity and periodic logical incoherence. Unlike the traditional explanation of the universality principle, according to which the crimes themselves are crimes under domestic law and international law supplies only the jurisdictional basis, La Forest seems compelled to recognize that war crimes and crimes against humanity are also crimes under international law. But if so, then why should they not be prosecuted under international law? Why would the Canadian legislation specifically invoke international law and require that the crimes prosecuted be war crimes and crimes against humanity without recognizing that these constitute distinct crimes from the underlying domestic offenses? Further, this account makes it difficult for domestic prosecutions under the statute to evolve as international law evolves.

Second, this approach often seems deeply counter-intuitive, to a troubling degree. La Forest stresses that the charges of war crimes and crimes against humanity, because they are based on domestic offenses, are no more serious than these domestic offenses: they require the same *mens rea* and they have no additional stigma.[81] This seems wrong. For all the problems associated with legislating international morality, all the cases in which contemporary courts have actually sought to exercise universal jurisdiction involve acts so horrible that they trigger a deep desire to vindicate our common humanity by seeking justice—however incomplete and imperfect it may be. To deny this moral element at the moment of potential conviction impoverishes the very concept of universal jurisdiction and misses a vital public opportunity to affirm the existence of genuine global norms.

A further difficulty here is that this account does not adequately explain why certain crimes have transcended the traditional boundaries of domestic jurisdiction and become subject to universal jurisdiction. While piracy may be easy to explain, because pirates were stateless and the offence occurred on the High Seas, outside the jurisdiction of any one state,[82] exercising universal jurisdiction in a case where another state has a more traditional basis for jurisdiction is more problematic. La Forest's attempt to ground universal jurisdiction in "practical necessity" is unsatisfying and potentially expansive in its turn. Surely universal jurisdiction cannot be exercised whenever the international community recognizes that the territorial state will be unlikely or unable to prosecute.[83] That may be a sufficient basis for the jurisdiction of an international criminal tribunal; a similar formulation commanded the consensus of the states that negotiated the statute for the International Criminal Court.[84] But it seems extremely unlikely that those same states would grant the power to prosecute on the same basis to any other national state. Indeed, even La Forest is ultimately driven to recognize that part of the basis for universal jurisdiction rests on the "international revulsion" associated with the underlying crimes.[85]

Finally, the La Forest account leads to awkward and even perverse results regarding the availability of defenses and degrees of punishment. On the one hand, all the procedural protections of the domestic legal system are available. La Forest stresses several times that the defendant will be able to avail himself of any defenses available under international law at the time. However, where the offense is the same as the domestic one, the protections will not be stronger. The absence of additional protections may be highly problematic in the politically charged atmosphere of some criminal prosecutions under universal jurisdiction.

On the other hand, grounding universal jurisdiction in domestic law may unduly restrict the punishments applicable to a convicted defendant. Judge Vandermeersch expressly argues that crimes against humanity "are of an unspeakable and unacceptable nature and the responsibility for their repression is shared by all."[86] Yet even he recognizes that where domestic criminal law is relied on to counter claims of retroactivity and to justify the application of universal jurisdiction, this must be combined with "the understanding that the applicable punishments will be those that were in force at the moment of the commission of the offences pursuant to the criminal law under the restriction of the possibly more favourable character of the new punishments (principles of legality of the punishments and of retroactivity of the mildest punishment)."[87]

In sum, the La Forest account raises as many problems as it solves. It might be argued that the contortions of the opinion flow from the need to counter the majority opinion in the context of the specific details of the Canadian war crimes legislation. However, the underlying issues debated between the majority and the dissent in *Finta* resonate around the world. The two opinions reflect a deep and determined effort to grapple with the problems posed by the exercise of universal jurisdiction in an actual case. They also expose the absence of consensus among international legal publicists and judges. The time may be thus ripe to propose something of a synthesis of the two approaches.

A Revised Standard Account: Combining International and Domestic Law

The distinction between crimes against international law and the universality principle in international jurisdiction, at least as operationalized in the *Finta* debate, is based on an outdated and essentially false dichotomy. Both accounts of universal jurisdiction presume a relatively fixed relationship between international and domestic law, one top-down and the other bottom-up. A better account would recognize an ongoing, dynamic relationship between international and domestic law, such that both continually feed into and supplement one another. That is the relationship in practice, as both international and domestic lawyers increasingly recognize. It is time to acknowledge it in theory and build on its implications.

Where, as in all cases likely to raise the question of universal jurisdiction, international law purports to regulate individuals as well as states, it makes moral and political sense to take as a point of departure the set of crimes prohibited under the domestic legal systems of virtually all nations.[88] Individuals can be presumed to have a role in defining these offenses through their domestic political systems and to internalize the resulting prohibitions. Where such domestic legal systems overlap, as in the case of murder, torture, kidnapping, or the deliberate shooting of civilians in wartime, international lawmaking rests on a strong foundation.

Moving from the domestic to the international level, states can be understood to come together as the representatives of their peoples and as the collective voice of global humanity to designate some subset of those crimes as worthy of additional prescription and condemnation. The conditions necessary for such a determination will inevitably involve both moral and pragmatic considerations. Designating specific offenses as international crimes must depend not only on the perception that their perpetrators are likely to go unpunished at home, but also on the deep sense that failure to punish them imperils values of justice and humanity as well as stability and security. Once such crimes have been designated, they should be deemed to carry with them a grant of universal jurisdiction, at least in the absence of a specific agreement or practice to the contrary.

The Princeton Principles grant universal jurisdiction over persons duly accused of committing serious crimes under international law.[89] However, the definition of such crimes in Principle 2(1)—piracy, slavery, war crimes, crimes against peace, crimes against humanity, genocide, and torture— selects offenses that are almost certain to be criminalized under the domestic law of virtually all nations. The Princeton Principles thus allow for any state to adopt the revised standard account suggested here as the basis for national legislation implementing the Principles. Such legislation need only set forth the presumed relationship between domestic and international law. Further, all states can be guided by this two-step process in defining additional crimes under international law, as envisioned by Principle 2(2).

The prosecution of crimes under international law, as defined here, can thus take place at the international or the domestic level.[90] Back at the domestic level, however, the particular domestic source of these international crimes can be recognized and relied on. The domestic criminal code is part of the basis for the prosecution. As Judge Vandermeersch recognized in the Belgian *Pinochet* case, it should not displace the international definition of the crime, but may supplement it.[91] Thus if the defendant cannot be shown to have the *mens rea* necessary to convict him of an international crime such as a crime against humanity, a war crime, or genocide, he can be prosecuted for the lesser included domestic offense. This was the result in *Djajic*,[92] a case based on the events in the former Yugoslavia that was ultimately decided by the Supreme Court of Bavaria. The defendant was found not to have the requisite *mens rea* for genocide, but was nevertheless found guilty of abetting murder and assisting murder.[93] These offenses were in turn punishable by Germany because they took place in the context of international armed conflict, putting the victims within the protections of Article 4 of the Fourth Geneva Convention.[94]

Conversely, Principle 3 authorizes national courts to rely on universal jurisdiction even in the absence of national legislation. Such reliance may be necessary, but from the perspective of encouraging a dynamic relationship between national and international law, it should be a stopgap measure.

Courts may have to take the lead in the absence of legislative action, but legislatures should then respond to judicial action and canvass both international law and the laws of other countries on universal jurisdiction before adopting a national statute. National judges will then be much more comfortable in building on the initial precedent. Principle 9 explicitly exhorts states to take this step.

A similar conception of an interactive relationship between domestic and international law should take place regarding procedural issues. Where international law has not specified the applicable procedure, the court should be able to fill the gaps with standard domestic procedures. Conversely, where a domestic statute has superseded applicable international law, it should be understood to have been enacted against a backdrop of international law that itself draws on domestic law. Domestic courts should thus be able to rely on international law where possible to fill gaps in domestic legislation or resolve ambiguities.

This account avoids many of the difficulties of the standard account. It acknowledges the moral dimension of international crimes while nevertheless anchoring them firmly in both domestic and international lawmaking processes. It may also help alleviate some of the concerns about needing positive law on which to found a prosecution, although such concerns are likely to continue as a reflection of fundamental concerns about judicial legitimacy and the need for protection against abuse of judicial power. Above all, this account provides a fallback for cases in which an attempted prosecution for a crime against international law fails or falls short. Incorporation of international crimes tends to be ad hoc.[95] This approach will ensure that courts and executives are not left without a means of filling in uncontemplated gaps in domestic law. Surely convicting an individual accused of war crimes or crimes against humanity for multiple murder, confinement, or kidnapping is better than no conviction at all.

Finally, this account improves on the La Forest account because it rejects the strict substance versus procedure and morality versus pragmatism distinctions that La Forest seeks to draw. It recognizes instead that international and domestic law interact in response to all these issues and concerns. It also allays the concern that judges take too little notice of the international legal and political context in which they are operating. The danger of believing that judges are simply applying domestic law is that this undermines the traditional boundaries on the exercise of jurisdiction and minimizes the offence being punished.

The synthesis offered here instead recognizes a distinct and critical role for the international legal system, one that buttresses and builds on domestic legal systems rather than potentially undermining domestic judicial legitimacy. The international law version of the crime is based on the consensus of as many nations as possible, a consensus that may water down what any one nation would want but that adds the imprimatur of the international community. The words of Judge Moore, dissenting in the *Lotus* case, are particularly apposite here in reference to piracy, which he, unlike many others, defines as an international crime: ". . . in the case of what is known as piracy by law of nations, there has been conceded a universal jurisdiction, under which the person charged with the offence may be tried and punished by any nation into whose jurisdiction he may come. I say 'piracy by law of nations,' because the municipal laws of many States denominate and punish as 'piracy' numerous acts which do not constitute piracy by law of nations, and which therefore are not of universal cognizance, so as to be punishable by all nations." He goes on to note that although domestic statutes "may provide for its punishment, it is an offence against the law of nations. . . ." It is the status of piracy as an international crime that allows the designation of the pirate "as the enemy of all mankind—*hostis humanis generis*—whom any nation may *in the interest of all* capture and punish."[96] Designation of a crime at international law thus assures each nation that they are acting on behalf of all others.

In sum, a more helpful account of universal jurisdiction emerges from a more subtle and complex understanding of the relationship between domestic and international law. Crimes recognized in domestic systems worldwide remain the starting point. Recognizing the role that domestic legal systems play without negating the role of international law in defining distinct and separate crimes legitimizes universal jurisdiction by simultaneous reference to a world of multiple polities and a global moral and legal community. At the same time, it provides more natural checks on the exercise of that jurisdiction. The account is one of a complex interaction of domestic law feeding into international law, which in turn both empowers and constrains domestic courts to develop their own synthesis of international and domestic rules and procedures. Many of the contributions to this volume emphasize this dynamic.[97] National legislators adopting the principles, and national judges seeking to apply them, should rely and build upon it.

A Process Solution: Global Judicial Dialogue

The revised standard account of universal jurisdiction developed above inevitably leaves many specific questions unanswered. However clear and compelling the underlying principles, they cannot generate clear and simple rules for courts grappling with many different cases in many different national legal systems. Different states have different constitutional structures. Further, despite the concentration in this article on the role of courts, courts are only one of the set of domestic actors involved in prosecutions based on universal jurisdiction. Consider the role of the prosecution—which in some countries comprises part of the executive branch and in others part of the judiciary—of other members of the executive branch and of the legislature.

In *Finta,* the executive may have been far more willing to prosecute than the court's final decision allowed. However, in most cases it is far more likely that the executive will be less willing to prosecute on the basis of universal jurisdiction than the judiciary. The legal procedure for initiating and pursuing criminal prosecutions may, therefore, affect the likelihood of such prosecutions. In Spain, the prosecuting judge responsible for the Pinochet extradition request was acting against the wishes of the Spanish government. Cases in France and Belgium have been initiated by victims of the alleged offenders and pursued by investigating judges with a central role in the case. By contrast, prosecutions in the United Kingdom are dependent on the independent Crown Prosecution Service, bound by the alternative principles of public interest and the likelihood of success. Decisions are discretionary and need not be explained.[98] The executive branch in all States is frequently faced with different pressures and issues, some of which are legitimate in the political arena but cannot be taken into account in the courtroom.[99]

Further, as was evident in the *Finta* case and the several Australian cases discussed above, domestic courts are often faced with trying to parse the intentions of the legislature. Dramatic prosecutions such as the Pinochet case, together with the well-publicized activity of international criminal tribunals, help mobilize public opinion in favor of legislation directly enabling, but also constraining, the exercise of universal jurisdiction by domestic courts. The actual prosecution of cases based on universal jurisdiction is a thus complex interaction between different state institutions. While national courts cannot rely on domestic law alone, they must operate within their own domestic framework, with international law only one factor in the decision-making process.

The alternative to generating uniform and determinate rules to address the myriad questions courts will inevitably face is a process solution. The revised standard account of universal jurisdiction assumes and thereby constitutes a community of domestic and international judges who bear equal responsibility for making universal jurisdiction operational.[100] In this context, judges can legitimately look to what other national judges are doing as well as to the decisions of international tribunals. The jurisprudence that is emerging is fact-based, contextual, and case-specific. At the same time, however, all judges seeking to exercise universal jurisdiction grapple with common problems. All would benefit from a more institutionalized process of transjudicial communication and consultation.

Principle 4 provides a doctrinal framework for this institutionalized process. Under the heading "Obligation to Support Accountability," it requires "states" to "provide[] other states investigating or prosecuting [crimes under international law] with all available means of administrative and judicial assistance."[101] This provision of course applies to prosecutors and other members of the executive branch engaged in criminal investigations; it could also apply to legislators, where national legislation authorizing such assistance is required. But it is most likely to apply to judges, and can be read as encouraging them to seek assistance from one another. The next step is to encourage them to see themselves as part of a broader community and common enterprise serving the ends of both national and international justice.

Courts should also be encouraged to take account of other courts' decisions, recognizing the accounts that form the basis for decisions and working toward answers to some of the most difficult issues. To some extent, this process has already begun, as the number of cases has grown in recent years.[102] The need for this dialogue and the likelihood of it happening will only increase as states enact legislation to implement the Statute of the International Criminal Court, with its provisions on complementary jurisdiction. This substantive interaction will contribute substantially to the international legislative process. In Diane Orentlicher's phrase, the judges involved will be "constructing a genuinely common code of humanity."[103]

Since domestic structures play such an important role, complete convergence is both impossible and undesirable. Rather, what is sought is a constructive dialogue that will take into account international law, comparative law and domestic law. Judges looking outside their own legal system can borrow one another's approaches and solutions to specific problems only as persuasive authority. It could be immensely valuable, however, even for judges to consider and reject approaches adopted by their foreign, regional and international counterparts, at least to the extent that they provided reasons for the rejection. The result could be a process of thoughtful convergence and informed divergence that provides for plenty of experimentation, including mistakes and rethinking.[104]

As judges participate in this global judicial dialogue, they will enhance their own legitimacy and create a sphere in which they are seen to operate within a legal rather than a political context.[105] This legitimacy will enable courts to expand their recognition of universal jurisdiction and develop constraints on the exercise of this jurisdiction that do not cut it off completely as a basis for prosecution. At the same time, the principles and approaches on which they converge will renew and invigorate the domestic sources of the international lawmaking process.

A process solution is a solution that has the potential to transform the imposition of multiple limits on universal jurisdiction by multiple national courts into a common global search for solutions to the problems that the exercise of such jurisdiction inevitably poses. As stated at the outset, universal jurisdiction is an awesome power that inevitably calls for limits. In fact, however, an equally pressing need is to find ways to overcome many of the limits that have already been imposed. The aim is to construct a process to help courts strike a balance among considerations that too often appear to conflict with each other: the desire to prosecute heinous international crimes versus the need to ensure that the defendant receives a fair and just process; international legal obligations versus domestic legal requirements; and the pragmatic versus the moral foundations for the exercise of universal jurisdiction.

Appendix:
Guidance for National Judges

Principle 1

Primacy of Domestic Law

1. These principles are intended to provide guidance to judges confronted with a case involving universal jurisdiction in their national courts and are without prejudice to the domestic law of the forum State.

Principle 2

Applying Universal Jurisdiction

1. Judges should be guided by relevant international law when presiding over a case involving universal jurisdiction in their national courts, insofar as that international law does not directly conflict with the domestic law of the forum State.
2. For the purposes of this principle, relevant international law should be understood to include conventions that deal with crimes subject to universal jurisdiction and customary international law. In recognition of the role of international and foreign national courts in the elaboration of international law regarding universal jurisdiction, relevant international law should also be understood to include decisions of such courts addressing equivalent questions in cases involving universal jurisdiction.
3. In determining the content of relevant international law for the purposes of this principle, judges are encouraged to consult with international law experts.
4. In deciding whether or not to draw on or rely on decisions of foreign national courts, judges should take account of any relevant differences between the legal system of the forum State and the legal system of the foreign court concerned.

Principle 3

Procedural Questions

1. Where the law of the forum State is insufficient to decide procedural questions arising in a case involving universal jurisdiction, judges dealing with such a case in their national courts are encouraged to consult relevant international law when seeking solutions to these questions.
2. For the purposes of this principle, relevant international law should be understood to include conventions that deal with crimes subject to universal jurisdiction as well as customary international law. In recognition of the role of international and foreign national courts in the elaboration of international law regarding universal jurisdiction, relevant international law should also be understood to include decisions of such courts addressing equivalent questions in cases involving universal jurisdiction.
3. In determining the content of international law for the purposes of this principle, judges are encouraged to consult with and be guided by international law experts.
4. In deciding whether or not to draw on or rely on decisions of foreign courts, judges should take account of any relevant differences between the legal system of the forum State and the legal system of the foreign court concerned.

Chapter 10
Universal Jurisdiction, National Amnesties, and Truth Commissions: Reconciling the Irreconcilable

Leila Nadya Sadat

Introduction

It is generally believed that the investigation and criminal prosecution of those who have ordered or have committed human rights atrocities is a desirable goal and may even constitute an international legal obligation. Requiring accountability for war crimes is posited as a remedy to impunity as well as a necessary, if not sufficient, condition for the reestablishment of peace.[1] Yet there are many challenges to the ideal of accountability: the desire to trade peace for justice in order to end a conflict more quickly, even if temporarily; the overwhelming task of bringing individual cases against hundreds or even thousands of individuals implicated in the commission of genocide or other mass atrocities; arguments that criminal trials may be counterproductive in bringing about reconciliation; and even the passage of time, which may cause authorities to hesitate in pursuing justice or extinguish otherwise valid cases through the application of statutes of limitations.[2]

The first two sections of this essay quickly survey these conflicting themes. The third evaluates the treatment of amnesties and other challenges to accountability from both a legal and a normative perspective, keeping in mind the principal goal of this project—to formulate principles that might guide or inform the responsible exercise of universal jurisdiction by states.[3] Ultimately, the issue becomes whether amnesties or other obstacles to prosecution created by one state have any binding effect outside of that jurisdiction. This problem has both a fascinating theoretical dimension and a practical consequence: putting it simply, can the beneficiaries of an amnesty (or some other bar to prosecution) travel abroad without losing the impunity they were granted at home?

The answer, it seems, subject to certain caveats, is no. Although truth commissions, lustration laws, and reparations have an important place in addressing human rights violations, they do so as a complement to legal accountability, which remains the foundation of international justice.[4] Realists would argue, of course, that this "legalistic" approach to the problem of atrocities is either hopelessly naive or simply wrong, that in the anarchy existent in the international order, law and legal aspirations have little place, and may even be counterproductive. Others have ably refuted the realist challenge to international law while at the same time pointing out the usefulness of realism as a form of auto-critique.[5] Rather than attempting to resolve this long-running *débat des sourds,* I suggest a jurists approach that employs a conflict-of-law analysis to accommodate the competing values and interests at stake. This mechanism preserves the essential role that international criminal accountability serves while at the same time accounting for the inescapable political realities that infuse the international legal order. The methodology suggested is that states confronted with challenges to accountability should treat them as presumptively invalid, a presumption that can be overcome if the state granting the immunity in question does so pursuant to a process that does not undermine the quest for accountability as a whole. In particular, blanket amnesties and any grant of immunity to a former leader should most likely be rejected out of hand.

Combating Impunity for International Crimes: The Accountability Paradigm

Devastated, demoralized, and depressed by war and the commission of atrocities on a massive scale, humankind has left the twentieth century desperately seeking new institutional and legal mechanisms capable of restraining its darkest impulses. The gravity of the problem cannot be overstated: it is estimated that 170 million people have been killed in more than 250 conflicts that have occurred since World War II.[6] The most obvious response would be to stop the atrocities before they have occurred or while they are occurring.[7] Unfortunately, the international legal community has not yet developed either the political institutions or the legal and logistical infrastructure that could effectively halt or prevent pathological disturbances of international *ordre public.*

One of the primary obstacles to establishing the rule of law has been the culture of impunity that has prevailed to date. Genocidal leaders flout their crimes openly, unconcerned about international reactions, which they suspect will probably range from willful blindness (at best, from their perspective) to diplomatic censure (at worst). Yet as Mary Robinson, UN high commissioner for human rights, recently noted: "Where domestic law and order has broken down, individuals may feel that they can commit even the most atrocious crimes without fear of legal sanction. When this happens, there is an urgent need to re-establish the principle of individual responsibility for crimes. If serious human rights violations are not addressed and a climate of impunity is permitted to continue, then the effect will be to stoke the fires of long-term social conflict. Where a community splits along religious or ethnic lines, such conflict can vent itself through cycles of vengeance over decades, and even centuries."[8]

The remedy proposed has been the establishment of international legal regimes and, more recently, international institutions that can bring about the transition from a culture of impunity to one demanding accountability. Although mechanisms such as truth commissions, reparations to victims, and civil proceedings have been proposed and used to address the problems suffered by societies victimized by mass atrocities, a cornerstone of the effort to combat impunity has been the traditional framework of the criminal law: the condemnation of certain behavior as *criminal*, not simply a breach of treaty or customary international law obligations, and the imposition of individual criminal responsibility therefore.[9]

This use of the criminal law is not accidental. Standard criminology was developed in the context of behavior that attacks norms established by the state, not in the context, as is so often the case in international crimes, of normatively unacceptable behavior *by* the state. Nevertheless, the international community, frustrated with the inability of civil sanctions, military reprisals, and the doctrine of state responsibility to deter atrocities,[10] has increasingly moved toward a criminal model that treats the commission of atrocities as unacceptably disruptive behavior, for which *individual* offenders must be tried and punished.[11]

Modern theories of criminal justice generally justify the punishment of criminals either on the basis of some benefit society can expect to receive as a result—to deter other criminals or to rehabilitate or incapacitate the offender (utilitarian theory)—or because the criminal "deserves" punishment for the injury he has inflicted on society (retributive justice).[12] Both utilitarian and retributive aspirations are found in international criminal justice. Certainly it is hoped, although not empirically demonstrable, that erecting a system of international criminal justice (including national and international prosecutions) will prevent the reoccurrence of abuses and assist in repairing the havoc wreaked upon society thereby.[13] The criminal justice apparatus is also designed to ensure respect for the rule of law as a value in and of itself.[14] Finally, by channeling accountability and punishment through an official mechanism, society hopes to avoid individual vigilantism as well as to provide an impartial forum where individuals accused of crimes during a prior regime may have their cases heard, with all the due process rights necessary to ensure that their treatment is not tantamount to a purge.[15] That is, the legitimacy of the trials require that the offenders receive all the benefits of due process and legality they themselves denied to their victims.[16] Public trials occurring in courts using rules of evidence and formalized procedures are invested with a solemnity and transparency often absent from other venues. It is hoped that this will not only provide a forum for the punishment of a particular defendant but also an arena in which the victims may be heard and an "official" version of the truth recorded.[17] In addition, there is no doubt that by employing the *criminal law*—the most coercive form of power generally available to a society to regulate social behavior—the international community (and its component states) is constructing a normative discourse that expresses deep condemnation of the behavior as well as support for its victims. As one scholar recently argued, the "documentary record clearly shows that the motivations for the trials at Leipzig, Constantinople, Nuremberg, Tokyo, The Hague and Arusha were not merely to purge. Victorious liberals saw their foes as war criminals deserving of just punishment."[18]

Challenges to the Accountability Paradigm: The Peace versus Justice Debate

The quest for accountability rests on the premise that there can be no real peace without justice. But accountability confronts many challenges. Because space is limited, this essay concentrates on some of the more serious challenges to accountability that may affect the exercise of universal jurisdiction by states. These include national amnesties, truth commissions, conditional amnesties, and international realpolitik.[19] Each of these can be seen as a variant on a common theme: is obtaining justice consistent with restoring peace?

National Amnesties

Amnesty is essentially an act of oblivion.[20] Derived from the Greek word *amnestia,* meaning forgetfulness, "[a]mnesty . . . connotes that the offender's crime has been overlooked because that course of action benefits the public welfare more than punishment would."[21] Unlike pardons, which imply forgiveness of the offender and are generally particularized in nature, amnesties typically apply to groups of offenders, and neither eradicate the offense nor the moral guilt that might be associated therewith.[22] They are thus practical, if somewhat unsatisfactory solutions to the problem of mass atrocities: justice is traded for peace, or at least a temporary truce, in the hopes that the atrocities will stop and the society will be able to move on.

Domestically, two principal justifications have been advanced for offering blanket amnesties for human rights violations committed by a regime in power against its citizens.[23] First, dictators and military leaders have often demanded impunity as a condition of relinquishing power.[24] In response, societies eager to end a conflict and fearful of repercussions from attempts to pursue accountability may shy away from criminal trials or other proceedings to hold responsible those accused of committing human rights violations in the former regime. New governments may also feel too fragile to take on former dictators and their followers.[25] Thus some societies emerging from periods of repression, such as El Salvador,[26] have offered blanket amnesties to perpetrators.[27] Morever, even without the passage of amnesty laws, nations may grant perpetrators amnesty de facto by simply failing to pursue them.[28]

Second, even if a new regime is committed to prosecuting past international crimes, it may face considerable obstacles in doing so. Rwanda is a case in point. As a result of the genocide, over 80 percent of Rwanda's justice system personnel, including judges and magistrates, simply and tragically disappeared.[29] Moreover, the judicial system faced serious shortages of resources, basic facilities, and equipment.[30] Rwanda attempted to address the problem by adopting a law under which the offenders would be punished that effectuated a four-part triage of offenses, ranging from the most serious[31] to the least egregious—those defendants who had committed crimes against property.[32] The law also provided for a "confession and guilty plea procedure" that would permit offenders in the second, third, and fourth categories to obtain significant reductions in penalties in exchange for a full confession.[33] Unfortunately, as at least some commentators have suggested, the sheer numbers of prisoners (estimated to be more than 100,000 at times), as well as the fact that the planners of the genocide are still reported to exert influence over the prison population,[34] rendered the confession and guilt procedures ineffective.[35] Finally, many of the trials which have occurred under the new law were severely criticized as unfair. Defendants often had little or no access to legal counsel during critical periods of the investigation or trial; trials have been unduly rapid and conducted in an atmosphere hostile to the defendants and have often resulted in death sentences that have expeditiously been carried out.[36] In such a case it is unclear whether imposing individual criminal responsibility is a viable strategy, an all-too-common scenario in cases involving mass atrocities.[37] Yet, as one author noted, to release the detainees and "admit that the task of processing the cases is impossible" would "itself constitute a major human rights violation" by promoting impunity.[38] Avoiding some of these difficulties, of course, is one reason the establishment of an international criminal tribunal for Rwanda appeared desirable,[39] but that tribunal has faced problems of its own.[40] In July 1999, Rwanda responded with the creation of "Gacaca Tribunals" comprised of ordinary citizens who will hear cases involving category 2, 3, and 4 offenses under the genocide law. Although based upon the traditional societal practice of Gacaca, the procedure created departs considerably from the traditional model, which was developed to handle property or marital disputes, not criminal trials or genocide. Under Gacaca, suspects will be brought before nineteen-member lay tribunals sitting in the village where the crimes occurred. Anyone can speak for or against those charged, and the accused may confess and seek forgiveness or deny the charges and defend themselves. The accused will not be protected by many of the rights normally available to criminal defendants, however, leading some international observers to express concern about the ultimate fairness of the result.[41] Rwanda's pursuit of the Gacaca process, however, suggests the continued importance of accountability and justice to Rwandan society.[42]

National Truth Commissions

Truth commissions need not pose a challenge to accountability, for they do not prejudice the subsequent application of the criminal law.[43] Indeed, truth commissions may facilitate accountability by serving as precursors to the adoption of measures of accountability that may include reparations, restitution, civil remedies, lustration laws, and even criminal prosecutions. Rather than focusing on individual criminality, truth commissions attempt to focus on the overall pattern of abuses occurring under a prior regime. They are thus sometimes referred to as the truth phase, after which the "justice phase" can begin.[44] Thus truth commissions are not alternatives to punishment. Some have argued that truth commissions generally have had a positive effect, "often reducing tension and increasing national reconciliation, and perhaps increasing the understanding of and respect for human rights issues by the general public and political leaders alike."[45] Others emphasize their therapeutic powers, as a form of restorative justice, asserting that because victims may be able to narrate the account of their victimization without the cumbersome baggage and ritualized procedures of the criminal trial, they serve a "victim-centered" vision of justice much more than criminal trials could.[46] Nevertheless, truth commissions may threaten accountability where they are established by unrepentant governments either to manipulate public perceptions at home or abroad, or attempt to whitewash past atrocities, as was the case with the first truth commission established by Idi Amin in Uganda in 1974, which was established partly as a result of international pressure, and disregarded thereafter, as Amin continued his "brutal" rule.[47] The same could be said, to a lesser degree, of the truth commission established in Chad in 1990, which, charged with the investigation of the Habré government's "Crimes and Misappropriations," was given for its headquarters space in the former secret detention center of the security forces where some of the worst abuses had occurred, thereby deterring many former victims from testifying before it. Moreover, although the commission "named names" and published a report, its findings were largely ignored, and it has been suggested that the commission was established largely to improve the new president's image.[48]

The South African Exception—Conditional Amnesties

Finally, the South African experience, as many have noted, has been unique, in part because the process embarked upon was established by a democratically elected legislature that included representatives of apartheid's victims and was not simply a matter of executive (or international) fiat.[49] The political transition from a regime of apartheid to a government guaranteeing full civil and political rights to all its citizens gave rise to the establishment of South Africa's Truth and Reconciliation Commission. As part of a negotiated settlement with the leaders of the apartheid regime, the 1993 interim constitution for the Republic of South Africa called for amnesty to be granted "in respect of acts, omissions and offences associated with political objectives committed in the course of the conflicts of the past."[50] Implementing this provision led to extensive debate between those who favored, at one extreme, blanket amnesties, and those who were opposed to amnesties of any kind.[51] The body that was finally established[52] attempted to forge a compromise between these two extremes.[53] As Richard Goldstone has written, it was "a political compromise more than a moral imperative."[54] Composed of three committees,[55] it was the task of the commission to "overcome the injustices of the past by promoting national unity and reconciliation,"[56] a goal to be achieved, according to the Promotion of National Unity and Reconciliation Act of 1995, which established the commission, by accomplishing four tasks:

> to provide for the investigation and establishment of as complete a picture as possible of the nature, causes and extent of gross violations of human rights committed during the period from March 1, 1960 to December 6, 1993, as well as the fate or whereabouts of the victims of such violations;
> to grant amnesty to persons who make full disclosure of all the relevant facts relating to acts associated with a political objective committed in the course of the conflicts of the past during such period;
> to afford victims an opportunity to relate the violations they suffered and take measures aimed to grant reparation to and rehabilitate and restore the human and civil dignity of victims; and
> to make a report about such violations and victims and recommend measures aimed at preventing such violations in the future.[57]

Pursuant to the act, amnesties may be granted only if the act, omission, or offence was committed with a political objective, in the course of the conflicts of the past.[58] Moreover, the applicant for amnesty must make full disclosure of all relevant facts.[59] The grounds for determining whether a crime was committed with a political objective are similar to those used in extradition law to decide if "an offense in respect of which extradition is sought is a political offense."[60] As of November 1, 2000, of the 7,112 amnesty applications that had been dealt with by the Amnesty Committee, 849 had been granted, and 5,392 had been rejected.[61] Those who do not come forward remain open to civil suits and criminal prosecutions.[62] Because the process became "judicialized" due to concerns about the due process rights of those named as alleged perpetrators, the commission hearings and amnesty applications came "to resemble criminal trials, with both victims or their families and the alleged perpetrators of human rights violations represented by lawyers determined to drag out the examination and cross-examination of witnesses."[63]

The Truth and Reconciliation Commission issued its report to Pres. Nelson Mandela on October 28, 1998.[64] An examination of public discussions on the work of the commission and the scholarly response to the amnesties granted by the commission suggest that reactions have been mixed.[65] The failure of former president Pieter W. Botha, many former cabinet ministers, and military officers to appear was disappointing, as was the acquittal of the former minister of defense, Magnus Malan, and his generals for murder arising from the KwaMakutha massacre. Moreover, most of those applying for amnesty were relatively low-level perpetrators, as opposed to high government officials.[66] On the other hand, prosecutors have brought cases against many who did not apply for amnesty, suggesting that the commission was not an attempt to whitewash crimes but to give those who committed them with a political motive the opportunity to avoid criminal sanctions at the cost of making a full disclosure of the facts. Additionally, justice in the South African context, many have argued, was restorative, not retributive, in nature, more appropriately suited to African, as opposed to Western culture.[67] Recent scandals involving a pardon of thirty-three prisoners by Pres. Thabo Mbeki, however, suggests that the ultimate success of the TRC is not yet assured.[68] As the South African minister of justice recently summed up:

We have a tradition of violence, a culture of violence, a history of violence, a history of people taking the law into their own hands, and a history of people who have not been held accountable for what they did. . . . So ending violence is a priority. Ending the culture of violence is a priority . . . if we committed human rights violations during the course of conducting our struggle, we must be held accountable because that is the only way we will send a signal to our people that every person who commits a violation in the future will be held accountable. *That is the only way we will establish peace and stability in our country and create an environment of safety and security for all our people* [emphasis added].[69]

International Realpolitik

The challenge here is not the fear of a particular society from sitting dictators, or the problem of mass atrocities flooding an inadequate criminal justice system. Rather, international negotiators eager to bring about a settlement in the hopes of ending a bloody conflict will often ignore calls for justice.[70] Negotiators in the Bosnian conflagration thus felt obligated to treat with Slobodan Milosevic, in spite of expert opinion and substantial evidence that implicated his leadership in the ethnic cleansing operations of the former Yugoslavia. Similarly, the international community negotiated with Foday Sankoh to try to bring about a settlement in the Sierra Leone conflict.[71] In both cases, as is well known, the two leaders went on, not to bring peace to their nations, but to renew their attacks on their countrymen and women, attacks for which both leaders were subsequently indicted.[72]

The political debate between the *realpoliticians* and those favoring accountability is paralleled by an academic debate along the same lines. Most scholarship has favored, and even advocated, adoption of the accountability paradigm in one form or another.[73] The strongest proponents of this view not only support the utility of criminal trials but also suggest a duty under both customary international law and treaties to try offenders or extradite them to jurisdictions where they will be tried.[74]

Recently, however, others have challenged the accountability paradigm. Some are skeptical of the utility value of international criminal trials, taking issue both with the normative claims for their value as well as their actual impact.[75] Others are critical of the two ad hoc tribunals, particularly the ICTR, suggesting that international criminal trials may even undermine "the preservation of accurate collective memory, the national rule of law, [and . . .] the realization of justice."[76] A different variation of this critique suggests that international law enforcement is so sporadic that it is unlikely to deter, and so plagued with "liberal" safeguards for criminal defendants, that international criminals, who often represent state power, are able to thwart the international tribunals' ability to mete out justice.[77] Finally, some recognize the value of criminal trials in theory but suggest that truth commissions that promote healing and truth telling may be more useful for societies than criminal trials, which they believe may be, in contrast, divisive, expensive, and possibly unfair.[78]

The Implication for Amnesties and Other Challenges to Accountability on the Exercise of Universal Jurisdiction by States

This section will: first, consider the nature of any legal obligations to disregard amnesties or other challenges to accountability; second, consider the desirability of accepting domestic immunization from prosecution for international crimes; and finally, third, propose how a state, confronted with an amnesty decision or similar obstacle to prosecution from a third state (or international body), might resolve the situation.

The Validity of Amnesties in International Law

As regards the validity of amnesties for war crimes, most commentators appear to make a distinction between international and noninternational armed conflict. With respect to international armed conflict, although amnesty clauses for war crimes committed in international armed conflict were generally incorporated in peace agreements prior to World War I,[79] they were vigorously rejected thereafter. The decision by the Allied powers to prosecute war criminals following the First World War (with little actual success) and following the Second World War brought about the expectation that war criminals would be punished, an expectation codified in the four Geneva Conventions of 1949, as discussed previously, and expanded upon in the 1977 Protocol Additional to the Geneva Conventions of 12 August 1949, and Relating to the Protection of Victims of International Armed Conflicts (Protocol I),[80] which extends the grave breaches regime substantially.[81] It is generally agreed that these conventions are now a source of customary international law. Thus, while it is certainly possible that only the substantive provisions of the conventions and not their procedural provisions have risen to the level of custom, most commentators have accepted that, at least with respect to war crimes committed in international armed conflict that fall within the grave breaches regime, a fair (but not watertight) case can be made not only for the existence of a customary international law duty to prosecute or extradite the offender but also, as a corollary,[82] for a rule prohibiting blanket amnesties.[83]

As regards noninternational armed conflicts, at least some take the view that general amnesties are not only permitted but are encouraged by existing law.[84] This view relies upon Article 6(5) of Protocol 2 relating to the Protection of Victims of Noninternational Armed Conflict, which provides: "At the end of hostilities, the authorities in power shall endeavor to grant the broadest possible amnesty to persons who have participated in the armed conflict, or those deprived of their liberty for reasons related to the armed conflict, whether they are interned or detained."[85]

Certainly, one could take the position that this language was intended to apply to those combating the state, not those acting as its agents.[86] Nonetheless, some courts have taken a different view. For example, a lower South African court held that this provision permitted the South African Truth and Reconciliation Commission to grant amnesties in regard to human rights violations committed under the apartheid regime.[87] The South African Constitutional Court affirmed, stating: "[In the case of] violent acts perpetrated during . . . conflicts which take place within the territory of a sovereign state in consequence of a struggle between the armed forces of that state and other dissident armed forces operating under responsible command, within such a state . . . there is no obligation on the part of a contracting state to ensure the prosecution of those who might have performed acts of violence or other acts which would ordinarily be characterized as serious invasions of human rights."[88]

This decision has been criticized on the grounds that it fails to analyze the crimes committed as crimes against humanity (of which apartheid is clearly one) and to establish whether there exists any customary international law duty to punish offenders of a prior regime for such crimes.[89] This criticism is consistent with the view, held by some, that there is an international duty to punish offenders after a civil war as a necessary corollary of the need to protect human rights.[90]

With respect to crimes against humanity and genocide, some commentators have strenuously argued for the existence of a duty to investigate and punish human rights violations committed under a prior regime.[91] Certainly, the Genocide Convention and the Torture Convention suggest that a duty is assumed by states parties to those conventions to pursue and punish (or extradite, in the case of the Torture Convention) those who violate the conventions' terms.[92] However, even those treaties are unclear as to the precise modalities of such punishment. They would thus appear to leave a certain degree of discretion to national legal systems in their implementation.

As to a generalized customary international law rule requiring punishment, the evidence of state practice seems weak. As Naomi Roht-Arrizia notes, in general, the human rights instruments that guarantee human beings a right to bodily integrity and to be free from torture and other abuses do not typically, by their terms, require states to investigate and prosecute abuses of rights.[93] A handful of decisions, however, emanating from the Human Rights Committee established to monitor compliance with the International Covenant on Civil and Political Rights and the Inter-American Court of Human Rights, charged with application of the American Convention on Human Rights, have imposed affirmative obligations on states to investigate human rights abuses stemming from provisions in the treaties that require states to respect and ensure to all persons subject to their jurisdiction the free and full exercise of the rights and freedoms contained in the treaties.[94] The European Commission of Human Rights has, similarly, suggested that states may have affirmative obligations to prevent and remedy breaches of the convention in quite limited circumstances, suggesting in one case that criminal prosecution could be required as part of that obligation.[95] Although these decisions are highly significant, they cannot, without more, establish that a duty to investigate and a prohibition against amnesties have become rules crystallized as a matter of general customary international law.[96] Many countries have granted amnesties to the perpetrators of atrocities under a prior regime, and while some lower national courts have overturned them, they have generally been sustained by higher courts.[97] Indeed, the international community "warmly welcomed" the decision of South Africa to pursue a course involving conditional amnesties "thereby casting doubts on the existence of an obligation upon successor regimes to prosecute those suspected of having committed international crimes."[98] Of course, the situation might have been different had South Africa, instead of adopting a course involving conditional amnesties, adopted a policy of blanket amnesties.[99]

The Rome Statute for the International Criminal Court is explicit on certain challenges to accountability such as superior orders,[100] head of state immunity,[101] and statute of limitations[102] but is silent both as to any duty to prosecute and with regard to amnesties.[103] Although the issue was raised during the Rome Conference at which the statute was adopted, no clear consensus developed among the delegates as to how the question should be resolved. This too suggests that customary international law has not yet crystallized on this point. According to the chairman of the Conference, the question was purposely left open by the drafters: while the statute does not condone the use of amnesties by its terms, presumably the prosecutor has the power to accept them if doing so would be "in the interests of justice."[104]

Are amnesties or other challenges to accountability generally desirable, from a normative perspective?

Although it is unclear whether international law clearly prohibits blanket amnesties for international crimes, it seems that if it does not already it should.[105] Blanket amnesties undermine the rule of law and are, for the most part, simply self-serving declarations by government officials exempting themselves from the reach of the law. They represent an attempt to trump the application of rules of law and as such constitute a threat to both the legitimacy and the fairness of the rules.[106] Justice Richard Goldstone has advocated this position, at least as regards international prosecutions, suggesting that although it would be appropriate to consider amnesty proceedings on a case by case basis, they should have "no standing" in international law and would not be a bar to prosecution in any court other than the court of the country granting the amnesty.[107] Moreover, the argument that amnesties are necessary due to the sheer volume of potential criminal cases does not appear to refute the overwhelming evidence that addressing the past is necessary for countries to break vicious cycles of human rights abuses—that there can be no real peace without justice. As one Rwandan lawyer poignantly stated: "We are in the process of falling into the trap that these murderers have set for us. This genocide is distinguished by the fact that a maximum number of people have been implicated in the killings—there is talk of a million killers. The Hutu extremists estimated that no court in the world could judge that many criminals, and they bet that they were going to get off. Are we going to say that they're right?"[108]

Conditional amnesties, such as those granted in the South African case, are of a different kind and would not appear to threaten accountability but to bring it about using a variation of the criminal process. Yet even the amnesty process in South Africa has been criticized, and it may be too early to tell whether the use of limited amnesties is more effective than criminal trials in bringing about reconciliation. Although some have suggested that the South African effort was a creative response to past atrocities,[109] the response within South Africa has arguably been mixed.[110] Due process concerns for perpetrators either named before the commission or brought before the commission have required the process be judicialized to the point that the proceedings resemble trials in fact, and scandals, perhaps inevitable in any human institution, have periodically tainted the process. Moreover, the South African experience is unique in that the two sides negotiated a power transition without the intervention of a civil war and the victory of one side or another. Where a country has emerged from a bloody genocide, as in Rwanda, the idea of amnesties, even conditional amnesties, for the perpetrators of genocide appears unthinkable, particularly for the leaders. If the international community truly believes that some behavior is *criminal,* indeed, pathological, with all that implies, amnesties would appear to be inconsistent with the reestablishment of peace and the rule of law.[111] Even those ultimately supporting the use of conditional amnesties have suggested that criminal trials, particularly international criminal trials, may be appropriate for the leaders, while other mechanisms of accountability, including the use of conditional amnesties, truth commissions, lustration laws, and reparations may be used for lower-level perpetrators.[112]

If these arguments prove persuasive as to the dubious value of immunities granted at the domestic level, they appear equally fruitful in evaluating international immunity agreements. Indeed, the case for trading justice for peace to bring about the international settlement of disputes appears to be quite weak. In addition to the moral repugnancy of turning a blind eye to the commission of atrocities, it may well be contrary to self-interest. Examples such as Milosevic and Sankoh suggest that granting impunity, rather than definitively settling a conflict, simply encourages the criminal behavior to reappear in the future. If one of the most important purposes of the criminal law is to remove dangerous individuals from society, it suggests that Slobodan Milosevic and Foday Sankoh should have been tried and indicted years ago.[113] Following the de facto immunity Milosevic received at Dayton,[114] he was finally indicted and is now on trial before the International Criminal Tribunal for the Former Yugoslavia for war crimes and crimes against humanity he committed in Kosovo as well as crimes arising out of the earlier conflicts for which he was subsequently indicted. Indeed, one expert recently suggested that the ICTY's failure to indict Milosevic for crimes he allegedly committed in Bosnia emboldened him to commit additional crimes in Kosovo.[115] In addition, it is hard to contemplate why it would be an effective law enforcement practice to offer deals to tyrants and the perpetrators of human rights atrocities while at the same time refusing to treat with terrorists or hostage takers. In domestic law and in other areas of international criminal law, government policy is clear: no ransom for hostages deals[116] and no immunity for terrorists.[117] Finally, if international law and state practice is increasingly moving toward rejecting blanket amnesties per se, and lower-level perpetrators are finding themselves in the dock in increasing numbers, it is difficult to support the notion that the leaders of a genocide or ethnic cleansing should receive immunity as a condition of relinquishing power while their followers will be prosecuted or otherwise held accountable.

Scholars who have critiqued the work of the two ad hoc tribunals or the inappropriateness of criminal trials generally have traditionally suggested that arguments supporting the establishment of a system of international criminal justice lack empirical foundation. Deterrence, they argue, is unproven. Because deterrence is also largely unproven in domestic legal orders,[118] it is not clear whether commentators relying on this argument believe that national, as well as international, criminal justice systems should be abandoned.[119] The key difference may be that if it is true that high probability of punishment generally deters more effectively than a severe sanction rarely applied,[120] the international criminal justice system has not yet reached the stage at which its deterrent value may be fairly assumed, largely to problems of interstate cooperation and state sovereignty. Yet, as Aryeh Neier has remarked, if there appears to be little decisive evidence as to whether disclosing the truth about past abuses or punishing those responsible will necessarily deter future abuses, there is equally little proof that amnesties promote reconciliation whereas criminal trials provoke relapses.[121] With neither side being able to stake a clear claim to the truth, what appears to be at issue is a competition over the values underlying the normative claims. Those supporting the use of criminal trials believe (even if they cannot show empirically) that changing the prevailing discourse about the commission of mass atrocities by condemning the behavior as criminal and punishing those that can be brought to justice will, over time, bring about a decrease in the number of situations involving the commission of mass atrocities. Those rejecting the accountability paradigm tender the opposite view: that "evil will always be with us . . . and genocide and mass violence are their case in chief."[122] Indeed, some suggest that the evils perpetrated are so terrible that "no legal norms can cope."[123] They also note that the much narrower scope of legal responsibility, as opposed to moral responsibility, may lead observers to regard the response of the law with suspicion, or even hostility.[124] Their solution, then, is not to waste resources pursuing the offenders but to establish mechanisms to comfort the victims.[125] It will be of small comfort to the victims, however, if the conflict resurges and leaders who were never punished become increasingly emboldened by their apparent impunity.

Finally, those scholars rejecting an international paradigm of accountability in favor of "bottom-up" solutions fail to recall that it was the inability of national legal systems to address the problem of mass atrocities that goaded the international community into action in the first place. Indeed, they ignore the pivotal role that international law can play in transitional justice. As Ruti Teitel has written, for successor regimes reeling from the shock of political upheaval and faced with the problem that the conduct of perpetrators under the law of the former regime was not only condoned but was lawful behavior, international law may offer an "alternate construction of law that, despite substantial political change, is continuous and enduring."[126] Given that the move to exercise of universal jurisdiction by states and the exercise of international universal jurisdiction by the international community began only a few years ago, it would appear injudicious to abandon the effort at this early stage of development.[127] Even those supporting the South African process concede that it is simply too soon to know whether the process will work.[128] The world has suffered from the reign of impunity since World War II, with the result of millions dead, tortured, or disappeared. Surely more evidence that the accountability paradigm is misguided would be necessary for the international community to conclude that it should be discarded. Rhetoric aside, what appears to be the most productive course is to identify the difficulties involved in the prosecution of war crimes and adopt creative solutions to address them. Thus a recent study examining the relationship between the Yugoslavia Tribunal and the Bosnian legal community identified some problems in the relationship between the tribunal and Bosnian legal professionals,[129] and suggested various means for improving the situation.[130] The difficulties underscored by the report suggest that framing the debate as "utter impunity v. individual trials" is largely counterproductive. Instead, justice and accountability need to "be conceptualized as but one aspect of a larger series of possible interventions."[131]

What considerations should amnesties or other challenges to accountability receive from states seeking to pursue individual perpetrators using universal jurisdiction to do so?

Having concluded that the accountability paradigm is normatively desirable (if not legally required), we are squarely faced with its operation through the mechanism of universal jurisdiction exercised either by states or the international community as a whole. States seeking to exercise universal jurisdiction over perpetrators do so pursuant to internal legislation adapted to that end. If faced with claims of a defendant's immunity, granted by domestic amnesty provisions, how should the state in question (the forum state) respond?[132]

With respect to amnesties or immunities granted by municipal law, the first question to be answered is the difficult question of what law applies. Public international law has not yet developed a system of conflicts of laws to address this question because it is largely operating under the *Lotus* paradigm: every state being an independent sovereign, every state may apply its law to a problem unless there is some rule prohibiting it from doing so.[133] Moreover, many states refuse to enforce foreign public law and would consider criminal proceedings as well as amnesty laws "public," applying what one writer has dubbed the "public law taboo."[134] Yet to the extent that national courts are using universal jurisdiction as the bases for the trial of perpetrators that otherwise have no connection to the forum (as in the *Pinochet* case, for example), they are already applying, through the medium of international law, an exception to the rule that penal jurisdiction is generally territorial in character. Thus the national court exercising universal jurisdiction has a dual role: to apply and interpret national law and to effectively sit as a court of the international community, applying international legal norms. Thus in considering what effect a national amnesty should have before a foreign court, it is appropriate to consider whether the applicable law should be the law of the forum state, the law of the state granting the defendant immunity, the law of the state of the defendant's nationality, the law of the state upon whose territory the crimes were committed (the territorial state), or international law to resolve the question.

While a full treatment of this subject is beyond the scope of this essay, I will nonetheless suggest some general parameters that may be of use. To begin with, surely, it would be paradoxical for the forum state to use the law of the state granting immunity as the measure of its own exercise of universal jurisdiction. First, as most of these crimes are committed in internal conflicts by regimes in power, the state granting immunity will typically be the state of the defendant's nationality as well as the territorial state. Since the defendant will presumably have violated clear norms of international law, there can be no issue relating to *nullum crimen, nullum poena sine lege*— no punishment without law—if an amnesty granted after the crime's commission is ultimately ineffective if the defendant travels abroad.[135] Moreover, many immunities are granted by regimes to themselves just before they step down, or are extracted from a successor regime with threats of rebellion and violence. The former situation is a classic example of law that is blatantly self-interested and illegitimate, and need not detain us further. The second situation, while involving amnesties granted by a presumably legitimate government, could appear to be an illegal contract, void *ab initio,* if the beneficiary seeks to enforce it, as against public policy and extracted by duress.[136]

Assuming then that it is not a state other than the forum state whose law should govern the question of whether the amnesty or other immunity is valid, the choices remaining are the law of the forum and international law. I discuss the last possibility first. As other essays in this volume have noted, the international law criminalizing gross abuses of human rights has developed considerably since World War II. There is general agreement that the substantive norms, whether initially established by treaty or by custom, are well-established norms of customary international law and, indeed, *jus cogens* norms that are nonderogable in nature.[137] This position was reaffirmed during the Rome Diplomatic Conference to establish the International Criminal Court, where most governments were comfortable codifying these norms and applying them universally in the event the Security Council referred a particular case to the court. A state investigating a nonnational for one of these crimes pursuant to an exercise of universal jurisdiction is thus applying, through the medium of its national law, international law. What is not clear is whether the state is bound, in the absence of a specific treaty obligation, to apply international rules *related to* the substantive norm. The most that can be said is that there is at least some evidence that a state is required to do so, at least as to certain rules.

First, the charter and judgment of the International Military Tribunal at Nuremberg clearly affirmed the primacy of international law over national law, at least insofar as crimes against peace, war crimes, and crimes against humanity were concerned. The charter essentially abolished the defense of superior orders and was explicit in rejecting municipal law as a defense to an international crime. The Nuremberg principles were adopted in a resolution by the United Nations General Assembly in 1946[138] and have not been seriously questioned since. It would seem odd for international law to prime national law, only for national law to extinguish the legal obligation imposed either through the application of a statute of limitations, amnesty, or some other form of domestic immunity. Although there was some doubt as to whether a rule concerning the statute of limitations existed in customary international law,[139] that doubt would seem to be laid to rest after the widespread adoption of the Rome Statute, which provides that the crimes therein do not expire.[140] Similarly, the issue of superior orders is clearly addressed in the Rome Statute, and its widespread adoption by states will presumably create clear legal rules on those issues. Thus, although the manner in which international law is applied by states is generally a question of national law, given that these particular rules of international law appear to be inextricably intertwined with the application of a *jus cogens* norm of fundamental importance, the better rule would be that national legal systems are bound, as a matter of international law, to apply international, and not national, rules regarding superior orders and statutes of limitation.

Head of state immunity presents a slightly different problem, as the House of Lords recognized in the *Pinochet* case, for if international law abolishes head of state immunity as regards the *international* prosecution of current, as well as former, heads of state, national prosecutions of current leaders (unlike their predecessors) might unduly strain the international legal system, which is still premised largely on the sovereign equality of states. The International Court of Justice took this view in its recent decision on the *Congo v Belgium* case, holding that Belgium's arrest warrant against an incumbent minister for foreign affairs of the Congo, alleging grave breaches of the Geneva Conventions of 1949 and the additional protocols thereto and crimes against humanity, violated international law by failing to respect his international immunity from jurisdiction.[141]

I turn now to the last issue, the difficult question of amnesty, either de facto or de jure. If our earlier analysis is correct, the most that can be said is that international law appears to reject amnesties with respect to grave breaches and perhaps other serious crimes committed in international armed conflict.[142] However, with respect to crimes against humanity, genocide, and other war crimes, a clear international rule does not appear. If we reject the law of the state granting the amnesty as a source of law to apply (for the reasons given above or through a simple refusal to accord the amnesty any extraterritorial effect), we must assume the relevant law to be the national law of the forum state.[143] Of course, it is quite likely, however, that the forum state may not have any law on the question, for its legislature probably has not considered the problem. Thus the remainder of this section proposes some policy considerations that a court in the forum state might use in evaluating a foreign amnesty, keeping in mind that it will need to balance the international community's interest in pursuing justice against concerns of comity and the importance of respecting the difficult choices a particular jurisdiction has made as to how it will treat the perpetrators of past atrocities.

Courts in the forum state should keep in mind that, as a general principle, amnesties should be disfavored, as argued above. Moreover, although international law may not yet have crystalized as to the legality of amnesties per se, to permit national amnesties to extinguish obligations imposed by international law would seem contrary to the foundational principles of international criminal law and stand in opposition to the clear weight of authority and much of the state practice emerging in this field. This should create a presumption that the forum state should refuse to accept the amnesty. This presumption would be rebuttable, however, in specific cases. First, even the Rome Statute for the International Criminal Court did not prohibit amnesties per se. Instead, as noted earlier, it left open the possibility that some amnesties might serve the interest of justice. Assuming the decision is made in good faith, national fora presumably should have the same margin of appreciation. Their courts may already be overburdened, the defendant may have already been placed "in jeopardy" of criminal prosecution elsewhere, or comity may require that the forum state abstain from prosecution in a specific case, particularly with respect to conditional amnesties that have resulted from a carefully negotiated and potentially fragile agreement entered into as part of a transition to democracy. Assuming the decision of the forum state is made without the influence of political pressure, and pursuant to sound jurisprudential reasoning, a case-by-case approach to the problem of amnesties would appear to serve the interest of justice more than a per se rule might.

Before concluding this section, it is worth noting that the conundrum posited by the application of international law by national legal systems is not new. All legal systems involving multiple and overlapping courts must address this problem. As an example, the United States Supreme Court has articulated a complex doctrine governing the application of state law by federal courts, a brief look at which may prove instructive. In the seminal case of *Erie Railroad v Tompkins*,[144] the Court held, for a variety of reasons having to do with the peculiarities of the United States Constitution and statutes granting federal jurisdiction, that federal courts sitting in diversity, meaning that they were essentially hearing cases involving citizens from different states, were required to apply state law to decide the case before them. The court was later faced with the difficult question, very similar to our problem here, of what the state law governing a case included. That is, if New York law was to be applied to govern the tort liability of a particular defendant, should New York's statute of limitations apply to the case, or was the federal court free to apply its own law to the problem? In a series of complicated decisions, the Supreme Court suggested that many factors would govern whether state or federal law would apply, in particular relying upon whether the application of one or the other would be "outcome determinative"[145] or bound up in the rights and obligations created by the state law to be applied.[146] Thus if the state law question was "substantive," state law applied. If it was simply procedural, federal law applied. The court has often suggested that the purpose of the *Erie* doctrine, aside from its constitutional underpinnings, was to avoid "forum shopping" and the "inequitable administration of the laws."[147] *Erie* and its progeny have plagued first-year law students ever since its elaboration, but there is no doubt that federal and quasi-federal systems in which many courts may potentially hear a case need to systematize the situation and balance the competing interests involved if the legal rules sought to be enforced are not to be undermined by inconsistent and widely varying application.

The European Court of Justice (ECJ) has developed similar doctrines governing the application of European Union (EU) law by national courts. (This is *Erie* in reverse.) Faced with the disparate application of EU law by national courts, the ECJ has, through a set of complex and sophisticated cases, developed doctrines that require national courts to apply EU law but allow them a certain degree of discretion in how they do so. A central point in the ECJ's jurisprudence, however, which the *Erie* doctrine also underscores, is that a national court's application of procedural rules to an EU cause of action may not discriminate against the application of community law, or completely vitiate the substantive right, nor render the right impossible to exercise in practice.[148]

The relationship between EU courts and national courts, and between federal and state courts in the United States are of course quite different than the diffuse and relatively informal links that characterize the relationship of national courts to each other, to other international tribunals such as the ICTY and ICTR, and to the International Criminal Court and the International Court of Justice. The treaties establishing the European Communities and the European Union form a nascent constitution constraining the member states, the communities, and the EU in a much more formal and legal relationship than exists in the international arena. Similarly, the balance between the federal and state courts in the United States is governed by a written constitution. Nevertheless, as the international legal system matures, and as projects such as this consider questions involving the multiple and conflicting application of the law by courts with concurrent jurisdiction, it may be instructive to consider case law elaborated in two well-developed two-tier legal systems as a guide to doctrines that might ultimately be useful to international criminal law.

Conclusion

Societies in transition and international negotiators are often tempted to suggest that justice should be traded, or at least postponed, in exchange for peace. They argue that prosecuting perpetrators of human rights atrocities from a former regime may plunge fragile societies back into chaos or bring about an endless cycle of recriminations. They also suggest that criminal trials may do more harm than good. Yet a thorough study of the literature suggests that the evidence to support this position is weak, although studies of the Rwanda and Yugoslavia Tribunals suggest that sensitivity to local context is important if international justice is to succeed. While it is impossible to try every perpetrator under a prior regime, criminal trials, particularly of the leaders, may serve many useful goals. Moreover, framing the peace versus justice debate in terms of absolutes is neither necessary nor useful— criminal trials need not replace other mechanisms of achieving national reconciliation or addressing victims' losses. Instead, they complement them.

Thus this paper concludes that the international community should stay the course set for itself since World War II and continue to demand legal accountability for human rights abuses. The legal regime applicable includes both the exercise of universal jurisdiction by the international community as a whole, a point not taken up in this essay, and the robust exercise of universal jurisdiction by states. It is suggested that states confronted with challenges to accountability should treat them as presumptively invalid, a presumption that can be overcome if the state granting the immunity in question did so pursuant to a process that did not undermine the quest for accountability as a whole. In particular, blanket amnesties and any grant of immunity to a former leader should most likely be rejected out of hand. As Tom Farer imaginatively suggests: "Negotiators, after all, can give no more than they have. They can guarantee Pinochet's ilk impunity at home but cannot assure their freedom to take tea abroad with honorable and right honorable persons or to exercise their human right to shop at Gucci in Miami. If the ICC stood alone as a threat to the pleasures of retirement, sociopathic leaders in states that had become parties . . . could simply withdraw. . . . The beauty of national tribunals enforcing international criminal law is their immunity to such ploys."[149]

The international community should, over time, develop a set of conflicts of law and conflicts of jurisdiction rules to assist states in considering amnesties or other immunities granted by other states with regard to the perpetrator(s) in a particular case. The law must retain flexibility yet not be so flexible that the progress made on the problem of impunity disappears entirely. Rather than abandon its recent effort to construct a regime of accountability premised largely (but not exclusively) on the application of the criminal law, the international community should redouble its efforts to make the system more effective. Justice should not be traded for peace; rather, justice should be given a chance.

Chapter 11
The Future of Universal Jurisdiction in the New Architecture of Transnational Justice

Diane F. Orentlicher

Although long established in international law, the principle of universal jurisdiction[1] had scant impact on state practice until recently. It has lately come to life. In the past decade, courts in Austria, Belgium, Canada, Denmark, France, Germany, the Netherlands, Senegal, Spain, Switzerland, and the United Kingdom have instituted criminal proceedings for atrocities in Europe, Africa, and South America. And while the United States has been reluctant to institute prosecutions based on universal jurisdiction,[2] its courts have seen a surge in civil litigation based on this principle.

For some, these trends herald a long-overdue era of enforcement of the law derived from Nuremberg. In their view, the task ahead is to dismantle remaining barriers to the use of universal jurisdiction. States must be lobbied to enact laws granting their courts a global remit, governments must be pressed to enforce laws already on the books, and concerted efforts should be made to track down potential defendants and bring them before the bar of justice.[3]

For others, recent trends present troubling questions. Some relate to the law itself: in view of the relative dearth of legal authority defining conduct subject to universal jurisdiction, should we leave the task of interpretation to the odd national court, whose judges may have scant experience enforcing the law of nations? The politically explosive nature of some prosecutions raises deeper issues touching on the links between legal process and political community. Above all, do courts of bystander states have either the wisdom or standing to pass judgment on crimes committed a world away—crimes that affect the deepest interests of the nation where they occurred? In larger perspective, we may wonder whether historic reckonings for past atrocity belong in court at all. At times, it may seem, courts have strayed beyond their proper sphere, addressing questions best resolved through political processes.

How these issues are settled will determine the basic architecture of the system of transnational justice now taking shape. That questions of such large scope are being resolved through a process that may seem scattershot points up the need for reasoned reflection on recent trends in the exercise of universal jurisdiction and on the desired path of its development.

With these considerations in mind, in this essay I address several front-burner issues raised by emerging trends in the use of universal jurisdiction.[4] In brief, I will argue that recent developments raise novel concerns about how jurisdictional authority should be allocated among states as well as between officials of states and officers of international tribunals. Most obviously, growing recourse to universal jurisdiction raises questions about whose claim should receive priority when more than one court seeks to prosecute an individual for the same crime. The question has been further complicated by the emergence of a new breed of court, fashioned out of international and national elements, which presents an alternative to familiar fora for prosecution. More vexingly, recent developments present a new variant on the familiar punish-or-pardon quandary: if a nation afflicted by mass atrocities forgoes punishment in the name of national reconciliation, how should other authorities that can prosecute the perpetrators take account of the domestic policy?[5]

Since it is no longer fanciful to suppose that several courts might assert jurisdiction with respect to the same crime, we need to forge a new consensus about *how to decide* which claim should prevail—and whether bystander states should stay the hand of justice in deference to national amnesty laws. We need, in short, principled rules for reconciling the claims of multiple communities—national, transnational and international.

Alternative Models and Supporting Principles

As a foundation for considering these issues, it is necessary first to identify core features of the system of global enforcement now taking shape. One of its most striking features is the seemingly infinite variety of courts that can enforce the law of humanity. Besides the familiar models of international tribunals and national courts, new courts are a hybrid of national and international elements. Each has been tailor-made to address unique circumstances.

The principle of universality is by no means the only jurisdictional basis for these courts. Even so, the expanding set of enforcement options has significant implications for the future course of universal jurisdiction. To begin, even when supported by other grounds of jurisdiction, the courts described in this section reinforce the conceptual underpinning of universal jurisdiction by expanding state practice in support of prosecuting internationally recognized crimes.[6] At the same time, the expanding range of tribunals empowered to enforce humanitarian law must be taken into account in determining whether universal jurisdiction is the preferred path in specific cases.

The trends I examine in this section also point up the limits to states' commitment to enforcing humanitarian law. Debates surrounding new institutions that draw on the principle of universality have highlighted questions concerning its legitimate use, a concern that looms especially large in respect of the newly established International Criminal Court (ICC). Challenges to the ICC, as well as to some countries' efforts to prosecute depredations committed beyond their borders, sound a cautionary note, highlighting the fragility and incompleteness of a global consensus on issues relating to universal jurisdiction.

The developments I examine here point the way toward principles that should guide future determinations of when it is appropriate to rely on universal jurisdiction. In particular, recent trends suggest that many states prefer to exercise universal jurisdiction when it is bolstered by other bases of jurisdiction—to rely, that is, on "universality plus." This preference may have significant implications for the development of a broad consensus in support of principles governing the exercise of universal jurisdiction, a subject I take up at the end of this essay.

International Tribunals: Ad Hoc and Permanent

If it is a mistake to suppose that there are only two venues for enforcing international criminal law—international and national courts—it would be equally wrong to believe that international tribunals are cast from a single mold. During the twentieth century, four distinct paths were taken to establish five international courts. As I will explain shortly, the asserted justifications for these tribunals illuminate the scope of states' commitment to universal jurisdiction.

The International Military Tribunal (IMT or Nuremberg Tribunal) was established by a four-party agreement[7] to which nineteen other countries adhered, while its counterpart in Tokyo, the International Military Tribunal for the Far East, was established through proclamation by U.S. general Douglas MacArthur.[8] The International Criminal Tribunal for the former Yugoslavia (ICTY) was established (in 1993) by the Security Council acting under Chapter VII of the UN Charter,[9] as was the International Criminal Tribunal for Rwanda (ICTR) (in 1994).[11] Finally, the Statute of the ICC,[11] adopted by an affirmative vote of 120 states at a diplomatic conference convened by the United Nations in 1998, entered into force on July 1, 2002, after acquiring the requisite number of states parties.[12]

It is widely thought that international tribunals derive their jurisdictional authority above all from the principle of universality.[13] In this view, states that have jointly established an international tribunal have in effect combined the authority each possessed singly to exercise universal jurisdiction.

But this view is not universally accepted. At least one writer has questioned whether states can readily transfer to an international court the jurisdictional power they possess one by one.[14] In any case, the extent to which a particular international tribunal is supported by the principle of universality may turn on how it was created.[15]

Recent controversy surrounding the International Criminal Court illustrates the point—and makes clear why these issues matter. The controversy derives from the fact that the ICC can theoretically assert jurisdiction over nationals of states that have not adhered to its statute, provided the state where the crime occurred (the territorial state) has accepted the court's jurisdiction and other preconditions have been satisfied.[16] The U.S. government has strenuously challenged this feature of the Rome Statute. While it has pressed political objections, the United States has also argued that ICC jurisdiction over nationals of nonconsenting states is legally impermissible.

Defenders of the Rome Statute counter that it is perfectly legitimate for states parties to confer upon the ICC the authority each of them could have exercised alone and that the Rome Statute permits nothing more than this. Behind this view lie several distinct theories concerning sources of the ICC's authority.

First, many have justified ICC authority over nationals of nonconsenting states on the ground that the Rome Statute enables the court to try only crimes that are already subject to universal jurisdiction. Since every state can prosecute these crimes, they argue, states can combine their respective authority and bestow it on the ICC. But as a justification for ICC jurisdiction over nationals of nonconsenting states, this argument runs up against a potential problem. Although most of the crimes that can be charged before the ICC are subject to universal jurisdiction, some aspects of the court's subject-matter jurisdiction represent progressive developments in international law.

Another view justifies ICC jurisdiction in terms of the territorial principle. This principle recognizes that states may apply their own law to conduct that occurs in their territory and may prosecute violations of that law even when the alleged perpetrator is a foreign national. As noted earlier, unless the UN Security Council has referred a situation to the ICC, the court can assert jurisdiction only with the consent of either the state of nationality of the accused *or the state where the crime occurred.* Thus if the state of nationality of the accused has not accepted ICC jurisdiction—the situation that concerns the U.S. government—the required consent can and must be provided by the territorial state. In these circumstances, some have argued, the ICC derives its authority to prosecute nationals of nonconsenting states from the delegated territorial jurisdiction of the state whose consent has been secured.[17]

Leila Nadya Sadat and S. Richard Carden offer a third account of the ICC's jurisdiction, which draws upon but extends and deepens the first two theories. In their view, the principal source of the court's prescriptive authority is universal jurisdiction—which, however, is transformed in the Rome Statute from a principle generally invoked to support national juris-diction to a form of "*universal international jurisdiction* which would permit the international community as a whole, in certain limited circumstances, to supplement, or even displace, ordinary national laws of territorial appli-cation with international laws that are universal in their thrust and un-bounded in their geographical scope."[18] When the state consent regime of the Rome Statute applies (that is, when the ICC's jurisdiction has not been triggered by the UN Security Council), jurisdiction is further bolstered by the territorial and/or nationality principle(s).[19] In these situations the court would exercise the international analogue to a state's exercise of "uni-versality plus" jurisdiction.[20]

As an explanation of what delegates to the Rome Conference believed they were doing, the second approach may come closest to the truth—with a modification inspired by Sadat and Carden's account. As an historical account, Sadat and Carden's interpretation runs up against two potential problems. First, delegates in Rome ultimately declined to adopt proposals put forth by Germany and South Korea, respectively, that were widely un-derstood to rely at least in part upon the principle of universality.[21] Also, key actors at Rome have countered the U.S. position by emphasizing the author-ity of territorial states to make their law applicable to non-nationals.[22]

Still, subject to one qualification, the Sadat-Carden account may work better as a *legal* account and justification of the Rome Statute. The core mandate of international courts is to try crimes of universal concern[23] and it may trivialize this role to suggest that the ICC is merely exercising a dele-gated form of territorial or nationality jurisdiction.[24] Also, many (perhaps most) delegates at Rome had no doubt that the German and South Korean proposals would have been legally sound. In their view, perhaps, the prin-ciple of universality reinforces the authority provided through the Rome Stat-ute's more modest reliance on the territorial and nationality principles.[25]

The qualification relates to the fact that the Rome Statute allows the ICC to try some crimes as to which universal jurisdiction is not clearly estab-lished.[26] While ICC jurisdiction over these crimes could not be justified on a theory of delegated universal jurisdiction, it might be supported as a form of delegated territorial and/or nationality jurisdiction.

The controversies that surfaced in Rome and the way they were resolved provide important insights into the current status and future development of universal jurisdiction. To begin, the fact that the Rome Statute does not vest the ICC with the international equivalent of "pure" universal jurisdic-tion may reflect reticence, at least among a significant bloc of states, to support prosecutions that rely solely on this principle. Thus if Rome reflects a new global commitment to universal jurisdiction, it also highlights the outer limits of that commitment. In particular, a global consensus with respect to universal jurisdiction may be possible only when its exercise is buttressed by another basis of jurisdiction.

The Rome Statute also embodies a contemporary (if incomplete) consensus among states about how competing claims of jurisdiction should be resolved. A central feature of the statute is that it subordinates the ICC's authority to that of states. The ICC prosecutor cannot proceed with an investigation or prosecution if another state that has jurisdiction is pursuing the crime in question, unless that state is unwilling or unable genuinely to conduct the criminal proceeding.[27] The Rome Statute thus reflects a strong preference for prosecution by national courts, allowing the ICC to exercise jurisdiction only as a last resort in cases involving "the most serious crimes of international concern."[28]

Hybrid Courts

Recent years have seen extraordinary experimentalism in the design of courts that enforce the law of humanity. In Kosovo, East Timor, and Sierra Leone, tribunals have been designed with national and international components. For several years, the United Nations and Cambodia have pursued negotiations aimed at creating a domestic court with international participation to judge Khmer Rouge–era atrocities.

Extraordinary Chambers in the Courts of Cambodia

On June 6, 2003, the United Nations signed an agreement with Cambodia to create a court, established under Cambodian law but operating with substantial international participation, to prosecute those most responsible for crimes committed by the Khmer Rouge when they ruled Cambodia in the mid- to late 1970s. The agreement was the product of vexed negotiations lasting over five years. The process reached a low point on February 8, 2002, when the UN announced that it was withdrawing from the negotiations because it had concluded that, "as currently envisaged, the Cambodian court would not guarantee independence, impartiality and objectivity, which is required by the United Nations for it to cooperate with such a court."[29]

Negotiations were revived at the urging of the UN General Assembly, which adopted a resolution in December 2002 requesting the secretary-general "to resume negotiations, without delay, to conclude an agreement with the Government of Cambodia" aimed at establishing the mixed court.[30] Several months earlier, UN secretary-general Kofi Annan had said he would resume talks if he received a mandate from the Security Council or General Assembly.[31] As this volume went to press, it remained for the Cambodian parliament to ratify the agreement. In the meantime, the UN-Cambodia negotiations have already introduced a new model of justice for mass atrocity, comprising national and international elements.[32]

The negotiating process was triggered by a letter to the UN secretary-general from Cambodia's two co–prime ministers, dated June 21, 1997, seeking "the assistance of the United Nations and the international community in bringing to justice those responsible for the genocide and crimes against humanity during the rule of the Khmer Rouge from 1975 to 1979."[33] Earlier that month the notorious leader of the Khmer Rouge, Pol Pot, had unexpectedly become available for trial. Since their ouster from power in 1979, the Khmer Rouge had continued to operate as a guerrilla force under Pol Pot's leadership. After an internal rebellion, Pol Pot's Khmer Rouge captors expressed their readiness to surrender him for prosecution. But no international court was available to try Pol Pot and no country was willing to seek his extradition.[34] The moment of opportunity soon passed, largely because of political upheavals in Phnom Penh.[35] Pol Pot's death one year later forever deprived Cambodians of the justice of seeing him brought to trial but provided fresh impetus for prosecuting surviving Khmer Rouge leaders.

In their letter seeking UN assistance in bringing Khmer Rouge leaders to justice, Cambodia's co–prime ministers explained that their country did "not have the resources or expertise to conduct this very important procedure" and asked the United Nations to provide the same assistance it had provided in response to atrocities in Rwanda and the former Yugoslavia—presumably meaning the creation of an international tribunal for Cambodia. But the government's consent to such a tribunal was later withdrawn. When a UN-appointed Group of Experts recommended that the United Nations establish a tribunal with jurisdiction over those most responsible for Khmer Rouge–era crimes, the Cambodian government rejected their proposal.[36] Prime Minister Hun Sen[37] said he would permit foreign participation in domestic trials but rejected a proposal put forth by the UN's Office of Legal Affairs to establish a "mixed tribunal" under predominantly non-Cambodian control. In the spring of 2000 the United Nations and the Cambodian government reached an agreement in principle to establish a novel court that would be dominated by Cambodian officials but would include non-Cambodians wielding an effective veto power by virtue of a "super-majority" voting requirement.[38]

After protracted delays, on August 10, 2002, Cambodian authorities enacted enabling legislation for the court. Pursuant to the Law on the Establishment of the Extraordinary Chambers in the Courts of Cambodia for the Prosecution of Crimes Committed during the Period of Democratic Kampuchea,[39] the office of the prosecutor would comprise two coprosecutors, one of whom must be Cambodian and the other "foreign."[40] Similarly, investigations would be "the joint responsibility of two investigating judges, one Cambodian and another foreign."[41] Judicial panels, too, would comprise a mix of Cambodian and foreign judges. At each level of the system envisaged for the Extraordinary Chambers, Cambodian judges would constitute a majority. For example, three of the five judges constituting a trial court must be Cambodian.[42] Further, all judges are supposed to be appointed by the Cambodian government, although foreign judges are generally supposed to be appointed based on nominations by the UN secretary-general.[43] But, reflecting the "super-majority" formula accepted by Cambodia in 2000, the law provides that the vote of at least one UN-appointed judge is necessary to secure a judgment of guilt.[44]

The international subject matter jurisdiction of the Extraordinary Chambers would comprise genocide as defined in the 1948 Convention on the Prevention and Punishment of the Crime of Genocide, crimes against humanity, and certain violations of the Geneva Conventions of 1949 and two other treaties.[45] The chambers' jurisdiction would also include three crimes proscribed by the 1956 Penal Code of Cambodia—homicide, torture, and religious persecution—when committed between April 17, 1975, and January 6, 1979.[46]

As the UN under-secretary-general for legal affairs, Hans Corell, observed, the court envisaged in the UN-Cambodia negotiations had no precedent.[47] Its unique features are best understood as the product of extremely difficult negotiations between the United Nations and the Cambodian government. Explaining the UN's willingness in February 2000 to participate in the hybrid court, Corell said that the institution embodied an acceptable balance between the sovereignty of Cambodia and the credibility of the United Nations.[48] Although Corell would have preferred that the UN exercise greater control over the proceedings, he explained that the organization could not force Cambodia to accept foreign control[49]—not, at any rate, without a Security Council resolution adopted under Chapter VII of the UN Charter, an option foreclosed by China's certain veto.

Two years later, Corell defended the UN's decision to pull out of negotiations on the ground that Cambodia was unwilling to commit itself to the supremacy of a UN-Cambodia agreement concerning the Extraordinary Chambers over domestic law. Under these circumstances, Corell said, the UN would be implicated in a "judicial process over which it would have had little or no control."[50] When negotiations resumed in 2003, UN negotiators were able to secure assurances addressing some of the key concerns that had led them to abandon talks in February 2002, but the agreed text fell short of UN aims.[51] Presenting the draft agreement to the UN General Assembly, the secretary-general warned that, "under the terms of the draft agreement, any deviation by the [Cambodian] Government from [its] obligations . . . could lead to the United Nations withdrawing its cooperation and assistance from the process.[52]

Independent Special Court for Sierra Leone

Although beset by its own problems, negotiations to establish a hybrid court for Sierra Leone were far less vexatious. Those negotiations were formally instituted by a letter dated June 12, 2000, from Ahmad Tejan Kabbah, the president of Sierra Leone, asking the United Nations to assist his country in bringing to justice those responsible for "crimes against the people of Sierra Leone and for the taking of United Nations Peacekeepers as hostages."[53] Ravaged by a decade of savage civil war, Sierra Leone did not have the resources to mount prosecutions itself. And yet, Sierra Leone's justice minister later explained, "[W]e came to realise . . . that without ending impunity by bringing to justice those who bear the greatest responsibility for the atrocities committed in this country, we were dooming ourselves to repeat them."[54]

On August 14, 2000, the United Nations Security Council adopted a resolution expressing its deep concern "at the very serious crimes committed within the territory of Sierra Leone" and requesting that the secretary-general "negotiate an agreement with the Government of Sierra Leone to create an independent special court" with jurisdiction over serious violations of international humanitarian law as well as crimes under Sierra Leonean law.[55] On January 16, 2002, the agreement contemplated in this resolution was concluded in Freetown, Sierra Leone.[56] Soon after, the parliament of Sierra Leone ratified the agreement and enacted implementing legislation.[57]

In the words of the UN secretary-general, the Special Court for Sierra Leone is "a treaty-based sui generis court of mixed jurisdiction and composition."[58] The subject matter jurisdiction of the Special Court is defined principally in terms of international criminal law, but includes two offenses proscribed by Sierra Leonean law.[59] Although the Special Court is based in Sierra Leone,[60] a majority of its judges, its prosecutor, and its registrar were appointed by the UN secretary-general.[61] The government of Sierra Leone appointed the remaining judges, who were not required to be nationals of Sierra Leone.[62] The only senior official required to possess Sierra Leonean nationality is the deputy prosecutor.[63] Thus the Special Court is perhaps not so much a court of "mixed jurisdiction and composition"[64] as an international court onto which national elements are grafted.[65]

*   *   *

As the contrasting details of the Extraordinary Chambers and the Special Court suggest, the two models were shaped by negotiations that unfolded in markedly different political contexts. In respect of Cambodia, the United Nations has had to reckon with a government determined to retain as much control over the proposed court as possible, and confident of its negotiating power. In contrast, the UN's negotiating partners in Sierra Leone were keen to establish an internationally legitimate process for prosecuting atrocities committed mainly by rebel forces opposing the government.

Both sets of negotiations have presented the United Nations with novel challenges: its officials have had to decide how far they are prepared to go in supporting criminal proceedings they cannot fully control. So far those challenges have stalled the creation of a hybrid court for Cambodia. Several prominent nongovernmental organizations (NGOs) have criticized the UN for what they consider its readiness to compromise international standards of fair process[66] and applauded its decision in February 2002—later reversed—to withdraw from negotiations.[67] For the United Nations, then, participating in mixed tribunals presents the risk of tarnishing its own credibility. But as UN officials have reminded critics, at least thus far they have not had the option of creating a UN-controlled tribunal for Cambodia.

Although they present special challenges, mixed tribunals may offer an attractive alternative to UN tribunals or to trials conducted by bystander states. Unlike the international tribunals for the former Yugoslavia and Rwanda, the court established in Sierra Leone will operate in the country most deeply affected by its proceedings and judgments. So too would the Extraordinary Chambers envisaged in the UN-Cambodia agreement. By bringing justice home, these courts might contribute more effectively to national processes of reckoning than the remote justice dispensed in The Hague and Arusha. And by including national judges, prosecutors, and staff, the mixed tribunals may help strengthen the sinews of law in countries whose systems of justice have been shattered. In this way the hybrid courts might realize the goals implicit in the Rome Statute's preference for national trials over prosecutions before the ICC. None of these goals can be realized, however, without adequate resources, training of court personnel, and an enduring commitment by the international community to insist upon fair process.

Internationalized National Courts: Ethiopia

Although an innovation, the mixed courts contemplated for Cambodia and established in Sierra Leone are a natural evolution of developments that have been under way for some time. Several countries that have instituted prosecutions for mass atrocities have sought guidance and support from other states, international organizations, and international NGOs.

Criminal proceedings in Ethiopia exemplify this trend. In 1992 the Ethiopian government established a Special Prosecutor's Office to prosecute individuals for certain crimes committed during the reign of the Dergue, the military junta led by Col. Mengistu Haile Mariam that ruled Ethiopia from 1976 until 1991. The special prosecutor has sought technical advice from the UN Centre for Human Rights and has received both technical and financial support from several Western governments. Charges in these trials have included national and international crimes, the latter as incorporated in Ethiopian law.[68]

The role of international actors in these prosecutions has been complex. Although supportive in principle of Ethiopia's effort to prosecute atrocious crimes, NGOs and others have criticized due process violations attending these prosecutions, particularly the lengthy time spent in pretrial detention without charge.[69]

UN-Administered Courts: Kosovo and East Timor

A third model of internationalized prosecutions has emerged as a byproduct of recent UN operations in postconflict regions. In two territories administered by the United Nations, human rights crimes have been prosecuted before courts established under UN auspices, with the involvement of local personnel.

Following the 1999 war between Yugoslavia and the North Atlantic Treaty Organization, the UN Security Council adopted a resolution pursuant to which Kosovo would be governed by the United Nations Mission in Kosovo (UNMIK) until the region's final status is determined.[70] As an interim governing authority, UNMIK has established local courts that prosecute crimes ranging from reckless driving to genocide. Like the Special Court for Sierra Leone and the Extraordinary Chambers contemplated in Cambodia, the UN-administered courts in Kosovo are an amalgam of local and international elements. The first international prosecutor was a U.S. national employed by the United Nations, and other "internationals" have served alongside local judges.[71]

A UN-administered court system was also established in East Timor by the United Nations Transitional Administration in East Timor (UNTAET), which administered East Timor during the period beginning shortly after East Timorese voted for independence from Indonesia in August 1999[72] and ending when East Timor became independent on May 20, 2002. UNTAET Regulation No. 2000/11 vested in the District Court of Dili exclusive jurisdiction over genocide, war crimes, and crimes against humanity as well as over torture, murder, and sexual offenses when committed between January 1, 1999, and October 25, 1999.[73] Pursuant to another UNTAET regulation, these crimes must be tried before special panels for serious crimes.[74] Panel judges apply a combination of domestic and international law.[75] Although numerically dominated by international judges, the special panels include local judges.[76]

To assist the new state during its first two years of independence, the United Nations has established a Mission of Support in East Timor (UNMISET).[77] Like UNTAET before it, UNMISET now administers the Serious Crimes Unit of the judicial system. During a transitional period this unit will continue to be headed by an international deputy prosecutor who reports to the East Timorese general prosecutor. The UN also foresees the continuing need for participation by international judges in special panels through 2003.[78]

In both Kosovo and East Timor the UN-administered courts have exercised jurisdiction that overlaps with that of purely national courts and, in the case of Kosovo, an international tribunal. How to reconcile potentially competing claims of jurisdiction among these courts presents novel questions. Consider this: in December 2000 the ICTY continued its investigation of Yugoslav atrocities committed in Kosovo in 1999—crimes for which the Hague Tribunal issued indictments against then-president Slobodan Milosevic and other senior Yugoslav officials in May 1999. Meanwhile, in early December 2000 a Serbian law student went on trial before a UN-administered court in the northern Kosovo town of Mitrovića on charges of genocide for mass murders committed in April 1999.[79] And on December 20, 2000, a Yugoslav court in the town of Niš convicted three Yugoslav soldiers of the double murder in late March 1999 of an ethnically Albanian couple in Šušića, Kosovo.[80]

Several time zones away, in September 2000, Indonesia's attorney general named nineteen suspects in connection with violent crimes surrounding East Timor's proindependence vote in August 1999.[81] In November 2000 the UN high commissioner for human rights warned Indonesian authorities that the United Nations might create a tribunal to try those behind the violence in East Timor if domestic trials did not deliver justice.[82] On December 11, 2000, UN prosecutors in East Timor indicted ten members of a pro-Indonesia militia group and an Indonesian army officer on the charge of crimes against humanity for their alleged role in atrocities surrounding the August 1999 referendum on independence.[83] Thus, as UNTAET proceeded with trials in East Timor, a top UN official was pressing Indonesian authorities to prosecute related crimes in Indonesian courts—under threat of being superceded by an international tribunal.[84]

Later, I take up the question of how potentially competing claims of jurisdiction over the same offenses should be resolved. First, however, two further models of justice merit brief note.

The *Lockerbie* Model

Another innovation was born of negotiations aimed at resolving a longstanding impasse between the governments of Libya, the United States, and the United Kingdom concerning the trial of two Libyan nationals believed to be responsible for the 1988 bombing of Pan Am Flight 103 as it flew over Lockerbie, Scotland, en route to the United States. The explosion caused the deaths of 259 people on board the flight and eleven residents of Lockerbie who were killed when the plane crashed. Both the United States and U.K. governments filed criminal charges against the two Libyan suspects and requested their extradition. France made a similar request in connection with a related case.

Libya refused to comply with these requests, arguing that its law prohibits it from extraditing Libyan nationals. The three requesting states next turned to the UN Security Council, which adopted a series of resolutions urging Libya to comply with the extradition requests[85] and imposing sanctions that were to remain in effect until Libya complied.[86]

The standoff ended in March 1999, when Libya accepted a U.S. and U.K. proposal to try the Libyan suspects before a Scottish court, applying Scottish law and largely following Scottish criminal procedure[87] but located in the Netherlands.[88] Under this novel arrangement, a patch of Dutch real estate would become Scottish territory for the duration of the proceedings. The Libyan suspects were transferred to the Netherlands on April 5, 1999.[89] After repeated delays, their trial finally began at Camp Zeist in the Netherlands on May 3, 2000.[90] On January 31, 2001, the Scottish court found one of the defendants guilty of murder but freed the second defendant because, it concluded, the prosecution had not proved his guilt beyond a reasonable doubt.[91] The convicted defendant lost his appeal on March 14, 2002, and is now serving his sentence in Scotland.[92]

The principal jurisdictional basis of the court convened at Camp Zeist was apparently the territorial principle.[93] As noted, parties to the dispute as well as the Dutch government agreed that Scotland, the site of the explosion, would extend its territorial jurisdiction to Camp Zeist for the duration of the trial. Even so, the arrangement may have significant implications for contemporary issues relating to international jurisdiction.

The *Lockerbie* innovation subtly bolsters the view that the ICC can exercise jurisdiction derived from the transferred authority of states, including states' authority to exercise universal authority—a claim that has figured prominently in legal justifications for the ICC's authority over nationals of non-party states. The analogy is, to be sure, imperfect. Theoretically, Scotland did not transfer its jurisdiction to the Netherlands; it extended Scottish sovereignty to territory in the Netherlands. Still, if this form of legal alchemy is acceptable, the claim that states cannot transfer their own jurisdictional authority to the ICC seems difficult to sustain.

The *Lockerbie* case also highlights the enduring importance of national ties in resolving jurisdictional conflicts over international crimes. It took a decade to resolve the impasse generated by Libya's insistence on its right—usually respected by international law—not to extradite its own nationals on the one hand and the determination of U.K. and U.S. authorities to prosecute those believed to be responsible for a terrorist attack against *their* nationals on the other.

Civil Litigation

In the past two decades, private litigants have brought hundreds of cases in U.S. courts seeking to establish civil liability on the part of foreign defendants accused of violating internationally recognized human rights. The

proliferation of these law suits highlights the relevance of universal jurisdiction for civil litigation as well as for criminal prosecution. At the same
time, this phenomenon underscores the central role of private parties in
enforcing international humanitarian law.

The principal basis for these cases has been the Alien Tort Claims Act
(ATCA),[94] which provides in full: "The district courts shall have original
jurisdiction of any civil action by an alien for a tort only, committed in violation of the law of nations or a treaty of the United States." Applying this
statute in cases alleging serious violations of human rights, U.S. courts have
invoked the principle of universality in support of federal jurisdiction.
Indeed, it is difficult to overstate the importance of this conceptual link in
ATCA jurisprudence.

The decision that transformed ATCA into a vehicle for litigating human
rights violations was rendered in the case of *Filartiga v. Pena-Irala*.[95] Ruling
that Paraguayan plaintiffs could use ATCA to sue a Paraguayan police official for torture allegedly committed in Paraguay, the Second Circuit Court
of Appeals analogized torture to piracy—the paradigmatic crime subject to
universal jurisdiction: "Among the rights universally proclaimed by all
nations, as we have noted, is the right to be free of physical torture. Indeed,
for purposes of civil liability, the torturer has become like the pirate and
slave trader before him *hostis humani generis,* an enemy of all mankind."[96]

While *Filartiga* evoked the imagery of piracy to transform torturers into
international outlaws, its progeny have invoked the metaphor of Nuremberg. Assessing the legal imprint of successful litigation against the estate
of former Philippine dictator Ferdinand Marcos, one writer has observed:
"At the least, the *Marcos* cases demonstrate that the Nuremberg principles
of criminal responsibility have left a civil legacy."[97]

Impact of International Tribunals on National Processes

Inevitably, the proliferation of courts newly able and willing to address serious violations of humanitarian law raises the question of how competing
claims should be addressed. If courts in Yugoslavia, Kosovo, The Hague,
and elsewhere bring charges for the same atrocities committed by Yugoslav
forces in Kosovo, whose claim should prevail?

However important this question, to which I will return later, the relationship among various courts enforcing the common law of humanity
cannot be reduced to matters of competition and coordination. A striking
feature of contemporary enforcement patterns is the dynamic impact that
international tribunals, national courts exercising universal jurisdiction,
and courts operating in countries where atrocious crimes occurred have
had on each other. The creation of international tribunals for the former
Yugoslavia and Rwanda has spurred courts in several European countries
to exercise universal jurisdiction over human rights crimes committed

during conflicts in both of those regions. In turn, the existence or looming prospect of international tribunals, along with the credible threat of prosecutions based on universal jurisdiction, have revitalized national processes of reckoning in countries afflicted by mass atrocity.

Although largely unforseen, this last development means that international criminal law is increasingly working just as it should. International human rights law does not—and should not—seek to displace national jurisdiction. The law that seeks to enforce the basic code of humanity works best when it widens the political and moral space for accountability in countries where atrocious crimes occurred.

In this sense, proceedings against former Chilean president Augusto Pinochet in Europe achieved striking success. By all accounts his arrest and detention in the United Kingdom at the behest of a Spanish magistrate several years ago enlarged the space in Chile for addressing crimes committed during Pinochet's tenure in office.[98] To be sure, even before Pinochet was arrested in England, Chilean society had made significant progress in its national process of reckoning with his crimes.[99] Even so, proceedings against Pinochet in Spain, England, and other countries had a catalytic effect in Chile. Many Chileans who believed they had pressed the question of accountability as far as the political environment could bear were inspired to reconsider their calculation. Some expressed a sense of shame over Chilean victims' belief that they could find justice for Pinochet-era crimes, if at all, only in courts an ocean away. Stung by what they regarded as an affront to their national honor, Chilean officials who had previously accepted Pinochet's untouchability pledged that Chilean courts would dispense justice.[100]

For a relatively brief time a similar dynamic seemed to be at play in respect of efforts by Indonesian authorities to prosecute those responsible for abuses committed in the period surrounding the 1999 plebiscite in East Timor. As the United Nations considered a proposal to create an international tribunal to judge those crimes, Indonesia instituted its own criminal proceedings.[101]

These developments provide a powerful if incomplete answer to the charge, sounded by critics of Pinochet's arrest in England, that universal and international jurisdictions invade the province of domestic politics. In this view, magistrates in Spain and courts in London had no business upending the decision made by Chilean society to grant Pinochet immunity in furtherance of Chile's transition to democracy.[102] While this concern must be taken seriously, it should be tempered by a keen awareness of the constraints Chile faced when its political leaders accepted Pinochet's self-amnesty. In effect, the proceedings outside Chile helped blunt the power of General Pinochet's threat to unleash destabilizing force if his amnesty were ever challenged.

Further, to suppose that the political leaders who accepted Pinochet's impunity represent "Chilean society" is to silence his victims and other Chileans who opposed the general's self-amnesty. Survivors of Pinochet's torture chambers and mothers of the disappeared did not make a deal with Pinochet, nor did they accept the bargain struck by politicians. They, after all, instituted the proceedings in Spain that led to Pinochet's arrest in London.[103]

Turning to the future, just as the prospect of proceedings against Pinochet in Spain made it more likely that he would be prosecuted in Chile, the ICC will doubtless inspire national prosecutors to pursue a greater measure of justice than they might otherwise have sought. As previously noted, the ICC may not try a case that is being or has been investigated or prosecuted by a state with jurisdiction, unless that state is unwilling or unable genuinely to carry out the proceeding. This limitation will help ensure that the court's very existence inspires more vigorous enforcement of international law by national courts.

Transjurisdictional Communication

The interplay among jurisdictions noted in the preceding section has another distinctive dimension: courts charged with enforcing the law of humanity are talking to each other, shaping each other's understanding of the law and, together, constructing a common code of humanity.[104] In its most important ruling on whether General Pinochet could be extradited to Spain, British law lords found persuasive authority on a key issue in a decision of a trial chamber of the Yugoslavia war crimes tribunal.[105] Each of the major decisions rendered by British courts in the *Pinochet* proceedings also cited decisions of U.S. and other national courts. For their part, the two UN ad hoc tribunals have repeatedly drawn upon case law of national courts, including courts exercising universal jurisdiction,[106] as well as decisions rendered by human rights treaty bodies.[107]

This phenomenon can alleviate a problem that may arise when courts exercise universal jurisdiction—they might render improper interpretations of international law. At a time when the Internet makes judicial opinions readily accessible across jurisdictions, patently incorrect interpretations are likely to be "corrected" by courts in other jurisdictions. Judicial communication across jurisdictional lines can also mitigate the risk of radically divergent interpretations of what is supposed to be a universal code.[108]

Nonstate Actors

Another distinctive feature of the contemporary era of universal jurisdiction is the influential role of nongovernmental actors. Private parties have been the driving force behind many of the recent human rights prosecutions based upon universal jurisdiction.

The most prominent example is, of course, the criminal proceedings in Spain against former Chilean president Augusto Pinochet, which led to his arrest in England at the behest of a Spanish magistrate. Although widely associated with the magistrate who brought charges against Pinochet, Baltasar Garzón, the criminal investigation of General Pinochet was initiated by private complainants—and was pursued by Judge Garzón over the objection of public prosecutors and the attorney general in Spain.[109] Similarly, proceedings in Spanish courts against various military officials associated with crimes committed during Argentina's "dirty war" were instituted by private parties.[110]

Individual victims and human rights organizations were also the engine behind criminal proceedings against former Chadian leader Hissène Habré in Senegal. Although charges were formally approved by an assistant state prosecutor, the case was triggered by a criminal complaint by private parties who had standing as civil parties. Notably, the case was prepared with the assistance of Chadian, Senegalese, and international NGOs that had closely collaborated with each other in support of the Chadian victims.[111]

These and other efforts of nonstate actors have provided a counterweight to the political calculations that often lead public authorities to forego prosecutions. Even when governments in principle support a policy of justice for atrocious crimes, they must rank this goal against other policies that compete for limited public resources. Prosecutorial efforts may falter or fail more because governments do not rank legal accountability high in their policy agenda than because they oppose prosecutions. In these circumstances victims and their supporters can overcome public inertia by mobilizing political pressure for state action or, where local procedure allows, by instituting criminal proceedings.

While the former phenomenon is familiar enough in the context of domestic politics, it has taken on a novel cast. Today, NGOs are cooperating across borders. Sometimes their audiences are government officials acting in an "internal" capacity, as when NGOs lobby national governments to institute prosecutions for crimes committed in their own territory. Transnational coalitions also target governments acting collectively, with growing success. As has often been noted, NGOs played a remarkably effective role at the diplomatic conference to establish a permanent international criminal court. And as the Hissène Habré case exemplifies, NGOs sometimes address national governments in the latter's capacity as transnational actors. Of particular relevance here, several prominent NGOs devote substantial resources to initiatives that seek to persuade governments to exercise universal jurisdiction.[112]

Through the efforts of nonstate actors, the law derived from Nuremberg is being transformed. Formerly associated with victors' justice, the law of humanity is increasingly being enforced by victims.

Reconciling Interests

This phenomenon and other trends examined in this essay present a new set of dilemmas. If the same crimes can be prosecuted in multiple jurisdictions, how shall we choose among them? Suppose that British authorities had determined General Pinochet medically fit to stand trial. In this (counterfactual) setting, should British authorities have extradited Pinochet to Spain, which made the first request for his surrender? To other European states that made subsequent requests for his extradition? Or to Chile, which sought his return? If a society that has endured the depredations of dictatorship decides to forego or limit prosecutions, should other legal systems defer to its policy by declining jurisdiction when victims seek justice abroad?

Familiar theories of universal jurisdiction provide surprisingly scant guidance, though their very diffidence tells us something important. To understand this point and its contemporary implications, it is helpful to return to the moment when universal jurisdiction was first made widely applicable to human rights crimes—the aftermath of World War II.

When law departs abruptly from its previous path, jurists typically seek support in the closest precedent they can plausibly cite. In the postwar period, Nazi war criminals were analogized to the pirate of another age—*hostis humanis generis,* enemies of all mankind who could be punished by any state that could establish jurisdiction.[113]

The image borrowed from piracy law—an enemy of mankind—served its immediate purpose and still provides a powerful metaphor in support of universal jurisdiction for human rights crimes. Yet the analogy is not entirely apt. For one thing, justifications for universal jurisdiction over piracy assume (perhaps not always correctly) that no state would consider prosecution an affront to its sovereignty. But when bystander states prosecute traveling dictators, indifference is the least likely response on the part of the defendant's home state. Further, piracy can be truly indiscriminate in its choice of victims; to say that the pirate is an enemy of all mankind may be an exaggeration, but it is more than a metaphor. In contrast, the claim that, "like the pirate . . . before him," the torturer is now an enemy of all mankind[114] is fundamentally a moral claim.

Rhetoric deployed by postwar tribunals makes this plain. Consider how a U.S. military tribunal justified its jurisdiction in the *Einsatzgruppen* case.[115] The tribunal emphasized that the defendants were accused "[n]ot [of] crimes against any specified country, but against humanity."[116] It followed that "humanity" itself could summon perpetrators to account through universal jurisdiction: "[T]he inalienable and fundamental rights of common man need not lack for a court . . . Humanity can assert itself by law. It has taken on the role of authority. . . . Those who are indicted . . . are answering to humanity itself, humanity which has no political boundaries and no geographical limitations."[117] With the Nuremberg precedent, the tribunal continued, "[I]t is inconceivable . . . that the law of humanity should ever lack for a tribunal. Where law exists, a court will rise. Thus, the court of humanity . . . will never adjourn."[118]

When an Israeli court rendered judgment against Adolf Eichmann in 1961 it too invoked the interests of mankind: "The abhorrent crimes defined in [Israeli] Law are not crimes under Israel [*sic*] law alone. These crimes, which struck at the whole of mankind and shocked the conscience of nations, are grave offences against the law of nations itself. . . ."[119]

But if the core justification for universal jurisdiction over inhumane crimes is a moral claim, an important corollary emphasizes practical concerns: By their nature, crimes against humanity are unlikely to be punished in the state where they occurred. This justification had strong resonance in the aftermath of Hitler's crimes; German courts were not to be trusted to prosecute major Nazi war criminals. Thus one U.S. military tribunal operating in Germany observed that surrendering the Nazi defendants before it for prosecution by German authorities would have been the "equivalent [of] a passport to freedom."[120]

More recently, this rationale for universal jurisdiction has been amplified by a distinct but related consideration. In many countries recently scourged by mass atrocity, the judicial system is in a state of wholesale collapse. Decades after the Khmer Rouge were routed from power, for instance, Cambodia was bereft of seasoned judges and lawyers, who had been targeted for extermination in the 1970s. In these circumstances the state where atrocities occurred may not be *able* to bring perpetrators to account.

In sum, legal justifications for universal jurisdiction over human rights crimes make two core claims: (1) certain crimes offend humanity writ large—a claim that translates into a global entitlement to bring perpetrators to account; and (2) unless every state assumes responsibility to prosecute the perpetrators of such crimes, they will elude the net of justice. Beneath the second rationale is an implied claim: universal jurisdiction provides an antidote to the impunity that accomplished despots are likely to enjoy in the countries that endured their crimes.

While this rationale explains why universal jurisdiction might be necessary, it may not fully reflect contemporary concerns about processes of transitional justice—truth commissions, trials, and other measures aimed at healing societies that have endured savage crimes and advancing their transition to constitutional democracy. At a time when dozens of countries are confronting the dilemmas of transitional justice and devising policies that reflect their unique experiences, the impunity rationale in support of universal jurisdiction may be too simplistic.

It does not, for example, readily accommodate the sophisticated policy devised by the postapartheid South African government led by Nelson Mandela. Eschewing a blanket amnesty, South Africa established a Truth and Reconciliation Commission (TRC) with several mandates. One TRC committee was empowered to grant amnesty for political crimes on an individual basis but could do so only if it was convinced that the applicant had fully confessed to his or her crimes. The TRC was also charged with establishing a comprehensive account of human rights violations committed during decades of apartheid and recommending reparations for victims.[121]

Suppose that an individual granted amnesty by the TRC traveled to Spain—where victims of his crimes instituted criminal proceedings against him for torture. Should Spanish judicial authorities honor South Africa's policy by declining to arrest the traveling torturer? Or should the victim petitioners, denied legal recourse in South Africa, be allowed to seek some measure of justice in Spain? I will return to these questions shortly. First, however, I would like to explore in broader perspective how the impunity rationale for universal jurisdiction might be refined in light of insights derived from contemporary experience.

Balancing Interests

My principal claim is that jurisdictional clashes over human rights crimes should be resolved by weighing the respective interests of relevant communities—an approach reflected in the Princeton Principles on Universal Jurisdiction. Normally, international legal principles concerned with allocating legal jurisdiction take nation states as the relevant communities of concern. But this approach needs to be enhanced to reflect one of the central claims of Nuremberg. Postwar prosecutions constituted "humanity itself," which "has no political boundaries and no geographical limitations,"[122] as a legal sovereign, the conceptual and moral fount of extraordinary jurisdiction. This radical move did not, however, displace the interests of other communities with substantial links to the crimes at issue.[123] Thus, Nuremberg is best understood as asserting that when no state is prepared to stand up for victims of ghastly crimes, "humanity itself" has legal standing.

In general, international law's commitment to the "interests of humanity" translates into support for prosecutions before impartial courts that operate in accordance with international standards of fair process.[124] Sometimes this will point toward prosecutions outside the state where atrocities were committed. As noted, countries ravaged by mass atrocities often cannot or will not dispense justice. Even so, core values of human dignity are best served when fair proceedings are instituted in the country that bears primary responsibility for atrocious crimes, generally the territorial state.[125] By averting or dispelling a culture of impunity, in-country justice provides the surest guarantee that human rights will be respected in the future. Also, prosecutions undertaken by the state that bears principal responsibility for atrocious crimes help repay the nation's moral and political debt to victims.

Complicating the interests analysis I am advocating, in an age that has spawned international and mixed tribunals operating alongside national courts, principles for resolving competing claims must take account of the respective merits of various *forms* of jurisdiction. When, for example, should an international tribunal have priority over national courts? Does it depend on *which* national court has asserted a competing claim?

International instruments concerned with criminal law provide a helpful point of departure for developing a more comprehensive interests-analysis approach. The Rome Statute provides especially relevant guidance in resolving conflicting claims of an international tribunal on the one hand and of national courts on the other. As for interstate conflicts, extradition treaties provide a useful starting point for resolving competing claims.

Conflicts between International and National Courts

As noted previously, the International Criminal Court can not try a suspect if a state with jurisdiction is pursuing the case unless that state is unwilling or unable genuinely to carry out the investigation or prosecution.[126] This restriction is likely to have a salutary effect: It will provide strong incentive for states to prosecute crimes they might have been disposed to entomb in a grave of silence and denial. That national trials will avert international prosecution may also provide domestic leaders with the political cover they need to prosecute those most responsible for notorious crimes. In this fashion the Rome Statute strikes just about the right balance—at least insofar as it resolves competing claims between the ICC and states with significant links to the crime in question. Far from undermining state responsibility, the ICC will likely invigorate governmental efforts to provide redress to victims. At the same time, the court remains available when national courts fail.

It is less clear that the Rome Statute deals adequately with situations involving the exercise of universal jurisdiction. Although the intention of the drafters is somewhat obscure, the Rome Statute conceivably could allow a state exercising universal jurisdiction to disable the ICC from prosecuting an individual.[127] This result may not be desirable, at least in some cases. The values underlying universal jurisdiction have generally been thought to be better served when an international tribunal acts on behalf of the international community than when a national court purports to act on its behalf.[128] This is not to deny the value and even necessity of national authorities sharing responsibility with the ICC for enforcing the law of humanity. That countries are now exercising universal jurisdiction to punish atrocious crimes has surely deepened international society's commitment to humanitarian law. Even so, national courts are embedded in particular political communities and to that extent may not be as well suited as international tribunals to enforce law on behalf of the international community (or, in the language of postwar case law, on behalf of "humanity").

Interstate Jurisdictional Conflicts

The possibility that a variety of states may be able to defeat ICC jurisdiction brings new urgency to a pressing task—developing consensus principles for resolving conflicting claims of jurisdiction among states. Normally, the question of how such conflicts should be resolved arises when a state receives multiple requests to extradite the same person or when a country seeks the extradition of an individual whom the requested state also wishes to try. Extradition treaties typically direct the requested state, in making its determination, to take into account a fairly standard set of considerations. For example, the European Convention on Extradition[129] specifies that when a state receives multiple extradition requests, the requested state should "make its decision having regard to all the circumstances and especially the relative seriousness and place of commission of the offences, the respective dates of the requests, the nationality of the person claimed and the possibility of subsequent extradition to another State."[130] The closest analogy in the Rome Statute, a provision that applies when a state party receives competing requests from the ICC on the one hand and another state that meets certain conditions on the other hand, directs the state party to "consider all the relevant factors," including:

(a) The respective dates of the requests;
(b) The interests of the requesting State including, where relevant, whether the crime was committed in its territory and the nationality of the victims and of the person sought.[131]

While these provisions provide a useful starting point, they do not provide sufficient guidance as to how relevant interests should be weighed when there are competing claims among states to prosecute the same person for crimes subject to universal jurisdiction. In these circumstances the following considerations should supplement the guidelines provided in standard extradition treaties: First, although a state's link of nationality to an alleged perpetrator normally counts in favor of its jurisdictional claim, the opposite may at times be true in respect of gross violations of human rights. As already noted, a chief justification for universal jurisdiction is that there is a heightened risk of impunity if, say, prosecution of a notorious dictator were left to national courts subservient to his authority. A principle requiring states to institute criminal proceedings if they decline to extradite their nationals would mitigate this risk,[132] but could not prevent states from staging sham proceedings. For the same reasons, the claims of territorial states are sometimes at odds with the "interests of humanity" as they have been conceived in the law derived from Nuremberg.

Yet human rights values themselves provide compelling reasons to give priority to prosecutions by the territorial state, *provided there are sufficient guarantees of fair process.* For one thing, this is the best assurance that human rights will be protected in every country through the rule of law, reliably enforced. In-country justice may also do more to advance a wounded nation's recovery in the aftermath of mass atrocity than the remote justice dispensed by international courts. Provided they enjoy legitimacy, trials in the territorial state are more likely than prosecutions abroad to inspire a sense of "ownership" by societies recently scourged by atrocious crimes. Thus, unless there is reason to doubt the fairness of their courts, the claims of territorial states should be given significant weight and support.[133] For reasons suggested earlier, in some circumstances that support might include international participation of the sort envisaged for Cambodia and already being provided in Sierra Leone. Mixed tribunals are especially appropriate in respect of countries that have the political will to institute credible prosecutions but lack the necessary resources and expertise.

Suppose, however, a credible (and safe) judicial process is not possible in the state where atrocities occurred. Suppose also that several other states wish to prosecute the perpetrator. How should their conflicting claims be resolved? Assuming that the judicial system of each state meets international standards of fairness, the claim of the state that has the most significant links to the crime in question should prevail. Since this approach would generally favor the state of nationality of the defendant and/ or victim,[134] this preference essentially amounts to a preference for "universality plus" over jurisdiction based solely on universal jurisdiction.[135] Giving priority to the claims of states that have substantial links to the crime in question can mitigate the appearance of hubris associated with universal jurisdiction and thereby enhance the legitimacy of prosecutions in fora outside the territorial state. By honoring enduring sensibilities of state sovereignty, "universality plus" may serve as a bridge to wider acceptance of jurisdiction based solely on the principle of universality.[136]

The Princeton Principles adopt essentially the approach I have advocated here while further elaborating the factors that should be considered in weighing competing jurisdictional claims of states. Principle 8 provides in full:

RESOLUTION OF COMPETING NATIONAL JURISDICTIONS
Where more than one state has [asserted] or may assert jurisdiction over a person and where the state that has custody of the person has no basis for jurisdiction other than the principle of universality, that state or its judicial organs shall, in deciding whether to prosecute or extradite, base their decision on an aggregate balance of the following criteria:
   (a) multilateral or bilateral treaty obligations;

(b) the place of commission of the crime;

(c) the nationality connection of the alleged perpetrator to the requesting state;

(d) the nationality connection of the victim to the requesting state;

(e) any other connection between the requesting state and the alleged perpetrator, the crime, or the victim;

(f) the likelihood, good faith, and effectiveness of the prosecution in the requesting state;

(g) the fairness and impartiality of the proceedings in the requesting state;

(h) convenience to the parties and witnesses, as well as the availability of evidence in the requesting state; and

(i) the interests of justice.

Amnesties

Returning to one of the most nettlesome issues raised in this essay, how should principles that address conflicting jurisdictional claims take account of domestic amnesty laws? Since this issue is addressed in depth in another contribution to this volume, I will only briefly touch upon several considerations.

As a matter of international law, states generally are not required to give extraterritorial effect to another state's amnesty for atrocious crimes. The state that enacts an amnesty is exercising only its own prescriptive jurisdiction; it is not enacting international law. When an amnesty covers crimes subject to universal jurisdiction, other states remain free to apply their own law to the conduct at issue. Still, the question remains: should they? Or should choice-of-law rules and prosecutorial policies governing this situation include a principle of deference to domestic amnesties?

The first point to be made here is that some amnesties may be inconsistent with international law. This is clearly true with respect to blanket amnesty laws covering atrocious crimes when enacted by states parties to certain human rights treaties, and some amnesties may be incompatible with states' obligations under customary law.[137] Addressing a hypothetical situation in which a state absolved perpetrators of torture through an amnesty law, a trial chamber of the International Criminal Tribunal for the former Yugoslavia has observed:

If such a situation were to arise, the national measures, violating the general principle [proscribing torture] and any relevant treaty provision, would . . . not be accorded international legal recognition. Proceedings could be initiated by potential victims if they had *locus standi* before a competent international or national judicial body with a view to asking it to hold the national measure to be internationally unlawful; or the victim could bring a civil suit for damage in a foreign court, which would therefore be asked *inter alia* to disregard the legal value of the national authorising act. What is even more important is that perpetrators of torture acting upon or benefiting from those national measures may nevertheless be held criminally responsible for torture, whether in a foreign State, or in their own State under a subsequent regime.[138]

Reflecting similar considerations, Principle 7 of the Princeton Principles provides in full:

PRINCIPLE 7—AMNESTIES
1. Amnesties are generally inconsistent with the obligation of states to provide accountability for serious crimes under international law as specified in Principle in 2(1).
2. The exercise of universal jurisdiction with respect to serious crimes under international law as specified in Principle 2(1) shall not be precluded by amnesties which are incompatible with the international legal obligations of the granting state.

Assuming for purposes of analysis that a state's courts were free to decide whether to give extraterritorial effect to another country's amnesty for torture, how should the foreign state's courts approach this issue?[139] The classic impunity rationale for universal jurisdiction would suggest that the bystander court should exercise jurisdiction despite—indeed, *in light of*—the domestic amnesty. But insights gleaned from the recent experience of societies that have instituted policies of transitional justice suggest this approach may be too rigid—perhaps even that bystander states should defer to domestic policies of national reconciliation that satisfy generally-accepted indicia of legitimacy.[140]

The complex considerations bound up in this issue are beyond the scope of this essay. I would, however, sound a cautionary note. The unexpected impact in Chile of European efforts to prosecute Pinochet is instructive: it highlights the value of maintaining pressure for legal accountability through the credible threat of universal jurisdiction. Had Spanish and British authorities declined to pursue torture charges in deference to Chilean amnesties, civil society in Chile would have lost a potent source of support. Instead, the proceedings outside Chile bolstered their efforts to secure Chile's future by confronting its past.

Conclusion

A new architecture of transnational justice is taking shape. Besides the familiar models of global tribunals and universal jurisdiction, hybrid courts are being fashioned out of national and international elements. Far from displacing national prosecutions, the expanding writ of justice across borders has invigorated efforts to bring justice home. In the process, in-country justice has been transformed. No longer operating exclusively within a national frame of law, domestic courts have become embedded in a transnational process of lawmaking and enforcement.

The proliferation of fora newly able and willing to enforce humanitarian law raises novel challenges. If more than one authority—national, international, or a blend of both—seeks to prosecute the same crime, which should prevail? When, if ever, should courts consider themselves free to disregard an amnesty conferred by another country? The task today is to forge a broad and deep consensus in support of principled guidelines for resolving these quandaries.

Chapter 12
Universal Jurisdiction and Judicial Reluctance: A New "Fourteen Points"

Michael Kirby

A Judge's Perspective

I want to explain why judges, at least those of the common-law tradition, respond with caution to the claim of universal jurisdiction. I want to identify the reasons, not from the perspective of a judge who thinks that there should be no innovation in substantive or procedural law, but from the viewpoint of one sympathetic to the advance of fundamental human rights through the common law and international law.

I am conscious of the capacity of the law to adapt to international human rights norms.[1] I am willing to consider novel legal responses to serious international crimes. All of us in the law today, but especially judges, need to set aside adolescent attitudes to formalism and to legal doctrines that have outgrown their usefulness or been overtaken by events.[2]

Other essays in this volume demonstrate that, without legislation specifically authorizing that course, judicial officers of the civil law tradition have, from time to time, asserted and exercised universal jurisdiction over persons accused of serious international crimes. They have not always done so. Occasionally, they have declined jurisdiction.[3] But at least there are instances where such jurisdiction has been exercised.

The same is not true of the judges of the common law. One can search the casebooks of the United Kingdom, the Commonwealth of Nations, the United States of America, and elsewhere and one will find very few instances where a higher court has upheld universal jurisdiction, absent explicit local legislation requiring or permitting it to do so. Occasionally, as in dicta of the Supreme Court of Israel in the *Eichmann* case,[4] universal jurisdiction has been mentioned as a basis for a court's authority over an accused, although a legislative foundation may also be available.[5] Occasionally, a judge expressing a minority opinion will support the notion.[6] Or a common-law judge will expressly reserve the point, commenting on it sympathetically.[7]

Sometimes the issue will be held over because the case can more easily be disposed of on other grounds.[8] One day, soon, the problem will be presented squarely to a final court of the common-law world. That court will then have to give answer.

To some extent the answer will be influenced by the temperament of the judge in question and the conception that the judge has of the judicial office. In most countries today, judges are more aware, and candid, than they were in the past about the choices they are obliged to make in discharging their functions.[9] Of course, some judges are more inclined than others to see leeways for choice in the expression and application of legal norms. They may view the constitutional provision or the statute in issue as ambiguous where other judges do not see the doubt or regard the ambiguity as insignificant or settled by past authority. Or they may regard the precedents of decisional authority as leaving a gap in the common law which they are entitled, or bound, to fill. In every jurisdiction the contemporary debates over the judicial function are vigorous. Some judges are labeled as activist, some as conservative. Such labels can often be misleading. Conservatives occasionally appear to become activists when an issue is perceived by them as very important. This, for example, has been said of some of the judges who participated in the decision of the United States Supreme Court in *Bush v Gore*.[10]

Few senior judges now hold the view of the judicial function formerly sustained by the declaratory theory.[11] In fact, that theory is all but dead in most common-law countries. Yet no judge, even in an apex court, is a complete legislator. To pretend to such a power would not only defy the judge's municipal mandate. It would be incompatible with the basic concept of the rule of law and also with international human rights norms.[12] The death of the declaratory theory may make it easier for the judge of the common law to give effect, at the margin, to novel notions, such as those about universal jurisdiction and to extend the legal boundaries. But margins and boundaries there still are.

I myself have faced a claim that purported to be based on universal jurisdiction, founded in the crime of genocide as expressed in the Genocide Convention of 1948. Australia is a party to that convention,[13] although it has not introduced legislation to give the convention municipal operation.

In 1997, soon after my appointment to Australia's highest court, an application came before me, sitting alone, to strike out an originating process brought by an Australian Aboriginal claiming declaratory relief against the Commonwealth, in other words, the federal polity. Amongst other declarations sought was one asserting that the Commonwealth owed a fiduciary obligation to "the original peoples of this land." Such obligation was alleged to have arisen by reason of "(b) [t]he general and continuing premeditated criminal genocide of [Aboriginal] people, and (c) the genocidal effect of the longstanding official lie of *terra nullius* and the complicity of lawmakers and the judicial system in this fictitious deception and only-recently overturned claim."

The Commonwealth moved to strike out this process as manifestly untenable.[14] The plaintiff resisted on the footing that the crime of genocide, of its nature, conferred on the court full jurisdiction and power to provide relief of the declaratory kind sought. It was true, as the process suggested, that Australian courts had then only recently overturned the rule that the interest of the indigenous peoples in land in Australia had been extinguished upon acquisition by the Crown of sovereignty over Australia as *terra nullius*.[15] It is also true that, in somewhat analogous cases, Canadian courts had upheld the suggestion that the Crown, apart from treaty, owed fiduciary obligations to the indigenous peoples.[16] However, the originating process before me presented numerous problems. They were not specifically those of jurisdiction, in the sense of power to decide the case because, under the Australian constitution the High Court undoubtedly enjoys original jurisdiction in all matters in which the Commonwealth is a party.[17]

Universal jurisdiction was, however, invoked by the plaintiff to meet the argument that the claim was not of its character such as to be susceptible to judicial determination. The open-ended declaration sought, by a person who had not established any particular authority to bring a representative action and who asked, essentially, for political remedies, bore some similarities to an earlier claim initiated in the court by another Aboriginal plaintiff.[18] In that case Justice F. G. Brennan had observed: "[W]hen one comes to a court of law it is necessary always to ensure that lofty aspirations are not mistaken for the rules of law which courts are capable and fitted to enforce. It is essential that there be no mistake between the functions that are performed by the respective branches of government."

In the end I dismissed the plaintiff's claim because the relief sought was outside that proper to the judicial branch and because the pleadings were hopelessly defective. In that sense the court lacked jurisdiction to give the relief claimed. This was not because it lacked jurisdiction and power over the party named as defendant. Universal jurisdiction, in that sense, was not required. Its boundaries were not therefore explored.

A like conclusion was reached in a later case in which I participated.[19] Here again, Aboriginal plaintiffs had brought proceedings to challenge government policy. They also contested matters considered in debates in the Australian parliament. Such debates enjoy a constitutionally privileged position not uncommon to like legislatures. The Federal Court of Australia had rejected the claim.[20] Special leave to appeal to the High Court of Australia was sought but refused. I participated in that rejection. The short reasons given by the court for the refusal of leave included these statements.[21]

We express no view on the correctness of the opinion of the majority of the Full Court of the Federal Court that the crime of genocide does not form part of the common law of Australia. Even if it does, it has not been shown that the Full Court erred in deciding that it is not arguable that conduct alleged to constitute genocide falls within the definition of "genocide" in international law. Counsel for the appellants could not point to any decision of any international court or tribunal or municipal court which suggested that it did. Nor could she point to any scholarly writing. Rather the history of the preparation of the Convention lends no support for the proposition that the Convention extends to the matters complained of here.

I mention these two cases to illustrate two propositions. First, invocations of universal jurisdiction are occurring in municipal courts in many parts of the common law world. They are being made in countries like Australia where relevant international crimes, stated in treaties or customary law, have not been given local application by municipal legislation. Second, the cases illustrate, in a sense, my credentials to write this essay. Although, as it happens, in neither of the matters described was universal jurisdiction essential to found the jurisdiction and power of the court over the parties and the issues, there is nothing that concentrates a judicial mind so much as an actual legal claim being propounded on a novel basis. When this happens, a judge of our tradition strives to reach a lawful and just conclusion. Moreover, he or she must ordinarily give reasons that are published to the parties and to the world.

The foregoing considerations allow me to collect some of the concerns that judges, faced with invocations of universal jurisdiction, will almost certainly feel. Those who look for an expansion of such jurisdiction and its application in appropriate cases, will do well to consider (and if possible to address) the sources of that such concern.

Reasons for Reluctance: Fourteen Points

1. Judicial Legitimacy Derives from a Legal System

It is for the judges of municipal courts to say when they will, or will not, exercise judicial power on the basis of an assertion of universal jurisdiction.[22] They do so by the application of the law. If there be doubt, it is a first rule of exercising judicial power that a judge should satisfy himself or herself that jurisdiction exists.[23] In most cases coming before judges, the issue passes *sub silentio*. Ordinarily, there is no real dispute about it. But an assertion of universal jurisdiction cannot be regarded as falling in that class. If not raised by a party, the judge would be bound to raise it if no other basis appeared to found the exercise of the court's jurisdiction.

Practicalities suggest that, unless there is some territorial connection with the jurisdiction in which the judge operates, it will usually be unlikely that a crime, international or otherwise, will come before a municipal court. In part, this is because, without such a connection, it is unlikely, in practice, that bodies with the competence, means, and motivation to investigate the crime, will gather the materials for a brief and initiate proceedings.[24] Yet nowadays even this assumption will not always be fulfilled. Civil society organizations, organizations of victims, human rights nongovernmental organizations (NGOs), and others may initiate proceedings, confronting courts with the obligation to decide whether or not they possess jurisdiction.[25] Because judges are used to dealing with cases in which they clearly have jurisdiction, on the basis that a crime was committed locally, it is natural for them to respond with hesitation to a suggestion that they enter upon "unchartered waters"[26] and exercise their powers over crimes alleged to have occurred in someone else's jurisdiction. The natural question is asked: why my court?—why not theirs?

A partial answer to such questions is that the litigant is actually invoking the judge's own law, being a municipal law that recognises and gives effect to principles of international law respecting universal jurisdiction.[27] Courts of the common law have long since abandoned the notion that they necessarily lack jurisdiction over events, even crimes, that occurred outside their territory.[28] However, in the matter of criminal law especially, lingering doubts will remain in the minds of many judges. A first source of the doubts will concern the legitimacy of the judge's intrusion into crimes that appear on their face to be the responsibility of the officials and judges of another legal jurisdiction. Sustaining this doubt is a notion about the sources of the legitimacy of judicial intervention in such matters.

Each judge, on appointment, receives a commission or equivalent document of authority of office. In the case of municipal judges, it is provided by the nation, state, or institution that legitimises the conferral of judicial power on the judge. Ordinarily, the source of such power could not rise higher than the stream. Accordingly, at least in most cases, a judge will think twice before he or she asserts coercive power over events and people that appear, on the face of the charges, to be the responsibility of the criminal (or civil) process of some other nation—one that has not conferred on the judge in question authority to deal with its citizens and their alleged wrongdoing occurring in their territory.

2. Municipal Legal Systems Operate in a World of Comity

The foregoing attitude is basically founded upon notions of comity and respect for the legitimate primacy of other legal systems operating within their own territory.[29] In part, it rests on knowledge that established legal procedures commonly exist, such as extradition, to hand criminals over to judicial authorities in other countries having clear jurisdiction over their crimes. In part, it depends upon practical matters that I will mention later. But its foundation lies in the judicial self-conception about the ultimate sources of legitimacy to make coercive orders affecting another human being.

To make such orders, a judge of the common-law tradition will usually require a firm satisfaction that there is a legitimate legal basis to do so.

Because that foundation ultimately derives, in law, from the judge's commission and own legal system, the assertion of judicial power over people and acts that ostensibly fall within the concerns of another jurisdiction, is not normally congenial. The judge will ask not why he or she should *not* act in the important matter in hand. Instead, the question will be, what right do I, a national judge, have to exercise jurisdiction over such a matter? The presence of the accused in the well of the court may afford jurisdiction in the sense of power over the party. But jurisdiction in the sense of legal authority with respect to a crime said to have occurred outside the territory of the judge's jurisdiction, will ordinarily require something more. At least it will usually do so in the absence of clear legislative authority, permitting the national judge to make coercive orders in such circumstances.

3. General Judicial Deference Is to Legislative Invention

Relatively little domestic legislation has been enacted authorizing national judges to exercise universal jurisdiction.[30] Nowadays, in the kinds of common-law countries of which I am writing, where the issues of universal jurisdiction are likely in the short term to be of chief practical concern, important new laws are ordinarily made by legislatures. They are enacted by representatives elected by the people and answerable to them in regular elections. Novel laws on large topics that are broad ranging, requiring detailed regulation, needing balances to be struck, and dealing with sensitive topics are not ordinarily invented by judges. In most countries, they are not accountable as legislators are.

The judicial role in expounding national constitutions, local legislation, and the common law is undoubted. Sometimes large steps are taken by courts.[31] However, a question that will naturally occur to a judge, faced with the invocation of universal jurisdiction that is not founded on parliamentary legislation, is why the judge should fill the gap in the law which the legislature has omitted to fill. Why, for example, should a judge in Australia, faced with a claim to jurisdiction based on the international crime of genocide, uphold an assertion of universal jurisdiction when not only has the Australian parliament omitted to enact such jurisdiction (where it could have done so) but where it has also withheld the general enactment of the Genocide Convention as part of Australia's domestic law?

Judges today, in every legal system, operate in the universe of statute law. Judges know, or can easily become aware, that statutes have been enacted, including in common-law countries, whose laws provide for jurisdiction in respect of international crimes.[32] Given that, in particular cases, legislation may accord jurisdiction to the courts in respect of certain crimes having their principal territorial connection with another place, a natural question to be asked by a judge, invited to assume jurisdiction without the enactment such legislation, is what "legitimizing connection"[33] exists, in default of express legislative authority, that permits the judge to assume control of the accused and the accusation. May it be that the legislature has held back deliberately, for reasons of international comity, concern about retaliation, opinions about judicial priorities or otherwise, to which the judge should also give deference? In the common-law tradition, judges are lawmakers, but in the minor key. Acknowledging that the legislature has the power (subject to any constitutional limitations) to confer upon them, explicitly, jurisdiction over particular international crimes or over international crimes generally, but has not chosen to do so, will cause many judges to stay their hand. In such a matter, why should a judge usurp the lawmaking function that belongs primarily to the legislature?[34]

Considerations such as these help to explain why, in default of national legislation, it has proved difficult to persuade most judges, at least in common-law countries, to assume universal jurisdiction over international criminals and their alleged crimes.[35] Such jurisdiction contemplates the potential exercise of "awesome power"[36] over the accused person. If such power is to be exercised, most judges will expect that it be authorized by elected lawmakers, not by other judges. At the heart of this feeling is a sense of the proper limits of judicial power and a belief that a point is quickly reached where judges should, in such matters, defer to legislators, directly accountable to the people.

4. The Basic Rule Is That Crime Is Local

An ingrained postulate both of international and municipal law is the principle of territoriality. According to this, jurisdiction is ordinarily "an incident of an independent nation."[37] The ultimate foundation for territorial jurisdiction is sovereignty. Although this notion can mean different things in international and municipal law, in relation to the latter, in an Australian decision, it has been said:[38] "Sovereignty is, by the law of all countries that have inherited the common law, regarded as territorial; because territorial boundaries ordinarily mark the limits of effective enforcement of municipal law. Territoriality (as an element on domicile, residence or presence) rather than political allegiance has by our law been recognised as the ordinary foundation of curial jurisdiction."

Earlier the same idea was expressed in England:[39] "It is an essential attribute of the sovereignty of this realm, as of all sovereign independent States, that it should possess jurisdiction over all persons and thing within its territorial limits and in all cases civil and criminal arising within those limits. This jurisdiction is exercised through the instrumentality of the duly constituted tribunals of the land."

In addition to these principles, which help to sustain the legitimacy of judicial orders, there is a particular principle that common-law courts have ordinarily upheld. It is sometimes expressed (not entirely accurately) in the aphorism "all crime is local."[40] Within the former British Empire, this principle was sometimes used to control the assertions of extraterritorial jurisdiction on the part of subordinate colonial legislatures.[41] By the end of the nineteenth century, with the growing ease of transport and telecommunications, new problems arose that challenged this hypothesis of the territoriality of crime in its original strictness.[42] By 1973 one law lord in England was pointing to the reality that crime "may originate in one country, be continued in another, produce effects in a third" allowing "no mechanical answer" to disputes over jurisdiction.[43] By 1991 another law lord was lamenting that "unfortunately in this century crime has ceased to be largely local in origin and effect. Crime is now established on an international scale and the common law must face this new reality."[44]

Nevertheless, enough remains of the former doctrine to cause a judge in country A to feel reluctance about the exercise of jurisdiction and power over an offender and an offense in country B, particularly where there is no legislation or settled law to authorize that course. Generally speaking, most judges (and not only of the common law)[45] recoil at the suggestion that they should exercise their power over the acts of foreigners performed in foreign countries. Such judges still feel the call of the basic rule that there should be some territorial nexus between the jurisdiction invoked and the place where the crime occurred.[46]

The territoriality of the locus remains the easiest and most traditional basis for the exercise of criminal jurisdiction. The heart of this continuing idea is a conception of the very nature of criminal jurisdiction. According to common-law beliefs, crime is not, as such, an offense against the victim who is wronged. That person (or that person's representatives) may or may not have civil or statutory remedies for compensation. But crime is, by its definition, an offense against the society in which it occurs. Originally, it was viewed as an affront to "the King's peace."[47] This is why crime is ordinarily (but not exclusively) prosecuted by the state or the Crown on behalf of the people. It is why, in many federal systems, crime is substantially a state responsibility, thereby acknowledging that different states may take different views about the conduct that is so antisocial that, if proved, it should be punished as criminal.

If this acceptance of particularity and specificity is acknowledged within the one federation, judges operating within federal systems especially may, by analogy, feel the same way about recognizing and punishing criminal acts that occurred in a foreign jurisdiction. Within a single federation, the recognition and enforcement of the criminal law of another jurisdiction may invite solutions derived from the language of the national constitution itself[48] or from a particular statute[49] or from a principle of the common law.[50] But in an international setting, in the absence of constitutional or statutory authority, many judges will feel diffident about expanding the ambit of their powers to render as offences of their jurisdiction crimes committed outside that jurisdiction. If they ask themselves whether such acts represent crimes against the local jurisdiction invoked, they may need some persuading to arrive at an affirmative answer. The presence in their jurisdiction of the offender, or of the victim, may lend color to the assumption of jurisdiction to decide the threshold issue. But, at least in respect of criminal wrongdoing, the exertion of judicial power over the offender (including the power to punish) may sometimes seem alien to inherited notions of the territoriality of crime. At least it may do so in the absence of express statutory law authorizing a larger jurisdiction.[51]

5. Judicial Creation of New Crimes Is Limited

There was a time when the judges of the common law did not hesitate to create, and define, new criminal offenses. After all, the original content of the common law of crime was a judicial invention. In some jurisdictions, a substantial part of the criminal law remains that of the common law, as modified by statute. However, in other jurisdictions the criminal law has been codified or substantially reduced to statutory form. In Australia, where the prime responsibility for the general criminal law is that of the states, we have each of these variants.[52]

In this situation, on the face of things, the willingness of municipal judges to enforce new crimes, beyond those provided in their jurisdiction by local codes and statutes, may depend upon the extent to which such legislation has excluded, expressly or by necessary implication, judicial innovation in the field of crime.

Apart from such considerations, there is, in many common-law jurisdictions, a particular inhibition on the creation of new crimes. The highest courts in some common-law countries have suggested that, in the matter of new criminal offenses, the common law is beyond childbearing. Such inventions must therefore be left to the legislature.[53] In part, this principle reflects the general judicial deference to elected lawmakers already mentioned. But in part, it also reflects contemporary judicial attitudes to due process and an increasing judicial distaste for legal fictions. Thus any "crime" recognized and enforced in a judge's own jurisdiction under the common law necessarily has operation retrospectively upon persons who might complain, with justification, that they were not on notice that the crime had become part of the body of law to which they were subject in that place.[54] The imposition of criminal offenses by legislation having retroactive effect raises, in some jurisdictions, constitutional or human rights questions about the requirements of due process and the limits of legislative power.[55] Many judges would feel that no lesser standards should be observed by judges themselves in effectively creating new crimes that have not previously been defined.

Most countries of the common law observe a bifurcation between international and municipal law.[56] Without legislation importing an international crime into the municipal legal system, international law will normally remain outside that system. In the case of international crimes of the kind that invoke universal jurisdiction, some judges will have no hesitation in treating the rule against retroactivity of new criminal offenses as overridden by a higher rule grounded in the common duties of humanity.[57] Others will even dispute the relevance of retroactivity, given that international law has long defined the ambit and application of the crimes in question. In this respect the debates of international law have moved on from the debates that surrounded the charges brought against the original defendants before the International Military Tribunal at Nuremberg.[58]

Yet for the ordinary municipal judge, facing the invocation of jurisdiction in respect of a crime that cannot be found in that judge's own criminal code, statute, or case books, such arguments may have the appearance of a fiction. To the assertion that the international crime in question is so horrendous that it is a crime against all people of the world, the average judge may respond with special hesitation. The bigger the crime, the greater the risk of emotion and antipathy to the accused. The greater the need, then, for procedural and substantive safeguards and clear legal authority to assume jurisdiction over such a crime and such a person.[59] Almost certainly, the judge will ask the questions: If it is such a horrendous crime, why is the accused not prosecuted and tried where the crime principally occurred? Why should jurisdiction be assumed here, when the local legislature has not bothered to make it a local crime?

6. New Retroactive Criminal Law Is Offensive

Municipal and international law have a bias against the retroactive enforcement of criminal offenses.[60] All retroactive laws have the potential to inflict injustice on those first rendered answerable to them. This is especially so where, as in the criminal law, a person's liberty and reputation are at stake. Considerations such as these were agitated on behalf of the Nuremberg defendants. They were raised in the *Eichmann* trial in Israel. How, for example, it was asked, could the courts of Israel, which did not even exist as a state at the time of Adolf Eichmann's offences, enjoy the legal authority to enforce, in relation to him, a local law passed only in 1950?[61]

These fundamental questions demonstrate the limits on the reliance upon the postwar Israeli legislation to render Eichmann accountable before Israeli courts.[62] In such courts, the legislation, being binding, would (subject to any constitutional challenge) have to be observed by the municipal courts. But it was this quandary that sent the Supreme Court of Israel (like the tribunal at Nuremberg) searching for a deeper, preexisting principle upon which to rely in rejecting the charge of an impermissibly retroactive imposition of criminal sanctions.

Various ways to circumvent this argument have been proposed.[63] However, it is not surprising to see judicial reservations where, without benefit of statute, a judge is asked to assume jurisdiction over an international crime. Often (but not always) the accused will be old because the wheels of justice will have moved slowly. Often the offenses will have happened long ago and far away. The victims will be foreigners. They may not speak the local language or understand fully local court procedure. The overworked prosecuting agencies of the state may have little or no interest in pursuing the matter.[64] If to these practical concerns is added the judge's intuitive resistance to the retroactive imposition of criminal offenses that are invoked in the municipal court, it is not difficult to understand why, in practice, few such cases have proceeded past first base.

7. Crimes of Uncertain Application Are Troubling

To attract universal jurisdiction it is clear enough that the crime must be one expressed by international law. It must be such as to found a compelling case for the exceptional invocation of jurisdiction although the crime has no other connection with the territory of the forum.[65] The precise crimes that are included in this class are a matter of dispute amongst experts. One list has identified twenty-nine crimes of this character.[66] Most lists, such as that provided by Cherif Bassiouni in his contribution to this volume, include such grave international crimes as war crimes, crimes against humanity, genocide, torture, and piracy.[67] But even these crimes occasionally attract criticism. Thus no provision is expressly made for universal jurisdiction in the case of the conventional law creating war crimes.[68]

Beyond this "core" list of truly serious international crimes there are other crimes in respect of which universal jurisdiction has sometimes been claimed. Crimes related to apartheid or certain offences against United Nations personnel or hostages are amongst these.[69] Where does the list end? Some would add crimes connected with the movement of obscene publications. Some would include certain crimes concerned with narcotic goods. Yet not everybody (and not every judge) would necessarily consider that such crimes are incontrovertibly serious, necessitating a novel assertion of jurisdiction. Some would feel disinclined to invent jurisdiction over strangers accused of such crimes having, otherwise, no territorial nexus with the forum.

The large number of potential crimes, and the disputes about many of them, present a further reason for judicial caution.[70] Some of the crimes propounded may be ill defined, involving uncertainties both of substance and procedure.[71] The international crime of piracy may be easy to justify as a crime of universal jurisdiction in a maritime, trading country such as the United States or Australia. But it may be less easy in other parts of the world.[72] Faced with the invocation of international law, municipal judges with little familiarity with such law could easily adopt incorrect interpretations.[73] Such judges will frequently be aware of that danger. It will provide another reason for proceeding with extreme caution.

8. Amnesty and Impunity Create Problems

Many of those accused who may be charged with an international crime, reliant on universal jurisdiction in a country other than their own, will find themselves in this predicament precisely because, at home, they are entitled to rely upon an amnesty, or impunity or some accountability mechanism which exempts them from criminal prosecution.[74] Sometimes such impunity will be reflected in the law.[75] Sometimes it will exist de facto because local prosecuting authorities will not pursue the accused.[76] Not infrequently, the impunity will have been provided as a condition for the relinquishment of power by a former ruler.[77] Occasionally the impunity will be claimed because the visitor is still the head of state of another nation or because he or she asserts that the crimes complained of were committed during a time when the accused enjoyed the immunity conventionally attributed to a head of state.[78] Occasionally there may be no legal amnesty that the accused can claim but, being regarded as a guest in the national forum (either of the government or of the head of state) there may be social or cultural reluctance to prosecute the accused even for grave international crimes.[79]

The extent of the exemptions from criminal liability provided in law or practice by these different forms of impunity cannot be underestimated. It is a problem regularly reported by a United Nations special rapporteur.[80] It is the subject of many complaints by victims, their families and civil society organizations.

A judge of the common law, asked to invoke universal jurisdiction in respect of an accused, entitled to impunity at home, will be confronted by a "nettlesome issue."[81] The judge may, of course, take a robust view: finding defects in the amnesty relied on,[82] rejecting the effectiveness of self-amnesty,[83] concluding that the international crimes charged fall outside the scope of head of state immunity[84] or that the domestic law of a nation cannot confer immunity against a serious international crime.[85]

On the other hand, the judge may feel that it is inappropriate to substitute his or her evaluation in a foreign court for an immunity that has been carefully negotiated in the jurisdiction where the criminal acts allegedly occurred. The judge may be concerned at the prospect of disturbing a compromise that reflects the settlement of extremely complex and sensitive local conflicts.[86] The judge may also be concerned that a refusal to recognize the impunity could sometimes have a serious destabilizing effect in a fragile political situation of which the judge knows little. Alternatively, if the impunity is based on the office which the accused held in the place having most connection with the crimes, the judge may be concerned that equivalent office holders of the court's own jurisdiction could be subject to retaliatory prosecutions when they travel internationally. To a large extent international law in the past has rested on a principle of comity.[87] That principle still sometimes informs judicial attitudes to assertions of extraterritorial jurisdiction.

9. Anxiety Exists about a New Imperialism of Rich Countries

Some judges, concerned about such issues of comity, will point out that the assertions of universal jurisdiction before courts have, so far, generally involved the courts of developed countries. It is in such countries that liberal ideas of personal accountability for international crimes and individual conformity with international law tend to have their most stalwart supporters. However, such judges might question whether this situation would remain the case if judicial assertions of universal jurisdiction became common. The principle must be tested by what would happen if the powers of courts in authoritarian countries were invoked by pliant prosecuting authorities to claim universal jurisdiction against a national of a developed country accused of trumped up war crimes, for example of genocide.[88] Such concern has been voiced in response to international seizures of alleged perpetrators of international crimes.[89] Immanuel Kant long ago taught the imperative of testing ethical propositions by what would happen if they became a universal rule. So we must do in the law.

Quite apart from the anxiety about retaliation and the fear, for example, that a United States president or British prime minister might be arrested and tried for war crimes against persons in the former Yugoslavia or Iraq when visiting a country whose courts uphold universal jurisdiction,[90] other observers (who would have their counterparts in the judiciary) might feel a sense of distaste at an intrusion by the governmental organs of developed countries into the political and legal affairs of, mostly, developing countries. Such intrusions are sure to be seen, or represented by some in developing countries, as an indictment of the capacity of their governmental organs to deal with their own national problems effectively and justly. That may indeed be the conclusion of many liberal observers in the developed world.[91] But a municipal judge may feel a disinclination to become engaged in a process that will often be presented as political interference in the internal affairs of another nation.[92] Considerations of this kind might convince many judges (members of a somewhat cautious profession anyway) that they should be extremely careful in upholding claims to universal jurisdiction lest they kill this delicate child in its cradle.[93]

10. Politically Controversial Cases Engender Caution

Reinforcing such judicial reactions will be the fact that, almost by definition, the kinds of cases in which universal jurisdiction will be invoked are likely to be highly controversial and potentially embarrassing. Thus they may involve a visiting head of state or former head of state selected precisely because of the embarrassment and publicity which the accusation and hoped-for arrest will occasion.[94] Such processes will commonly be brought not on the initiative of official prosecutors but by highly motivated NGOs, urged on by the expatriate victims of wrongdoing and their families.[95] It should not be overlooked that the Spanish law minister opposed the investigation by a Spanish magistrate of the Chilean general Pinochet.[96] Moreover, it was the persistence of international NGOs that led to the initiation of proceedings before the Senegal courts against former president Habré.[97] The role of such bodies, and especially bodies visibly led by foreigners, may sometimes occasion resentment in the country of the forum which spills over to the members of the judiciary who are, after all, citizens of that country.[98] While it is true that well-motivated NGOs can constitute a counterweight to political and institutional complacency, judges may sometimes view them as irresponsible, effectively unaccountable, and prone to cause wildfires that imperil orderly legal process and foreign relations.[99]

Such attitudes may arise within the complacency that not infrequently accompanies the judicial life. But it can sometimes also be explained by judicial concern about being seen to be too active in responding to prosecutions of this character. Concern about reprisals against members of the judiciary, who reach conclusions in such sensitive cases uncongenial to their governments, has already been expressed by the relevant United Nations special rapporteurs.[100] Such cases will commonly be extremely sensitive. Inescapably, their prosecution might affect the relations between the forum and the country having most connection with the crimes charged. Judges are not blind. They will be aware of such sensitivities. However unconsciously, such considerations may provide another reason for caution.

11. Preference Is for International Tribunals

Yet another reason for judicial hesitation will be the municipal judge's knowledge of the growing number of international tribunals with statute or treaty-based jurisdiction to try persons accused of crimes against international law. No judge today would be unaware of the special Scottish tribunal, conducted in the Netherlands, that tried two accused in respect of the *Lockerbie* disaster.[101] Many would know generally of the International Criminal Tribunals for the Former Yugoslavia and Rwanda.[102] A few would be aware of the proposed mixed tribunals for Sierra Leone and Cambodia,[103] established with United Nations backing. Some may know of the United

Nations–organized courts in Kosovo, East Timor, and elsewhere.[104] Most judges would have some idea of the adoption of the Rome Statute for the Creation of an International Criminal Court.[105] Many municipal judges would consider that this is the proper course to follow: invoking jurisdiction before courts and tribunals with clear international authority rather than attempting to persuade municipal courts to assert novel authority although it has not been expressly conferred on them.

Reasoning of this kind will not satisfy the scholar who will know that the jurisdiction of such international and transnational bodies rests on their constituting instrument not upon notions of universal jurisdiction as such.[106] Moreover, the creation of special courts and tribunals cannot, of its nature, replace the argument for universal jurisdiction before municipal courts. Universal jurisdiction is complementary to the jurisdiction of international bodies, not a substitute for them.

Supporters of the idea of universal jurisdiction will point to the limitations on the focus and resources of specialist bodies and the need to supplement them with the ever-present authority of municipal courts. Apart from anything else, if this is not done, powerful or recalcitrant states will be able effectively to immunize themselves and their wrongdoers from accountability to international criminal law by simply refusing to participate in the activities of specialist international bodies.[107] The sequence of events involving the prosecution of General Pinochet in the United Kingdom (although strictly an application under local extradition law, pursuant to statute, not an invocation of universal jurisdiction under the common law) undoubtedly encouraged the courts of Chile (to whom the general was ultimately returned) to assume a role in his case that had previously seemed impossible.[108]

The International Criminal Court will only be as effective as the judges elected to it, and the resources devoted to it, permit.[109] Nevertheless, it is an understandable reaction on the part of a municipal judge, faced with an unusual assertion of universal jurisdiction, to consider that this is not a role that a municipal court should assume. In a world of proliferating international bodies having jurisdiction over various international crimes, the municipal judge may feel that the foundation for universal jurisdiction should be more solidly based. It should have a surer footing in international treaty law and local statute law than is typically the case in common-law countries.

When invited to assume universal jurisdiction, the municipal judge's own hesitations may be reinforced by knowledge of the fact that, where the international community is firmly of the opinion that crimes of an international character should be prosecuted, it has moved to create courts or tribunals with defined powers whose jurisdiction is specified and not dependant on an affirmative and exceptional decision of a municipal judge.

12. Judges Respect Democratic Responsibility

An additional reason for hesitation may be a judge's sense of respect for the nation, and the courts of the nation, having the closest territorial connection with the crimes alleged. Knowing the important part that courts play in a country in upholding and reinforcing the democratic process,[110] the judge may feel a proper sense of inhibition in intruding into an area that can readily be perceived as primarily the concern of the institutions (including the courts) of the country most concerned.[111] Most judges would not want, by asserting their own jurisdiction in a doubtful case, to undermine efforts to rebuild national sovereignty, democratic institutions, and self-respecting courts, in countries that have lately suffered from catastrophic events that include international crimes.[112]

The participation in a national response to such crimes may itself be an important part of the acceptance of responsibility for grave wrongdoing. The assumption of that responsibility by the courts of a foreign country may, at least in some cases, interfere in the institutional renewal of the country most affected.[113] Thus the public conduct of trials in countries such as Cambodia and Sierra Leone, which have suffered from terrible instances of international crimes, and the involvement in such trials of local judges, may be an important step in reinforcing the rule of law. Of course, in most cases, an appeal to universal jurisdiction will only occur where domestic institutions have failed to bring alleged wrongdoers to justice in the place of the alleged crimes. Moreover, as in the case of Chile, foreign initiatives may occasionally strengthen those at home.[114] Nevertheless, a judge, asked to exercise judicial power in respect of events having their most natural connection with another country, will commonly be anxious to avoid intruding into a circumstance of which the judge may know little with consequences that the court cannot easily predict.

13. Judges Lack Clear Precedents

Judges of the common law, by virtue of their office and habits, tend to feel most comfortable when they are applying settled law. State practice on universal jurisdiction has not yet risen to the point at which it can be described as part of customary international law.[115] Therefore, neither in the precedents of the common law nor in the authorities of international law are there indisputable norms that a judge can invoke and apply when an appeal is made to universal jurisdiction. In so far as international law has spoken through the voice of the International Court of Justice, it has been very cautious: reflecting some of the concerns identified in this essay written before that court's decision was delivered.[116]

A judge without a clear precedent, or an available constitutional or statutory norm, will often feel at sea. Because of the preceding considerations courts, especially final courts, will commonly have many potential reasons for postponing an authoritative ruling on the ambit and contours of the rules of universal jurisdiction. Because, as a matter of practicality, the invocation of such jurisdiction will ordinarily come before a trial court, at a lower tier in the municipal judicial hierarchy, additional reasons for caution and hesitation exist. Without clear leadership in the face of an accused protesting the jurisdiction, trial courts are likely to respond with a measure of reluctance to assume it.

14. Judges Have Heavy Case Lists and Plenty to Do

A final point should not be overlooked. Judges at every level of the hierarchy in municipal systems are usually hard-pressed. They have plenty of tasks to occupy their time. In virtually all of those tasks there will be no challenge to their jurisdiction. When suddenly presented with an unusual case, perhaps agitated by unusual prosecutors, making an accusation against foreigners temporarily within the jurisdiction in respect of events that happened far away and long ago, the busy national judge may respond with impatience. Such a judge would be less than human if he or she did not feel irritation.

Even a judge who may feel sympathy for the victims, empathy for human rights, and support for the advance of international law may be so weighed down by the pressure of court lists as to seek some respite from an unusual case in which an uncertain jurisdiction is invoked, resting not on clear treaty and statute law but on the judge's uncertain interpretation of the common law. This may be an unfortunate truth. But reality often controls legal outcomes, not least in the highly practical systems of the common law. More perhaps than judges of other traditions, the judges of the common law are, by tradition, pragmatic. They tend to be suspicious of grand theories and hesitant about vague principles, especially where such principles impinge on the liberty of an accused person before them.

Conclusions

The foregoing are fourteen reasons for hesitation and inaction about universal jurisdiction. Many of them overlap. However, judges in municipal courts will also be well aware that, if they decline to exercise such jurisdiction, the practical consequence, in most cases, will be that persons accused of truly heinous crimes will probably go unpunished by law. To insist on their prosecution by the state in whose territory the crimes have been committed will often be unrealistic, given that such states are frequently themselves implicated in the crimes or in the deals done with criminals to exempt them from legal responsibility.[117]

Every judge is well aware of the importance of affording an impartial public forum in which the victims of serious criminal wrongdoing can tell their stories and have them recorded.[118] The notion that one's own jurisdiction may become a safe haven for those who have grossly offended against fellow human beings would be offensive to most judges whose lives are dedicated to law and justice, not the protection of tyranny and oppression.[119] In the age of global media, the impartial courtroom provides an important metaphor for compelling those charged with the gravest of crimes to make answer.[120] It would have been perfectly possible for the Israeli agents to have murdered Adolf Eichmann in Argentina. A trial, based on evidence and conducted in public before professional judges had a deep symbolic significance, and not only for Eichmann's victims.[121]

Nowadays there are fewer Nazi perpetrators and victims around. But there are plenty of others from Cambodia, the Balkans, Rwanda, the Congo, and other lands. Victims may have no confidence in their own courts but look with hope, the accused being in the jurisdiction, to judges of countries that observe the rule of law and conduct a manifestly fair and speedy trial.

Such judges, faced with the alternatives, may feel a moral compulsion to respond to such pleas. But can they do so consistently with law? In many parts of the world, municipal judges are becoming accustomed to drawing upon international law and giving it effect in their own decisions. Normally, it is true, in countries of the "dualist" tradition, they will need to be sustained by local legislation or regulations made under legislative power.[122] But within common-law systems, judges too have a lawmaking function. In the exercise of that function, increasingly it is realized that judges of the common law may draw upon the principles of international law and in particular international human rights norms.

This process was expounded in the context of the important decision which, for the first time, accorded recognition to Aboriginal native title: *Mabo v Queensland*.[123] In the course of that decision, Justice F. G. Brennan explained why earlier propositions of the common law, denying respect to native title, were no longer true expressions of the common law of Australia. One of the steps in the argument (which gathered the support of the majority of the High Court of Australia) made reference to the deep principle against racial discrimination contained in international law. Justice Brennan said:[124]

The opening up of international remedies to individuals pursuant to Australia's accession to the Optional Protocol to the International Covenant on Civil and Political Rights brings to bear on the common law the powerful influence of the Covenant and the international standards it imports. The common law does not necessarily conform with international law, but international law is a legitimate and important influence on the development of the common law, especially when international law declares the existence of universal human rights. A common law doctrine founded on unjust discrimination in the enjoyment of civil and political rights demands reconsideration. It is contrary both to international standards and to the fundamental values of our common law. . . .

So far as the interpretation of laws, even the Constitution, by reference to developments of international law is concerned, the approach that I have mentioned, often favored by judges of Commonwealth countries,[125] has recently gathered some support in the Supreme Court of the United States. In ruling that the carrying into effect of a sentence of death upon a prisoner who was severely mentally handicapped would constitute "cruel and unusual punishment," contrary to the United States Constitution, Justice Stevens, for the majority of the Court, called in aid options concerning the requirements of international human rights law.[126]

Against the background of this principle, the question is whether, without legislative or executive incorporation into municipal law of a general principle of universal jurisdiction (or specific jurisdiction over particular crimes) a judge of our tradition would be entitled to do so. In *Mabo*, Justice Brennan, and the High Court of Australia, took a bold step. They did so under the pressure of serious demonstrated injustice that legislatures and executive governments had failed adequately to cure. Of course, they acted in relation to people who lived in Australia, wrongs done locally, and in respect of land and conduct indubitably within the court's jurisdiction. But do equal wrongs done to other human beings forfeit the demand for judicial creativity because those wrongs were done in another country to people who, at the time, were not of one's own nation? If victims and the accused are before the court, is that enough? Will the common law take this extra step?

These questions have not yet been conclusively answered in Australia or in most countries of the common law. To some extent there are precedents that would encourage a common-law judge to uphold universal jurisdiction. Courts of the common-law tradition have done so in the past in relation to pirates[127] and slaves.[128] Such people were respectively the perpetrators, or victims, of grave crimes against all humanity. To this extent the notion of universal jurisdiction is not entirely novel nor extralegal.[129] What is new is the expansion of the crimes to which universal jurisdiction is said to apply. Supporters suggest that all that has changed is the recognition that there are now more crimes *contra omnes*[130] whose alleged perpetrators will be rendered accountable wherever they are and wherever their crimes took place.[131] To wait for international tribunals with clear jurisdiction will be to wait to the Greek calends. According to supporters of universal jurisdiction, some international crimes are just so serious that, in law, they override territorial limitations on the jurisdiction of municipal courts. The right of the judge to assert jurisdiction comes from the presence in the forum of the accused and from the judge's act of importing into his or her own legal system the international human rights norms that are part of the common heritage of humanity.

In my own country the question of whether judges may take this extra step is still a matter of controversy and uncertainty.[132] As that question may one day come before me for decision, I will refrain from expressing a concluded view. Both opinions have been stated in Australian courts, as elsewhere. Each view has persuasive supporters and opponents. Of this there is no doubt. The twenty-first century will see a growing rapprochement, in common-law countries, between municipal legal systems and international law, specifically the international law of human rights. Indeed, this is one of the largest challenges that every legal system has to resolve.

In the resolution of this tension, the legislatures and executive governments will have the largest role to play. But the genius of the common law lies in the creative function that it accords to its judges. They also have a part to play. Their daily involvement in the search for justice under law makes them sensitive to the call for justice where they can respond to it. The ultimate question is whether, in the hands of such judges, universal jurisdiction, long discussed in the texts of international law, will have a life in municipal law under conditions which the judges proclaim.[133] Will this be a further step in the building of a global rule of law? Or will the judges hold back, leaving it to the primary lawmakers in the legislature to afford redress? Will they refuse jurisdiction, knowing that the result will usually be that nothing is done and that grave injustices go unrepaired? For the answers to these questions, watch this space.

Chapter 13
Afterword: The Politics of Advancing International Criminal Justice

Lloyd Axworthy

The reflections that follow describe the public and political process that animated Canada's experience in asserting universal jurisdiction over crimes against humanity and war crimes. I should emphasize that I see universal jurisdiction not as merely a legal concept but additionally as an important political value and a tool to achieve an important public policy objective.

My perspective is clearly not a juridical one. Over the past twenty-one years I have served as a member of Parliament, both in opposition and in government. During that time the issue of war criminals was a constant item on the public agenda and a source of deep concern to many of my constituents who wished to see an end to the impunity for perpetrators of terrible human rights violations. The matter came before Parliament, the courts, and was the subject of a Royal Commission study. I also served as foreign minister when Canada chaired the Rome Conference in 1998, and I introduced in the House of Commons Bill C-19, which gave the federal government full legislative power to implement the Statute of Rome and the International Criminal Court it creates. The bill amended provisions of the Criminal Code to address these issues and to pursue allegations and prosecution of war crimes. As a result, when I look at the Princeton Principles of Universal Jurisdiction under consideration here, it is comforting to know that what we were attempting in the political trenches up north is now receiving broad confirmation and deep examination. I only wish that the research and analysis that these essays provide had been available at the time.

By any account the principle of universal jurisdiction must be inextricably linked to the value that some crimes are so horrific, so offensive, that they are perpetrated not only against their victims but against humanity. This value is the basis for asserting jurisdiction over all offenders of these crimes, no matter where they take place. This principle is an immeasurably important one. It underlies the Nuremberg Charter and the Statute of

Rome. It is also a principle embraced by a majority of Canadians, a fact that I feel confident in asserting because the public debates we held in Canada confirmed it.

The principle of universal jurisdiction also reflects the human security agenda of Canadian foreign policy. Simply put, the Canadian government has advanced the notion that the risk to individuals was as great a security risk as that faced by nation states. This led us to champion such causes as the land mines treaty, the protection of civilians in peacekeeping missions, small-arms trade restrictions, war-affected children, and, most notably, the International Criminal Court. Central to the agenda was not only protecting the individual from risk but also holding the offender accountable for his or her actions. The use of universal jurisdiction for enforcing criminal responsibility was viewed as a crucial way to pursue these objectives.

To illustrate the point, the indictment of Milosevic and his accomplices during the Kosovo conflict had a dramatic effect on changing the dynamics of negotiation, led to a settlement and, as we have seen, to his eventual fall from power. The very act of indictment isolated Milosevic and convinced many Serbs that they could never become an accepted participant in international discourse as long as there was a pariah in their midst. This recognition provided a dramatic example of the power of shaming as an effective tool of conflict resolution. On the other hand, I should add that universal jurisdiction as an instrument of domestic criminal law to respond to war crimes and crimes against humanity has proven to be somewhat more unwieldy and difficult. Let me share a brief illustration.

In the mid-1980s a public inquiry headed by Justice Deschenes was mandated to examine the prosecution of suspected World War II–era war criminals who were then residing in Canada. The public mood was animated by shock and disbelief. There had been many allegations in the media of war criminals living undetected in Canada for the previous forty years or so. As a member of Parliament, I found that my constituents were troubled very deeply by the thought that war criminals could have been living in their midst for so long. These and other Canadians called upon the government to show leadership in the international community by ensuring that Canada was doing its part to bring war criminals to justice.

Justice Deschenes delivered his report in 1986. He recommended that the following tools be used to pursue alleged war criminals: extradition, criminal prosecutions in Canada, and denaturalization and deportation. The Canadian government responded by outlining a new policy reiterating that Canada would not be a haven for war criminals. In my opinion there were two distinct policy objectives in play. The first was to keep Canada free of war criminals—in other words, to prevent war criminals from entering and removing war criminals if they were found residing here. The other policy objective was to bring war criminals to justice—in other words, to investigate allegations and prosecute or extradite to other jurisdictions.

To accommodate criminal prosecutions of suspected war criminals in Canada, the Criminal Code was amended to assert universal jurisdiction over war crimes and crimes against humanity and apply these amendments retrospectively to crimes committed outside of Canada.

The Royal Canadian Mounted Police (RCMP) launched several investigations. The result of one of the investigations led to charges against Imre Finta, a Canadian citizen from Hungary who was accused of participating in the deportation of Hungarian Jews to Auschwitz and elsewhere during World War II. Finta was acquitted, and the Crown appealed the case all the way to the supreme court of Canada. The court upheld the acquittal on the grounds that it interpreted the statute as drafted to require that prosecutors demonstrate that the offense was a violation of both international and domestic law. This ruling set an almost impossibly high standard for prosecution. The court also stated that certain defenses were admissible to avoid conviction. An alleged offender could avoid conviction, the court asserted, if he was acting on superior orders provided that those orders were not known by the accused to be manifestly unlawful. Finta had pleaded that he was acting strictly in accordance with a Hungarian order requiring the deportation of all Hungarian Jews. The court expressed serious concern about the use of jury trial and how it could be manipulated on behalf of the defendant. Many legal scholars criticized the decision, and there were renewed calls for more effective criminal laws including provision for some international universal jurisdiction regime.

Setting aside some of the specific repercussions of this decision, it became clear that collecting enough evidence to successfully prosecute, in Canada, a war crime committed in another part of the world, and some fifty years earlier, was impossibly difficult. The practical difficulties were and still are apparent. Successful investigations require the cooperation of other governments, some of which Canada may not have mutual legal assistance treaties with. For example, prior to the lifting of the Iron Curtain, obtaining evidence from Eastern Bloc countries was practically impossible.

The same obstacles apply to modern-day conflicts. The regimes that engage in crimes against humanity or war crimes are not likely to cooperate with our investigations. Throughout the 1990s the media published rumors that Somali war criminals had entered into Canada, allegations that raise two interesting issues. One is that while we may not be able to gather enough evidence to prosecute a war criminal who is found in Canada, it is a much easier task to surrender a suspect to an international tribunal mandated to investigate and gather evidence against criminals as well as prosecute them. The second issue is that the difficulties in prosecuting foreign war criminals have become painfully clear as the years have progressed. In the fourteen years since Canada asserted universal jurisdiction over crimes against humanity and war crimes, we have not seen a single criminal conviction for these crimes. We have only had one extradition of a suspect to

Germany. In all other cases where Canada has acted to pursue war criminals and crimes against humanity, it has been through our Immigration Act, by denaturalization or deportation of suspects found in Canada, or by refusing to admit suspects applying to enter Canada. So if we revisit Canadian public policy goals, it is clear that the goal of getting war criminals out and keeping them out is more easily done, but the policy of prosecuting war criminals through the assertion of universal jurisdiction has proven to be practically impossible.

The current Canadian government, on which I served, did attempt to remedy this problem. But before I elaborate on actions we took in the late 1990s, I would like to reflect on how what I have described thus far about Canada's experience echoes the inability or unwillingness of most nations to prosecute war criminals from the days of Nuremberg and Tokyo until the present. After Nuremberg, despite the new international law created, and despite the Universal Declaration on Human Rights, the world has seen some of the most tragic and despicable crimes ever committed, most of them with complete impunity. Some estimate that Stalin's purges resulted in the deaths of more innocent people than the Holocaust. There is also the agony of the Biafra, the killing fields of Cambodia, the horrific crimes of Sierra Leone, and the list goes on and on . . . with impunity for all. Unless we have an enforceable system in place, all the precedents and genocide conventions, and indeed all our progress in international law, makes no difference. To quote Bert Rolling, "The road to hell is paved with good conventions."

Since Nuremberg and Tokyo, only two criminal tribunals have been established by the international community, one for the former Yugoslavia and the other for Rwanda. The creation of these tribunals occurred because of political conditions and Security Council dynamics. I believe that if we want justice for all, not just when it is convenient or when the stars align, the world needs a permanent tribunal—in other words, an International Criminal Court. The obligations of the Statute of Rome will be enforceable through national criminal codes and through the pending creation of the International Criminal Court in the Hague. The statute and its obligations are already having a definite impact on criminal codes around the world. As I discuss these issues presently, states are amending their penal codes to allow prosecution of individuals for genocide, crimes against humanity and war crimes. States are creating and improving capacity to punish war criminals as a result of the complementarity principles of the International Criminal Court. (Complementarity presumes that domestic jurisdiction will prosecute alleged criminals unless they are unwilling or unable to do so, and then the international court has the opportunity to assume jurisdiction.) This was certainly the Canadian experience. The act of ratifying the statute in and of itself gave rise to an extensive examination of the entire domestic regime of codes and courts in order to provide a system for applying universal jurisdiction much clearer and more comprehensive than in the past.

Incredibly, states where short years ago terrible atrocities were taking place are signing and ratifying the statute. The very fact that new leaders of Sierra Leone and the Federal Republic of Yugoslavia are embracing the International Criminal Court sends out a powerful message to their own people: these horrendous criminal acts will not be tolerated in the future. Indeed, it sends the message to the international community that these nations are working to bring accountability to their leaders and that victims and witnesses should see the perpetrators of terrible atrocities be held responsible for their crimes. As more and more nations agree to sign and ratify the Rome Statute, they further emphasize that international law *will* begin to penetrate immunities that no national system of universal jurisdiction can.

All of these arguments illustrate why Canada made the policy decision to support and indeed vigorously pursue the creation of the International Criminal Court. On December 10, 1999, Human Rights Day, I introduced into the House of Commons Bill C-19, which would implement the Statute of Rome and strengthen the foundation for criminal prosecution in Canada. It addressed the supreme court ruling in *R. v Finta* by clarifying criminal offenses as well as permissible defenses. In brief, the bill repealed the previous war crimes provisions in the Criminal Code and replaced them with new crimes of genocide, crimes against humanity, and war crimes to reflect definitions outlined in the Statute of Rome. The bill created a new criminal offense of breach of responsibility by military commanders and civilian superiors. Failure to exercise control over persons under their authority, which then results in subordinates committing a war crime or crime against humanity, could entail the superior's criminal responsibility if that superior officer fails to take measures to prevent the crime. The defense of superior orders was thus withdrawn as a permissible defense against conviction for genocide.

As it progressed through the legislative process, this bill fostered a very interesting and useful parliamentary and public debate about the International Criminal Court and Canada's prosecution of war criminals. The parliamentary committee that considered the bill included several eminent experts in international law, including Professors of Law Bill Graham, the chair; Daniel Turp; and Irwin Cotler. The committee received as witnesses everyone who applied to appear including legal scholars, human rights workers, individuals, Ukrainian and Jewish groups, and even a conservative profamily group. National newspapers weighed in with their editorials, which were frequently followed by letters to the editor.

I will not elaborate on the specifics of these debates, as they are a matter of public record. Instead, I will briefly refer to two issues of interest. First, there was no argument opposing the government's decision to more firmly assert universal jurisdiction over war crimes and crimes against humanity. Indeed, a surprising number of organizations and even politicians from several political parties urged the government to adopt a broader definition of universal jurisdiction—in other words, something similar to the current Belgian model. One amendment was accepted, but in the end the government took the position that it did not want to assert "super universal jurisdiction" on the grounds that the government wanted to keep war criminals *out* rather than bring them all here for trials or to create a surrogate International Criminal Court in Canada. The definition that the government accepted required the presence of the alleged offender in Canada but does not require the offense to have taken place in Canada.

A larger debate unfolded about the International Criminal Court itself. While there was unanimity in the belief that it was necessary to create such a court, there were many concerns expressed about the loss of national sovereignty. This is, in fact, one of the main issues still animating the debate in the United States about the International Criminal Court. Following the debates in Canada, I believe that most Canadians were confident that the complementarity principle of the Statute of Rome preserves Canadian sovereignty at its most fundamental root since it allows the Canadian government to have the first opportunity to prosecute a Canadian national accused of crimes covered under the statute.

The conclusion of the parliamentary debate in the House of Commons was that four out of the five political parties in Canada supported the ICC as the preferred option of prosecuting war criminals. This is, of course, my personal conclusion as well as the view of the government that I served. This fact highlights other benefits in bringing the ICC into the public arena: the benefit of having serious legislative debate and the benefit of building an open transparent process for considering the court's purpose and provisions. Mythology, misperception, misrepresentation are the enemies of a clear case for prosecuting war criminals. These myths must be exposed to the glaring light of scrutiny.

Before concluding, I would like to touch on one last issue: now that the world has chosen to adopt an International Criminal Court, what will the role of the United States be? Obviously, world justice would be much stronger if the largest and most powerful nation in the world joined the internationally sanctioned, comprehensive, criminal justice system that punishes the most heinous crimes known to humanity. I would also argue that this position is more than consistent with American leadership of the past. After World War II, when some actors such as Winston Churchill were advocating the public summary execution of Nazi leaders, the United States argued in favor of the rule of law. I need not overemphasize how greatly the Nuremberg Charter advanced justice and the principles of international law.

Without the efforts of Eleanor Roosevelt, the world would not now have the Universal Declaration on Human Rights as adopted in 1948. It is important to note that Article 48 reads: "Everyone is entitled to a social and international order in which the rights and freedoms set forth in this declaration can be fully appreciated." That was, in my view, a direct call for an international enforcement system, something we are still struggling to build today. But what also resonates in this document is the echo of the American Declaration of Independence, which refers to the inalienable rights of man, rights that no political power can remove. And most recently, given American leadership in creating the Rwanda and Yugoslav tribunals, it is entirely fitting that the United States signed the Statute of Rome on December 31. It is also important to note that this institution is mutually beneficial. U.S. ratification of the ICC will provide some significant advantages. It will, for example, allow the United State to assert jurisdiction over any crimes involving its armed forces, something it cannot do previous to ratification. Ratification will also mean that the United States can participate in the international criminal justice system and contribute some of its most talented judges and jurists.

I am aware of the many domestic concerns and I know that many efforts were made to address them. But I believe that it is necessary for there to be a full, intellectually honest, public debate in all countries about the Criminal Court, and particularly in the United States. I believe that it is incumbent upon all those who can make a contribution to the debate to do so. And these Principles of Universal Jurisdiction go a long way in promoting that end.

In conclusion, if Canada's experience can be a useful lesson to other nations, the lesson would be that universal jurisdiction is a crucial concept for crafting good public policy and for effectively pursuing world justice. As a tool of criminal law, it can be unwieldy and problematic. But despite the hurdles that may lie ahead, it is essential that we generate good public debate to sharpen the tool and prepare for its use. Canada's leaders and the Canadian public have largely embraced the International Criminal Court as the most viable way of creating a system of enforcement in the world of war crimes, crimes against humanity and genocide. To quote from Michael Ignatieff's recent book on the rights revolution: "The rights revolution since 1945 has widened the bounds of community so that our obligations no longer cease at our frontiers." The Princeton Principles will help advance us all to that desired end.

Postscript

Time-defining changes have taken place since a distinguished group of international scholars and jurists met to discuss and refine an important concept for the development of international law: universal jurisdiction.

These discussions and the product they created known as the Princeton Principles on Universal Jurisdiction are already regarded as an important contribution to international legal discourse and development. Since the time I delivered my speech at Princeton University printed above, the events of September 11 have made the work of this Princeton Project even more prescient and urgent. The United States in particular, and the world in general, has had to focus even greater attention and resources on addressing the increasingly present and formidable opponent of international terrorism. This heightened attention has uncovered and will continue to uncover new and perpetual obstacles to deterring and prosecuting a body of crime that has no recognizable face and no permanent home. International terrorism has and will continue to illustrate that new institutions, new laws, and a new willingness to use and enforce existing laws will be critical to deter if not defeat the scourge of international crime. Critical to this arsenal of weaponry to combat terrorism is both the perception and the reality that there is no safe haven for terrorists. Equally critical is the focus on the rule of law as an institutionalized, apolitical, and tenacious long-term strategy against international crime, whatever form it takes. If the rule of law is going to be effective, states will need to embrace and use one of international law's most powerful deterrents: universal jurisdiction.

As the Princeton Project has progressed, so too has the initiative for an International Criminal Court as outlined in the Statute of Rome. As there are far more than the necessary sixty states that have ratified the statute, the ICC has become a reality and international criminal law has another effective weapon against international crime. It is important to remember, however, that the International Criminal Court will be no panacea. It has many obstacles to overcome and many tests to pass before its effectiveness is proven. And although no effort should be spared to make the ICC an effective, apolitical and tenacious mechanism for thwarting international crime, other complementary and necessary components of the international rule of law must be promoted. This includes the widespread promotion, acceptance and use of the principle of universal jurisdiction.

Application of universal jurisdiction will also face serious challenges. Although several states have already amended their Criminal Codes or other relevant legislation to allow for some form of universal jurisdiction, few states have taken the initiative to assume universal jurisdiction over certain serious crimes allegedly committed by individuals residing within its borders or extraditable to its jurisdiction. Other challenges to universal jurisdiction arise from the recent move in the United Nations Security Council to grant the United States a one-year exemption from ICC jurisdiction for peacekeeping missions. Whereas Principle 5 of the Princeton Principles on Universal Jurisdiction suggests that an effective system of international criminal law would afford no immunities from prosecution and no exemption from accountability, it would seem that an erosion of our commitment to the Principles may already be underway on that issue. What immunities, if any, should be built into the architecture of the International Criminal Court? Will other nations be granted ad hoc immunities as well?

Although there has been some recent progress in the expanded application of the universal jurisdiction principle, there have been setbacks. Much optimism was created when several European countries prosecuted individuals accused of international crimes during the Yugoslav conflict. More optimism was created by the decision in the British House of Lords in the *Pinochet* case. That optimism may have been tempered somewhat by the unsuccessful attempt by the Belgian government to assume jurisdiction over the minister of foreign affairs of the Democratic Republic of Congo for serious violations of international humanitarian law. The international community holds conflicting views on the legality of states using universal jurisdiction to prosecute nonnationals who have committed serious human rights crimes outside of that state's jurisdiction. The incongruent models of universal jurisdiction from the *Pinochet* case and from the *Congo* case need to be either reconciled, or preferably, reconsidered in a future case that will strongly assert the legality of universal jurisdiction and specify when it can be applied.

The discourse on universal jurisdiction must continue and states must be given the legal tools to use the principles of universal jurisdiction as a front line attack against international crime. States must also create the resources and the domestic legal infrastructure to use the power of universal jurisdiction to its greatest effect. Furthermore, states must be willing and adept navigators of international politics which frequently challenge the effective use of universal jurisdiction. The application of universal jurisdiction does not entail the diminution of state sovereignty but rather the enforcement of a collective and fundamental international system of criminal justice.

Notes

Introduction

1. See Gary Jonathan Bass, *Stay the Hand of Vengeance: The Politics of War Crimes Trials* (Princeton, N.J. : Princeton University Press, 2000).

2. I draw here on Richard A. Falk, "Assessing the Pinochet Litigation: Whither Universal Jurisdiction?," this volume.

3. The complaint was filed on September 10, 2001; see "Kissinger Sued over Chile Death," *The Guardian* (U.K.), September 12, 2001, http://www.guardian. co.uk/international/story/0,3604,550375,00.html

4. Christopher Hitchens, *The Trial of Henry Kissinger* (New York: Verso, 2001).

5. A BBC documentary called "The Accused" (which aired in the summer of 2001) included an interview suggesting that Sharon could be indicted for the massacres by Lebanese Phalangist militia groups of unarmed Palestinians in the refugee camps of Sabra and Shatilla in 1982. An investigating magistrate in Belgium has considered such charges.

6. My thanks to Diane Orentlicher for her guidance here. On Belgium see Marlise Simons, "Sharon Faces Belgian Trial After Term Ends," *The New York Times,* February 13, 2003, http://www.nytimes.com/2003/046162052.

7. At least temporarily. The *Wall Street Journal* editorial page later expressed reservations about universal jurisdiction.

8. http://www.afrol.com/News2001/rwa010_nuns_genocide.htm.

9. See "The Princeton Principles on Universal Jurisdiction," below, Principle 1(1).

10. Our thanks to the Permanent Missions of Canada and the Kingdom of the Netherlands to the United Nations for their role in securing UN translation and publication of the Princeton Principles under Agenda Item 164, Establishment of the International Criminal Court, Fifty-Sixth Session of the United Nations, December 4, 2001. Copies of *The Princeton Principles on Universal Jurisdiction* (Princeton, N.J.: Program in Law and Public Affairs, Princeton University, 2001) can also be obtained by contacting the University Center for Human Values, Louis Marx Hall 302, Princeton University, Princeton, NJ 08544.

11. See paragraph 4 of the preamble and article 5(1) of the Rome Statute creating an International Criminal Court.

12. See Principle 7.

13. This text is contained in a letter from Brown-Wilkinson to William J. Butler,

and it can be found in the commentary to the Princeton Principles, note 20. The case against Pinochet in London was Regina v. Bartle and the Commissioner of Police for the Metropolis and others Ex Parte Pinochet, judgment delivered on March 24, 1999; see www.parliament.the-stationery-office.co.uk/pa/ld199899/ldjudgmt/jd990324/pino1.htm.

14. See Principles 1 (especially Paragraphs 3 and 4), 9, and 10.

15. The decision was rendered on February 14, 2002, and is available on the website of the International Commission of Jurists at www.icj-cij.org. Jonathan H. Marks, barrister, Matrix Chambers, London, and visiting lecturer in Public and International Affairs, Princeton University (2000–2001) has prepared an important commentary on Democratic Republic of Congo v. Belgium and some other matters related to universal jurisdiction, from which I have benefited.

Preface

This preface is reprinted here as it was first published in the summer of 2001 in *The Principles on Universal Jurisdiction* (Princeton: Program in Law and Public Affairs, Princeton University, 2001).

The Princeton Principles on Universal Jurisdiction

"The Princeton Principles on Universal Jurisdiction" is reprinted as it was first published in *The Principles on Universal Jurisdiction* (Princeton: Program in Law and Public Affairs, Princeton University, 2001).

1. See list of participants at the end of this volume.
2. One participant did not join in the adoption; see the comment, note 18.

Commentary

This commentary was prepared by Steven W. Becker under the direction of Prof. M. Cherif Bassiouni and with the assistance of Stephen Macedo, Stephen A. Oxman, and others.

1. The first meeting, in November 2000, was attended by leading academics who wrote and discussed scholarly papers on various aspects of universal jurisdiction. The assembly at the second meeting, in January 2001, was composed of distinguished legal scholars including some of the academics who attended the first meeting. See "Participants" at the end of this volume.

2. See Richard A. Falk, "Assessing the Pinochet Litigation: Whither Universal Jurisdiction?," this volume.

3. See, e.g., Principle 3, which encourages judicial organs to rely on universal jurisdiction; Principle 11, which calls upon legislatures to enact laws enabling the exercise of universal jurisdiction; and Principle 12, which exhorts governments to include provisions for universal jurisdiction in new treaties and protocols to existing treaties.

4. See Michael Kirby, "Universal Jurisdiction and Judicial Reluctance: A New 'Fourteen Points,'" this volume.

5. See Attorney General of Israel v. Eichmann, 36 I.L.R. 5 (Isr. D.C., Jerusalem, December 12, 1961), aff'd, 36 I.L.R. 277 (Isr. S. Ct., May 29, 1962), which is often

cited as representing the exercise of universal jurisdiction by Israel, although many argue that the decision was more fundamentally predicated upon the passive personality doctrine and the protective principle under a unique Israeli statute passed by the Knesset in 1950. See Gary J. Bass, "The Adolf Eichmann Case," this volume.

6. See the International Court of Justice's order in the case of Arrest Warrant of April 11, 2000 (Democratic Republic of Congo v. Belgium) (December 8, 2000), in which these issues feature prominently. On March 20, 2001, the Senegalese Cour de Cassation held that Hissène Habré, the former president of Chad, could not be tried on torture charges in Senegal. See Stephen P. Marks, "The Hissène Habré Case: The Law and Politics of Universal Jurisdiction," this volume.

7. See Principle 9. Note also that the drafters intended the international due process norms in Principle 1(4) to be illustrative and not exhaustive. The right to reasonable bail (cf. Principle 14[2]) and the right to counsel were also referred to as being included among the essential due process guarantees. See also Universal Declaration of Human Rights, December 10, 1948, arts. 10, 11, G.A. Res. 217A (3), U.N. Doc. A/810 (1948); International Covenant on Civil and Political Rights, December 19, 1966, arts. 14, 15, 999 U.N.T.S. 171 (hereinafter ICCPR).

8. See Principle 2(1).

9. See, e.g., Convention on the High Seas, April 29, 1958, art. 19, 450 U.N.T.S. 82, 13 U.S.T. 2312 ("On the high seas, or in any other place outside the jurisdiction of any state, every state may seize a pirate ship or aircraft, or a ship taken by piracy and under the control of pirates, and arrest the persons and seize the property on board."); United Nations Convention on the Law of the Sea, December 10, 1982, art. 105, U.N./CONF.62/122, 21 I.L.M. 1261. See also M. Cherif Bassiouni, "The History of Universal Jurisdiction and Its Place in International Law," this volume.

10. *Cf.* Convention for the Suppression of the Traffic in Persons and of the Exploitation of the Prostitution of Others, March 21, 1950, art. 11, 96 U.N.T.S. 271 ("Nothing in the present Convention shall be interpreted as determining the attitude of a Party towards the general question of the limits of criminal jurisdiction under international law"); Convention Relative to the Slave Trade and Importation into Africa of Firearms, Ammunition, and Spiritous Liquors, July 2, 1890, art. 5, 27 Stat. 886, 17 Martens Nouveau Recueil (ser. 2) 345; Treaty for the Suppression of the African Slave Trade, December 20, 1841, arts. 6, 7, 10, and annex B, pt. 5, 2 Martens Nouveau Recueil (ser. 1) 392.

11. September 7, 1956, 266 U.N.T.S. 3, 18 U.S.T. 3201.

12. See Geneva Convention for the Amelioration of the Condition of the Wounded and Sick in Armed Forces in the Field, August 12, 1949, art. 50, 75 U.N.T.S. 31, 6 U.S.T. 3114, T.I.A.S. No. 3362; Geneva Convention for the Amelioration of the Condition of Wounded, Sick and Shipwrecked Members of Armed Forces at Sea, August 12, 1949, art. 51, 75 U.N.T.S. 85, 6 U.S.T. 3217, T.I.A.S. No. 3363; Geneva Convention Relative to the Treatment of Prisoners of War, August 12, 1949, art. 130, 75 U.N.T.S. 135, 6 U.S.T. No. 3316, T.I.A.S. No. 3364; Geneva Convention Relative to the Protection of Civilian Persons in Time of War, August 12, 1949, art. 147, 75 U.N.T.S. 287, 6 U.S.T. 3516, T.I.A.S. No. 3365; Protocol I Additional to the Geneva Conventions of August 12, 1949, December 12, 1977, art. 85, U.N. Doc. A/32/144, Annex I.

13. See Charter of the International Military Tribunal, August 8, 1945, art. 6(a), 82 U.N.T.S. 284, 59 Stat. 1546 (hereinafter Nuremberg Charter), annexed to Agreement for the Prosecution and Punishment of the Major War Criminals of the European Axis, August 8, 1945, 82 U.N.T.S. 279, 59 Stat. 1544.

14. July 17, 1998, art. 7, U.N. Doc. A/CONF.183/9, 37 I.L.M. 999 (hereinafter ICC Statute).

15. Convention on the Prevention and Punishment of the Crime of Genocide, December 9, 1948, art. 6, 78 U.N.T.S. 277.

16. G.A. Res. 39/46, Annex, U.N. GAOR, 39th Sess., Supp. No. 51, U.N. Doc. A/39/51 (1984), entered into force June 26, 1987 (hereinafter Torture Convention), draft reprinted in 23 I.L.M. 1027, modified 24 I.L.M. 535.

17. Id. arts. 5, 7(1).

18. Lord Browne-Wilkinson provided the following reasons for his dissent from the Princeton Principles:

> I am strongly in favour of universal jurisdiction over serious international crimes if, by those words, one means the exercise by an international court or by the courts of one state of jurisdiction over the nationals of another state with the prior consent of that latter state, i.e. in cases such as the ICC and Torture Convention. But the Princeton Principles propose that individual national courts should exercise such jurisdiction against nationals of a state which has not agreed to such jurisdiction. Moreover the Principles do not recognize any form of sovereign immunity: Principle 5(1). If the law were to be so established, states antipathetic to Western powers would be likely to seize both active and retired officials and military personnel of such Western powers and stage a show trial for alleged international crimes. Conversely, zealots in Western States might launch prosecutions against, for example, Islamic extremists for their terrorist activities. It is naïve to think that, in such cases, the national state of the accused would stand by and watch the trial proceed: resort to force would be more probable. In any event the fear of such legal actions would inhibit the use of peacekeeping forces when it is otherwise desirable and also the free interchange of diplomatic personnel. I believe that the adoption of such universal jurisdiction without preserving the existing concepts of immunity would be more likely to damage than to advance chances of international peace.

19. Nuremberg Charter, supra note 15, art. 7.

20. See Statute of the International Criminal Tribunal for the Former Yugoslavia, art. 7(2), S.C. Res. 808, U.N. SCOR, 48th Sess., 3175th mtg., U.N. Doc. S/RES/808 (1993), annexed to Report of the Secretary-General pursuant to Paragraph 2 of U.N. Security Council Resolution 808 (1993), U.N. Doc. S/25704 & Add.1 (1993) (hereinafter ICTY Statute); Statute of the International Criminal Tribunal for Rwanda, art. 6(2), S.C. Res. 955, U.N. SCOR, 49th Sess., 3453d mtg., Annex, U.N. Doc. S/RES/955 (1994) (hereinafter ICTR Statute).

21. See ICTY Statute, supra note 22, art. 7(2); ICTR Statute, supra note 22, art. 6(2). Article 27 of the ICC Statute similarly provides:

> 1. This Statute shall apply equally to all persons without any distinction based on official capacity. In particular, official capacity as a Head of State or Government, a member of a Government or parliament, an elected representative or a government official shall in no case exempt a person from criminal responsibility under this Statute, nor shall it, in and of itself, constitute a ground for reduction of sentence.
> 2. Immunities or special procedural rules which may attach to the official capacity of a person, whether under national or international law, shall not bar the Court from exercising its jurisdiction over such a person.

ICC Statute, supra note 16, art. 27. Article 98 of the ICC Statute, however, yields to the primacy of other multilateral treaties in assessing immunity:

> 1. The Court may not proceed with a request for surrender or assistance which would require the requested State to act inconsistently with its obligations

under international law with respect to the State or diplomatic immunity of a person or property of a third State, unless the Court can first obtain the cooperation of that third State for the waiver of the immunity.

2. The Court may not proceed with a request for surrender which would require the requested State to act inconsistently with its obligations under international agreements pursuant to which the consent of a sending State is required to surrender a person of that State to the Court, unless the Court can first obtain the cooperation of the sending State for the giving of consent for the surrender.

Id. art. 98. Note that article 27 is located in part 3 of the ICC Statute; while article 98 is contained in part 9 of the statute, which contains no prohibitions on immunities and thus seems to permit a head of state, diplomat, or other official to invoke procedural immunity where applicable.

22. See Vienna Convention on Diplomatic Relations, April 18, 1961, 500 U.N.T.S. 95, 23. U.S.T. 3227; see also United States Diplomatic and Consular Staff in Tehran (U.S. v. Iran), 1980 I.C.J. 3 (May 24). These temporary immunities are not revoked by this subsection. Such doctrines, however, may be in the process of erosion. See infra note 25 and accompanying text.

23. Prosecutor v. Milosevic (Indictment) (May 24, 1999), at www.un.org/icty/indictment/english/mil-ii990524e.htm.

24. See Principle 6.

25. See Convention on the Non-Applicability of Statutory Limitations to War Crimes and Crimes against Humanity, November 26, 1968, 754 U.N.T.S. 73; European Convention on Non-Applicability of Statutory Limitations to Crimes against Humanity and War Crimes (Inter-European), January 24, 1974, Europ. T.S. No. 82.

26. See Principle 7(1).

27. This method of listing relevant factors has been employed in other similar contexts, such as in determining jurisdictional priority over extraterritorial crime. See Restatement (Third) of Foreign Relations Law of the United States § 403 (1987). In resolving conflict of laws problems, see Restatement (Second) of Conflict of Laws § 6 (1971).

28. It is also included in the ICCPR, supra note 9, art. 14(7), and the American Convention on Human Rights, November 22, 1969, art. 8(4), 1144 U.N.T.S. 123, O.A.S. T.S. No. 36.

29. See Torture Convention, supra note 18, art. 1.

30. Arrest Warrant of April 11, 2000 (Democratic Republic of Congo v. Belgium) (December 8, 2000).

Chapter 1. The History of Universal Jurisdiction and Its Place in International Law

The research assistance of Steven Becker is gratefully acknowledged.

1. See generally *The Pinochet Precedent: How Victims Can Pursue Human Rights Criminals Abroad,* Human Rights Watch Update (Human Rights Watch, September 2000); *Universal Jurisdiction: Fourteen Principles on the Effective Exercise of Universal Jurisdiction; Universal Jurisdiction in Europe: Criminal Prosecutions in Europe Since 1990 for War Crimes, Crimes against Humanity, Torture, and Genocide* (Redress, June 1999). A recent example of this unfortunate phenomenon is the lengthy *Universal Jurisdiction: The Duty of States to Enact and Implement Legislation* (Amnesty International, September 2001). Such efforts only lead to false expectations and disappointment.

2. See Robert Jennings and Arthur Watts, eds., *Oppenheim's International Law,*

9th ed. (Boston: Addison-Wesley, 1992), 462–88. Entities exercising some of the attributes of state sovereignty include military forces legitimately occupying foreign territories in accordance with international humanitarian law in their lawful exercise of jurisdictional power over such territories and persons on these territories; statelike entities exercising legitimate attributes over certain territories and their inhabitants, which are under their dominion and control; and the United Nations in its exercise of jurisdictional power over certain territories and their inhabitants pursuant to a mandate of the Security Council. International criminal law proscribes certain conduct that states are bound to enforce, particularly those proscriptions arising out of general customary international law of *jus cogens*. See M. Cherif Bassiouni, "The Sources and Content of International Criminal Law: A Theoretical Framework," in *International Criminal Law,* 2d rev. ed., vol. 1, ed. M. Cherif Bassiouni (New York: Transnational Publishers, 1999), 3–126; M. Cherif Bassiouni, "International Crimes: Jus Cogens and Obligatio Ergo Omnes," *Law and Contemporary Problems* 59 (1996): 9–28 (hereinafter "Jus Cogens Crimes").

3. Territorial jurisdiction is referred to as a principle because of its universal recognition. See The S.S. Lotus (France v. Turkey), 1927 P.C.I.J. (Ser. A) No. 9, 25; 2 Manley O. Hudson, *World Court Reports* 20 (1935). Other jurisdictional bases are referred to as theories because they are not universally recognized, but their recognition is sufficiently well established to warrant their acknowledgment as constituting part of customary international law. For a discussion of theories of jurisdiction, see Christopher Blakesley, "Extraterritorial Jurisdiction," in *International Criminal Law,* 2d rev. ed., vol. 2, ed. M. Cherif Bassiouni (New York: Transnational Publishers, 1999), 33–105; M. Cherif Bassiouni, *International Extradition in United States Law and Practice,* 4th rev. ed. (Dobbs Ferry, N.Y.: Oceana Publications, 2002), 313–459.

4. Most writers on private international law barely touch on conflicts of criminal laws. The same is true of U.S. writers on conflicts of law. For conflict of criminal law, see the seminal early work of Henri Donnedieu De Vabres, *Les Principles modernes du droit pénal international* (Paris: Librarie du Recueil Sirye, 1928). It is mostly European criminal law experts who write on that subject.

5. August 8, 1945, 8 U.N.T.S. 279; 59 Stat. 1544 (hereinafter IMT Charter).

6. January 19, 1946, T.I.A.S. No. 1589 at 3, 4 Bevans 20; amended April 26, 1946, T.I.A.S. No. 1589 at 11, 4 Bevans 27 (hereinafter IMTFE Amended Charter).

7. IMT Judgment, September 30, 1946, reprinted in 22 *Trial of The Major War Criminals before the International Military Tribunal* (1948) 411, 461.

8. Charter of the United Nations, signed at San Francisco, June 26, 1945, ch. 7, 59 Stat. 1031, 3 Bevans 1153.

9. S.C. Res. 808, U.N. SCOR, 48th Sess., 3217th mtg., U.N. Doc. S/RES/808 (1993) (hereinafter ICTY Statute), annexed to Report of the Secretary-General Pursuant to Paragraph 2 of U.N. Security Council Resolution 808 (1993), U.N. Doc. S/ 2–5704 and Add. 1 (1993). See M. Cherif Bassiouni and Peter Manikas, eds., *The Law of the International Criminal Tribunal for the Former Yugoslavia* (Ardsley Park, N.Y.: Transnational Publishers, 1996); Virginia Morris and Michel P. Scharf, eds., *An Insider's Guide to the International Criminal Tribunal for the Former Yugoslavia: A Documentary History and Analysis,* 2 vols. (Ardsley Park, N.Y.: Transnational Publishers, 1995).

10. S.C. Res. 955, U.N. SCOR, 49th Sess., 3453d mtg., Annex, U.N. Doc. S/ RES/955 (1994) (hereinafter ICTR Statute). See Virginia Morris and Michel P. Scharf, eds., *The International Criminal Tribunal for Rwanda,* 2 vols. (Ardsley Park, N.Y.: Transnational Publishers, 1998).

11. These Security Council decisions are, however, described by United Nations and government legal advisers, as well as by some publicists, as different from the exercise of sovereignty.

12. The establishment of these two tribunals evidenced a new concept in the exercise of judicial jurisdiction by an organ of the United Nations.

13. This is evidenced in "Harvard Research in International Law: Jurisdiction with Respect to Crime," *American Journal of International Law* 29 (Supp. 1935): 443. See also *Restatement (Third) Foreign Relations Law of the United States* 402 (Boston: American Law Institute: 1987) (hereinafter *Restatement*); Donnedieu De Vabres, *Les Principles modernes.* Under the active personality theory, a state may prosecute a person who committed a crime in another state provided that the crime in question also constitutes a crime in the state of nationality. That is referred to as "double criminality." See Bassiouni, *International Extradition,* 366; Blakesley, "Extraterritorial Jurisdiction," 43. In such cases, however, the enforcing state relies on its own law, but that is essentially because of ease and consistency in application. States are not, however, obligated to require "double criminality." National enforcement may require that international legal proscriptions are enacted into national legislation depending on national constitutional requirements and other national laws. This is the case with respect to states that follow the "dualistic" approach to national application of international legal obligations and also with respect to "monistic" states in connection with non–self-executing treaties.

14. States, however, rely on extradition as a means of securing in personam jurisdiction in order to subject a national to their enforcing jurisdiction. Bassiouni, *International Extradition,* 3.

15. Ibid., 353; Blakesley, "Extraterritorial Jurisdiction," 50.

16. Bassiouni, *International Extradition,* 370; Blakesley, "Extraterritorial Jurisdiction," 54. This is based on the notion that states have a right to protect their citizens when a criminal act harms them irrespective of the locus of the criminal conduct's occurrence. But that presupposes that the criminal act is proscribed by the enforcing state or the territorial state. That theory is based on a connection between the enforcing state and the victim of the proscribed conduct.

17. For example, in *Attorney General of Israel v. Eichmann,* 36 I.L.R. 5, 5–57 (Israel D.C., Jerusalem, December 12, 1961) (hereinafter *Eichmann*), the Israeli district court referred to universal jurisdiction *in dictum* but relied on Israel's national legislation conferring upon its courts jurisdiction over "crimes against the Jewish people," based on a law it passed in 1950 that includes genocide and crimes against humanity whenever committed against the "Jewish people" wherever they may be. See Nazi and Nazi Collaborators (Punishment) Law, August 1, 1950, 4 L.S.I. No. 64, 154. Israel's jurisdictional reach is, under its law, universal, but it is based on a nationality connection to the victim that places such jurisdictional basis under the "passive personality" theory. Admittedly, that law purports to apply to acts that took place before that sovereign state existed, that is, 1948, but that does not alter the basis of the theory relied upon. Furthermore, there is no historical legal precedent for such a retroactive application of nationality, but that goes to the issue of the law's international validity and the jurisdictional theory relied upon. In its judgment, the district court stated: "All this applies to the crime of genocide (including the 'crime against the Jewish people') which, although committed by the killing of individuals, was intended to exterminate the national as a group. . . . The State of Israel, the sovereign State of the Jewish people, performs through its legislation the task of carrying into effect the right of the Jewish people to punish the criminals who killed its sons with intent to put an end to the survival of this people. We are convinced that this power conforms to the subsisting principles of nations." *Eichmann,* I.L.R. at 57 (para. 38). In affirming the district court's judgment, the supreme court of Israel, while noting full agreement on the protective principle of jurisdiction, insisted upon the universal jurisdiction argument, as this applied not only to Jews, in whose

name Israel claimed to exercise protective jurisdiction, but also to Poles, Slovenes, Czechs, and gypsies. Attorney General of Israel v. Eichmann, 36 I.L.M. 277, 304 (para. 12) (Israel S. Ct., May 29, 1962). Ibid. ("The State of Israel . . . was entitled, pursuant to the principle of universal jurisdiction and in the capacity of a guardian of international law and an agent for its enforcement, to try the appellant"). In *Demjanjuk v. Petrovsky*, 776 F.2d 571 (6th Cir. 1985), the Sixth Circuit referred to universal jurisdiction over crimes of genocide and crimes against humanity but relied on the same Israeli law that was based on the theory of passive personality. Ibid., 582 ("Israel is seeking to enforce its criminal law for the punishment of Nazis and Nazi collaborators for crimes universally recognized and condemned by the community of nations. The fact that Demjanjuk is charged with committing these acts in Poland does not deprive Israel of authority to bring him to trial"). See Yoram Sheftel, *Defending Ivan the Terrible: The Conspiracy to Convict John Demjanjuk* (Washington, D.C.: Regnery Publishing,1996).

18. See Resolution of the Third International Congress of Penal Law (Palermo 1933) in *Revue internationale de droit pénal* 10 (1933): 144, 157; International Law Association, Report of the 34th Conference 378, 383–84 (1926); Resolution of the International Congress of Comparative Law (The Hague, 1932); International Conference for the Unification of Penal Law, Article 7 (Warsaw, 1927). Summarizing this policy desideratum, Donnedieu De Vabres aptly stated: "Il est dés lors inutile de pénétrer le détail des spéculations philosophiques par lesquelles on a voulu l'étayer *utile*-Binternationalement, universellement utile-Bet *juste,* cette compétence répond aux *desiderata* don't s'inspire, pour organiser la répression, la doctrine neo-classique, fondement de presques toutes les législations positives." Donnedieu De Vabres, *Les Principles modernes,* 69. "L'attribtution d'une compétence très subsidiaire au juge du lieu d'arrestation donne satisfaction à un besoin de sécurité, à un sentiment élémentaire de justice." Ibid., 445. See also Maurice Travers, 1 *Le Droit pénal international* 1 Section 73 (1920); Mercier, Rapport, *Annuaire de l'institute de droit international,* 87, 136 (1933).

19. These issues are discussed in M. Cherif Bassiouni and Edward M. Wise, *Aut Dedere Aut Judicare: The Duty to Prosecute or Extradite in International Law* (Dordrecht: Martinus Nijhoff Publishers, 1995), 3–69. The case for an international *civitas maxima* supporting the duty to prosecute or extradite is valid, but whether that includes the theory of universal jurisdiction is doubtful. In fact, *aut dedere aut judicare* may well be argued as the substitute for a theory of universal jurisdiction. In this writer's opinion, universal jurisdiction complements *aut dedere aut judicare* in that whenever a state does not extradite and proceeds to prosecute it may need to rely on universality.

20. This is why the Ayatollah Khomeni in 1989 issued an edict of death for blasphemy against author Salman Rushdie for his book *The Satanic Verses* (New York: Viking Penguin, 1988). The majority of the world's states reacted negatively to the extraterritorial reach, as did many scholars. See M. Cherif Bassiouni, "Speech, Religious Discrimination, and Blasphemy," *Proceedings of the American Society of International Law* (1989): 432–35. This is an example of why universal jurisdiction should be carefully circumscribed.

21. For a synopsis of the views on this point, including those of Grotius, Heineccius Burlamaqi, De Vattel, Rutherford, Kent, and others, see Henry Wheaton, *Elements of International Law,* 8th ed. (London: B. Fellowes, 1836), 181.

22. Cesare Beccaria-Bonesan, *An Essay on Crimes and Punishment* (1819; reprint, Brookline Village, Mass.: Branden Publishing, 1992).

23. Ibid., 135; Bassiouni and Wise, *Aut Dedere Aut Judicare.*

24. See Donnedieu De Vabres, *Les Principles modernes,* 135–36 .

25. Most of them relating to piracy. See Alfred Rubin, *The Law of Piracy,* 2d ed.

(Irvington on Hudson: Transnational Publishers, 1998). Some cases reported by scholars refer to post–WWII prosecutions but could not be found by this writer. See William A. Schabas, *Genocide in International Law: The Crimes of Crimes* (Cambridge: Cambridge University Press, 2000), 360–68. *Cf.* Human Rights Watch, "Pinochet Precedent," 9–10.

Following the genocides in the former Yugoslavia and Rwanda, a number of European countries brought perpetrators to trial on the basis of universal juris-diction. In Belgium, a Rwandan, Vincent Ntezimana, was arrested and charged with genocide. In Germany, the Bavarian high Court sentenced a Bosnian Serb, Novislav Djajic, to five years imprisonment in 1997 under the Geneva Conventions for aiding and abetting the killing of fourteen Muslim men in Bosnia in 1992. A former leader of a paramilitary Serb group, Nikola Jorgic, was convicted on eleven counts of genocide and thirty counts of murder, and sentenced to life imprisonment by the Düsseldorf high court. A third case is pending against a Bosnian Serb charged with genocide before the Düsseldorf High Court. In Denmark, Bosnian Muslim Refik Saric is currently serving an eight-year sentence for war crimes, charged under the Geneva Conventions with torturing detainees in a Croat-run prison in Bosnia in 1993. In April 1999, a Swiss military court convicted a Rwandan national of war crimes, but held it had no jurisdiction over genocide and crimes against humanity. A Bosnian Serb was indicted but acquitted of war crimes. The Netherlands is prosecuting a Bosnian Serb for war crimes before a military court. France is currently prosecuting a Rwandan priest, Wenceslas Munyeshyaka, for genocide, crimes against humanity, and torture. In addition, in July 1999, French police arrested a Mauritanian colonel, Ely Ould Dah, who was studying at a French military school, on the basis of the U.N. Convention against Torture, when two Mauritanian exiles came forward and identified him as their torturer. Ould Dah, free on bail, slipped out of France in March 2000, however. In February 2000, a Senegalese court indicted the exiled dictator of Chad, Hissène Habré, on torture charges. In 1997, the United Kingdom arrested a Sudanese doctor residing in Scotland for alleged torture in Sudan, but later dropped the charges, apparently for lack of evidence. In August 2000, Mexico arrested Ricardo Miguel Cavallo, a former Argentine military official. Judge Garzón of Spain has filed an extradition request for Cavallo based on the torture and "disappearance" of over 400 people.

A. Hays Butler, "Compilation of Documents" (unpublished compilation of documents on universal jurisdiction, prepared for the Princeton Project on Universal Jurisdiction).

26. Report of the European Committee on Crime Prevention, Council of Europe (1990). The report was prepared by the Select Committee of Experts on Extraterritorial Jurisdiction (PC-R-EJ), set on by the European Committee on Crime Problems (CDPC) in 1984.

27. Ibid., 14–16.

28. Bassiouni, "Sources and Content," 3–126.

29. "In its classic statement, however, the universality theory encompasses acts committed beyond *any* country's territorial jurisdiction, the paradigm offense being piracy on the high seas." Rena Hozore Reiss, "The Extradition of John Demjanjuk: War Crimes, Universality Jurisdiction, and the Political Offense Doctrine," *Cornell International Jaw Journal* 20 (1987): 281, 303 (citing M. Cherif Bassiouni).

30. M. Cherif Bassiouni, "General Principles of International Law," *Michigan Journal of International Law* 11 (1990): 768–818; see also Révé David, *Les Grands Systémes de droit contemporaries,* 5th ed. (Paris: Dallos, 1973), 22–32.

31. M. Cherif Bassiouni, *International Criminal Law Conventions and Their Penal Provisions* (Ardsley Park, N.Y.: Transnational Publishers, 1997) (hereinafter *ICL Conventions*).

32. M. Cherif Bassiouni, "From Versailles to Rwanda in Seventy-Five Years: The Need to Establish a Permanent International Criminal Court," *Harvard Human Rights Journal* 10 (1997): 11.

33. See Rome Statute of the International Criminal Court, July 17, 1998, U.N. Doc. A/CONF.183/9 (hereinafter ICC Statute), reprinted in 37 I.L.M. 999 (1998); see also M. Cherif Bassiouni, *The Statute of the International Criminal Court: A Documentary History* (Ardsley Park, N.Y.: Transnational Publishers, 1998).

34. ICC Statute, arts. 6, 7, and 8.

35. Ibid., art. 14.

36. Ibid.

37. Ibid., art. 12(3).

38. Ibid., art. 13(b).

39. See Bassiouni, *ICL Conventions*. That research refers only to twenty-five categories—three more were added since 1997.

40. Ibid., 20–21, which refers only to 274 since seven conventions were adopted between 1997 and 2001.

41. Ibid.

42. Ibid., 5, 20–21.

43. Ibid., 20–21.

44. Bassiouni, "Jus Cogens Crimes." It is noteworthy that several international criminal law conventions that apply to crimes that have not risen to *jus cogens* contain a provision on universal jurisdiction.

45. Homer, *The Illiad*, trans. A. T. Murray (Cambridge, Mass.: Harvard University Press, 1971).

46. Homer, *The Odyssey*, trans. A. T. Murray (Cambridge, Mass.: Harvard University Press, 1960).

47. Thucydides, *The Peleponnesian War*, trans. C. M. Smith (Cambridge, Mass.: Harvard university Press, 1969).

48. Cicero, *Contra Verres II*, trans. L. H. G. Greenwood (Cambridge, Mass.: Harvard University Press, 1953). See also Cicero, *De Officii*, trans. L. H. G. Greenwood (Cambridge, Mass.: Harvard University Press, 1953); Cicero, *De Re Publica*, trans. C. W. Keyes (Cambridge, Mass.: Harvard University Press, 1928).

49. Coleman Philippson retraces that historical evolution, both as to its substantive meaning and as to exercise of jurisdiction in Greece and Rome. Coleman Phillipson, *The International Law and Custom of Ancient Greece and Rome*, vol. 2 (Salem, N.H.: Ayer, 1911).

50. Hugo Grotius, *De Jure Belli AC Pacis*, trans. Francis W. Kelsey (Oxford: Clarendon Press, 1925). Grotius also relied on the Old and New Testaments and on Aristotle and Cicero for a universal perspective. See also Bassiouni, *Crimes against Humanity*, 108 n. 71.

51. Rubin, *Law of Piracy*. Alfred Rubin authoritatively documents this history up to contemporary times.

52. Gentili, *De Ivre bellicis libri tres*, trans. J. C. Rolfe (Buffalo, N.Y.: W. S. Hein, 1933). See, for example, Gentili's work, *De Jure Belli* (1612), reprinted in *Classics of International Law* no. 16, vol. 1 (Washington, D.C.: Carnegie Institution, 1933); Grotius, *De Jure Belli AC Pacis*. For a brief assessment of these works, see Peter Haggenmacher, "Grotius and Gentili: A Reassessment of Thomas E. Holland's Inaugural Lecture," in *Hugo Grotius and International Relations*, ed. Hedley Bull, Adam Roberts, and Benedict Kingsbury (Oxford: Oxford University Press, 1992); G. I. A. D. Draper, "Grotius' Place in the Development of Legal Ideas about War," in *Hugo Grotius and International Relations*.

53. See Balthazar Ayala, *Three Books on the Law of War and on the Duties Connected with War, and on Military Discipline,* trans. John Pawley Bate (Washington D.C.: Carnegie Institution, 1912), 88.

54. See Rubin, *Law of Piracy.* The Constitution in Article 1(8,10) refers to "Piracies" and the Judicature Act of September 24, 1789. "An Act to Establish the Judicial Courts of the United States," ch. 20, sect. 9, 1 stat. 73, 76–77, gives each of the thirteen original "district courts" exclusive jurisdiction for such crimes. The first time, however, that piracy was deemed a crime of universal jurisdiction arose under Jay's Treaty of 1794, signed at London, November 19, 1794, art. 21, 8 stat. 116, 12 Bevans 13, 27.

55. See U.S. v. Palmer, 16 U.S. (3 Wheat.) 610 (1818). U.S. v. Klintock, 18 U.S. (5 Wheat.) 144 (1820). All other U.S. cases involving piracy had a "contact" with U.S. law because the acts of piracy were committed either against a U.S. vessel or against U.S. nationals.

56. This may be due to the fact that piracy has for all practical purposes disappeared as of the nineteenth century, and during the twentieth century there is only one instance that occurred in the Western world. Thus the international community found it more readily acceptable to recognize universal jurisdiction for piracy. See Thomas Franck, "To Define and Punish Piracies: The Lessons of the Santa Maria: A Comment," *New York University Law Review* 36 (1961): 839. Conversely, there have been many manifestations of piracy in Southeast Asia. See Gerhard O. W. Muller and Freida Adler, *Outlaws of the Ocean* (New York: William Morrow and Co., 1985).

57. April 25, 1958, 450 U.N.T.S. 82, 1 U.S.T. 2312, T.I.A.S. No. 5200.

58. United Nations Convention on the Law of the Sea, October 7, 1982, U.N. Doc. A/CONF.62/122, art. 150.

59. Bassiouni, *ICL Conventions,* 637–734.

60. Ibid.

61. M. Cherif Bassiouni, "Enslavement as an International Crime," *New York University Journal of International Law and Politics* 23 (1991): 445.

62. See Treaty for the Suppression of the African Slave Trade, signed at London, December 20, 1841, arts. 6, 7, 10, and Annex B, pt. 5, 2 Martens Nouveau Recueil (ser. 1) 392. See Convention for the Suppression of the Traffic in Persons and of the Exploitation of the Prostitution of Others, opened for signature at Lake Success, New York 21 March 1950, art. 11, 96 U.N.T.S. 271 ("Nothing in this Convention shall be interpreted as determining the attitude of a Party towards the general question of the limits of criminal jurisdiction under international law").

63. International Agreement for the Suppression of the "White Slave Traffic," May 18, 1904, 1 L.N.T.S. 83, 35 Stat. 1979; International Convention for the Suppression of the White Slave Traffic, May 4, 1910; International Convention for the Suppression of the Traffic in Women and Children, September 30, 1921, 9 L.N.T.S. 415.

64. Convention Concerning Forced or Compulsory Labour (Forced Labour Convention, 1930) June 28, 1930, 39 L.N.T.S. 55; Convention (No. 105) Concerning the Abolition of Forced Labour, June 5, 1957, 320 U.N.T.S. 291.

65. 96 U.N.T.S. 271.

66. Art. 13.

67. International Convention for the Suppression of the Traffic in Women of Full Age, October 11, 1933, 150 L.N.T.S. 431; Protocol to Amend the Convention for the Suppression of the Traffic in Women and Children, concluded at Geneva on September 30, 1921, and the Convention for the Suppression of Traffic in Women of Full Age, concluded at Geneva on October 11, 1933, 53 U.N.T.S. 13; Annex to the Protocol to Amend the Convention for the Suppression of the Traffic in Women and Children, concluded at Geneva on September 30, 1921, and the Convention for the

Suppression of Traffic in Women of Full Age, concluded at Geneva on October 11, 1933; International Convention for the Suppression of the Traffic in Women and Children, concluded at Geneva on September 30, 1921, amended by the Protocol Signed at Lake Success, New York, on November 12, 1947, 53 U.N.T.S. 39; International Convention for the Suppression of the Traffic in Women of Full Age concluded at Geneva on October 11, 1933, amended by the Protocol Signed at Lake Success, New York on November 12, 1947, 53 U.N.T.S. 49; Annex to the Protocol Amending the Agreement for the Suppression of the White Slave Traffic signed at Paris on May 18, 1904, and the International Convention for the Suppression of the White Slave Traffic, signed at Paris on May 4, 1910; International Agreement for the Suppression of the White Slave Traffic, signed at Paris on May 18, 1904, amended by the Protocol Signed at Lake Success, New York on May 4, 1949, 92 U.N.T.S. 19, 2 U.S.T. 1997; International Convention for the Suppression of White Slave Traffic, signed at Paris on May 4, 1910, and amended by the Protocol, signed at Lake Success, New York, May 4, 1949, 98 U.N.T.S. 101; Convention for the Suppression of the Traffic in Persons and of the Exploitation of the Prostitution of Others, 21 March 1950, 96 U.N.T.S. 271; Supplementary Convention on the Abolition of Slavery, the Slave Trade, and Institution and Practices Similar to Slavery, September 7, 1956, 266 U.N.T.S. 3, 18 U.S.T. 3201. See Bassiouni, *ICL Conventions.*

68. But see Draft Protocol on International Traffic in Women and Children to the Draft United Nations Convention on Organized Crime, U.N. Doc. A/AC.254/4/Add.3/Rev.6 (2000). This Protocol applies to traffic in women and children in the context of organized crime. See M. Cherif Bassiouni and Eduardo Vetere, *Organized Crime* (Ardsley Park, N.Y.: Transnational Publishers, 1998). That Draft Protocol does not, however, contain a provision on universal jurisdiction.

69. Bassiouni, *ICL Conventions,* 285.

70. Geneva Convention for the Amelioration of the Condition of the Wounded and Sick in Armed Forces in the Field, signed at Geneva, August 12, 1949, 75 U.N.T.S. 31, 6 U.S.T. 3114, T.I.A.S. 3362 (hereinafter First Geneva Convention); Geneva Convention for the Amelioration of the Condition of Wounded, Sick, and Shipwrecked Members of Armed Forces at Sea, signed at Geneva, August 12, 1949, 75 U.N.T.S. 85, 6 U.S.T. 3217, T.I.A.S. 3363 (hereinafter Second Geneva Convention); Geneva Convention Relative to the Treatment of Prisoners of War, signed at Geneva, August 12, 1949, 75 U.N.T.S. 135, 6 U.S.T. 3316, T.I.A.S. No. 3364 (hereinafter Third Geneva Convention); Geneva Convention Relative to the Protection of Civilian Persons in Time of War, signed at Geneva, August 12, 1949, 75 U.N.T.S. 287, 6 U.S.T. 3516, T.I.A.S. No. 3365 (hereinafter Fourth Geneva Convention).

71. Protocol I Additional to the Geneva Conventions of August 12, 1949, opened for signature at Berne, December 12, 1977, U.N. Doc. A/32/144, Annex I (hereinafter Protocol I); Protocol II Additional to the Geneva Conventions of August 12, 1949, opened for signature at Berne, December 12, 1977, U.N. Doc. A/32/144, Annex II.

72. Bassiouni, *ICL Conventions,* 416–45, 457–94.

73. Convention with Respect to the Laws and Customs of War on Land (First Hague, II), signed at The Hague, July 29, 1899, 32 Stat. 1803, 26 Martens Nouveau Recueil (ser. 2) 949. See M. Cherif Bassiouni, ed., *A Manual on International Humanitarian Law and Arms Control Agreements* (Ardsley Park, N.Y.: Transnational Publishers, 2000).

74. Bassiouni, *ICL Conventions,* 286.

75. For particular provisions regarding the enacting of legislation by contracting parties for the repression of grave breaches, see First Geneva Convention, art. 49; Second Geneva Convention, art. 50; Third Geneva Convention, art. 129; Fourth Geneva Convention, art. 146.

76. Following WWII, Allied military tribunals referred to the exercise of univerality with respect to war crimes and crimes against humanity, but these cases were prosecuted pursuant to Control Council Law No. 10. These gave the four major Allies "sovereignty" over their respective zones of occupation. Thus the tribunals exercised national jurisdiction.

77. IMT Charter, art. 6(c).

78. IMTFE Amended Charter, art. 5(c).

79. Allied Control Council Law No. 10, Punishment of Persons Guilty of War Crimes, Crimes against Peace and against Humanity, December 20, 1945, Official Gazette of the Control Council for Germany, No. 3, Berlin, 31 January 1946, art. 2(c), reprinted in Benjamin B. Ferencz, *An International Criminal Court: A Step toward World Peace* (London: Oceana Publications, 1980), 488.

80. ICTY Statute, art. 5; ICTR Statute, art. 3 and ICC Statute, art. 7.

81. ICC Statute, art. 7.

82. See M. Cherif Bassiouni, "Crimes against Humanity: The Need for a Specialized Convention," *Columbia Journal of Transnational Law* 31 (1994): 457–94; Bassiouni, *Crimes against Humanity.*

83. See Criminal Code, Section 7(3.71) (Can.); see also Regina v. Finta, [1994] 1 S.C.R. 701, 811.

84. See Nazi and Nazi Collaborators (Punishment) Law, August 1, 1950, 4 L.S.I. No. 64, at 154; see also Attorney General of Israel v. Eichmann, 36 I.L.R. 5 (Israel D.C., Jerusalem, December 12, 1961), aff'd, 36 I.L.R. 277 (Israel S. Ct., May 29, 1962).

85. See Criminal Code art. 212 (Ger.); German Bundesgerichtshof, Urteil vom. Apr. 30, 1999, 3StR 215/98; see also M. Cherif Bassiouni, "Crimes against Humanity," *International Criminal Law,* 2d ed., vol. 1, ed. M. Cherif Bassiouni (Ardsley Park, N.Y.: Transnational Publishers, 1999): 521, 584–86.

86. *Code Pénal* art. 212–1 (Paris: Dalloz, 2000). For a discussion of France's three major prosecutions of Barbie, Touvier, and Papon, see Leila Sadat Wexler, "The French Experience," in *International Criminal Law,* 2d ed., vol. 3, ed. M. Cherif Bassiouni (Ardsley Park: Transnational Publishers, 1999), 273–300. See also Leila Sadat Wexler, "Prosecutions for Crimes against Humanity in French Municipal Law: International Implications," in *Proceedings of the American Society of International Law* (Washington, D.C.: ASIL, 1997), 270–76; Leila Sadat Wexler, "Reflections on the Trial of Vichy Collaborator Paul Touvier for Crimes against Humanity in France," *Journal of Law and Social Inquiry* 20 (1995): 191; Leila Sadat Wexler, "The Interpretation of the Nuremberg Principles by the French Court of Cassation: From Touvier to Barbie and Back Again," *Columbia Journal Transnational Law* 32 (1994): 289.

87. Act Concerning the Punishment of Serious Violations of International Humanitarian Law, Section 7 (Belgium); as amended by the law of 5 April 2003.

88. See Christian Favre, Marc Pellet, and Patrick Stoudmann, *Code Penal Annote* (1997).

89. *Finta,* [1994] 1 S.C.R. at 811 (Cory, J.) (first emphasis added) (citation omitted).

90. Convention on the Prevention and Punishment of the Crime of Genocide, December 9, 1948, 78 U.N.T.S. 277 (emphasis added). While an intellectual campaign for the crime of genocide was begun in 1946, the word did not make its way to the public arena prior to 1948.

91. Ibid., art. 6 (emphasis added).

92. See ICTY Statute.

93. See ICTR Statute.

94. See ICC Statute.

95. ICTY Statute, art. 4.

96. ICTR Statute, art. 2.

97. ICC Statute, art 6.

98. See Schabas, *Genocide in International Law*, 353–78; Matthew Lippman, "Genocide," *International Criminal Law*, 2d ed., vol. 1, ed. M. Cherif Bassiouni (Ardsley Park, N.Y.: Transnational Publishers, 1999), 589–613.

99. Theodor Meron, "International Criminalization of Internal Atrocities," *American Journal of International Law* 89 (1995): 554, 570. But see Christopher C. Joyner, "Arresting Impunity: The Case for Universal Jurisdiction in Bringing War Criminals to Accountability," *Law and Contemporary Problems*. 59 (1996): 153, 159–60; Jordan J. Paust, "Congress and Genocide: They're Not Going to Get Away with It," *Michigan Journal of International Law* 11 (1989): 90, 91–92 ; Kenneth Randall, "Universal Jurisdiction under International Law," *Texas Law Review* 66 (1988): 785, 837. These and other authors, including this writer, have consistently asserted that universal jurisdiction applies to genocide as a *jus cogens* international crime. See Bassiouni, "Jus Cogens Crimes." It is because of scholars' influence that the *Restatement of the Foreign Relations Law of the United States* explains: "Universal jurisdiction to punish genocide is widely accepted as a principle of customary law." *Restatement*, para. 404, reporter's n. 1.

100. Prosecutor v. Tadic, Case No. IT-94-1–AR72, Decision on the Defence Motion for Interlocutory Appeal on Jurisdiction, para. 62 (October 2, 1995).

101. Prosecutor v. Ntuyahaga, Case No. ICTR-90–40–T, Decision on the Prosecutor's Motion to Withdraw the Indictment (March 18, 1999).

102. G.A. Res. 3068 (XXVIII), U.N. GAOR, 28th Sess., Supp. No. 30, at 75, U.N. Doc. A/9030 (1973) (hereinafter "Apartheid" Convention). See Roger S. Clark, "Apartheid," in *International Criminal Law*, 2d ed., vol. 1, ed. M. Cherif Bassiouni (Ardsley Park: Transnational Publishers, 1999), 643–62. A draft statute was prepared by this author in 1979.

103. "Apartheid" Convention, art. 4.

104. Ibid., art. 5.

105. It should also be noted that 101 states have ratified the "Apartheid" Convention, which is significantly less than the 186 member states of the United Nations. See *Study on Ways and Means of Insuring the Implementation of International Instruments Such as the International Convention on the Suppression and Punishment of the Crime of Apartheid, Including the Establishment of the International Jurisdiction Envisaged by the Convention*, U.N. Doc. E/CN.4/1426 (1981); M. Cherif Bassiouni and Daniel Derby, "Final Report on the Establishment of an International Criminal Court for the Implementation of the Apartheid Convention and Other Relevant International Instruments," *Hofstra Law Review* 9 (1981): 523.

106. Convention against Torture and Other Cruel, Inhuman, or Degrading Treatment or Punishment, G.A. Res. 39/46, U.N. GAOR 39th Sess., Supp. No. 51, U.N. Doc. A/39/51 (1984), entered into force June 26, 1987, draft reprinted in 23 I.L.M. 1027 (1985) (hereinafter Torture Convention). See Daniel H. Derby, "Torture," in *International Criminal Law*, 2d ed., vol. 1, ed. M. Cherif Bassiouni (Ardsley Park: Transnational Publishers, 1999), 705–49; J. Herman Burgers and Hans Danelius, *The United Nations Convention against Torture: A Handbook on the Convention against Torture and Other Cruel, Inhuman, or Degrading Treatment or Punishment* (Dordrecht: Martinus Nijhoff Publishers, 1988).

107. Torture Convention, art. 5.

108. See Bassiouni and Wise, *Aut Dedere Aut Judicare*.

109. Torture Convention, art. 7(1).

110. R. v. Bow Street Stipendiary Magistrate and others, ex parte Pinochet Ugarte, [1998] 4 All ER 897, [1998] 3 W.L.R. 1456 (H.L.). Reed Brody and Michael Ratner, *The Pinochet Papers: The Case of Augusto Pinochet in Spain and Britain* (The Hague: Kluwer Internal Law, 2000) Human Rights Watch, "When Tyrants Tremble," http://

www.hrw.org/reports/1999/Chile. See also "The Prosecution of Hissène Habré, an 'African Pinochet,'" in Human Rights Watch, http://www.hrw.org/editorials/2001/habre0515.htm *Cf.* Human Rights Watch, http://www.hrw.org/campaigns/Chile98/precedent.htm What Is Universal Jurisdiction (citing the *Filartiga* case for the proposition that "the torturer has become like the pirate and slave trader before him hostis humanis generis, an enemy of all mankind").

111. Convention on Offences and Certain Other Acts Committed on Board Aircraft (Tokyo Hijacking Convention), signed at Tokyo, September 14, 1963, art. 3(3), 704 U.N.T.S. 219, 20 U.S.T. 2941.

112. Convention for the Suppression of Unlawful Seizure of Aircraft (Hague Hijacking Convention), signed at The Hague, December 16, 1970, art. 4(3), 860 U.N.T.S. 105, 22 U.S.T. 1641.

113. Ibid., art. 7.

114. Convention for the Suppression of Unlawful Acts against the Safety of Civil Aviation (Montreal Hijacking Convention), signed at Montreal, September 23, 1971, art. 5(3), 974 U.N.T.S. 177, 24 U.S.T. 564.

115. Protocol for the Suppression of Unlawful Acts of Violence at Airports Serving International Civil Aviation, done at Montreal, adopted by the International Civil Aviation Organization, February 24, 1988, art. 3, 27 I.L.M. 627.

116. Convention for the Suppression of Unlawful Acts against the Safety of Maritime Navigation, done at Rome, March 10, 1988, art. 7(4, 5), 27 I.L.M. 668.

117. Ibid., art.10(1).

118. Protocol for the Suppression of Unlawful Acts against the Safety of Fixed Platforms Located on the Continental Shelf, done at Rome, March 10, 1988, art. 3, 27 I.L.M. 685.

119. Convention on the Prevention and Punishment of Crimes against Internationally Protected Persons, Including Diplomatic Agents (New York Convention), opened for signature at New York, December 14, 1973, art. 3, 1035 U.N.T.S. 167, 28 U.S.T. 1975.

120. Convention on the Safety of United Nations and Associated Personnel, opened for signature at New York, December 15, 1994, art. 10, U.N. Doc. A/49/742 (1994).

121. International Convention against the Taking of Hostages, concluded at New York, December 17, 1979, art. 5, 18 I.L.M. 1456.

122. Single Convention on Narcotic Drugs (Single Convention), signed at New York, March 30, 1961, art. 36(4), 18 U.S.T. 1407, referenced in 14 I.L.M. 302. For an amendment to Article 36, see Article 14 of the Protocol Amending the Single Convention on Narcotics Drugs, 1961, signed at Geneva, March 25, 1972, 976 U.N.T.S. 3, 26 U.S.T. 1430.

123. Convention on Psychotropic Substances (Psychotropic Convention), signed at Vienna February 21, 1971, art. 22(5), 1019 U.N.T.S. 175, T.I.A.S. No. 9725. See also ibid., art. 27 (regarding territorial application).

124. Hague Convention for the Protection of Cultural Property in the Event of Armed Conflict, signed at The Hague, May 14, 1954, art. 28, 249 U.N.T.S. 240.

125. Convention on the Means of Prohibiting and Preventing the Illicit Import, Export, and Transfer of Ownership of Cultural Property (UNESCO Cultural Convention), signed at Paris, November 14, 1970, art. 12, 823 U.N.T.S. 231.

126. International Convention for the Suppression of the Circulation of and Traffic in Obscene Publications, opened for signature at Geneva, September 12, 1923, art. 2, 27 L.N.T.S. 213, 7 Martens Nouveau Recueil (ser. 3) 266. See also International Convention for the Suppression of the Circulation of and Traffic in Obscene Publications, signed at Geneva, September 12, 1923, amended by the Protocol, signed at Lake Success, New York, November 12, 1947, art. 2, 46 U.N.T.S. 169.

127. International Convention for the Suppression of Counterfeiting Currency, signed at Geneva, April 20, 1929, art. 17, 112 L.N.T.S. 371.

128. Convention for the Protection of Submarine Cables, signed at Paris, March 14, 1884, arts. 1, 8, 9, 24 Stat. 989, 11 Martens Nouveau Recueil (ser. 2) 281.

129. International Convention against the Recruitment, Use, Financing, and Training of Mercenaries, adopted at New York, December 4, 1989, art. 9(2, 3), 29 I.L.M. 89.

130. See Bassiouni, "Sources and Content," 27–31.

131. Ibid., 46–100.

132. M. Cherif Bassiouni, "Enforcing Human Rights through International Criminal Law and through an International Criminal Tribunal," in *Human Rights: An Agenda for the Next Century*, eds. Louis Henkin and Lawrence Hargrove (Washington, D.C.: American Society for International Law, 1994), 347.

133. The category of war crimes continues to be augmented to reflect different practices and more detailed regulations; slave-related practices have not, as mentioned above. International crimes are a result of a historic evolution, which begins with the enunciation of certain rights or the expansion of certain "prescriptions" in treaties. These prescriptions do not contain any penal characteristics, and thus they do not criminalize the conduct. At a subsequent stage, that particular prescription is embodied in a "proscription," a norm that not only prohibits but criminalizes the violation.

134. For that historical evolution, see Bassiouni, *Crimes against Humanity*.

135. The only logical method of dealing with these problems of uneven development of international criminal law is to codify it, but it regrettably appears that governments do not support this proposition; consequently international criminal law will continue to suffer from a number of legislative and other deficiencies. See, e.g., M. Cherif Bassiouni, *A Draft International Criminal Code and a Draft Statute for an International Criminal Tribunal* (Dordrecht: Martinus Nijhoff Publishers, 1987).

136. See M. Cherif Bassiouni, "Searching for Peace and Achieving Justice: The Need for Accountability," *Law and Contemporary Problems* 59 (1996): 9; Madeline H. Morris, "International Guidelines against Impunity: Facilitating Accountability," *Law and Contemporary Problems* 59 (1996): 29; Michael Scharf, "The Letter of the Law: The Scope of the International Legal Obligation to Prosecute Human Rights Crimes," *Law and Contemporary Problems* 59 (1996): 41; Bassiouni, "Jus Cogens Crimes"; W. Michael Reisman, "Legal Responses to Genocide and Other Massive Violations of Human Rights," *Law and Contemporary Problems* 59 (1996): 75; Stephan Landsman, "Alternative Responses to Serious Human Rights Abuses: Of Prosecution and Truth Commissions," *Law and Contemporary Problems* 59 (1996): 81; Naomi Roht-Arriaza, "Combating Impunity: Some Thoughts on the Way Forward," *Law and Contemporary Problems* 59 (1996): 93; Jennifer L. Balint, "The Place of Law in Addressing International Regime Conflicts," *Law and Contemporary Problems* 59 (1996): 103; Neil J. Kritz, "Coming to Terms with Atrocities: A Review of Accountability Mechanisms for Mass Violations of Human Rights," *Law and Contemporary Problems* 59 (1996): 127; Joyner, "Arresting Impunity"; Priscilla B. Hayner, "International Guidelines for the Creation and Operation of Truth Commissions: A Preliminary Proposal," *Law and Contemporary Problems* 59 (1996): 173; Mark S. Ellis, "Purging the Past: The Current State of Lustration Laws in the Former Communist Bloc," *Law and Contemporary Problems* 59 (1996): 181; Douglass Cassel, "Lessons from the Americas: Guidelines for International Response to Amnesties for Atrocities," *Law and Contemporary Problems* 59 (1996): 197; see also *Reining in Impunity for International Crimes and Serious Violations of Fundamental Human Rights: Proceedings of the Siracusa Conference, September 17–21, 1998, Nouvelles Études pénales* 14 (1998);

Diane F. Orentlicher, "Settling Accounts: The Duty to Prosecute Human Rights Violations of a Prior Regime," *Yale Law Review* 100 (1991): 2537.

137. The series of restatements of certain aspects of U.S. law is an interesting model. However, since there is no restatement on criminal law, the closest analogy is the *Restatement (Second) of Conflict of Laws*, 2d ed. (Boston, Mass.: American Law Institute, 1971), which, in Section 6, includes a policy-oriented approach to choice of law. It states:

(1) A court, subject to constitutional restrictions, will follow a statutory directive of its own state on choice of law.
(2) When there is no such directive, the factors relevant to the choice of the applicable rule of law include
    (a) the needs of the interstate and international systems,
    (b) the relevant policies of the forum,
    (c) the relevant policies of other interested states and the relative interests of those states in the determination of the particular issue,
    (d) the protection of justified expectations,
    (e) the basic policies underlying the particular field of law,
    (f) certainty, predictability and uniformity of result, and
    (g) ease in the determination and application of the law to be applied.

Restatement (Second) of Conflict of Laws, 2d, Section 6, at 10 (1971). While such a choice-of-law approach can work in a federal system linked by a constitution that contains a "full faith and credit" clause, U.S. Const. art. 4, sect. 1, it may not work effectively at the international law level. Consequently, a more hard-fast normative approach may be more appropriate in the international context.

138. While this writer strongly supports this outcome, it must be noted that a similar effort undertaken in 1967 by the International Association of Penal Law resulted in the adoption of the 1968 UN Convention on the Non-Applicability of Statutes of Limitations to War Crimes and Crimes against Humanity, opened for signature at New York, November 26, 1968, 754 U.N.T.S. 73. Forty-three states ratified it. See *Revue international de droit pénal* 37 (1966). It can thus be assumed that at most the same number of states would support a convention on universal jurisdiction. The more recent European Convention on Non-Applicability of Statutory Limitations to Crimes against Humanity and War Crimes (Inter-European), Europ. T.S. No. 82 has only a disappointing two ratifications.

Chapter 2. Comment: The Quest for Clarity

1. M. Cherif Bassiouni, "The History of Universal Jurisdiction and Its Place in International Law," this volume.
2. Ibid.
3. Ibid.
4. Princeton Principles on Universal Jurisdiction, Principle 1(1), this volume.
5. Comments made in the course of the preparatory process for the Princeton Project.
6. Ibid.
7. Bassiouni, "History of Universal Jurisdiction," this volume.
8. Ibid.
9. Richard A. Falk, "Assessing the Pinochet Litigation: Whither Universal Jurisdiction?," this volume.

Chapter 3. The Growing Support for Universal Jurisdiction in National Legislation

The author would like to express his gratitude to Prof. Roger S. Clark of Rutgers University School of Law–Camden for his assistance in the preparation of this essay.

1. U.N. Doc. A/CONF.183/9 (1998), available at www.un.org/law/icc/statute/romefra.htm.

2. International law recognizes a number of instances where courts may be permitted to exercise extraterritorial jurisdiction. Courts may exercise jurisdiction over crimes committed outside the territory of the state committed by the state's own nationals (active personality jurisdiction), over crimes that threaten the security interests of the state (protective principle jurisdiction), and over crimes against a state's citizens (passive personality jurisdiction). *Cf.* Ian Brownlie, *Principles of International Law,* 5th ed. (Oxford, U.K.: Clarendon Press 1990), 303–9. In addition, where the only link between the state and the criminal conduct is custody over the offender, international law has recognized a "universal jurisdiction" over a limited class of very serious offenses. The Restatement (Section 404) defines "universal jurisdiction": "A state has jurisdiction to define and prescribe punishment for certain offenses recognized by the community of nations as of universal concern, such as piracy, slave trade, attacks on or hijacking of aircraft, genocide, war crimes, and perhaps certain acts of terrorism."

3. While states that ratify the Rome Statute are not required to make the offenses provided for in Articles 6 through 8 of the statute crimes in their territory, many states may consider it useful to do so. If a state wishes to invoke the principle of complementarity, then the state must align its domestic law with the provisions of the Rome Statute. As the commentary on the International Crimes and International Criminal Court Act recently enacted in New Zealand (available at http://www.legislation.govt.nz) explains: "The ICC is intended to be a court of last resort. It will act only where national systems that have jurisdiction are genuinely not willing or able to investigate or prosecute these crimes. Its jurisdiction is underpinned by the principle of 'complementarity' which seems to mean that if a state party wishes to exercise jurisdiction over the crimes, the ICC must defer to the state in the first instance. In order for a state party to exercise jurisdiction in respect of international crimes, its domestic law must therefore contain the relevant offenses."

4. See, e.g., International Convention on the Suppression and Punishment of Apartheid, 1015 U.N.T.S. 243, 13 *I.L.M.* 50 (1974); Convention against Torture and Other Cruel, Inhuman, or Degrading Treatment or Punishment ("Convention against Torture"), 23 *I.L.M.* 1027 (1984); Convention on the Prevention and Punishment of the Crime of Genocide ("Genocide Convention"), 78 U.N.T.S. 277; Geneva Convention for the Amelioration of the Condition of the Wounded and Sick in Armed Forces in the Field, signed at Geneva on August 12, 1949, 75 U.N.T.S. 31, 6 U.S.T. 3114, T.I.A.S. 3362; Geneva Convention for the Amelioration of the Condition of the Wounded, Sick, and Shipwrecked Members of the Armed Forces at Sea, signed at Geneva August 12, 1949, 75 U.N.T.S. 85, 6 U.S.T. 3217, T.I.A.S. 3363; Geneva Convention Relative to the Protection of Civilian Persons in Time of War, signed at Geneva August 12, 1949, 75 U.N.T.S. 135, 6 U.S.T. 3316, T.I.A.S. No. 3364; Convention on Offenses and Certain Acts Committed on Board Aircraft, signed at Tokyo on September 14, 1963, 704 U. N. T. S. 219 (1969); and Convention for the Suppression of Unlawful Seizure of Aircraft, signed at The Hague on December 16, 1970, 10 *I.L.M.* 1233 (1970).

5. The *Audiencia,* created in 1977, is a special centralized court in Madrid with

extraordinary powers, including extraterritorial jurisdiction, to prosecute cases such as international terrorism and narcotics trafficking. See Reed Brody and Michael Ratner, ed., *The Pinochet Papers: The Case of Augusto Pinochet in Spain and Britain* (Boston: Kluwer Law International: 2000), 24.

6. Amnesty International issued a CD-ROM last year containing a survey of national legislation on universal jurisdiction, titled *Universal Jurisdiction: The Duty of States to Enact and Implement Legislation.* The work is designed to assist legislatures in drafting legislation providing for universal jurisdiction and contains a comprehensive survey of state practice concerning universal jurisdiction at the national level, including national legislation, case law, and other materials. A number of special features make this resource particularly valuable, including extensive quotations from pertinent statutes in many different countries in English as well as an extensive analysis of the manner in which many nations have implemented universal jurisdiction over international crimes in their domestic courts.

7. Act Concerning the Punishment of Serious Violations of International Humanitarian Law, *Moniteur Belge,* March 23, 1999 (available at http://staatsblad.fgov.be) (English translation reprinted in 38 *I.L.M.* 918 with introductory note by Stefan Smis and Kim Vander Borght).

8. Article 7. Such jurisdiction is subject to the immunity for senior government officials from prosecution in national courts. The continuing importance of this immunity was recognized recently by the International Court of Justice in its decision in *Democratic Republic of the Congo v. Belgium* holding that an incumbent minister is immune from prosecution under the Belgian statute. Arrest Warrant of April 11 (D.R. Congo v. Belgium), 2002 I.C.J. Rep. (Judgment of February 14, 2002), available at www.icj-cij.org/icjwww/idocket/icobe/icobeframe.htm. This important decision supports the conclusion in the commentary to the *Princeton Principles* that "procedural" immunity remains in effect before national courts during a senior government official's term in office. For a more extensive discussion of the difference between "procedural" and "substantive" immunity, see the analysis below of the United Kingdom's universal jurisdiction legislation.

9. Article 6 of the Genocide Convention provides for jurisdiction against genocide offenses either in the territory where the offense is committed or before an international tribunal: "Persons charged with genocide or any of the acts enumerated in Article II shall be tried by a competent tribunal of the state in the territory in which the act was committed, or by such international penal tribunal as may have jurisdiction with respect to the contracting parties which shall have accepted jurisdiction." While it has occasionally been argued that the convention implicitly denies universal jurisdiction over genocide offenses, a number of states, such as Canada, Ethiopia, and Spain, have asserted universal jurisdiction over genocide. See Luc Reydams, "Universal Jurisdiction: The Belgian State of Affairs," *Criminal Law Forum* 10 (2000): 183, 196 n. 58. In addition, a number of courts have held that the Genocide Convention should not be interpreted to deny states the right to assert universal jurisdiction over the crime. For example, the *Audiencia* noted in its decision finding extraterritorial jurisdiction over genocide in the *Pinochet* proceeding: ". . . [I]t would be contrary to the spirit of the convention—which seeks a commitment on the part of the contracting parties to use their respective criminal justice systems to prosecute genocide as a crime under international law, and to prevent impunity in the case of such a grave crime—to interpret Article 6 as limiting the exercise of jurisdiction by excluding any jurisdiction not treated therein." *In Re Pinochet: Order of the Criminal Chamber of the Spanish Audiencia Nacional Affirming Spanish Jurisdiction,* November 5, 1998, reprinted in Brody and Ratner, *The Pinochet Papers,* 95, available at http://derechos.org/nizkor/chile/juicio/denu.html.

10. A recent law review article explains: "As for war crimes, the Act applies also to armed conflicts not of an international character, whereas the treaty obligation is limited to international armed conflicts. The Geneva Conventions and Additional Protocols require that state parties search for and punish persons, regardless of their nationality, alleged to have committed 'grave breaches' thereof, but the term 'grave breaches' only appears in the four Geneva Conventions and the Additional Protocol I, applicable only to international armed conflicts. By including Additional Protocol II, which applies to non-international armed conflicts, in the original title and body of the law, the legislature decided to criminalize acts which were not 'grave breaches' but merely 'prohibited' under the Conventions and Additional Protocols." Reydams, "Universal Jurisdiction," 197.

11. Piracy is covered by the Convention on the High Seas, April 9, 1958, art. 19, 450 U.N.T.S. 82, 13 U.S.T. 2312 ("On the high seas, or in any other place outside the jurisdiction of any state, every state may seize a pirate ship or aircraft, or a ship taken by piracy and under the control of pirates, and arrest the persons and seize the property on board"); see also United Nations Convention on the Law of Sea, December 10, 1982, art. 105, U.N. A/Conf. 62/122, 21 *I.L.M.* 1261.

12. Extradition rules govern the official surrender of an alleged criminal by one state to another jurisdiction over the crime charged. The "double criminality rule," a common extradition requirement, provides that the act charged must be criminal under the laws of both the state of refuge and the requesting state. *Cf.* Brownlie, *Principles of International Law,* 319.

13. For example, Article 8(6) of the Danish Criminal Code establishes universal jurisdiction over genocide, crimes against humanity, and violations of the Geneva Conventions but only where another state has requested extradition of the person, extradition has been refused, and the alleged behavior is a crime under Danish law. *Cf.* Fiona McKay, "The Redress Trust: Universal Jurisdiction in Europe since 1990 for War Crimes, Crimes against Humanity, Torture, and Genocide" (Annex) (1999), 6 (available at www.redress.org/publications.unijeur.html).

14. See Reydams, "Universal Jurisdiction," 190–91.

15. "The Pinochet Precedent: How Victims Can Pursue Human Rights Criminals Abroad," *Human Rights Watch Update,* September 2000, 8.

16. R.S.C. (2000), chapt. 24, available at http://laws.justice.gc.ca/en; on this legislation *cf.* William A. Schabas, "Canadian Implementing Legislation for the Rome Statute," *Yearbook of International Humanitarian Law* 3 (2000): 337.

17. R.S.C. (1985), c. C-46, § 7 (3.71).

18. See R. v. Finta (LaForest, J, dissenting), [1994] 1 S.C.R. 701, 736. This fiction eliminated the "obstacle of extraterritoriality" and enabled Canada to serve as the forum for domestic prosecution of these crimes. Thus it was necessary to prove both that the offense was an international crime, as defined in the statute, and a violation of domestic law.

19. Among the requirements imposed on the prosecution under the Court's interpretation of the statute was the Court's insistence that the defendant could be convicted only if the jury found that he knew subjectively that his acts were of the serious nature of war crimes and/or crimes against humanity. R. v. Finta, [1994] 1 S.C.R. 701, 783, 819. See the analysis of the *Finta* decision in Anne-Marie Slaughter's contribution to this volume.

20. Another purpose of enacting these crimes in Canada is to facilitate the surrender of suspects to the International Criminal Court. The double criminality requirement generally requires that conduct for which extradition is sought be an offense in the jurisdiction from which extradition is requested. By making these international crimes also domestic offenses under Canadian law, it cannot be argued that a crime under ICC jurisdiction is not also a crime under Canadian

law. *Cf.* "Bill C-19: Crimes Against Humanity and War Crimes Act," available at www.parl.gc.ca/common/bills_ls.asp?lang=e&parl=36&ses=2&ls=c19&source=bills.

21. R.S.C. 2000, c. 24, § 4.

22. The Rome Statute offenses thus form a baseline of customary international law starting July 17, 1998. Canadian courts need only determine the relevant developments in international law after that date. Ibid.

23. In a fashion similar to the Belgian and Canadian legislation, the International Crimes and International Criminal Court Act recently adopted in New Zealand (available at http://www.legislation.govt.nz) provides broad universal jurisdiction over genocide, crimes against humanity, and war crimes. A similar statute has been adopted in Germany. *Cf.* Draft of an Act to Introduce the Code of Crimes against International Law ("International Criminal Code") (available at www.iuscrim.mpg.de/forsch/legaltext/vstgbleng.pdf) (see note 41). South Africa, the Netherlands, Argentina, and Australia (among other countries) have also either enacted or are in the process of enacting legislation incorporating international crimes in their penal codes and providing their courts with some form of universal jurisdiction. The Coalition for an International Criminal Court has prepared a country-by-country ratification report that describes such legislation (available at http://iccnon.org/countryinfo.html).

24. *Cf.* Geneva Conventions Act of 1957, § 1.

25. *Cf.* Geneva Conventions Act of 1957, Sch. 1, Art. 50; see also "Final Report on the Exercise of Universal Jurisdiction in Respect of Gross Human Rights Offenses," International Law Association, Committee on International Human Rights Law and Practice (2000), 6.

26. "Each High Contracting Party shall be under the obligation to search for persons alleged to have committed, or to have ordered to be committed, such grave breaches, and shall bring such persons, regardless of their nationality, before its own courts. It may also, if it prefers, and in accordance with the provisions of its own legislation, hand such persons over for trial to another High Contracting Party concerned, provided such High Contracting Party has made out a *prima facie* case." Articles 49, 50, 129, and 146 of the First, Second, Third, and Fourth Geneva Conventions.

27. Chapter 17, available at www.hmso.gov.uk/acts/acts2001/20010017.htm.

28. The statute repeals the Genocide Act of 1969 (whose provisions have been subsumed within part 5 of the new legislation). The new statute, however, does not repeal the Geneva Conventions Act of 1957, as the explanatory notes discuss: "Certain war crimes . . . (notably grave breaches of the Geneva Conventions) also constituted existing domestic offenses in identical terms. However, as the Geneva Conventions Act of 1957 takes wider jurisdiction than this act (and, by virtue of the Geneva Conventions [Amendment] Act of 1995, also covers grave breaches of Additional Protocol 1 of the Geneva Conventions), it remains in force subject to the amendments specified in section 70."

29. § 51(1), International Criminal Court Act.

30. § 51(2)(b), International Criminal Court Act; see also § 68(1) ("This section applies in relation to a person who commits acts outside the United Kingdom at a time when he is not a United Kingdom national, a United Kingdom resident or a person subject to United Kingdom service jurisdiction and who subsequently becomes resident in the United Kingdom").

31. As discussed in note 3 above, the "complementarity" provisions of the Rome Statute require the United Kingdom to make ICC crimes domestic offenses in order to assure its citizens the right to trial before British Courts. Robin Cook explained (in the address noted above): "Members on both sides of the House should have robust confidence that the British legal system has adequate remedies for crimes against

humanity and can satisfactorily demonstrate to the International Criminal Court that any such allegations have been properly investigated and, where appropriate, prosecuted. In short, British service personnel will never be prosecuted by the International Criminal Court because any bona fide allegation will be pursued by the British authorities."

32. J. D. Van der Vyer, "Universal Jurisdiction in International Criminal Law," *South African Journal of International Law* 24 (1999): 107; see also Reg. v. Bow St. Metro Stipendiary and Others, ex parte Pinochet Ugarte *(No. 3),* [1999] 2 All E.R. 97 (H.L. 1999) (available at www.parliament.the-stationery-office.co.uk/pa/ld199899/ldjudgmt/jd990324/pino1.htm).

33. See § 23, International Criminal Court Act. The immunity rules set forth in the Rome Statute distinguish between signatories and nonsignatories, as the explanatory notes to the International Criminal Court Act explain: "Article 27 [of the Rome Statute] states that the Statute shall equally apply to all persons without any distinction based on official capacity and that all immunities attaching to the official capacity of a person, whether under national or international law, shall not bar the ICC from exercising its jurisdiction over such a person. Article 98.1 provides that the ICC may not proceed with a request for surrender or assistance which would require the requested state to act inconsistently with its obligations under international law with respect to the State or diplomatic immunity of a person or property of a third State, unless the ICC can first obtain the third state's co-operation for the waiver of the immunity. These articles mean that a State Party to the ICC Statute, in accepting Article 27, has already agreed that the immunity of its . . . officials . . . including its Head of State, will not prevent the trial of such persons before the ICC. . . . But non-State Parties have not accepted this provision and so immunity of their representatives would remain intact unless an express waiver were given by the non-State Party concerned to the ICC."

34. See discussion on immunity in the commentary to *Principles,* this volume.

35. *In Re Pinochet: Order of the Criminal Chamber of the Spanish Audiencia Nacional Affirming Spanish Jurisdiction,* November 5, 1998, printed in Brody and Ratner, *The Pinochet Papers,* 95; see also Article 65 of the Organic Law of the Judicial Branch, which provides that Spanish courts have jurisdiction over acts committed abroad where Spain is obliged to exercise jurisdiction under international treaties.

36. Ibid.

37. Principle 9 recognizes that, in exercising universal jurisdiction, "a state or its judicial organs shall ensure that a person who is subject to criminal proceedings shall not be exposed to multiple prosecutions or punishment for the same criminal conduct where the prior criminal proceedings have been conducted in good faith and in accordance with international norms and standards."

38. Richard J. Wilson, "Prosecuting Pinochet: International Crimes in Spanish Domestic Law," *Human Rights Quarterly* 21 (1999): 927, 955.

39. "Regardless of the law of the place of commission, the German criminal law is also applicable to the following acts committed outside Germany: (1) Genocide . . ." and ". . . [A]cts which, on the basis of an international treaty binding on the Federal Republic of Germany, are to be prosecuted even in cases when such acts have been committed abroad." *Strafgesetzbuch (StGB),* § 6, available at www.icrc.org/ihl-nat.nsf.

40. For example, in the prosecution against *Novislav Djajic,* Djajic was charged with genocide, murder, and deprivation of liberty, according to sections 211, 220a, and 239 of the German penal code, which defines the crimes, and section 6(9), dealing with jurisdiction, in connection with Articles 3, 146, and 147 of the Fourth Geneva Convention. On May 23, 1997, the Bavarian High Court convicted Novislav Djajic, a Bosnian Serb, to five years imprisonment for his role in aiding and abetting the killing of fourteen Muslim men in Eastern Bosnia in April 1992. See Public

Prosecutor v. Djajic, Bayrisches Oberlandesgericht, May 23, 1997; see also McKay, "The Redress Trust," 24.

41. The statute provides domestic jurisdiction over such crimes "even when the offense was committed abroad and bears no relation to Germany." Article I, International Criminal Code. This legislation is unique in several respects. Prosecutions are generally mandatory if the suspect is either present in the jurisdiction or even *expected* to be present. However, in a fashion similar to the Rome Statute's "complementarity" provisions, German courts will not assume jurisdiction over a case being prosecuted in the territory where the crime was committed. See §§ 153f (1, 2) of the German Code of Criminal Procedure, Article 3, § 5 of the International Criminal Code.

42. C. PEN., art. 211(1) and 212(1) (Dalloz, ed., 2000).

43. After an extensive discussion of these provisions, Bassiouni concludes in his contribution to this volume that France does not provide for universal jurisdiction for genocide and crimes against humanity. Article 113[6], however, does permit French courts to exercise jurisdiction over persons who commit felonies abroad and subsequently become French citizens: "French criminal law is applicable to any felony committed by a French national outside the territory of the Republic. . . . This present article applies even though the accused acquired French nationality subsequent to the conduct imputed to him or her." C. PEN, art. 113(6) (English translation in *The French Penal Code of 1994* (Littleton, Colo.: Rothman, 1999)). This article would apply to genocide committed after 1993, the date that genocide became a crime under French law. See Amnesty International, *Universal Jurisdiction: The Duty of States to Enact and Implement Legislation* (CD-ROM), ch. 4: 84, ch. 8: 28.

44. "Whoever outside the territory of the Republic, commits acts qualified as crimes or offenses which constitute torture within the meaning of Article 1 of the Convention Against Torture and Other Cruel, Inhuman or Degrading Treatment or Punishment, adopted at New York on 10 December 1984, may be prosecuted and tried by French Courts if he is found in France."

45. *Munyeshyaka*, Cour de Cassation of the French Republic, Chambre Criminelle, January 6, 1998, Nr. X 96–82.492 (Cass. Crim. January 6, 1998, *Bull. Crim.*, n. 2, Rep. Pen. Dalloz, 2000); see also McKay, "The Redress Trust," 9. Bassiouni notes in his contribution to this volume that if universal jurisdiction over genocide and crimes against humanity exists based on France's implementation of the Security Council Resolution establishing the ICTR, then, based on the same reasoning, France's implementation of the Rome Statute could also justify the exercise of universal jurisdiction.

46. See "The Prosecution of War Criminals," *Virginia Journal of International Law* 29 (1989): 887, 922–26 (student note).

47. The United Kingdom also enacted a War Crimes Act in 1991 giving British courts jurisdiction over "certain offenses committed during the Second World War. Jurisdiction is limited to offenses of homicide constituting a violation of the laws and customs of war, committed by a British citizen or resident, and committed in Germany or German occupied territory between September 1939 and June 1945." McKay, "The Redress Trust," 24. In order to be subject to prosecution under the statute, the accused must have been or subsequently become a British citizen on March 8, 1990. War Crimes Act § 1(1).

48. *Cf.* Principle 11 ("A state shall, where necessary, enact national legislation to enable the exercise of universal jurisdiction and the enforcement of these principles.")

49. The Arrest Warrant of April 11, 2000 (D.R. Republic of Congo v. Belgium), 2002 I.C.J. Rep. (Judgment of February 14, 2002), Joint Separate Opinion of Higgins, Kooijmans, and Buergenthal, slip op. at 18.

50. This quotation can be found on the United Nations web page devoted to the International Criminal Court. See www.un.org/law/icc/general/overview.htm.

Chapter 4. The Adolf Eichmann Case: Universal and National Jurisdiction

I am grateful to Cherif Bassiouni, Lori Damrosch, Richard Falk, Jeff Herbst, Steve Macedo, Stephen Marks, Martha Minow, Diane Orentlicher, Leila Sadat, Anne-Marie Slaughter, and the other participants in the Princeton Project on Universal Jurisdiction for their thoughtful and helpful advice. My thanks to Chandra Sriram for superb research assistance.

1. Louis Henkin, *How Nations Behave: Law and Foreign Policy* (New York: Columbia University Press, 1979), 276–77.

2. "War Crimes Tribunal Accused of Eichmann-like Abductions," *Associated Press,* August 4, 2000.

3. See Amnon Rubenstein, *The Zionist Dream Revisited: From Herzl to Gush Emunim and Back* (New York: Schocken Books, 1984), 89.

4. I am grateful to Martha Minow for this point.

5. Laqueur, "Hannah Arendt in Jerusalem: The Controversy Revisited," in Lyman H. Legters, *Western Society after the Holocaust* (Boulder: Westview, 1983), 113. Laqueur thought that this distinction was not particularly important. For an overview of jurisdictional arguments, see Steven R. Ratner and Jason S. Abrams, *Accountability for Human Rights Atrocities in International Law: Beyond the Nuremberg Legacy* (Oxford: Clarendon, 1997), 133–89.

6. Tom Segev, *The Seventh Million: The Israelis and the Holocaust,* trans. Haim Watzman (New York: Hill and Wang, 1994), 329.

7. Telford Taylor, "Large Questions in the Eichmann Case," *New York Times Magazine,* January 22, 1961, 11.

8. Taylor, "Eichmann Case," 22.

9. Ibid.

10. Ibid., 23.

11. Ibid., 25.

12. Segev, *Seventh Million,* 325; Isser Harel, *The House on Garibaldi Street* (New York: Viking, 1975), 3.

13. Hannah Arendt, *Eichmann in Jerusalem: A Report on the Banality of Evil* (London: Penguin, 1994), 14.

14. Martha Minow, *Between Vengeance and Forgiveness: Facing History after Genocide and Mass Violence* (Boston: Beacon, 1998), 135–36.

15. British Public Records Office, Kew, London, CAB 23/43, Imperial War Cabinet 39, November 28, 1918, 11:45 A.M., 7.

16. CAB 28/5, I.C.-98, Allied conversation, London, December 2, 1918, 11 A.M., 7.

17. See James F. Willis, *Prologue to Nuremberg: The Politics and Diplomacy of Punishing War Criminals of the First World War* (Westport, Conn.: Greenwood Press, 1982); and Gary Jonathan Bass, *Stay the Hand of Vengeance: The Politics of War Crimes Tribunals* (Princeton: Princeton University Press, 2000), 58–105.

18. "The Moscow Declaration," in Bradley F. Smith, ed., *The American Road to Nuremberg: The Documentary Record, 1944–1945* (Stanford, Calif.: Hoover Institution Press, 1982), 13.

19. W. P. (43) 496, Churchill, "The Punishment of War Criminals," November 9, 1943, CAB 66/42, 266.

20. Smith, "The Moscow Declaration," 13.

21. Ibid.

22. Ibid., 14.

23. Judith N. Shklar, *Legalism: Law, Morals, and Political Trials* (Cambridge: Harvard University Press, 1986), 170–71.

24. See Bradley F. Smith, *The Road to Nuremberg* (New York: Basic Books, 1981).

25. See Howard M. Sachar, *A History of Israel: From the Rise of Zionism to Our Time*, vol. 1 (New York: Knopf, 1989), 556.

26. Segev, *Seventh Million*, 330–31.

27. Arendt, *Eichmann in Jerusalem*, 270–71.

28. Ibid., 263.

29. Segev, *Seventh Million*, 325–26.

30. David Ben-Gurion, "The Eichmann Case as Seen by Ben-Gurion," *New York Times Magazine*, December 18, 1960, 7, 62. On the uniqueness of the Holocaust and what is at stake in the debate, see Charles S. Maier, *The Unmasterable Past: History, Holocaust, and German National Identity* (Cambridge: Harvard University Press, 1988).

31. Ben-Gurion, "Eichmann Case," 7.

32. Segev, *Seventh Million*, 332–33.

33. Arendt, *Eichmann in Jerusalem*, 7.

34. Segev, *Seventh Million*, 327.

35. Ibid., 332–33.

36. Sachar, *History of Israel*, vol. 1, 558.

37. Segev, *Seventh Million*, 326–29.

38. Theodor Meron, "Public International Law Problems of the Jurisdiction of the State of Israel," *Journal du Droit International*, vol. 88, pt. 2 (July–December 1961), 1054–56.

39. Meron, "Public International Law Problems," 1056.

40. Segev, *Seventh Million*, 334–35.

41. Meron, "Public International Law Problems," 1056–58.

42. Ibid., 1058.

43. Segev, *Seventh Million*, 329–30.

44. Ibid., 356.

45. Pnina Lahav, *Judgment in Jerusalem: Chief Justice Simon Agranat and the Zionist Century* (Berkeley and Los Angeles: University of California Press, 1997), 153.

46. Lahav, *Judgment in Jerusalem*, 154.

47. Ibid.

48. Arendt, *Eichmann in Jerusalem*, 264. Parentheses removed from original text. See also Milton Katz, "Eichmann: International Problem," *Harvard Law Record*, vol. 32, no. 3 (February 16, 1961), 9–15.

49. Harel, *House on Garibaldi Street*, viii.

50. Zvi Aharoni and Wilhelm Dietl, *Operation Eichmann*, trans. Helmut Bögler (New York: John Wiley and Sons, 1997),168–70.

51. Ibid., 169–70.

52. Harel, *House on Garibaldi Street*, viii–ix.

53. Ibid., 39.

54. Aharoni and Dietl, *Operation Eichmann*, 79. The Mossad, not sure where Mengele was in 1960, considered nabbing him as well as Eichmann (149–52).

55. Bob Woodward, *The Commanders* (New York: Simon and Schuster, 1991), 87.

56. Ibid., 113.

57. Ibid., 159.

58. Ibid., 170.

59. United States v. Humberto Alvarez-Machain, 504 U.S. 655 (1992). See also Michael J. Glennon, "State-Sponsored Abduction: A Comment on United States v. Alvarez-Machain," *American Journal of International Law* 86 (1992): 746; J. Bush, "How Did We Get Here?: Foreign Abduction after *Alvarez-Machain*," *Stanford Law Review* 45 (1993): 939. I am grateful to Asli Bali for pointing out this case to me.

60. Taylor, "Eichmann Case," 25.

61. Lahav, *Judgment in Jerusalem*, 107–8.

62. Ibid., 113–17.

63. Arendt, *Eichmann in Jerusalem*, 4–5. For a criticism of Arendt's controversial emphasis on Jewish passivity, see Gershom Scholem, "On Eichmann," in his *On Jews and Judaism in Crisis: Selected Essays* (New York: Schocken Books, 1976), ed. Werner J. Dannhauser, 298–306.

64. Segev, *Seventh Million*, 342–43, 353–54, 356; Sachar, *History of Israel*, vol. 1, 557.

65. Taylor, "Eichmann Case," 11.

66. Arendt, *Eichmann in Jerusalem*, 265.

Chapter 5. Comment: Connecting the Threads in the Fabric of International Law

1. Compare T. M. Franck, *The Power of Legitimacy among Nations* (Oxford University Press, 1990), 147–48. Legitimacy depends upon "coherence," defined in part as the extent to which a rule is connected to a "lattice of principles in use to resolve different problems."

2. Letter of June 15, 1960, from the representative of Argentina to the president of the Security Council, U.N. Doc. S/4336.

3. S.C. Res. 138, 15 U.N. SCOR, Resolutions and Decisions, 4. See also S/4349 (June 1960).

4. Joint Communiqué of August 3, 1960, cited in Lori F. Damrosch et al., *International Law: Cases and Materials*, 4th ed. (St. Paul, Minn.: West Group, 2001), 1138.

5. See judgments in Attorney General of Israel v. Eichmann (Dist. Ct. Israel 1961, affirmed Sup. Ct. Israel 1962), reprinted at 36 Int'l L. Repts. 18, 277 (1968).

6. Hannah Arendt, *Eichmann in Jerusalem: A Report on the Banality of Evil* (New York: Penguin Books, 1994), 264. Arendt's passage continues: "Those who are convinced that justice, and nothing else, is the end of law will be inclined to condone the kidnaping act, though not because of precedents, but, on the contrary, as a desperate, unprecedented and no-precedent-setting act, necessitated by the unsatisfactory condition of international law" (264–65).

7. Only a handful of legal articles seek to justify abduction in aid of criminal jurisdiction, notably Malvina Halberstam, "In Defense of the Supreme Court Decision in Alvarez-Machain," *American Journal of International Law* 86 (1992): 736. Even so, the brunt of Halberstam's argument is not so much in favor of abduction as supportive of the *male captus* rule under which a court overlooks irregularities in the manner in which the accused arrived in the jurisdiction. Of the many articles criticizing the practice of abduction, see especially Andreas F. Lowenfeld, "U.S. Law Enforcement Abroad: The Constitution and International Law," *American Journal of International Law* 83 (1989): 880; Lowenfeld, "U.S. Law Enforcement Abroad, Continued," *American Journal of International Law* 84 (1990): 4; Lowenfeld, "Kidnaping by Government Order: A Follow-up," *American Journal of International Law* 84 (1990): 712.

8. See Arendt, *Eichmann in Jerusalem*, 240–42 ("No drugs, no ropes, no handcuffs were used . . . as no unnecessary violence had been applied; he was not hurt." Eichmann wrote a statement while tied to a bed in a Buenos Aires suburb, "which was the only aspect of the whole affair that he complained about"). For an account by the former head of the Mossad who organized the operation, see Isser Harel, *The House on Garibaldi Street* (New York: Viking, 1975), 150–54.

9. Lowenfeld, "U.S. Law Enforcement Abroad, Continued," 446.

10. See generally Antonio Cassese, *Terrorism, Politics, and Law: The Achille Lauro Affair* (Princeton: Princeton University Press, 1989).

11. 504 U.S. 655, 112 S. Ct. 2188 (1992).

12. Compare I.L.C. Draft Statute for International Criminal Court (1994) and its

annex of proposed crimes to fall within the jurisdiction of the court, derived from treaties containing prosecute-or-extradite obligations.

13. Within just the last few years, the United Nations has added to the catalog of prosecute-or-extradite obligations through an International Convention for the Suppression of Terrorist Bombings and a convention on the financing of terrorist activities.

14. [1966] 11 Y.B.I.L.C. 169, 247–249. The context was the proposal for what became Article 53 of the Vienna Convention, rendering invalid any treaty in conflict with a peremptory norm (*jus cogens*) defined (circularly) as "a norm accepted and recognized by the international community of States as a whole as a norm from which no derogation is permitted."

15. Restatement (3rd) of the Foreign Relations Law of the United States, § 102, Comment *k* and Reporters' Note 6. See also § 702, Comment *n* ("Not all human rights norms are peremptory norms (*jus cogens*), but those in clauses (a) to (f) of this section are. . . ."). Section 702(a)-(f) identifies (a) genocide, (b) slavery or slave trade, (c) the murder or causing the disappearance of individuals, (d) torture or other cruel, inhuman, or degrading treatment or punishment, (e) prolonged arbitrary detention, and (f) systematic racial discrimination.

16. A current favorite is the application of the death penalty to juveniles. The Inter-American Commission on Human Rights considers that "in the member States of the OAS there is a recognized norm of *jus cogens* which prohibits the State execution of children." Quoted in T. Meron, *Human Rights and Humanitarian Norms as Customary Law* (Oxford: Clarendon Press, 1989), 99.

17. Compare 1996 Draft Articles on State Responsibility and commentary thereto with the latest reports of James Crawford as Special Rapporteur on State Responsibility and the issuance of a final draft in August 2001. A few governments, notably France, have distanced themselves from the very concept of *jus cogens*. See 1999 Report of the I.L.C., 165, para. 311:

> Reference was further made to the strong doubts about *jus cogens* expressed by a number of Governments, which could not be overlooked. It was noted in this regard that the doubts related not so much to the substantive values embodied in *jus cogens* norms, such as those prohibiting genocide, slavery, war crimes, crimes against humanity and others, but rather to the uncertainty surrounding peremptory norms and to the risk of destabilizing treaty relations. It was observed that the International Court of Justice had up to now not used the term *jus cogens* in any judgment or advisory opinion, while endorsing the concept of "intransgressible rules" in its Advisory Opinion on the *Threat or Use of Nuclear Weapons*. Hence caution was advised in deciding whether compliance with peremptory norms should be included (in Chapter 5 of the Draft Articles on State Responsibility).

18. *Cf. Tehran Hostages* case, 1980 I.C.J. 3.

19. See, e.g., Oscar Schachter, *International Law in Theory and Practice* (Dordrecht: Martinus Nijhoff Publishers, 1991), 342–45 (on human rights as *jus cogens* and obligations *erga omnes*).

20. Restatement, § 404.

21. The effort to arrest General Aideed derived formal legitimacy from a resolution of the UN Security Council authorizing "all necessary measures against all those responsible" for the attacks on the Pakistani peacekeepers "including to secure the investigation of their actions and their arrest and detention for prosecution, trial and punishment." S.C. Res. 837 (1993). Legitimacy in the eyes of Somali or U.S. or international public opinion is another matter.

22. The obligation to cooperate is established in the ICTY Statute promulgated by

compulsory resolution of the Security Council. S.C. Res. 827 (1993), para. 4, and Article 29 of ICTY Statute annexed thereto. See also Prosecutor v. Blaskic, Case No. IT-95–14–AR I 08bis (Judgment of Appeals Chamber, October 29, 1997). Compare the dispute over whether fugitives involuntarily transferred can contest the regularity of their rendition, as noted in Gary Bass's essay, this volume.

23. Other projects are doing so, with participants overlapping with those at the Princeton Project on Universal Jurisdiction meeting.

24. Princeton: Princeton University Press, 2000.

25. Arendt, *Eichmann in Jerusalem*, 265.

Chapter 6. Assessing the Pinochet Litigation: Whither Universal Jurisdiction?

I would like to thank Chandra Sriram for invaluable research assistance, as well as helpful substantive suggestions. Also, I am grateful to Reed Brody, Elisabeth Hillbink, Stacy Jonas, and Stephen Macedo for specific suggestions, and especially to Pablo De Greiff for a stimulating set of comments made at the Princeton University Conference on Universal Jurisdiction, November 10–11, 2000.

1. Henry Steiner and Philip Alston, eds., *International Human Rights in Context,* 2d ed. (New York: Oxford University Press, 2000), 1199.

2. Howard Ball, *Prosecuting War Crimes and Genocide: The Twentieth Century Experience* (Lawrence: University Press of Kansas, 1999), 232.

3. Quoted in ibid., 232.

4. Tunku Varadarajan, Wall Street Journal, November 14, 2000, A43.

5. Several other allegedly criminal heads of state had been previously indicted in domestic courts but with far less publicity and with less emphasis on crimes of state that seemed to qualify as crimes against humanity. Legal proceedings in foreign domestic courts against Manuel Noriega (Panama), Ferdinand Marcos (Philippines), and Alfredo Stroessner (Paraguay), are examples.

6. See Daniele Archibugi and David Held, eds., *Cosmopolitan Democracy: An Agenda for a New World Order* (Cambridge: Polity, 1995); also Martha Nussbaum's lead essay in *For Love of Country: Debating the Limits of Patriotism* (Boston: Beacon Press, 1996).

7. The *Milosevic* indictment and prosecution will remain controversial because it is intertwined with both the NATO War of 1999 relating to Kosovo and to the overall status of Serbian nationalist claims.

8. In the absence of a Security Council referral, the prosecutor can only initiate a proceeding if either the state where the crime occurred or if the nationality of the accused is itself a party or gives its consent to ICC jurisdiction. This seemingly crippling constraint was established to placate the sovereignty-oriented insistence of several states, especially the United States and France.

9. Richard J. Goldstone, review of *War Crimes Law Comes of Age* by Theodor Meron, *American Journal of International Law* 94, no. 2 (2000): 417.

10. For assessment, see Falk, *Human Rights Horizons: The Pursuit of Justice in a Globalizing World* (New York: Routledge, 2000), esp. 1–56.

11. The same time, the Chilean picture remained clouded for several years. The Chilean military establishment exerted considerable pressure on the Lagos administration to avoid prosecutions of Pinochet and other officials associated with Pinochet-era policies. There was a complex series of legal developments in Chile after Pinochet's return in March of 2000. These developments included due process objections to the mode of interrogation in Britain as well as continuing objections to Pinochet's prosecution based on his ill health. As indicated above, the supreme

court of Chile has finally resolved the fitness issue in Pinochet favor, ending the prospect of further litigation and any substantive decision. For a journalistic account of these Chilean maneuverings, see Mark Mulligan, "Appeal against Pinochet Charges Upheld," *Financial Times,* December 21, 2000, 3.

12. See "When Tyrants Tremble: The Pinochet Case," *Human Rights Watch* 11, no. 1 (October 1999): 2.

13. For an argument to this effect, see Gregory Weeks, "Waiting for Cincinnatus: The Role of Pinochet in Post-Authoritarian Chile," *Third World Quarterly* 21, no. 5 (2000): 725–38.

14. "When Tyrants Tremble," 3.

15. For an important clarification, see José Zalaquett's introduction to the Report of the Chilean National Commission on Truth and Reconciliation of 1993 in Steiner and Alston, eds., *International Human Rights,* 1221–24.

16. A summary account of Chilean crosscurrents with respect to Pinochet during the presidency of Ricardo Lagos is contained in Clifford Krauss, "In Chile, Democracy Depends on a Delicate Balance," *New York Times,* December 31, 2000, §4, 5. Krauss calls attention to the Chilean use of the word *convivencia,* or living together, as a way of expressing a search for some middle ground between pro- and anti-Pinochet tendencies in Chile.

17. See the strong argument for maximal flexibility in the application of legal standards in Pinochet-type situations put forward in Boot, "When 'Justice' and 'Peace' Don't Mix."

18. This presentation of the Spanish phase of the *Pinochet* proceedings relies heavily on María del Carmen Márquez Carrasco and Joaquín Alcaide Fernández, "In re Pinochet," *American Journal of International Law* 93 (1999): 690.

19. The Criminal Division of the National Court indicated that more than five hundred Spanish subjects had disappeared or were killed in Argentina and another fifty in Chile. Ibid., 691. It is not clear why the events in Argentina should have been included in an inquiry legally concerned only with Chile.

20. For evaluation of the Spanish proceedings, see ibid., 694–96; for parallel consideration of investigation, indictment, and extradition requests in the French Tribunal de grande instance (Paris), see Brigette Stern, "In re Pinochet," *American Journal of International Law* 93 (1999): 696; for Belgian proceedings, which included allegations of crimes against humanity, that took place in the Belgian Tribunal of First Instance of Brussels, see Luc Reydams, "In re Pinochet," *American Journal of International Law* 93 (1999): 700. Only in Spain did the proceedings commence *before* the detention of Pinochet.

21. For summary and references, see footnote 2 of Luc Reydams's report on the Belgian experience in 1998, ibid., 703.

22. It may be that a mutation on the general moral climate of world politics occurred in this interim. Such a ruptured continuity has been noted, with particular reference to reparations and restitutions claims being acted upon around the world. Elazar Barkan considers this pattern, noting that "on or about March 5, 1997, world morality—not to say, human nature—changed. The reason was unexpected: In response to accusations of profiting from Jewish suffering during World War II, Switzerland announced its intention to sell substantial amounts of its gold to create a humanitarian fund of five billion dollars." Barkan, *The Guilt of Nations: Restitution and Negotiating Historical Injustices* (New York: Norton, 2000), xv. I would argue that issues of restitution are cut from the same moral climate as the sort of questions of criminal accountability raised by the claims against Pinochet.

23. The French experience is summarized by Stern, "In re Pinochet," 696–700.

24. Ibid., 699.

25. Interestingly, in 1998 the Belgian Parliament amended the 1993 statute, qualifying

crimes against humanity and genocide as international law crimes under Belgian law. See ibid., 701 n. 7.

26. Ibid., 703.

27. Ibid.

28. Ibid.

29. *Cf.* Ibid., n. 11, for citations and reference to Antonio Cassese's reliance on Scelle's ideas within the contemporary setting.

30. See an overview of the British litigation provided by Christine M. Chinkin, "In re Pinochet," *American Journal of International Law* 93 (1999): 703.

31. R. v. Bow Street Metropolitan Stipendiary Magistrate and Others, ex parte Pinochet Ugarte, [1998] 3 WLR 1456; it should be noted that the House of Lords, which is formally the senior chamber of the British Parliament, contains the highest court in the United Kingdom, consisting of twelve law lords appointed for life and known as life peers. The panel of judges that hears a particular case is designated by the presiding law lord, who during the Pinochet proceedings was Lord Browne-Wilkinson.

32. See Steiner and Alston, eds., *International Human Rights*, 1198–1216.

33. Regina v. Bartle and the Commissioner of Police for the Metropolis and others Ex Parte Pinochet, session 1998–99. All England Law Reports, vol. 1998 pt. 1, p. 97 ff (1999).

34. Regina v. Bartle.

35. Lord Hoffman was a director of AI's charity division, and his wife was a member of the AI administrative staff.

36. R. v. Bow St. Stipendiary Magistrate and Others, ex parte Pinochet Ugarte (No. 2), [1999] 2 WLR 272.

37. See "When Tyrants Tremble," 21, stressing "self-amnesty," Pinochet's senatorial immunity, and the jurisdiction of military tribunals.

38. For details, see Chinkin, "In re Pinochet," 705 n. 11.

39. 38 International Legal Materials 581, 583 (1999).

40. Quoted in "When Tyrants Tremble," 17.

41. 38 International Legal Materials (1999), 588, more fully explained in Lord Hope's opinion, 613–15.

42. Ibid.

43. Ibid., 591.

44. Ibid., 594.

45. Ibid., 595–609.

46. Ibid., 609–27.

47. Attorney-General of Israel v. Eichmann (1962) 36 I.L.R. 5; also noted was the American extradition case of Demjanjuk v. Petrovsky (1985) 603 F. Supp. 1468, aff'd 776 F. 2d 571.

48. 38 International Legal Materials (1999), 648.

49. Ibid., 649.

50. Isolated offense by political leaders would not pass the test. Ibid.

51. Ibid., 650.

52. Ibid., 652.

53. Civil charges against heads of state for official wrongdoing have been previously accepted, and without much international fanfare. For instance, in various proceedings in American courts against the former Filipino leader, Ferdinand Marcos. See Republic of the Philippines v. Marcos, 806 F.2d 344 (2d Cir. 1986). See also on drug charges used to convict Noriega for acts committed while he was head of state. United States v. Noriega, 746 F. Supp 1506 (S.D. Fla. 1990) and 117 F.3d 1212 (11th Cir., 1997).

54. A new important challenge to the ethos of accountability arose as a result of Milosevic's fall from power in the Federal Republic of Yugoslavia and Kostunica's initial pledge of noncooperation with the International Criminal Tribunal for the Former Yugoslavia in The Hague. For an argument that this is an unacceptable retreat from accountability, see Michael Ignatieff, "The Right Trial for Milosevic," *NewYork Times*, October 10, 2000, A27. In the end Belgrade facilitated the arrest of Milosevic and his transfer to The Hague for prosecution, succumbing to pressures relating to much-needed economic assistance that would not be forthcoming unless Milosevic was made available as a criminal defendant to face international charges.

Chapter 7. Comment: Universal Jurisdiction and Transitions to Democracy

1. See Diane F. Orentlicher, "The Future of Universal Jurisdiction in the New Architecture of Transnational Justice," this volume. See also Anne-Marie Slaughter, "Defining the Limits: Universal Jurisdiction and National Courts," this volume. M. Cherif Bassiouni, in his "The History of Universal Jurisdiction and Its Place in International Law," this volume, claims explicitly that "the *Pinochet* case . . . does not stand for the proposition of universal jurisdiction, nor for that matter is the extradition request from Spain for torture based on universal jurisdiction."

2. See Leila Nadya Sadat, "Universal Jurisdiction, National Amnesties, and Truth Commissions: Reconciling the Irreconcilable," this volume.

3. In talking about the three stages of the case, I am following, as Falk does, Christine M. Chinkin's account of the British litigation in her "In re Pinochet," *American Journal of International Law* 93 (1999): 703–11.

4. Only one of the lords was willing to stake the position that *jus cogens* itself provides ground for universal jurisdiction.

5. Ruth Wedgwood, "International Criminal Law and Augusto Pinochet," *Virginia Journal of International Law* 40 (2000): 836.

6. The National Commission of Truth and Reconciliation found that most of the violence took place in the early years of the dictatorship. According to the commission, 1,261 were killed or disappeared in Chile in 1973; 309 in 1974; 119 in 1975; 139 in 1976; and 25 in 1977. See Phillip E. Berryman, trans., *Report of the Chilean National Commission on Truth and Reconciliation* (Notre Dame: University of Notre Dame Press, 1993).

7. Richard A. Falk, "Assessing the Pinochet Litigation: Whither Universal Jurisdiction?," this volume.

8. Orentlicher, "Future of Universal Jurisdiction," this volume.

9. The relative paucity of references to democracy in the human rights literature may be explained by both factual and theoretical reasons. The former have to do with the cold war in the recent past and with multicultural (and specifically, "Asian") concerns in the present. Both have understandably made democracy such a contested concept that human rights activists may, understandably, have felt the need to separate the defense of some fundamental rights from discussions about democracy. The theoretical reasons have to do with ongoing discussions about the relationship between classical individual rights and rights to democratic, political participation. Ultimately, I think that those, like Jürgen Habermas, who argue that individual and political rights are internally related, are fundamentally correct. In a nutshell the argument is that individual rights are secure only in contexts in which people have political rights that allow them to define, for example, the scope of privacy rights and that political rights are secure only in contexts in which there are

meaningful freedoms of thought, speech, religion, etc. See Jürgen Habermas, "On the Internal Relationship between Democracy and Rights," in *The Inclusion of the Other,* Ciaran Cronin and Pablo De Greiff, eds. (Cambidge: MIT Press, 1998), 253–64. Henry Shue, *Basic Rights* (Princeton: Princeton University Press, 1976).

10. For a fuller treatment of this argument, see my "Deliberative Democracy and Group Representation," *Social Theory and Practice* 26, no. 3 (2000): 397–415. The general approach stems from the work of Jürgen Habermas. See especially his *Between Facts and Norms,* trans. William Rehg, (Cambridge: MIT Press, 1993).

11. John Rawls, "Kantian Constructivism and Moral Theory," in *Journal of Philosophy* 67 (1980): 543.

12. Falk, "Assessing the Pinochet Litigation," this volume.

13. Orentlicher, "Future of Universal Jurisdiction," this volume.

14. In addition to all sorts of procedural irregularities, the plebiscite did not offer much of a choice to the electorate. The ballot read: "In the face of international aggression unleashed against the government of the fatherland, I support President Pinochet in his defense of the dignity of Chile, and I reaffirm the legitimate right of the republic to conduct the process of institutionalization in a manner befitting its sovereignty." Pinochet won 75 percent of the vote. For a generally useful account of the Pinochet years, from which I took this translation of the ballot, see Mark Ensalaco, *Chile under Pinochet: Recovering the Truth* (Philadelphia: University of Pennsylvania Press, 2000), 128.

15. For a concise but useful account of justice in Chile after 1990, see Jorge Correa Sutil, "No Victorious Army Has Ever Been Prosecuted: The Unsettled Story of Transitional Justice in Chile," *Transitional Justice,* ed. James McAdams (Notre Dame: University of Notre Dame Press, 1999), 123–54.

16. Interview with *Las Ultimas Noticias* (Santiago), October 14, 1989. A few days later, on October 22, the commander in chief of the air force, Fernando Matthei, in an interview with *El Mercurio,* said: "I hope that everyone has good sense and that they behave in the future in such a way as to permit the country to look forward and build a new country. It is very difficult to walk forward safely when you are looking backward. Probably you will fall on something. I do not think this is a good [approach]." Both passages quoted in Correa, "No Victorious Army," 151.

17. Augusto Pinochet U., *Camino recorrido: memorias de un soldado,* vol. 2 (Santiago: Instituto Geográfico Militar de Chile, 1991), 145ff. Ensalaco, *Chile under Pinochet,* 126ff., provides a good narrative of the context in which the Chacarillas speech, as it came to be known, was given.

18. The term became a critical expression in Chile. See, for example, Manuel Antonio Garreton, "Chile, 1997–1998: Las Revanchas de la Democratización Incompleta," in *FLACSO-Chile Entre la II Cumbre y la detención de Pinochet* (Santiago: FLACSO-CHILE, 1999): 153–66.

19. *Report of the Chilean National Commission on Truth and Reconciliation,* Art. 1.

20. See Francesc Relea, "Las víctimas vivientes de la dictadura," *El País* (Madrid), January 16, 2000.

21. Ibid.

22. Fuerzas Armadas y de Orden, "Respuesta de las Fuerzas Armadas y de Orden al informe de la Comisión Nacional de Verdad y Reconciliacion," reprinted in *Estudios Públicos* (Santiago) 38 (1990).

23. See Prudencio García, "La falsa aceptación de responsabilidad de Pinochet," *El País* (Madrid), November 29, 2000.

24. Paraphrasing Patricio Aylwin Azócar, *La transición chilena: discursos escogidos marzo, 1990–1992.* (Santiago: Editorial Andrés Bello, 1992), 21.

Chapter 8. The *Hissène Habré* Case: The Law and Politics of Universal Jurisdiction

The author wishes to express his gratitude for the background information and substantive comments provided by Reed Brody, Hurst Hannum, Jeffrey Herbst, Pascal Kambale, Stephen Macedo, Peter Rosenblum, Oscar Schachter, and Bacre Wally N'Diaye.

1. The name of the Chadian head of state from 1982 to 1990 is variously spelled Hissein Habre, Hissen Habre, Hissane Habre, Hissene Habre, and Hissène Habré. The latter spelling will be used in this essay, except where another spelling is used in the original of passages quoted.

2. Human Rights Watch, *The Pinochet Precedent: How Victims Can Pursue Human Rights Criminals Abroad,* March 2000 (hereinafter HRW, *Pinochet Precedent*); "An African Pinochet," *New York Times,* February 11, 2000, A30. Tina Rosenberg, "The Power Balance Tilts toward Chile's Victims." *New York Times,* August 23, 2000, 9; Alexander MacLeod, "Pinochet Goes Free but Sets a Precedent;" *Christian Science Monitor,* March 3, 2000, World, 1.

3. The information in this section is summarized from various articles appearing in the online edition of the *Encyclopedia Britannica,* 1999–2000, Britannica.com Inc. See also Jacques Le Cornec, *Histoire politique du Tchad de 1900 à 1962* (Paris: R. Pichon and R. Durand), 1963; Samuel Decalo, *Historical Dictionary of Chad* (Lanham, Md.: Scarecrow), 1997; Virginia M. Thompson and Richard Adloff, *Conflict in Chad* (Berkeley and Los Angeles: Institute of International Studies), 1981; Michael P. Kelley and Robert Buijtenhuijs, *Le Frolinat et les révoltes populaires du Tchad, 1965–1976* (The Hague: Martin, 1978); Robert Buijtenhuijs, *Le Frolinat et les guerres civiles du Tchad, 1977–1984: la révolution introuvable* (Paris: Karthala, 1987).

4. The population is currently around 7.9 million, with a life expectancy at birth estimated at 45.2 years, adult literacy at 42.6 percent, and infant mortality at 118 per 1,000 live births. Gross national income per capita was $200 in 2000, down from $252 in 1975. United Nations Development Programme (UNDP), *Human Development Report 2002* (New York: Oxford University Press, 2002), 165, 177, 185; and World Bank, *2002 World Development Indicators* (Washington, D.C.: World Bank, 2002), 18. These figures are for the year 2000.

5. Also spelled Weddeye.

6. *Les crimes et détournements de l'Ex-Président Habré et de ses complices, Rapport de la Commission d'Enquête du Ministère Tchadien de la Justice,* L'Harmattan1993 (hereinafter *Commission of Inquiry*), 18.

7. Ibid., 19.

8. Decree No. 005/PR January 26, 1983, cited in ibid., 21.

9. Ibid., 25.

10. Interview with Saleh Younouss, former DDS Director, quoted in *Commission of Inquiry,* 22.

11. Ibid., 24.

12. Ibid.

13. Ibid., 27. The report lists the number of postcards and letters from national sections of Amnesty International received by the government, amounting to a total of over fifty thousand. Ibid., 92–93.

14. Ibid., 216–17.

15. "Chadian Rebel Chief Assumes Presidency," *New York Times,* December 5, 1990, A3, col. 1.

16. Decree No. 014/P.CE.CJ90 of December 29, 1990, cited in *Commission of Inquiry,* 8.

17. Ibid.

18. Ibid., 10.

19. Ibid., 11.

20. The initial deadline of six months was extended for another four months. Decree No. 382/PR/MJ/91of July 29, 1991. The commission was still working in February 1992, when it conducted an exhumation. The report was published by the Ministry of Justice in May 1992. Ibid., 10.

21. Ibid., 13.

22. Ibid., 97. Many journalistic accounts refer to 40,000 political killings and 200,000 victims of torture, directly or indirectly citing the commission's report. The plaintiffs' brief appears to misread the commission's report when it states, "Selon un rapport de la Commission d'enquête nationale du ministère tchadien de la Justice (1992), plus de 40 000 personnes auraient été sommairement exécutées ou seraient mortes en détention et 200 000 autres auraient été soumises à la torture." Plainte avec Constitution de Partie Civile (private prosecution submitted by eight Chadian individuals and the Association of Victims of Crimes and Political Repression in Chad— AVCRP) (hereinafter Plainte), 3. The wording used by the commission suggests that a more accurate estimate is 40,000 victims of political killing, disappearances, and torture, and 200,000 left without means of support ("personnes se trouvant, du fait de cette répression, sans soutien moral et matériel"). *Commission of Inquiry,* 97. The meaning the commission gave to the category of victims is clarified in a section titled "Les chiffres parlent d'eux-mêmes," in which the commission mentions 3,780 Chadian and 26 foreigners dead, and estimates that its work could only account for 10 percent of the victims. Ibid., 69. The commission also counted over 54,000 political prisoners (dead or alive). Regarding the category of persons left without support, the commission, in its section titled "Les personnes à charge sont dépourvues de tout soutien," speaks of a social disaster of homeless people without resources, due primarily to the loss of the father of the family leaving behind children, wives, fathers, mothers, uncles, aunts, cousins, nieces, and nephews. Ibid., 85. This is the category it estimates at 200,000. The only exception that could be found of a news article indicating that the figure of 40,000 rather than 200,000 applied to killing and torture was Brigitte Breuillac, "La justice sénégalaise annule l'inculpation d'Hissene Habre pour complicité d'actes de torture," *Le Monde,* July 6, 2000.

23. "D'engager sans délai des poursuites judiciaires contre les auteurs de cet horrible génocide, coupables de crimes contre l'humanité." Commission of Inquiry, 98.

24. Ibid. The motion to dismiss indicates that Habré lives in Ouakam Cité Africa in Dakar and declares as his legal domicile the legal office of Madicke Niang, his lawyer (and advisor to Pres. Abdulaye Wade), at 114 Avenue Peytavain in Dakar. While president, Habré allegedly received millions of dollars in weapons and equipment from the United States and France and brought over $11 million with him to Senegal in 1990. Karl Vick, "African Eyes Opened by Ex-Leader's Indictment," *Washington Post,* February 3, 2000, A13, col. 1. Another source indicates that he took seven billion CFA francs ($11.5 million). Agence France Presse, "Chad Seeks Extradition of Ex-President," January 17, 1998, Lexis-Nexis. See also notes 14 and 15 and accompanying text.

25. Information provided by Pascal Kambale on October 21, 2000. Contradicting the position of the UNHCR, the Senegalese Ministry of Justice informed the UN High Commissioner for Human Rights in November 2000 that Habré is "a person who does after all enjoy the right of asylum in Senegal." "Observations et commentaries sur 'l'affaire Hissene Habre," communicated by the Permanent Mission of Senegal to the Office of the High Commissioner for Human Rights (OHCHR) on

November 9, 2000, translated by the OHCHR as document HR/NONE/2001/1, GE.01–40051 (E), on file with the author.

26. The Declaration on Territorial Asylum of 1967 provides that "states shall not grant asylum to any person with respect to whom there are serious reasons for considering that he has committed a . . . crime against humanity." A similar position was affirmed by the General Assembly in Resolution 3074 (XXVII) of December 3, 1973, setting out principles of international cooperation in the detection, arrest, extradition, and punishment of persons guilty of war crimes and crimes against humanity.

27. Michael Scharf, "The Amnesty Exception to the Jurisdiction of the International Criminal Court," *Cornell International Law Journal* 32 (1999): 139.

28. "A recommendation is thus no more than a resolution without legal value or binding force." Jean-Pierre Cot and Alain Pellet, *La Charte de Nations Unies* (Paris: Economica and Brussels: Bruylant, 1985), 331.

29. On this, Oscar Schachter observes that "several resolutions have asserted rules or principles of general international law when the practice was negligible or inconclusive and these resolutions have been regarded as sufficient evidence of the legal character of the norm asserted." Oscar Schachter, *International Law in Theory and Practice* (Dordrecht: Martinus Nijoff, 1991), 87, 88. The principle of denial of asylum to persons against whom there is evidence of involvement in serious crimes of international law also appears in the Refugee Convention. Convention relating to the Status of Refugees, concluded July 28, 1951, entered into force on April 22, 1954, 189 U.N.T.S. 150, Article 1(F). It is also reaffirmed in the Set of Principles for the Protection and Promotion of Human Rights through Action to Combat Impunity. Sub-Commission on Prevention of Discrimination and Protection of Minorities, Forty-ninth session, Final report prepared by Mr. Joinet pursuant to Sub-Commission decision 1996/119, U.N. Doc. E/CN.4/Sub.2/1997/20/Rev. 1 (October 2, 1997) (hereinafter Joinet Report), Annex II, Principle 26. Although the principles were not formally endorsed by the commission or the General Assembly, the commission did "recall" them and invited "States, international organizations and non-governmental organizations to provide the Secretary-General with their views and comments on the report" and states "to provide information on any legislative, administrative or other steps they have taken to combat impunity for human rights violations in their territory and to provide information on remedies available to the victims of such violations." Commission on Human Rights Resolution 1999/34, U.N. Doc. E/CN.4/RES/1999/34 (April 23, 1999).

30. The comprehensive peace agreements with respect to Cambodia, El Salvador, Angola, Colombia, and others either contain provisions requiring prosecution for past abuses or otherwise do not endorse amnesties. See also Scharf, "The Letter of the Law: The Scope of the International Legal Obligations to Prosecute Human Rights Crimes, *Law and Contemporary Problems* 41 (1996): 57–58, 59.

31. See on this subject, Martha Minow, *Between Vengeance and Forgiveness* (Boston: Beacon, 1998). See also the special issue on international justice of the *Journal of International Affairs* 52, no. 2 (spring 1999).

32. In the recent case of Sierra Leone, while the UN initially sought a compromise that might have allowed amnesty, it excluded international prosecution from the clause on immunity from prosecution and subsequently created a tribunal to try those responsible for atrocities. See U.N. SCOR, 56th Sess., 4500th mtg. at 2–3, U.N. Doc. S/RES/1400 (2002); see also Report of the Secretary General on the Establishment of a Special Court for Sierra Leone, at 3, U.N. Doc. S/2000/915 (2000).

33. For example, Jack Snyder argues that a "golden parachute" is preferable to prosecution because "where elites have felt most threatened, notably in Rwanda,

human rights disasters have only intensified. Punishment is a prudent strategy only when the human rights abusers are too weak to wreak such havoc." Jack Snyder, *From Voting to Violence: Democratization and Nationalist Conflict* (New York: Norton, 2000), 41.

34. HRW, *Pinochet Precedent*, 16–18.

35. Joinet describes four stages in the combat against impunity, the third of which in the early 1990s showed some interest in peace negotiations stressing reconciliation, whereas we are now in the fourth stage in which "the international community realized the important of combating impunity." Joinet Report, Par. 4–5.

36. Agence France Presse, "Chad Seeks Extradition of Ex-President," January 17, 1998.

37. The Restatement summarizes this exception as follows: "A person will not be extradited if the offense with which he is charged or of which he has been convicted is a political offense." Restatement (Third) of the Foreign Relations Law of the United States (hereinafter Restatement) §476 (2).

38. According to the Restatement, practice distinguishes "pure" political acts, such as treason, sedition, espionage, and conspiracy to overthrow a government, prohibited political expression or travel and "relative" political offenses, such as assassination of a political leader, robbery to support a political movement, etc. Ibid., Reporters' Notes 4 and 5.

39. Principle 27 on Restrictions on Extradition states that "[p]ersons who have committed serious crimes under international law may not, in order to avoid extradition, avail themselves of the favourable provisions generally relating to political offenses or of the principle of non-extradition of nationals. Extradition should always be denied, however, especially by abolitionist countries, if the individual concerned risks the death penalty in the requesting country." Joinet Report. The death penalty, mentioned in the same principle, could be a bar to extradition since Senegal is an abolitionist state in practice (last execution having taken place in 1967) and Chad is retentionist. Amnesty International, *The Death Penalty: List of Abolitionist and Retentionist Countries* (January 1, 2000), AI INDEX: ACT 50/05/00, April 2000.

40. On this point the Restatement says that extradition "is generally refused if the requested state has reason to believe that extradition is requested for purposes of persecution, or because the person sought belongs to a particular political movement or organization or if there is substantial ground for believing that the person sought will not receive a fair trial in the requested state." Restatement, §476, Comment h.

41. Model Treaty on Extradition, Adopted by the Eighth Crime Congress, Havana, August 27–September 7, 1990, Article 3.

42. The Torture Convention provides that "1. No State Party shall expel, return ("refouler") or extradite a person to another State where there are substantial grounds for believing that he would be in danger of being subjected to torture. 2. For the purpose of determining whether there are such grounds, the competent authorities shall take into account all relevant considerations including, where applicable, the existence in the State concerned of a consistent pattern of gross, flagrant or mass violations of human rights." Convention against Torture and Other Cruel Inhuman or Degrading Treatment or Punishment, concluded December 18, 1984, entered into force, June 26, 1987, G.A. Res. 39/46 (Annex), U.N. GAOR, 39th Sess., Supp. No. 51, at 197 U.N. Doc. A/RES/39/51 (1985), 23 I.L.M. 1027 (1984), Article 3. The convention was ratified by Senegal on June 16, 1986 (Law 86–26) and entered into force on June 26, 1987. Chad acceded to the convention on June 9, 1995.

43. Committee against Torture, "Implementation of Article 3 of the Convention in the Context of Article 22," CAT General Comment No. 1 of November 21, 1997, U.N. Doc. A/53/44, Annex IX.

44. Amnesty International, for example, reported in 1996 that the human rights record of Pres. Idriss Deby's administration was "marked by the same 'thirst for power' and tendencies toward domination and terror that characterized the regime of former President Hissein Habre," including numerous acts of violence and torture. "Human Rights Group Attacks Chad's Record," *Christian Science Monitor,* October 10, 1996.

45. "An African Pinochet," *New York Times,* February 11, 2000, A30.

46. Amnesty International, "CHAD: Empty Promises: Human Rights Violations Continue with Impunity," AI Index: AFR 20/03/95, consulted online at www.amnesty.org/ailib/aipub/1995/AFR/200395.AFR.txt.

47. HRW, *Pinochet Precedent,* 11.

48. Written statement submitted by the International Federation of Human Rights Leagues, a nongovernmental organization in special consultative status, submitted to the Commission on Human Rights at its 55th session, January 11, 1999, para. 125.

49. UN Integrated Regional Information Network (IRIN), "Torture Victims File Criminal Charges at Home," All Africa, Inc., *Africa News,* November 1, 2000. The news item contains the disclaimer that it "is delivered by the UN's IRIN humanitarian information unit (e-mail: irin@ocha.unon.org; fax: +254 2 622129; Web: http:/www.reliefweb.int/IRIN), but may not necessarily reflect the views of the United Nations."

50. "Le Gouvernement exploitera d'autres procédures de poursuites." Communication du Garde des Sceaux, Ministre de la Justice au Conseil des Ministres sur l'Affaire Hissène Habré, July 6, 2000, quoted in Reed Brody, "The Prosecution of Hissène Habré—An 'African Pinochet,'" *New England Law Review* 35, no. 2: 58.

51. Torture Convention, art. 8, paras. 1 and 2.

52. Ibid., para. 3.

53. Ibid., para. 4.

54. Ibid., art. 5. The measures to which this provision refers are set out in Article 6: "The State Party must examine available information, take the accused present on its territory into custody or otherwise ensure his/her presence, make a preliminary inquiry into the facts, assist the accused in communicating immediately with the nearest appropriate representative of his/her State of nationality, and notify the States where the acts were committed or of the nationality of the accused or the victims and report its findings to those States, indicating whether it intends to exercise jurisdiction."

55. Michael P. Scharf, "The Amnesty Exception to the Jurisdiction of the International Criminal Court," *Cornell International Law Journal* 32 (1999): 514–21, reproduced in part in Paust et al., *International Criminal Law* (Durham, N.C.: Carolina Academic Press, 2000), 137.

56. Ibid., 137–38.

57. Ibid., 138, n. 3. The following texts are pertinent: G.A. Res. 2312: 1967 Declaration on Territorial Asylum (requiring states to refuse asylum to persons who participated in crimes against humanity); G.A. Res. 2712: 1970 Resolution on War Criminals (calling on states to bring to trial persons guilty of crimes against humanity); G.A. Res. 2840: 1971 Resolution on War Criminals (affirming as contrary to the U.N. Charter and "to generally recognized norms of international law" the refusal by a state "to cooperate in the arrest, extradition, trial and punishment" of persons responsible for crimes against humanity); G.A. Res. 3074: 1973 Principles of International Cooperation in the Detection, Arrest, Extradition, and Punishment of Persons Guilty of War Crimes and Crimes against Humanity (affirming states' duty to investigate crimes against humanity and to trace, arrest, try, and, where the accused are found guilty, to punish persons against whom there is evidence of such

crimes); G.A. Res. 44/162, endorsing Economic and Social Council Resolution 1989/65: 1989 Principles on the Effective Prevention and Investigation of Extra-Legal, Arbitrary and Summary Executions (affirming the obligation of states to bring to justice those who participated in such executions or to extradite them); G.A. Res. 47/133: 1992 Declaration on the Protection of All Persons from Enforced Disappearances (requiring states to try persons suspected of having perpetrated involuntary or enforced disappearances, characterized as crimes against humanity). See also International Law Association, Report of the Sixty-first Conference, 1985, Resolution 7.

58. Brody, "Prosecution," 324 and n. 13.

59. Ibid., 324 and note 14.

60. The date is not certain. Brigitte Breuillac, "L'ex-président tchadien Hissene Habre fait l'objet d'une plainte pour torture et crimes contre l'humanité," *Le Monde,* January 27, 2000, indicates January 25 as the date of filing. The Human Rights Watch Press Release "Senegal Opens Investigation against Ex-Chad Dictator," found at www.hrw.org/hrw/press/2000/01/hab127.htm, refers to Tuesday" [January 25], whereas Brody's law review article states that the complaint was filed on January 26. Brody, "Prosecution," 324.

61. HRW, *Pinochet Precedent,* 12.

62. Norimitsu Onishi, "An African Dictator Faces Trial in His Place of Refuge," *New York Times,* March 1, 2000, Foreign Desk, downloaded from New York Times Archives. Further information on Guengueng's case is in Norimitsu Onishi, "He Bore up under Torture, Now He Bears Witness: An African Survivor Fights Back, Fearless," *New York Times,* March 31, 2001, A3. See also Plainte, 5.

63. Breuillac, "L'ex-président."

64. Brigitte Breuillac, "La justice sénégalaise annule l'inculpation d'Hissene Habre pour complicité d'actes de torture," *Le Monde,* July 6, 2000; English translation in "Dakar Court Drops Charges against Habre," *Manchester Guardian Weekly,* July 19, 2000, 27.

65. Brigitte Breuillac, "Hissène Habré est inculpé de complicité d'actes de torture; L'ancien président tchadien est placé en résidence surveillée à Dakar," *Le Monde,* February 5, 2000.

66. Ibid.

67. Information provided by Human Rights Watch in a letter addressed to the Special Rapporteur on the Independence of Judges and Lawyers dated July 6, 2000, on file with the author.

68. The judge ordered him not to leave the two municipal zones where he had houses, to turn over his firearms and passport, and not to make public declarations. Brody, "Prosecution," 326 and n. 20.

69. The three grounds for the motion to dismiss were 1) lack of jurisdiction of Senegalese courts according to domestic law, in particular Article 669 of the Code of Criminal Procedure; 2) lack of a legal basis, since the Criminal Code, specifically Article 295(1), was modified to incorporate a provision on torture by law No. 96(15) of August 28, 1996, published in the Journal Official on October 5, 1996, after the alleged facts of the indictment, and the Senegalese constitution at Article 6, Paragraph 4, prohibits retroactivity of laws, as does the Torture Convention; and 3) expiration of statute of limitations concerning the facts of the case, in accordance with Article 7 of the Code of Criminal Procedure, which had not been modified to provide for the nonapplication of the statute to torture.

70. "Observations de la partie civile sur la requête en annulation déposée par Hissein Habré," text provided by Human Rights Watch (hereinafter cited as "Observations").

71. The letter to Chad asked an investigating judge to interview witnesses, and

the letter to France asked for a deposition of Helène French researcher, who had collected affidavits of torture. These affidavits were provided in September 2000. Brody, "Prosecutions," 327 n. 23.

72. Réquisitoire No. 75 of April 12, 2000.

73. Information provided by Human Rights Watch in a letter addressed to the special rapporteur on the Independence of Judges and Lawyers, dated July 6, 2000, on file with the author.

74. République du Sénégal, Court d'appel de Dakar, Chambre d'Accusation, Arrêt No. 135 of July 4, 2000 (hereinafter cited as "Appellate Judgment"). Manuscript on file with the author.

75. The principal objection of this nature was the fact that the motion was addressed to the president of the Indicting Chamber rather than to the president and all the members thereof.

76. Reference by the indicting judge to Articles 45, 46, 294 bis, and 288 of the Criminal Code and to Articles 77 and 130 of the Code of Criminal Procedure appears to have been the handle which the Court used to consider that the judge was acting in accordance with domestic law, which has no place for universal jurisdiction. The Appellate Judgment refers to "articles 45–46–294 bis 288 du Code Penal," making it ambiguous whether the punctuation is intended to be inclusive or enumerative. For present purposes, the reference to Article 288 is adequate to underscore the Court's focus on the indicting judge using domestic law.

77. Law 96(15) of August 28, 1996, which adds torture to the crimes punishable under Article 295(1) of the Criminal Code.

78. Appellate Judgment. Article 5 of the Torture Convention "contrairement à l'accord de Londres du 08 novembre 1945 et de la charte du Tribunal Militaire ancêtre de la convention des Nations unies du 09 décembre 1948 sur le génocide ne détermine aucune compétence juridictionnelle." The Court also distinguished primary and secondary rules of penal law ("règles de fond" and "règles de forme"), the former establishing the crimes and punishments and the latter the jurisdiction, access to, and functioning of criminal courts and notes that the nature of criminal law requires procedural formalism. Excluding comparison with other branches of law, neither the convention nor domestic law established jurisdiction of Senegalese courts over acts of torture by a foreigner outside of Senegal.

79. Constitution of the Republic of Senegal, art. 79, to be examined below.

80. An AFP dispatch states that "les partisans de Habré avaient toujours défendu l'idée selon laquelle le procès avait été 'monté de toutes pièces' par le régime de l'ancien président Abdou Diouf à des fins politiques, avec la complicité d'ONG à la recherche d'une jurisprudence visant à asseoir le concept de justice pénale internationale." *Agence France Presse,* "Des experts de l'ONU déplorent la levée des poursuites contre Hissene Habre," August 4, 2000, Lexis-Nexis.

81. Norimitsu Onishi, "An African Dictator Faces Trial in His Place of Refuge," *New York Times,* March 1, 2000, A3.

82. HRW, *Pinochet Precedent.*

83. Ibid., 4.

84. Alexander MacLeod, "Pinochet Goes Free but Sets a Precedent: Britain Yesterday Released the Former Chilean Dictator, Others Are on Notice," *Christian Science Monitor,* March 3, 2000, 1

85. Norimitsu Onishi, "An African Dictator Faces Trial in His Place of Refuge," *New York Times,* March 1, 2000, A3.

86. "Tous les êtres humains sont égaux devant la loi," Constitution of Republic of Senegal, art. 7., www.jurisen.sn/institutions/ass/123.htm.

87. For example, International Covenant on Civil and Political Rights, art. 14(1): "All persons shall be equal before the courts and tribunals."

88. Onishi "An African Dictator."

89. Ibid.

90. On April 6, 2000, *La lettre du Continent,* a publication of Indigo Publications, reported under the title "Tidjani Yahya Abakar (Tchad/Senegal)" the story as follows:

En marge de l'instruction en cours contre Hissene Habre, la justice sénégalaise a découvert la "disparition" de l'ancien garde du corps de l'ex-président tcha-dien. Originaire—comme Habre—de Faya Largeau, ou il est né le 11 janvier 1964, Tidjani Yahya Abakar était aux cotes de Habre lors de leur fuite en décem-bre 1990. Avec sa femme et ses cinq enfants, il s'est installe à Dakar, dans une Sicap aux Castors, en continuant à percevoir un salaire de 300 000 F CFA par mois. Que s'est-il passé par la suite entre Habre et son principal garde du corps, bien connu de tous les services du monde pour avoir accompagne le président tchadien lors de ses voyages a l'étranger depuis 1982 . . . ? Le fait est que, n'étant plus payé par Habre, Abakar a poursuivi son patron en justice début 1994 devant un tribunal de travail pour rupture abusive de contrat. Or, la procédure n'a jamais abouti, le plaignant ayant "disparu" peu après: éliminé ou, l'hypothèse la plus optimiste, exfiltre par les autorités sénégalaises? L'enquête suit son cours.

Document retrieved on Nexis-Lexis, Foreign Language, News, visited on September 16, 2000.

91. "Le pouvoir judiciaire est indépendant du pouvoir législatif et du pouvoir exécutif." (The judicial authority is independent of the legislative and executive authority.) Constitution of Senegal, art. 80, www.jurisen.sn/institutions/ass/128.htm.

92. Arrêté No. 004706 du 12 avril 2000 portant nomination de Me Madické Niang en qualité de conseiller chargé des Affaires juridiques à la présidence de la République, cited by Human Rights Watch in a letter of July 6, 2000, from Reed Brody, Advocacy Director, Human Rights Watch to Dato' Param Cumaraswamy, Special Rapporteur on the Independence of Judges and Lawyers, on file with the author. See also Brigitte Breuillac, "La justice sénégalaise annule l'inculpation d'Hissene Habre pour complicité d'actes de torture," *Le Monde,* July 6, 2000.

93. Arrêté No. 006501 of June 1, 2000, appointing him "avocat-conseil de la présidence de la République . . . chargé de fournir des consultations juridiques en toutes matières et, en rapport avec l'Agence judiciaire de l'Etat, de diligenter et de faire diligenter les procédure impliquant la présidence de la République, tant en action qu'en défense." Quoted in ibid., letter of July 6, 2000, note 92. In the copy on file with the author, "Eta" appears for "État" and "dilengenter" for "diligenter"; these errors have been corrected in the above quotation.

94. Ibid., letter of July 6, 2000, note 92.

95. Ibid.

96. Ibid.

97. Brody, "Prosecutions," 329. See also Human Rights Watch, letter of July 6, 2000, n. 92.

98. "Les juges ne sont soumis dans l'exercice de leurs fonctions qu'à l'autorité de la loi." Constitution of Senegal, art. 80 ter.

99. Human Rights Watch, letter of July 6, 2000, n. 136. Human Rights Watch also cites allegations that Habré's agents bribed "editors to run articles" and "put money into the judicial system." Brody, "Prosecutions," 327 n. 26.

100. "Sénégal: Arrêt des poursuites judiciaires contre Hissen," Schweizerische Depeschenagentur AG (SDA), Service de base français, July 4, 2000.

101. Interview with Panafrican News Agency, reported by *Africa News,* July 4, 2000, "Senegal: Judge Dismisses Habre's Case," Lexis-Nexis.

102. "Affaire Habre: Annulation de l'inculpation, la saga judiciaire continue," *Agence France Presse,* July 4, 2000.

103. Brigitte Breuillac, "La justice sénégalaise annule l'inculpation d'Hissene Habre pour complicité d'actes de torture," *Le Monde,* July 6, 2000.

104. Ibid. This translation from "Dakar Court Drops Charges against Habre," *Manchester Guardian Weekly,* July 19, 2000, 27, loses the play on the word *magistral* (judicial and enormous) of the original, which is "C'est une gifle magistrale administrée à la justice sénégalaise."

105. U.N. High Commissioner for Human Rights, Press Release of August 2, 2000, www.unhchr.ch/huricane/huricane.nsf/framepage/pressroom?opendocument.

106. Ibid.

107. Brigitte Breuillac, "La justice sénégalaise annule l'inculpation d'Hissene Habre pour complicité d'actes de torture," *Le Monde,* July 6, 2000.

108. Sud Quotidien, February 21, 2001 (text provided by Human Rights Watch). See also "Sénégal: Un procès de Hissène Habré paraît de nouveau possible," *Le Monde,* February 22, 2001; Hamadou Tidiane Sy, "Victims of Chad Regime Applaud Moves on Habre Torture Charges," *Agence France Presse,* February 21, 2001, Lexis-Nexis.

109. ". . . que les juges relèvent qu'aucune modification de l'article 669 du code de procédure pénale n'est intervenue et en déduisent que les juridiction sénégalaises sont incompétentes pour connaître des actes de torture commis par un étranger en dehors du territoire quelle que soit la nationalité des victimes." Cour de Cassation, Première chambre statuant en matière pénale, arrêt No. 14 du 20–3–2001 Pénal, provided online by Human Rights Watch at www.hrw.org/french/themes/habre-cour_de_cass.html.

110. ". . . l'article 79 de la Constitution ne saurait recevoir application dès lors que l'exécution de la Convention nécessite que soient prise par le Sénégal des mesures législatives préalables." Ibid.

111.

. . . la violation du principe de compétence universelle en ce que la chambre d'accusation a déclaré les juridictions sénégalaises incompétentes au motif que la compétence universelle ne peut être admise sans modification de l'article 669 du code de procédure pénale alors que cet article ne peut faire échec à l'application d'une convention internationale édictant une compétence universelle ni aux dispositions de la Convention de Vienne, applicable au Sénégal, notamment en ses articles 27 et 53 qui ne permettent pas à un État signataire d'une convention internationale de s'abriter derrière les lacunes et les insuffisances de son droit interne pour se soustraire à ses engagements internationaux.

Ibid.

112. "[Q]u'aucun texte de procédure ne reconnaît une compétence universelle aux juridictions sénégalaises en vue de poursuivre et de juger, s'ils sont trouvés sur le territoires de la République, les présumés auteurs ou complices de faits qui entrent dans les prévisions de la loi du 28 août 1996 portant adaptation de la législation sénégalaise aux dispositions de l'article 4 de la Convention lorsque ces faits one été commis hors du Sénégal par des étrangers." Ibid. The reference to Article 53 of the Vienna Convention (jus cogens) is not addressed by the Court.

113. "[L]a présence au Sénégal d'Hissène Habré ne saurait à elle seule justifier les poursuites intentées contre lui." Ibid.

114. Human Rights Watch, www.hrw.org/french/press/2001/habrecatfr0423.htm. On other applications of the Belgian law, see notes 126 and 210 below.

115. The text of the communication appears at www.hrw.org/french/themes/habre-cat.html.

116. Letter from Hamid Gaham to Reed Brody of April 27, 2001, available at www.hrw.org/french/themes/images/guengueng_small.jpg.

117. See ibid., 6.

118. *Commission of Inquiry,* 17–34, 157–62.

119. Plainte, 12–14.

120. Ibid., 13.

121. See Peter Evan Bass, "Ex-Head of State Immunity: A Proposed Statutory Tool of Foreign Policy," *Yale Law Journal* 97: 299.

122. Opinions of the lords of appeal for judgment in the Cause Regina v. Bartle and the commissioner of police for the metropolis and others (appellants) ex parte Pinochet (respondent) (on appeal from a divisional court of the queen's Bench Division); Regina v. Evans and another and the commissioner of police for the metropolis and others (appellants) ex parte Pinochet (respondent) (on appeal from a divisional court of the queen's Bench Division) on November 25, 1998, 37 I.L.M. 1302 (1998) 1338.

123. Judgment, Regina v. Bartle and the Commissioner of Police for the Metropolis and Others ex parte Pinochet; Regina v. Evans and Another and the Commissioner of Police for the Metropolis and Others ex parte Pinochet (on appeal from a Divisional Court of the queen's Bench Division) on March 24, 1999, 38 I.L.M. 581, 594–95.

124. "Chandra Lekha Sriram and Jordan J. Paust, "Universal Jurisdiction and the Cases: Current, Impending, and Potential," unpublished manuscript of September 1, 2000, 5.

125. International Court of Justice, year 2002, Case Concerning the Arrest Warrant of 11 April 2000 (Democratic Republic of the Congo v. Belgium), General List, No. 121, February 14, 2002.

126. Face à la colère declenchée en Israël par l'affaire Sharon, la Belgique réagit avec sérénité," *Le Temps,* February 14, 2003; Marlise Simons, "Sharon Faces Belgian Trial After Term Ends," *New York Times,* February 13, 2003, A12.

127. Kadić v. Karadžić, 70 F.3d 232, 240 (2d Cir. 1995), cert. denied 518 U.S. 1005, 116 S.Ct. 2524, 135 L. Ed.2d 1048 (1996), cited in Restatement (Third), Suppl. § 404, 221–22. See also note 210 below.

128. "Immunity Provided Peruvian Charged with Torture," *American Journal of International Law* 94: 535–36.

129. Interview with Bacre Wally N'Diaye, former attorney at the Dakar bar, October 20, 2000.

130. "La ratification par une loi no. 9626 du 16.06.1996 de la convention contre la torture et autres traitements dégradants ne saurait suffire, pour asseoir la compétence des juridictions sénégalaises." Requête en Annulation dated February 18, 2000, on file with the author. The highly misleading confusion between the adoption of implementing legislation and ratification is repeated in "Observations et commentaries sur 'l'affaire Hissene Habre,'" communicated by the Permanent Mission of Senegal to the Office of the High Commissioner for Human Rights (OHCHR) on November 9, 2000, translated by the OHCHR as document HR/NONE/2001/1, GE.01–40051 (E), on file with the author. That texts says: "This Convention was ratified by Senegal by Act No. 96–26 of 16 June 1996. However, the offences in question date from the period from June 1982 to December 1990 and were already subject to prescription because the Convention did not affect the periods of prescription in force in the States Parties."

131. Press statement by Madické Niang, counsel for Habré, *Agence France Presse,* March 3, 2000. "Senegal must drop charges against Habre: lawyer," Lexis-Nexis.

132. The Senegalese Constitution refers to the entry into force of treaties on their publication in the Journal Officiel, which occurred for the Torture Convention on August 8, 1986, although it entered into force on the thirtieth day after the date of

the deposit of the twentieth instrument of ratification or accession, pursuant to Article 27, on June 26, 1987.

133. Status of The Convention against Torture and Other Cruel, Inhuman, or Degrading Treatment or Punishment, Report of the Secretary General, U.N. Doc., E/CN.4/2000/59, December 11, 1999, Annex: List of States that have signed, ratified, or acceded to the Convention against Torture and Other Cruel, Inhuman, or Degrading Treatment or Punishment as at November 1, 1999.

134. Torture Convention, preamble.

135. Ruth Wedgewood anticipated the problem of ratification by both Chad and Senegal after the alleged criminal acts. She wrote: "The Habre trial may turn on the very issues of customary law and jus cogens in relation to universal jurisdiction and official acts immunity that were sidestepped in Pinochet. For Chad did not ratify the Torture Convention until five years after Habre left power in 1990. It will be hard to rest the prosecution upon Chad's contemporaneous consent by treaty." Wedgewood, "40th Anniversary Perspective: International Criminal Law and Augusto Pinochet," *Virginia Journal of International Law* 40: 829, 846. For reasons explained in the text, unlike Prof. Wedgewood, the present author sees no need for Chad's contemporaneous consent by treaty.

136. Human Rights Watch said two months before the judgment dismissing the charges that the theory behind Habré's argument on this point, which the Court eventually followed, "would turn Senegal's ratification of this key treaty into an empty gesture with no real effect." Human Rights Watch, "Senegal Must Try Ex-Chad Dictator," May 10, 2000, www.hrw.org/rw/press/2000/05/habre0509.htm.

137. Plainte, 5–11.

138. Martha Minow has written on this subject, "Even when marred by problems of retroactive application of norms, political influence, and selective prosecution, however, trials can air issues, create an aura of fairness, establish a public record, and produce some sense of accountability. Then claims for the power of the rule of law can grow, even in the face of demonstrable failures in is implementation." Minow, *Between Vengeance and Forgiveness*, 50.

139. Human Rights Watch, "Case against Ex-Chad Dictator Debated: Decision Due on June 15," listserv from hrw-news posted May 16, 2000.

140. "La prescription est suspendue par tout obstacle de droit ou de fait empêchant l'exercice de l'action publique." Code of Criminal Procedure, art. 7(2).

141. This issue arose in the context of efforts to prosecute those responsible for murder and other acts committed before the fall of Communist Party rule in Eastern Europe. In Hungary, for example, parliament enacted a law declaring that the statute of limitations for such crimes did not begin until May 2, 1990, but the president of Hungary refused to sign it, and the Constitutional Court declared it unconstitutional on the grounds that law—including the statute of limitations—should be viewed as continuous and the political motivation for failure to prosecute in the past should not lead to a dangerous precedent applying a different political motivation to disregard for the law in the form of the statute of limitations. Carlos Nino, *Radical Evil on Trial* (New Haven, Conn.: Yale University Press, 1995), 24, cited in Minow, *Between Vengeance and Forgiveness*, 38.

142. Interview with Bacre Waly N'Diaya, October 20, 2000.

143. See note 13 above and accompanying text.

144. Convention on the Nonapplicability of Statutory Limitations to War Crimes and Crimes against Humanity, adopted and opened for signature, ratification, and accession by General Assembly resolution 2391 (XXIII) of November 26, 1968, entry into force November 11, 1970, in accordance with Article 8, Official Records of the General Assembly, Twenty-third Session, Supplement No. 18 (A-7218), 40. Senegal has not ratified this. www.unhchr.ch/html/menu3/b/treaty6.htm.

145. Restatement (Third), § 404. The bases of jurisdiction as set out in § 402 are the territoriality principle, the effects principle, the nationality principle, the protective principle, and the passive personality principle. The Restatement further indicates that "[a] state may enforce its criminal law within its own territory through the use of police, investigative agencies, public prosecutors, courts, and custodial facilities, provided (a) the law being enforced is within the state's jurisdiction to prescribe; (b) when enforcement is through the courts, the state has jurisdiction to adjudicate with respect to the person who is the target of enforcement; and (c) the procedures of investigation, arrest, adjudication, and punishment are consistent with the state's obligations under the law of international human rights." Restatement (Third), § 432. The nonexhaustive enumeration of "serious crimes under international law" of the Princeton Principles includes piracy, slavery, war crimes, crimes against peace, crimes against humanity, genocide, and torture.

146. Restatement (Third) § 702, Reporters Note 12.

147. *Commission of Inquiry*, 18.

148. Plainte, 16. The definition in Article 1 of the Torture Convention reads:

'[T]orture' means any act by which severe pain or suffering, whether physical or mental, is intentionally inflicted on a person for such purposes as obtaining from him or a third person information or a confession, punishing him for an act he or a third person has committed or is suspected of having committed, or intimidating or coercing him or a third person, or for any reason based on discrimination of any kind, when such pain or suffering is inflicted by or at the instigation of or with the consent or acquiescence of a public official or other person acting in an official capacity. It does not include pain or suffering arising only from, inherent in or incidental to lawful sanctions.'

149. *Commission of Inquiry*, 136–55.

150. The seven methods of torture are described in *Commission of Inquiry*, 41–42; the conditions in detention centers, which appear to amount to torture in themselves, are discussed on 46–51, and the drawings of the methods of torture appear on 111–23.

151. The Rome Statute defines these crimes as:

any of the following acts when committed as part of a widespread or systematic attack directed against any civilian population, with knowledge of the attack: (a) Murder; (b) Extermination; (c) Enslavement; (d) Deportation or forcible transfer of population; (e) Imprisonment or other severe deprivation of physical liberty in violation of fundamental rules of international law; (f) Torture; (g) Rape, sexual slavery, enforced prostitution, forced pregnancy, enforced sterilization, or any other form of sexual violence of comparable gravity; (h) Persecution against any identifiable group or collectivity on political, racial, national, ethnic, cultural, religious, gender as defined in paragraph 3, or other grounds that are universally recognized as impermissible under international law, in connection with any act referred to in this paragraph or any crime within the jurisdiction of the Court; (i) Enforced disappearance of persons; (j) The crime of apartheid; (k) Other inhuman acts of a similar character intentionally causing great suffering, or serious injury to body or to mental or physical health.

Rome Statute of the International Criminal Court of July 17, 1998 [as corrected by the procés-verbaux of November 10, 1998, and July 12, 1999], U.N. Doc. A/CONF.183/9, art. 7(1).

152. Ibid., art. 7(2).

153. On the elements of crimes against humanity and the intensity and scope of

acts that are required the meet the definition, see Cherif Bassiouni, *Crimes against Humanity in International Criminal Law,* 2d rev. ed. (The Hague: Kluwer Law International, 1999), 369–447.

154. Ibid.

155. "War crimes and crimes against humanity, wherever they are committed, shall be subject to investigation and the persons against whom there is evidence that they have committed such crimes shall be subject to tracing, arrest, trial and, if found guilty, to punishment." G.A. Res. 3074 (XXVIII), operative para. 1. The reference to the right of every state to "try its own nationals" in the next principle makes it clear that the first principle quoted above refers to persons of any nationality.

156. Ibid., operative para. 9. Emphasis added.

157. See definition, note 151 above, particularly Paragraph k.

158. See definition, note 148 above.

159. G.A. Res. 47/133 of December 18, 1992, by which the assembly adopted the Declaration on the Protection of All Persons from Enforced Disappearance.

160. The commission specifically reminded governments

(a) That all acts of enforced or involuntary disappearance are crimes punishable by appropriate penalties which should take due account of their extreme seriousness under penal law; (b) Of the need to ensure that their competent authorities proceed immediately to conduct impartial inquiries in all circumstances where there is reason to believe that an enforced disappearance has occurred in territory under their jurisdiction; (c) That, if such belief is borne out, all the perpetrators of enforced or involuntary disappearances must be prosecuted; (d) That impunity is simultaneously one of the underlying causes of enforced disappearances and one of the major obstacles to the elucidation of cases thereof.

Commission on Human Rights Resolution 1999/38 of April 26, 1999, UN Doc. E/CN.4/RES/1999/38.

161. E/CN.4/Sub.2/1998/19, Annex. This draft was considered by an open-ended working group established by the Commission on Human Rights in 2001 to draft "a legally binding normative instrument" on the subject. See Commission on Human Rights Resolution 2001/46 of April 23, 2001, and "Report of the Intersessional Open-Ended Working Group to Elaborate a Draft Legally Binding Instrument for the Protection of All Persons from Enforced Disappearance," UN Doc. E/CN.4/2003/71, February 12, 2003.

162. "[F]orced disappearance is considered to be the deprivation of a person's liberty, in whatever form or for whatever reason, brought about by agents of the State or by persons or groups of persons acting with the authorization, support or acquiescence of the State, followed by an absence of information, or refusal to acknowledge the deprivation of liberty or information, or concealment of the fate or whereabouts of the disappeared person." Draft International Convention on the Protection of All Persons from Forced Disappearance E/CN.4/Sub.2/1998/19, Annex, (August 19, 1998), art. 1. See Commission on Human Rights Resolution 2001/46 of April 23, 2001.

163. Article 6(1) reads:

1. Forced disappearance and the other acts referred to in article 2 of this Convention shall be considered as offences in every State Party. Consequently, each State Party shall take the necessary measures to establish jurisdiction in the following instances: (a) When the offence of forced disappearance was committed within any territory under its jurisdiction; (b) When the alleged perpetrator or the other alleged participants in the offence of forced disappearance or the

other acts referred to in article 2 of this Convention are in the territory of the State Party, irrespective of the nationality of the alleged perpetrator or the other alleged participants, or of the nationality of the disappeared person, or of the place or territory where the offence took place unless the State extradites them or transfers them to an international criminal tribunal.

164. A/CONF.183/9, art. 7 (2)(1).

165. Plainte, Annexes 6 and 17.

166. In a section titled "Plus qu'un massacre, Habré a commis un génocide contre le peuple tchadien," the *Commission of Inquiry* stated that over eight years of bloody dictatorship, "Hissein Habré a commis un véritable génocide contre le peuple tchadien. Jamais dans l'histoire du Tchad il n'y a eu autant de morts. Jamais il n'y a eu autant de victimes innocentes." *Commission of Inquiry,* 68. As to the ethnic nature of the mass killing, the reports says, "Aucun groupe ethnique, aucune tribu, aucune famille n'a été épargnée, exceptés les Goranes et leurs alliés." Ibid. On the relation between genocide and impoverishment, the report says, "Le génocide commis par Hissein Habré sur le peuple tchadien a privé un grand nombre de personnes de leur soutient moral et matériel." Ibid., 85.

167. Convention on the Prevention and Punishment of the Crime of Genocide [hereinafter Genocide Convention], adopted by the General Assembly on December 9, 1948. G.A. Res. 260 A(3), art. 2 (c).

168. *Commission of Inquiry,* 55–56.

169. Plainte, 15.

170. Ibid., 16.

171. The text explicitly includes attempted torture and complicity in torture along with responsibility for acts of torture, an important point since Habré is accused primarily of complicity.

172. Article 9 reads: "1. States Parties shall afford one another the greatest measure of assistance in connection with criminal proceedings brought in respect of any of the offences referred to in article 4, including the supply of all evidence at their disposal necessary for the proceedings. 2. States Parties shall carry out their obligations under paragraph I of this article in conformity with any treaties on mutual judicial assistance that may exist between them. . . ."

173. See note 77 above and accompanying text.

174. Appellate Judgment.

175. Observations.

176. "La justice pénale . . . a toujours manifesté son autonomie par rapport aux autres normes juridiques, . . . cette particularité est due au caractère sanctionnateur du droit pénal qui tend à la protection des intérêts de la société comme ceux des individus en cause et exige un certain formalisme de procédure." Appellate Judgment.

177. "[A]utomatique et indépendant de tout autre acte juridique." Nguyen Quoc Dinh, Patrick Daillier, Alain Pellet, *Droit International Public,* 4th ed., 1992, 225.

178. Like Article 55 of the 1958 French Constitution, Article 79 of the Constitution of the Republic of Senegal reads: "Les traités ou accords régulièrement ratifiés ou approuvés ont, dès leur publication, une autorité supérieure à celle des lois, sous réserve, pour chaque accord ou traité, de son application par l'autre partie." (Duly ratified or approved treaties or agreements prevail over statutes subject to reciprocity by the other party to any treaty or agreement.) Article 26 of the French Constitution of 1946 made it clear that implementing legislation was not required: "[L]es traités régulièrement ratifiés et publiés une force de loi sans qu'il soit besoin d'autres dispositions législatives que celle qui auraient été nécessaire pour assurer sa ratification." (Treaties duly ratified and published have the force of law without

need for legislative measures other than those that might be necessary to ensure the ratification thereof.) Notwithstanding this monist system, there have been French cases in which international treaties, including human rights treaties, have been deemed non–self-executing. The Appellate Court of Paris found that Articles 6 and 13 of the European Convention on Human Rights were non–self-executing. Arrêt du 29 février 1980, GP 1980, II, 697, N. Junoszasdro-Jewski, cited in Quoc Dinh, Daillier and Pellet, *Droit International,* 226. However, most other parties to the European Convention and the European Court consider all the provisions of the convention self-executing. Quoc Dinh et al., *Droit International,* 226.

179. One of the lawyers supporting jurisdiction in this case, Me Boukounta Diallo, correctly pointed out that "aucun Etat ne peut invoquer les lacunes de son droit interne pour échapper à ses engagements conventionnels, lesquels ont une force supérieure a la loi interne selon la Constitution sénégalaise. " See Brigitte Breuillac, "La justice sénégalaise annule l'inculpation d'Hissene Habre pour complicité d'actes de torture," *Le Monde,* July 6, 2000. Translation in the *Manchester Guardian Weekly,* July 19, 2000, 27: "No state can argue that short-comings in its own legal system can justify a failure to respect its commitments under the convention, which according to the Senegalese constitution carry greater weight than the country's own legal provisions."

180. "Seuls les tribunaux nationaux peuvent contribuer à une solution plus efficace, soit en accueillant les recours fondés sur l'inobservation de cette obligation par le pouvoir réglementaire, soit en faisant prévaloir une convention internationale sur le droit interne malgré l'insuffisance des mesures d'application: leur attitude sera en partie commandée par leur conception de l'application directe du traité considéré." Quoc Dinh et al., *Droit International,* 227.

181. Ibid.

182. Ibid., citing L. Dubouis, "Le juge administratif français et les règles de droit international," Annuaire français de droit international, 1971, 19–21. Specifically, they note that "le juge français se montre souvent réticent pour reconnaître aux particuliers le droit de se prévaloir en justice des droits qui semblent leur conférer les traité." Ibid., 228.

183. C. Hennau and J. Verhaegen, *Droit pénal général,* 2d ed. (Brussels: Bruylant, 1995), 48 ff. Emphasis by Professor David. Cited in Observations, Annex II. Author's translation.

184. The relevant provision of Article 8(2) reads: "If a State Party which makes extradition conditional on the existence of a treaty receives a request for extradition from another State Party with which it has no extradition treaty, it may consider this Convention as the legal basis for extradition in respect of such offences."

185. International Council on Human Rights Policy, *Hard Cases: Bringing Human Rights Violators to Justice Abroad, A Guide to Universal Jurisdiction,* 1999, 38.

186. Question of the impunity of perpetrators of human rights violations (civil and political), revised final report prepared by Mr. Joinet pursuant to subcommission decision 1996/119 E/CN.4/Sub.2/1997/20/Rev.1, October 2, 1997.

187. See notes 91–106 above and accompanying text.

188. See "Observations et commentaries sur 'l'affaire Hissene Habre,'" Plainte, 137. This analysis refers to the French Constitution of 1946, not the current one. The reference to public international law in that constitution is presumably to Paragraph 14 of the preamble: "La République française, fidèle à ses traditions, se conforme aux règles du droit public international. Elle n'entreprendra aucune guerre dans des vues de conquête et n'emploiera jamais ses forces contre la liberté d'aucun people." Of equal value, however, would be the preamble to Senegal's Constitution, according to which, "Le peuple du Sénégal proclame solennellement son indépendance et son attachement aux droits fondamentaux tels qu'ils sont

définis dans la Déclaration des Droits de l'Homme et du Citoyen de 1789 et dans la Déclaration universelle du 10 décembre 1948."

189. Under French criminal law, "Les auteurs ou complices d'infractions commises hors du territoire de la République peuvent être poursuivis et jugés par les juridictions françaises . . . lorsqu'une convention internationale donne compétence aux juridictions françaises pour connaître de l'infraction." (Perpetrators of or accomplices in offenses committed outside the territory of the Republic may be prosecuted and judged by French courts when an international convention establishes the competence of French courts over the offense.) Article 689 of the Code of Criminal Procedure. http://admi.net/code/cprocpel-689.html. The subarticles of this article of the code specify the conventions in questions, beginning with the Torture Convention. Ibid., art. 689(1, 2). The failure of the Senegalese parliament to adopt a similar provision was part of the reasoning of the appellate and supreme courts of Senegal in rejecting jurisdiction.

190. HRW, *Pinochet Precedent,* 16–18.

191. E/CN.4/RES/1999/32, torture and other cruel, inhuman, or degrading treatment or punishment, April 23, 1999.

192. E/CN.4/RES/2000/68, impunity, April 27, 2000.

193. See note 186 above and accompanying text.

194. Principle 21, on "[m]easures to strengthen the effectiveness of treaty clauses concerning universal jurisdiction," reads:

(a) An appropriate clause concerning universal jurisdiction should be included in all relevant international human rights instruments. (b) In ratifying such instruments, States shall undertake, by effect of that clause, to seek out and prosecute persons against whom there are specific, consistent accusations of violations of human rights principles laid down in those instruments, with a view to bringing them to trial or extraditing them. They are consequently bound to take legislative or other measures under domestic law to ensure the implementation of the clause on universal jurisdiction.

Joinet Report, note 186 above.

195. Principle 22, concerning "[m]easures for determining extraterritorial jurisdiction in domestic law" stipulates that "[i]n the absence of a ratification making it possible to apply a universal jurisdiction clause to the country where a violation was committed, States may take practical measures in their domestic legislation to establish extraterritorial jurisdiction over serious crimes under international law committed outside their territory, which by their nature fall within the scope not only of domestic criminal law but also of an international punitive system which disregards the concept of frontiers." Joinet Report, note 186 above.

196. Senegal signed the ICC Statute on July 18, 1998, and ratified it on February 2, 1999. Ruth Wedgewood placed the initial indictment in the context of Senegal's attitude regarding the expansion of international criminal liability of state perpetrators of massive violations of human rights. "The indictment follows ten years' asylum for Habre in Dakar - an arrest perhaps occasioned by Senegal's standing as the first country to ratify the International Criminal Court statute." Wedgewood, "Pinochet."

197. HRW, *Pinochet Precedent,* 12.

198. Human Rights Watch, "Senegal President Urged to Back Rights Prosecution," September 5, 2000, www.hrw.org/rw/press/2000/09/wade905.htm.

199. Ibid.

200. Adama Dieng left his positing at the ICJ and is now at the ICTR; Pierre Sané left AI and is now at UNESCO; and Ibrahima Fall left the Office of the High

Commissioner of Human Rights to become assistant secretary-general in the Department of Political Affairs of the UN. The tradition of Senegal furnishing outstanding jurists who have greatly influenced the evolution of international human rights law and practice is perhaps best exemplified by Kéba M'Baye, former first president of the supreme court of Senegal, vice president of the International Court of Justice, president of the International Commission of Jurists, president of the UN Commission on Human Rights, president of the International Institute of Human Rights, and principal author and promoter of the African Charter of Human and Peoples Rights.

201. "Quand la politique entre dans le prétoire, le droit en sort."

202. Application Instituting Proceedings filed in the Registry of the Court on October 17, 2000. Arrest Warrant of April 11, 2000 (Democratic Republic of the Congo v. Belgium). See also note 125 above

203. "Un juge au-dessus de tout soupçon," *Jeune Afrique l'Intelligent*, February 15–21, 2000, cited in Brody, "Prosecutions," 329 n. 34.

204. See the essay by Falk, present volume.

205. See the cases against Radovan Karadžić, President of Republika Srpska, and Li Peng, former Chinese premier, both brought under the Torture Victims Protection Act and the Alien Tort Claims Act. The former resulted in two default judgments and awards of $745 million and $4.2 billion. "Award of Damages against Bosnian Serb Leader Radovan Karadžić," *American Journal of International Law* 95 (2001): 143–44. The latter was filed on August 31, 2001, by four Chinese dissidents and victims of the 1989 crackdown at Tiananmen Square and led to process being served by order of Judge Casey of the U.S. District Court for the Southern District of New York and trial proceedings under Judge William H. Pauley III. "Global Justice: The Li Peng Lawsuit and Universal Jurisdiction over Violation of Rights," *China Rights Forum* (winter 2000–01): 22–29. On these and other cases, see William Glaberson, "U.S. Courts Become Arbiters of Global Rights and Wrongs," *New York Times,* June 21, 2001, A 1.

206. Michael Kirby, "Universal Jurisdiction and Judicial Reluctance: A New 'Fourteen Points,'" this volume.

207. Among the issues U.S. courts have held to be political questions and not justiciable is the determination by the executive of whether to grant or deny sovereign immunity. See Restatement, §1, Reporter's Note 4.

208. Kirby, "Judicial Reluctance."

209. See Pierre Chambon, *Le Juge d'instruction: Théorie et practique de la procedure,* 4th ed. (Paris: Dalloz, 1997), 75–96.

210. Reed Brody, "Justice Comes to Chad," March 20, 2002, on the Human Rights Watch website at www.hrw.org/editorials/2002/justicetochad.htm; "Belgian Senate Approves Changes to 'Universal Competence' Law," *Agence France Presse,* January 31, 2003; Simons, "Sharon Faces Belgian Trial After Term Ends"; Daphne Eviatos, "Debating Belgium's War-Crime Jurisdiction," *New York Times,* January 25, 2003, B7.

211. 28 U.S.C. § 1350 (1994). The significance of this legislation for universal jurisdiction is discussed in Hari M. Osofsky, "Domesticating International Criminal Law: Bringing Human Rights Violators to Justice," *Yale Law Journal* 107 (1997): 191–92, 198–201.

212. Public Law No. 103–236, § 506(a), 108 Stat. 382, 463–64 (1994), codified at 18 U.S.C. 2340 (West Suppl 1997).

213. "The Princeton Principles on Universal Jurisdiction," Principle 3(30), this volume.

214. HRW, *Pinochet Precedent,* 17. See also Marwan Macon-Markar, "Rights: Victims of Dictatorship Begin Quest for Justice," *Intern-Press Service,* May 25, 2000, Lexis-Nexis.

215. "Peru's Ambassador to Japan May Seek to Have Former President Fujimori's

Citizenship Revoked," Associated Press, July 11, 2001, Lexis-Lexis. Associated Press also reported that Japan and Peru have no extradition treaty and that Japanese authorities "have no intention of sending him back to Peru, where he faces a charge of dereliction of duty." Further, "Japan will not deport Fujimori because he is a Japanese citizen," according to a foreign ministry official, who also said that Japanese law does not permit deportation of its nationals. Scott Stoddard, "Despite Pressure in Peru, Japan Has No Intention of Extraditing Fujimori," Associated Press, June 28, 2001, Lexis-Nexis. See also Marlise Simons, "Interpol Issues a Wanted Notice for Peru's Former President," *New York Times*, March 27, 2003, A8; Yuri Kageyama, "Peru's Ex-Leader Says He Will Return," *Boston Globe*, March 29, 2003, A13.

216. *Commission of Inquiry,* 89.

217. Ibid., 54–55.

218. Ibid., 43.

219. See note 49 above.

220. Ibid. Human Rights Watch said, "This is the first time that members of Habre's government have been brought to court in Chad."

221. Hari Osofsky mentions the hypothetical of a former head of a Chinese prison visiting the United States to attend his daughter's wedding only to find himself subject to civil suit under the Alien Tort Claims Act and the Torture Victim Protection Act and indictment under 28 U.S.C. 1350, notwithstanding U.S. foreign policy interest in good relations with China. See Osofsky, "Domesticating International Criminal Law," 191 n. 201.

222. Oscar Schachter, *International Law in Theory and Practice* (Dordrecht: Nijhoff, 1991), 270.

223. Hervé Gattegno, "DC10 d'UTA: le juge Bruguère est autorisé a poursuivre M. Kadhafi; La cour d'appel estime que l'immunité des chefs d'Etat ne s'applique pas." *Le Monde*, October 21, 2000.

224. Accusation of war crimes and other violations of international law were made by Yugoslavia against Canada, France, Germany, Italy, the Netherlands, Portugal, Spain, the United Kingdom, and the United States of America, in its application to the International Court of Justice of February 21, 2001 (General List No. 113, Case Concerning Legality of Use of Force).

225. Bass, "Ex-Head of State Immunity," 306.

226. Ibid., 316.

227. Report submitted by El Hadji Guissé pursuant to subcommission resolution 1996/24 of August 29, 1996, on the question of impunity of perpetrators of violations of economic, social, and cultural rights, U.N. Doc.E/CN.4/Sub.2/1997/8.

228. Commission on Human Rights, impunity of perpetrators of violations of economic, social, and cultural rights, E/CN/4/RES/1999/58 of April 28, 1999, adopted by a vote of 21 to 9 with 22 abstentions.

229. Bass, "Ex-Head of State Immunity," 316.

Chapter 9. Defining the Limits: Universal Jurisdiction and National Courts

I am greatly indebted to Annecoos Wiersema, S.J.D. candidate, Harvard Law School, both for research assistance and for many valuable suggestions and contributions.

1. Jack Goldsmith and Stephen D. Krasner, "The Limits of Idealism," *Daedalus* (winter 2003): 47–63.

2. M. Cherif Bassiouni, "The History of Universal Jurisdiction and Its Place in International Law," this volume.

3. Michael Kirby, "Universal Jurisdiction and Judicial Reluctance: A New 'Fourteen Points,'" this volume.

4. The judges in the *Pinochet* case, for example, did not tackle some of the trickiest and most contentious questions about universal jurisdiction, including its relationship to customary international law. Ruth Wedgwood, "International Criminal Law and Augusto Pinochet,"*Virginia Journal of International Law* 40 (2000): 829, 836.

5. See Ian Brownlie, *Principles of Public International Law,* 5th ed. (Oxford: Oxford University Press, 1998), 307–8. Brownlie observes that punishment of crimes under international law by states "is often expressed as an acceptance of the principles of universality, but this is not strictly correct, since what is punished is the breach of international law; and the case is thus different from the punishment, under national law, of acts in respect of which international law gives a liberty to all states to punish, but does not itself declare criminal." Other commentators have drawn a distinction between vicarious jurisdiction and universality. See Rüdiger Wolfrum, "The Decentralized Prosecution of International Offences through National Courts," in *War Crimes in International Law,* ed. Yoram Dinstein and Mala Tabory (Boston: M. Nijhoff Publishers, 1996), 233, 235. See also Christoph Safferling, "International Decisions: Public Prosecutor v. Djajic," *American Journal of International Law* 92 (1998): 528, 529–30 (hereinafter Djajic) (drawing a distinction between vicarious jurisdiction and universality in discussion of the Djajic case).

For a further account of this distinction in the evolution of universal jurisdiction, see Bassiouni's contribution to this volume, "The History of Universal Jurisdiction and Its Place in International Law." Bassiouni uses a different terminology, referring to the "historic idealistic universalist position" versus the "pragmatic policy position," but the underlying ideas are the same.

6. See "Attorney-General v. Eichmann," *International Law Review* 36 (1961): 18, 26.

7. Sometimes this approach is expressed as referring to offenses recognized as illegal by all "civilized" nations. See, e.g., R. v. Finta, [1994] 1 S.C.R. 701, 783 (La Forest, J., dissenting) (hereinafter Finta), citing George Schwarzenberger, *The Law of Armed Conflict* (London: Stevens and Sons, 1968). Although La Forest used the term "civilized" nations interchangeably with the idea of offenses prohibited in all nations, the distinction can have significant consequences. See infra note 87.

8. Brownlie categorizes the crime most commonly associated with universal jurisdiction, piracy, as a crime over which universality can be exercised, not as a crime under international law. Brownlie, supra note 5.

9. Bassiouni, "History of Universal Jurisdiction."

10. Finta, supra note 7.

11. Not all legal systems recognize passive personality as a legitimate ground for the exercise of jurisdiction, and some commentators also do not recognize it as an internationally accepted basis for the exercise of jurisdiction. See Christopher L. Blakesley, "Introduction: Brief Overview of the Traditional Bases of Jurisdiction over Extraterritorial Crimes," *International Criminal Law* 2 (1999): 33, 67–70. See also Brownlie, *Principles of Public International Law,* supra note 5.

12. See "Polyukhovich v. Commonwealth of Australia," *American Law Review* 101 (1991): 545, 583 (Brennan, J., dissenting) (hereinafter Polyukhovich). The issue becomes more complex when the defendant has subsequently become a national of the state exercising jurisdiction. See ibid., 571.

13. Indeed, as we shall see, many judges argue that this is precisely when and why universal jurisdiction may be exercised. See, e.g., Finta, supra note 7, 732–33 (La Forest, J., dissenting); R. v. Bow Street Magistrate, Ex. p. Pinochet (No. 3), (1999) 2 All ER 97, 179 (H. L.) (Lord Millett) (hereinafter Pinochet [No. 3]).

14. Bassiouni and Orentlicher both make a similar point in their contributions to this volume; indeed, Orentlicher explicitly refers to the pattern of "universal

jurisdiction plus." See their contributions to this volume. Interestingly, Principle 8 takes account of this practice and intuitive preference, instructing judges in cases where more than one state has or may assert jurisdiction to canvass an array of factors such as the place the crime was committed and the nationality of the victim and the perpetrator in deciding where the case should ultimately be tried.

15. In re Javor, Cass. crim., March 26, 1996, Bull. crim. 1996, No. 132, 379, summarized and discussed in Brigitte Stern, "International Decisions: Universal Jurisdiction over Crimes against Humanity under French Law," *American Journal of International Law* 93 (1991): 525 (hereinafter Stern, "In re Javor and In re Munyeshyaka"). The requirement that the accused be on the territory of the prosecuting state is a commonly stated restriction on the exercise of universal jurisdiction. See, e.g., Polyukhovich, supra note 12, 650 (Toohey, J.).

16. See Stern, "In re Javor and In re Munyeshyaka," supra note 15, 696. See also "French Extradition Request for Argentine Military Officer Ready," *Agence France Presse*, August 11, 2000 (reporting France's request for extradition from Italy of the Argentine former military officer, Jorge Olivera, in connection with the disappearance of a French national during Argentina's military dictatorship). See also Fiona MacKay, "The Redress Trust, Universal Juridsiction in Europe: Criminal prosecutions in Europe since 1990 for War Crimes, Crimes against Humanity, Torture, and Genocide" (Annex) (1999), www.redress.org/unijeur.html (hereinafter "Universal Jurisdiction in Europe") (describing, in the section on France, the conviction in absentia of Argentine Captain Alfredo Astiz and the request for a provisional warrant for the arrest of General Pinochet, both based on the passive personality principle); Brigitte Stern, "International Decisions: Universality and Passive Personality Principles of Jurisdiction in French Law," *American Journal of International Law* 93 (1999): 696 (hereinafter Stern, In re Pinochet) (discussing the Pinochet case in France).

17. "Attorney-General v. Eichmann," supra note 6, 50–57. See also Attorney-General v. Eichmann, 36 I.L.R. 277, 304 (S. Ct. 1962) (Isr.) (affirming that the protective principle and the passive personality principle were valid grounds on which to base prosecution in addition to the universality principle).

18. Public Prosecutor v. Jorgic, discussed in Sascha Rolf Lüder and Gregor Schotten, "Correspondent's Reports: Germany," Y.B. *International Humanitarian Law*, 2 (1999): 366. *Cf.* Djajic, supra note 5, where the nexus required was even more minimal than in Jorgic.

19. War Crimes Amendment Act 1988, § 11 (Austl.); War Crimes Act 1991, c. 13, § 2 (Eng.); Canadian Criminal Code, R.S.C., ch. C-46, §§ 7(3.71)-(3.73) (1985) (Can.).

20. See Hari M. Osofsky, Note, "Domesticating International Criminal Law: Bringing Human Rights Violators to Justice," *Yale Law Journal* 107 (1997): 191, 221–25. Osofsky proposes a three-step process for decision making, which he terms "comparative forum non conveniens." The first and second steps involve consideration of whether any other State is considering criminal or civil action and whether that State is adequate. The third step is a balancing test where prosecutors should consider the level of jurisdictional ties to the United States." Ibid.

21. Ibid., 223. When an international criminal law violation occurs within another country, involves nonnationals who are not located in the United States, and does not directly threaten U.S. interests, the case for taking jurisdiction may be less strong than that of another state. If all states granted jurisdiction for every international criminal law violation, the absurd result of hundreds of parallel prosecutions might occur. Universal jurisdiction thus is a necessary but not a sufficient condition for the appropriateness of prosecution. Ibid.

22. Finta, supra note 7, 788 ff.

23. The "Baky Order" process consisted of several stages: first, Jews were isolated by being identified and having to wear a yellow star; second, their property was

expropriated; third, they were removed to ghettoes; fourth, they were brought to a large concentration center where valuables were removed; fifth, they were put onto trains; and sixth, they were transported, mostly to Auschwitz-Birkenau. See David Matas, "The Case of Imre Finta," *University of New Brunswick Law Journal* 43 (1994): 281. See also Finta, supra note 7, 790.

24. R. v. Finta, (1992) 53 O.A.C. 1.

25. Ibid.

26. In two previous libel cases concerning accusations that Finta was a war criminal, one initiated by Finta and another brought against Finta after he called the accuser a liar, Finta also failed to produce any evidence on his behalf. See Matas, supra note 23, 281. The only evidence introduced on his behalf at trial was called by the judge.

27. Finta, supra note 7, 758 (La Forest, J., dissenting). In addition to his legal arguments, La Forest found no moral problem in arguing that this *mens rea* would be sufficient: "From the sheer viewpoint of our moral responsibility, I fail to see any injustice in prosecuting these crimes in accordance with our normal criminal procedures." Ibid., 772.

28. Ibid., 813–18 (Cory, J.).

29. Matas, supra note 23, 296.

30. Ibid., 296.

31. See supra note 7, 724 (La Forest, J., dissenting) and 788 (Cory, J.). Canadian Criminal Code, R.S.C., ch. C-46, §§ 7(3.71)-(3.73) (1985) (Can.). The Supreme Court also considered whether these provisions of the Criminal Code violated the Canadian Charter of Rights and Freedoms. Canada Act (U.K.), R.S.C., ch. 11, §§ 1, 7, 11(a, b, d, f, g), 12, 15, 24(1) (1982) (hereinafter Canadian Charter of Rights and Freedoms) (providing for, inter alia, principles of fundamental justice, the right to trial by jury, the prohibition of retroactive legislation, the prohibition of cruel and unusual punishment, the prohibition of vagueness). The Court was unanimous in upholding the legislation's constitutionality.

32. Ibid., 814 (Cory, J.). See also ibid., 810 ("It is readily apparent that the jury could find that the accused was guilty of manslaughter and yet have reasonable doubts as to whether his actions and state of mind were such that his actions amounted to crimes against humanity or war crimes. If the appellant's submission were accepted, the jury would nonetheless be forced to convict").

33. Cory even refers to Brownlie's distinction between universality and crimes under international law, placing the offenses being prosecuted in the case at bar in the category of crimes under international law. Ibid., 806 (Cory, J.), citing Ian Brownlie, *Principles of Public International Law,* 4th ed. (Oxford: Clarendon Press; New York: Oxford University Press, 1990), and citing Gillian Triggs, "Australia's War Crimes Trials: A Moral Necessity or Legal Minefield?," *Melbourne University Law Review* 16 (1987): 382, 389. Cory further quotes Bassiouni for the proposition that "a war crime or a crime against humanity is not the same as a domestic offense." Finta, supra note 7, 811 (Cory, J.), citing M. Cherif Bassiouni, *Crimes against Humanity in International Criminal Law* (Boston: M. Nijhoff, 1992).

34. Finta, supra note 7, 812 (Cory, J.).

35. Finta, supra note 7, 873 (Cory, J.), citing Hans Kelsen, "Will the Judgment in the Nuremberg Trial Constitute a Precedent in International Law?," *International Law Quarterly* 1 (1947): 153, 165. See also Triggs, "Australia's War Crimes Trials," supra note 33, 394 (noting that commentators have "long debated the question, whether individuals can commit crimes under international law"). See generally ibid., 394–95 (discussing the evolution of international law regarding individual criminal responsibility and the adoption of individual criminal responsibility in the Charter of the Nuremberg Tribunal and subsequent conventions). The question of whether international law provides for individual responsibility is also one affected

by the account adopted of universal jurisdiction. If the crimes prosecuted are based on international law alone, the problem of individual responsibility arises because international law has traditionally been concerned only with States. *Cf.* Pinochet (No. 3), supra note 13, 170, 180 (Lord Millett) (arguing that the classical view of international law as only applicable to states is no longer appropriate but must give way to a more individualized account of international law). By contrast, if the account adopted bases the jurisdiction on domestic crimes, there is no question that these have always applied to individuals.

36. In the *Finta* case, this concern flows directly from Cory's finding that the Canadian Code introduced two new offences, previously unknown in domestic law. See Finta, supra note 7, 870 (Cory, J.). Justice La Forest, as discussed below, avoids this problem by arguing that the crimes were already crimes under Canadian law at the time the offence was committed. See ibid., 781–84 (La Forest, J., dissenting).

37. See ibid., 870–72 (Cory, J.). The Canadian Charter of Rights and Freedoms' prohibition on retroactive legislation includes reference to international law and general principles of law recognized by the community of nations:

> Any person charged with an offence has the right . . . (g) not to be found guilty on account of any act or omission unless, at the time of the act or omission, it constituted an offence under Canadian or international law or was criminal according to the general principles of law recognized by the community of nations; . . .

Canadian Charter of Rights and Freedoms, supra note 31, § 11(g).

38. See Finta, supra note 7, 872–74 (Cory, J.). Cory does not explain his rejection of this approach, other than implicitly by citing Kelsen's view that the Nuremberg and Tokyo Charters were not declarative of already existing international law "but were merely meant to punish the atrocious behaviour of the Nazi and Japanese regimes because their deeds could not go unpunished." Ibid. Other judges have been similarly unconvinced that all of these acts were criminal under international law during the Second World War. See, e.g., Polyukhovich, supra note 12, 667 (Toohey, J.) (arguing that war crimes were criminal under international law between 1939 and 1945 but that crimes against humanity were not criminal under international law during the same period).

39. See Finta, supra note 7, 872–74 (Cory, J.).

40. Cory accepts this approach without further elaboration. Finta, supra note 7, 873–74 (Cory, J.), citing Kelsen, "Will the Judgment," supra note 35.

41. Finta, supra note 7, 819 (Cory, J.). See generally ibid., 813–23 (discussing the mental element required for war crimes and crimes against humanity and the trial judge's instruction to the jury regarding the requisite mental element).

42. Ibid., 818 (Cory, J.).

43. See, e.g., Stern, "In re Javor and In re Munyeshyaka," supra note 15. See also the Swiss case, *N*, discussed in "Universal Jurisdiction in Europe," supra note 16.

44. Pinochet (No. 3), supra note 13. See also supra note 4.

45. Pinochet (No. 3), supra note 13, at 177–78 (Lord Millett). *Cf.* ibid., 100 (Lord Browne-Wilkinson).

46. Extradition Act, 1989, c. 33 (Eng.).

47. Lord Hope accepted that the terms of the Extradition Act are unclear on this point but adopted this interpretation in order to avoid retroactivity. Pinochet (No. 3), supra note 13, at 136 (Lord Hope). Lord Goff even refused to read a term into a treaty without an explicit statement in international law that sovereign immunity is not to apply in cases of torture. Ibid., 126 (Lord Goff).

48. Nulyarimma v. Thompson, Buzzacott v. Minister for the Environment (1999) 165 A.L.R. 621 (hereinafter Nulyarimma).

49. See, e.g., ibid., 637 (Whitlam, J.).

50. Polyukhovich, supra note 12. Writing in dissent, Brennan declined to uphold war crimes legislation on the ground that the difference between the international law and the definitions of the crimes contained in the relevant portion of the domestic law indicated that the Australian legislation had not been exercised in accordance with the external affairs power.

51. For striking examples of this, see generally ibid., Nulyarimma, supra note 48.

52. Stern, "In re Javor and In re Munyeshyaka," supra note 15.

53. See Stephen P. Marks, "The *Hissène Habré* Case: The Law and Politics of Universal Jurisdiction," this volume.

54. Pinochet (No. 3), supra note 13, 177.

55. Ibid.

56. Ibid.

57. See also Finta, supra note 7, 788 ff. (Cory, J.).

58. See "Correspondent's Reports: Canada," Y. B. *International Humanitarian Law* 2 (1999): 345 (hereinafter "In Re Pinochet").

59. See Finta, supra note 6, 745–46 (La Forest, J., dissenting) ("The question of the presence of war crimes or crimes against humanity is thus one of jurisdiction. The offence with which the accused is charged, on the other hand, is the underlying domestic offence, drawn from the already existing Canadian criminal law at the time of commission.")

60. Finta, supra note 7, 741–42 (La Forest, J., dissenting). La Forest draws an analogy with provisions in Canadian law on conspiracy. Ibid., 742.

61. Ibid., 744–45.

62. Ibid., 737.

63. Ibid., 735.

64. Ibid.

65. Ibid., 746.

66. Ibid., 734.

67. Ibid., 728. Here too, however, La Forest adds a bottom-up element, going on to note that these acts are "universally recognized as criminal according to general principles of law recognized by the community of nations." Ibid. This is one of the sources of international law under the Statute of the International Court of Justice, art. 38.

68. "Since war crimes and crimes against humanity are crimes against international prescriptions and, indeed, go to the very structure of the international legal order, they are not under international law subject to the general legal prescription . . . that crimes must ordinarily be prosecuted and punished in the state where they are committed." Finta, supra note 7, 731–32 (La Forest, J., dissenting). This recognition appears to undermine La Forest's general approach, although he does acknowledge that "the principle of territoriality simply responds to the structure of the international order." Ibid., 747.

69. Ibid., 732–33 (La Forest, J., dissenting). In Austria, Article 65(1) of the Penal Code specifically allows for jurisdiction for offences committed abroad where there is double criminality, the person is present on Austrian territory, and he/she cannot be extradited for reasons unrelated to the nature and characteristics of the offence. In *Dusko Cvjetkovic*, the prosecutor relied on this provision, arguing "that judicial co-operation with Bosnia-Herzegovina [the state with territorial jurisdiction] was not possible since there were no mail or telephone communications between the judicial authorities of the two countries due to the war, and that there was no orderly administration of criminal justice in the place where the offences were committed." The court accepted the basis for jurisdiction, finding that Article 65(1) "presupposed that there was a functioning criminal justice system in the state where the crime was committed. "Universal Jurisdiction in Europe," supra note 16.

70. See Finta, supra note 7, 745–46 (La Forest, J., dissenting) (arguing that the question of whether the crimes were committed in circumstances that allow them to come under Canada's extraterritorial jurisdictional provisions as war crimes or crimes against humanity are jurisdictional questions for the judge, not the jury, to determine).

71. "These types of actions have been so widely banned in societies that they can truly be said to fall to the level of acts that are *mala in se*." Ibid., 784. La Forest refers to writers such as Schwarzenberger who "have emphasized that the strongest source in international law for crimes against humanity was the common domestic prohibitions of civilized nations." Ibid., 783. See also ibid., 764.

72. "In Re Pinochet Ugarte," District of Brussels, Tribunal of First Instance of Brussels (investigating magistrate), November 8, 1998. For an unofficial translation, see "Documentation: National Courts: Belgium" (hereinafter "Documentation"), 475. For analysis of the decision, see Luc Reydams, "International Decisions: In Re Pinochet," *American Journal of International Law* 93 (1999): 700.

73. See "Documentation," supra note 72, 478, 482.

74. "When examining the validity of prosecutions under the War Crimes Act 1945 it would be wise to found jurisdiction upon the international breach rather than upon a violation of Australia's legislation. This is not because of any doubts about Australia's international personality during the war, but because of the retrospective nature of the Australian legislation." Triggs, "Australia's War Crimes Trials," supra note 33, 389. It can be argued, however, that this relates only to the Australian legislation because it does not even purport to deal with future acts and may not correspond to international law. See generally Polyukhovich, supra note 12, 585 (Brennan, J., dissenting) (arguing that the lack of conformity of the domestic legislation with the international legislation makes it entirely retrospective) and 662 (Toohey, J.) (concluding that crimes against humanity were not contrary to international law during the time which the Australian legislation purports to regulate).

75. See Polyukhovich, supra note 12, 673 (Toohey J.) (arguing that since these acts were crimes under Australian law and under Ukraine law at the time of their commission, the policy concerns which lead to a prohibition on retroactive criminal law are not at issue). See also Rosalyn Higgins, "Time and International Law," *International and Comparative Law Quarterly* 46 (1997): 501, 509 (arguing that the U.K. war crimes legislation is not truly retroactive).

76. "Documentation," supra note 72, 482.

77. Finta, supra note 7, 772 (La Forest, J., dissenting).

78. Ibid., 738.

79. Ibid., 734.

80. Ibid.

81. "The normal *mens rea* for confinement, robbery, manslaughter, kidnapping, whether it be intention, knowledge, recklessness or wilful blindness, would be adequate." Finta, supra note 7, 765 (La Forest, J., dissenting). See generally ibid., 753–66, especially 753, 754.

82. See U.S. v. Smith, 18 U.S. 153, 162 (1820), U.S. v. Klintock, 18 U.S. 144, 152 (1820).

83. Brennan in Polyukhovich is particularly concerned about allowing a state to impose its domestic law on non-nationals without a requirement that that domestic law conform to international law. See Polyukhovich, supra note 12, 585 (Brennan, J., dissenting).

84. See Rome Statute of the International Criminal Court, art. 17, U.N. Doc. A/CONF. 183/9 (1998), 37 I.L.M. 999, available at www.un.org/law/icc/statute/romefra.htm.

85. See supra note 67. Elsewhere in the decision, La Forest also recognizes: "In

my view, Canada always has an interest, or a moral claim, in bringing those who commit acts that it regards as offensive behaviour to justice. Conduct is not viewed as any less culpable merely because it is committed abroad; murder of anybody anywhere is something we find abhorrent." Finta, supra note 7, 770 (La Forest, J., dissenting).

86. "Documentation," supra note 72, 483.

87. Ibid., 478.

88. I deliberately avoid the language of Article 38 of the ICJ Statute, referring to "general principles of law recognized by civilized nations." The adjective "civilized" is offensive to many nations, recalling first Christian and later colonial supremacy of select and self-appointed states. Moreover, efforts to translate "civilized" into more modern language, such as suggestions that it now be read to encompass democratic nations or nations with a tradition of respect for human rights, are highly controversial.

89. Principle 1(2).

90. See Pinochet (No. 3), supra note 13, 120–21 (Lord Goff) (arguing that non-recognition of sovereign immunity by international tribunals does not translate to nonimmunity before domestic courts).

91. "Documentation," supra note 72.

92. Djajic, supra note 5.

93. Ibid., 529.

94. Ibid., 530.

95. See "Universal Jurisdiction in Europe," supra note 16.

96. The Lotus Case, PCIJ, Ser. A, no. 10 (1927), 70, cited in Brownlie, *Principles of Public International Law*, supra note 5, 235 (emphasis added). Oddly, given his citation of this passage, Brownlie treats piracy an example of an offence which is subject to the principle of universality, as opposed to a crime against international law. See ibid., 307–8. His logic would seem to be contradicted by Judge Moore's analysis. *Cf.* Wedgwood, supra note 4, 836. For a view challenging both Moore and Brownlie, see Alfred Rubin, *The Law of Piracy* (Newport, RI: Naval War College Press, 1988) (questioning international law as a direct source of law and jurisdiction in piracy).

97. See, e.g., the contribution by Diane Orentlicher, which makes this point very forcefully and effectively. "Future of Universal Jurisdiction," this volume.

98. See, e.g., the Scottish case regarding a Sudanese doctor accused of acts of torture in Sudan. Dr. Mahgoub was arrested in Dundee in 1997. The case was dropped without explanation by the Crown Office in Edinburgh in 1999. See James Rougvie, "Sudan Torture Charges Dropped," *Scotsman*, May 28, 1999. See also "Universal Jurisdiction in Europe," supra note 16. In the U.K., Home Sec. Jack Straw was ordered by the High Court to release the medical report that formed the basis of his decision that Augusto Pinochet was medically unfit to stand trial. See Warren Hoge, "British Court Orders Disclosure of Pinochet's Medical Records," *New York Times*, February 16, 2000, A12. Straw's final decision to release Augusto Pinochet on medical grounds was not, however, challenged in the courts. Warren Hoge, "After 16 Months of House Arrest, Pinochet Quits England," *New York Times*, March 3, 2000, A6. See also Terence Shaw, "Pinochet Freed: Straw Takes Pains to Avoid Further Legal Challenge," *Daily Telegraph* (London), March 3, 2000, 6.

99. South Africa resisted calls for the arrest and prosecution of the Ethiopian dictator Mengistu Haile Mariam while he was in South Africa, arguing that such a prosecution would contravene its own domestic policy of reconciliation. See Avril McDonald, "The Year in Review," Y. B. *International Humanitarian Law*, 2 (1999): 213, 241. South Africa also denied a request by Ethiopia to extradite Mengistu on the grounds that there was no extradition treaty between the two states. Ibid. South Africa

has since agreed to review this decision. "South Africa Will Review Extradition of Former Ethiopia Dictator for Genocide," *International Enforcement Law Reporter* 16 (2000): 558. South Africa has requested that states recognize its amnesties. John Dugard, "South Africa's Truth and Reconciliation Process and International Humanitarian Law," Y. B. *International Humanitarian Law* 2 (1999): 254, 262–63.

100. Again, Diane Orentlicher makes a similar point in "Future of Universal Jurisdiction," this volume.

101. Principle 4(1).

102. See, e.g., Nulyarimma, supra note 48, 650–51 (Merkel, J.), citing Lord Millett in Pinochet (No. 3), supra note 13.

103. Orentlicher, "Future of Universal Jurisdiction," this volume.

104. Laurence Helfer and Anne-Marie Slaughter, "Toward a Theory of Effective Supranational Adjudication," *Yale Law Journal* 107 (1997): 371, 373, 376.

105. See ibid.

Chapter 10. Universal Jurisdiction, National Amnesties, and Truth Commissions: Reconciling the Irreconcilable

1. For a fine treatment of the subject, see Martha Minow, *Between Vengeance and Forgiveness: Facing History after Genocide and Mass Violence* (Boston: Beacon Press, 1998).

2. The doctrines of head of state immunity, diplomatic immunity, and superior orders also surface in this connection. Because space is limited and these issues have either been fairly clearly addressed by international law already (particularly superior orders) or are the subject of another essay, I will take them up only briefly in part 3, below.

3. Because this essay, and indeed this project, focuses mostly on the exercise of universal jurisdiction by states, challenges to accountability that might affect the universal international jurisdiction exercised by the international community were not addressed. For a discussion of this topic, see Leila Nadya Sadat and S. Richard Carden, "The New International Criminal Court: An Uneasy Revolution," *Georgetown Law Journal* 88 (2000): 406–9; and Leila Nadya Sadat, "Redefining Universal Jurisdiction," *New England Law Review* 35 (2001): 241–63.

4. Carlos Santiago Nino, *Radical Evil on Trial* (New Haven: Yale University Press, 1996), x.

5. Gary Jonathan Bass, *Stay the Hand of Vengeance* (Princeton: Princeton University Press, 2000), 10–20.

6. M. Cherif Bassiouni, "The Normative Framework of International Humanitarian Law: Overlaps, Gaps, and Ambiguities," *Transnational Law and Contemporary Problems* 8 (1998): 203.

7. W. Michael Reisman, "Legal Responses to Genocide and Other Massive Violations of Human Rights," *Law and Contemporary Problems* 59 (1996): 75. But see Payam Akhavan, "Justice and Reconciliation in the Great Lakes Region of Africa: The Contribution of the International Criminal Tribunal for Rwanda," *Duke Journal of Comparative and International Law* 7 (1997): 338 (arguing that because cataclysmic violence requires extensive planning it is both foreseeable and preventable).

8. Mary Robinson, "Genocide, War Crimes, Crimes against Humanity," *Fordham International Law Journal* 23 (1999): 277–78.

9. In 1996 the United Nations Commission on Human Rights issued a report to which was attached a set of principles defining and attacking the culture of impunity. The report defined impunity as "the impossibility, *de jure* or de facto, of bringing the perpetrators of human rights violations to account whether in criminal,

civil, administrative or disciplinary proceedings since they are not subject to any inquiry that might lead to their being accused, arrested, tried and, if found guilty, convicted, and to reparations being made to their victims." *Question of the Impunity of Perpetrators of Human Rights Violations (Civil and Political)* U.N. Doc. E/CN.4/Sub.2/1997/20 (1997), at Annex II, Definitions, A (hereinafter *U.N. Impunity Guidelines*). Although it appears to leave room for a variety of legal responses to the commission of atrocities by referring to "criminal, civil, administrative or disciplinary proceedings," the definition clearly contemplates that "criminal proceedings" are the most appropriate response to atrocity.

10. Antonio Cassese, "On the Current Trends towards Criminal Prosecution and Punishment of Breaches of International Humanitarian Law," *European Journal of International Law* 9 (1998): 3–4; Leila Nadya Sadat, "The Establishment of the International Criminal Court: From the Hague to Rome and Back Again," *Detroit Journal of International Law and Practice* 8 (1999): 102–7.

11. See Theodor Meron, "Is International Law Moving towards Criminalization," *European Journal of International Law* 9 (1998): 18.

12. Leila Nadya Sadat (formerly Wexler), "Reflections on the Trial of Vichy Collaborator Paul Touvier for Crimes against Humanity in France," *Journal of Law and Society Inquiry* 20 (1995): 210. Retributive justice has many variants, as wonderfully explained in Joshua Dressler, "Hating Criminals: How Can Something That Feels So Good Be Wrong?," *Michigan Law Review* 88 (1990): 1451–53, reviewing Jeffrie G. Murphy and Jean Hampton, *Forgiveness and Mercy* (Cambridge: Cambridge University Press, 1998). The most widely supported variant is what he calls "negative retributivism," which holds that it is morally wrong to punish an innocent person even if society might benefit from the action (but does not require the guilty be punished, which "positive retributivism" does). Ibid., 1451. For a critique of modern retributive theory, see David Dolinko, "Three Mistakes of Retributivism," *University of California Los Angeles Law Review* 39 (1992): 1623. See also generally *Israel Law Review* 25 (1991): 283–791, for a wonderful collection of essays on justice and punishment.

13. Stanley Cohen, "State Crimes of Previous Regimes: Knowledge, Accountability, and the Policing of the Past," *Journal of Law and Society Inquiry* 20 (1995): 22.

14. Indeed, "the idea that wrongs should be redressed, that reparation should be made to the injured is among the most venerable and most central of legal principles." Naomi Roht-Arriaza, "Punishment, Redress, and Pardon: Theoretical and Psychological Approaches," in *Impunity and Human Rights in International Law and Practice,* ed. Naomi Roht-Arriaza (New York: Oxford University Press, 1995), 17.

15. Purges have been another traditional response of societies in transition. As Mark Osiel notes, many societies have seen a "quick, decisive purge of enthusiastic collaborators" to be an effective alternative to criminal trials. Osiel mentions Argentina and de-Nazification in Germany as examples, and notes the serious due process and other problems that attend the use of purges by a society. Mark J. Osiel, "Why Prosecute? Critics of Punishment for Mass Atrocity," *Human Rights Quarterly* 22 (2000): 133. In postwar Europe they were common, the purge in France resulting in as many as forty thousand extrajudicial executions. Sadat Wexler, "Reflections," 197 n. 34. Indeed, the purge in France, while perhaps understandable, probably increased tensions in postwar France that, in combination with other factors, created a deep schism in French society that persists to this day. See generally John F. Sweets, *The Politics of Resistance in France* (Dekalb: Northern Illinois University Press, 1976), 213–17.

16. Cohen, *State Crimes,* 22. For a critique of this position, suggesting that many safeguards afforded to defendants in national courts should not be extrapolated to the international arena, see Tom J. Farer, "Restraining the Barbarians: Can International Criminal Law Help?," *Human Rights Quarterly* 22 (2000): 92–98.

17. For a superb treatment of many of the issues surrounding the use of criminal trials following mass atrocities, see Mark Osiel, *Mass Atrocity, Collective Memory, and the Law* (New Brunswick: Transaction Publishers, 1997).

18. Bass, *Stay the Hand,* 12.

19. For the view that state sovereignty is the principle obstacle to the enforcement of international humanitarian law, see Antonio Cassese, "Reflections on International Criminal Justice," *Modern Law Review* 61 (1998): 1.

20. Fania Domb, "Treatment of War Crimes in Peace Settlements: Prosecution or Amnesty," *Israel Yearbook of Human Rights* 24 (1994): 253.

21. Daniel T. Kobil, "The Quality of Mercy Strained: Wrestling the Pardoning Power from the King," *Texas Law Review* 69 (1991): 576.

22. Ibid., 575–77. Recent surveys of the pardoning power worldwide suggest that "this institution remains an integral part of the constitutional scheme in almost every jurisdiction." Leslie Sebba, "The Pardoning Power: A World Survey," *Journal of Criminal Law and Criminology* 68 (1977): 120.

23. This section addresses blanket amnesties, that is, amnesties granted pursuant to a general law or decree that do not require the recipient to account in any way, through confession or other method, for the crime of which he or she is accused. Amnesties granted after a judicial or quasi-judicial official proceeding of some kind are similar to pardons and are therefore considered in connection with the South African experience, outlined below.

24. See Michael P. Scharf, "The Amnesty Exception to the Jurisdiction of the International Criminal Court," *Cornell International Law Journal* 32 (1999): 509 (arguing that civilian rule was restored to Haiti because the members of the military regime that had been accused of massive human rights abuses received amnesty for their crimes pursuant to the Governors Island Agreement negotiated in July 1993 under international auspices). But see Irwin P. Stotzky, "Haiti: Searching for Alternatives," in *Impunity and Human Rights,* ed. Roht-Arriaza, 185, 189 (stating that the "Governors Island Agreement was a total failure. Neither Cédras [the military leader] nor François resigned. Instead Cédras broke every part of the brokered deal and employed every kind of delay while subordinates known as attachés continued to terrorize the population" and that the only way the military leaders were ousted was the threat of invasion by the United States, which ultimately sent U.S. troops to Haiti under an agreement that also required Cédras and François to leave their posts and receive amnesty for their crimes).

25. Diane F. Orentlicher, "Settling Accounts: The Duty to Prosecute Human Rights Violations of a Prior Regime," *Yale Law Journal* 100 (1991): 2546.

26. Priscilla B. Hayner, "Fifteen Truth Commissions, 1974 to 1994: A Comparative Study," *Human Rights Quarterly* 16 (1994): 627–29. Orentlicher notes that in addition to El Salvador, amnesty laws or decrees were adopted by Argentina, Brazil, Chile, Uruguay, Guatemala, Nicaragua, Namibia, and Suriname. Orentlicher, "Settling Accounts," 2548 n. 36.

27. Naomi Roht-Arriaza and Lauren Gibson, "The Developing Jurisprudence on Amnesty," *Human Rights Quarterly* 20 (1998): 849–51 (describing the El Salvadoran amnesty law).

28. In her classic study of fifteen truth commissions, Priscilla Hayner notes that "prosecutions are very rare after a truth commission report; in most cases there are no trials of any kind, even when the identity of violators and the extent of the atrocities are widely known." Hayner, "Fifteen Truth Commissions," 604. See also Orentlicher, "Settling Accounts," 2548 n. 36 (noting that de facto immunity was conferred in the Philippines and Haiti).

29. Evelyn Bradley, "In Search for Justice: A Truth and Reconciliation Commission

for Rwanda," *Journal of International Law and Practice* 7 (1998): 140. Akhavan, "Justice and Reconciliation," 339–40.

30. Bradley, "In Search for Justice," 140.

31. Category 1 offenders include organizers or planners of the genocide, persons in positions of authority, and "notorious murderers who by virtue of the zeal or excessive malice with which they committed atrocities, distinguished themselves. . . ." and persons who committed "acts of sexual torture." Ibid., 134–35.

32. Ibid.

33. William A. Schabas, "Justice, Democracy, and Impunity in Post-Genocide Rwanda: Searching for Solutions to Impossible Problems," *Criminal Law Forum* 7 (1996): 536–39.

34. If true, it is arguable that Rwanda would be worse off if it released prisoners still under the influence of the *génocidaires*. Indeed, it suggests that Rwanda must be constantly vigilant if not to lose control to the forces of violence once more.

35. Bradley, "In Search for Justice," 135.

36. Ibid., 144–45. Minow, *Between Vengeance and Forgiveness,* 124–25.

37. John Dugard suggests an alternative reason that criminal prosecutions may be thwarted following a transition to democracy: sufficient evidence may simply be unavailable to support a criminal conviction, given that the repressive regime in question may quite probably have operated under a shroud of secrecy that makes information gathering after the fact quite difficult. He suggests South Africa is a case in point. John Dugard, "Reconciliation and Justice: The South African Experience," *Transnational Law and Contemporary Problems* 8 (1998): 286–87.

38. Schabas, "Post-Genocide Rwanda," 547–48.

39. Cassese, "Reflections"; Akhavan, "Justice and Reconciliation," 336. As Schabas notes in his article, the Security Council resolution establishing the tribunal expressly speaks to the need "to strengthen the courts and judicial system of Rwanda, having regard in particular to the necessity for those courts to deal with large numbers of suspects." Schabas, "Justice, Democracy, and Impunity," 551, citing S.C. Res. 955, U.N. SCOR, 49th Year, 1994 S.C. Res. and Dec. at 15, U.N. Doc. S/INF/50 (1994).

40. Schabas, "Post-Genocide Rwanda," 552–54.

41. Leah Werchick, "Prospects for Justice in Rwanda's Citizen Tribunals," *Human Rights Brief* 8, no. 3: 15.

42. Sudarsan Raghavan, "Rwanda Prepares to Use Tribunals for Genocide but Community Courts Ill-Prepared," *San Jose Mercury News,* June 20, 2002.

43. Much of the literature posits truth commissions as alternatives to prosecutions. Dugard, "Reconciliation and Justice," 287. But the question of whether to establish a truth commission is quite separate from the issue whether any or all of the regimes' former leaders (or lower level offenders) will ultimately be prosecuted. Indeed, in the El Salvadoran case, the fear was apparently that the truth commission process would lead to prosecutions, and the Commission's report was immediately followed by a "sweeping amnesty that extinguished civil and criminal responsibility for political crimes by the FMLN and the government." Roht-Arriaza, "Developing Jurisprudence," 850.

44. Cohen, *State Crimes,* 12. As Cohen notes, the truth phase of social transitions "is an onslaught on all [the] forms of denial—personal and collective, the conscious coverup and the convenient forgetting, the euphemistic renaming. This process can be as painful as its common metaphors imply: digging up graves, opening wounds."

45. Hayner, "Fifteen Truth Commissions," 610. Peter A. Schey, Dinah Shelton, and Naomi Roht-Arriaza, "Addressing Human Rights Abuses: Truth Commissions and the Value of Amnesty," *Whittier Law Review* 19 (1997): 337–38.

46. Elizabeth Kiss, "Reflections on Restorative Justice," in Truth v. Justice: The

Morality of Truth Commissions, ed. Robert I. Rotberg and Dennis Thompson (Princeton: Princeton University Press, 2000), 70–74.

47. Hayner, "Fifteen Truth Commissions," 608. The commission, which was known as the Commission of Inquiry into "Disappearances" of People in Uganda, held public hearings into disappearances that occurred under the Amin government and issued a report, which President Amin refused to publish. Indeed, the four commissioners who comprised the commission were targeted by the state for reprisals, and one was ultimately executed on trumped-up murder charges. Ibid., 611–12. A second, and better-known, truth commission was established in Uganda in 1986, which, although more active than the first commission, was beset with financial and logistical problems. Neil J. Kritz, ed., *Transitional Justice: Country Studies*, vol. 2 (United States Institute of Peace, Washington, D.C., 1995), 513–31. The report was issued in 1994 and has received little attention, as most copies are apparently languishing in Ugandan warehouses. Neil J. Kritz, "Coming to Terms with Atrocities: A Review of Accountability Mechanisms for Mass Violations of Human Rights," *Journal of Law and Contemporary Problems* 59 (1996): 142.

48. Hayner, "Fifteen Truth Commissions," 607, 624–25. The United Nations, in its work on Impunity Guidelines, proposed a set of principles for the conduct of truth commissions that would set a minimum internationally acceptable standard for their operation. See *Set of Principles for the Protection and Promotion of Human Rights through Action to Combat Impunity*, U.N. Subcommission for Prevention of Discrimination and Protection of Minorities, 48th Sess., Annex II, Agenda Item 10, at 12, U.N. Doc. E/CN.4/Sub.2/1996/18 (1996). Osiel is particularly critical of truth commissions. See Osiel, "Why Prosecute." For a more positive assessment, see Thomas Buergenthal, "The United Nations Truth Commission for El Salvador," *Vanderbilt Journal of Transnational Law* 27 (1994): 497–544.

49. On the South African experience generally, see Richard J. Goldstone, *For Humanity: Reflections of a War Crimes Investigator* (New Haven: Yale University Press, 2000), 59–73; Dugard, "Reconciliation and Justice"; Jeremy Sarkin, "The Trials and Tribulations of South Africa's Truth and Reconciliation Commission," *South African Journal of Human Rights* 12 (1996): 617; Schey, "Addressing Abuses"; Justin M. Schwartz, "South Africa's Truth and Reconciliation Commission: A Functional Equivalent to Prosecution," *DePaul Digest of International Law* 3 (1997): 13.

50. The Constitution of the Republic of South Africa Act 200 of 1993, Postamble.

51. Sarkin, "The Trials and Tribulations of South Africa's Truth and Reconciliation Commission," 620; Dugard, "Reconciliation and Justice," 279. Interestingly, prior to the political transition that finally occurred, it had been contemplated that the leaders of the apartheid regime would be tried either by an international criminal court, à la Nuremberg, or in states to which they might flee. Thus the apartheid convention criminalized apartheid as a crime and provided for the trial of offenders either by states parties to the convention or an international tribunal. Dugard, "Reconciliation and Justice," 290.

52. Law No. 34 of July 26, 1995, "Promotion of National Unity and Reconciliation Act," available at www.doj. gov.za/trc/legal/act9534.htm.

53. Dugard, "Reconciliation and Justice," 292. South Africa looked to Chile as a model both as to what to avoid and what mechanisms might be successful as regards a truth commission. Richard Goldstone, "Past Human Rights Violations: Truth Commissions and Amnesties or Prosecutions," *North Ireland Legal Quarterly* 51 (2000): 164, 166–67.

54. Goldstone, "Past Human Rights Violations," 169.

55. The Committee on Human Rights Violations, the Committee on Amnesty, and the Committee on Reparation and Rehabilitation.

56. For a fine discussion of the meaning of reconciliation in the South African

context, see Abdullah Omar, "Truth and Reconciliation in South Africa: Accounting for the Past," *Buffalo Human Rights Law Review* 4 (1997): 5.

57. Law of 1995, Preamble.

58. Ibid., Section 20(1)(b).

59. Ibid., Section 20(1)(c).

60. Dugard, "Reconciliation and Justice," 294.

61. Despite the hope that the Amnesty Committee would finish its work by June of 2000, hearings continue today. www.doj.gov.za/trc/amntrans/index.htm.

62. The difficulty of obtaining evidence suitable for prosecutions is often cited as another factor supporting the South African solution. Cassese, "Reflections," 4. As others have noted, the South African Truth and Reconciliation Commission is quite different than virtually all other commissions in its effort to establish mechanisms of accountability in the face of severe political constraints. Kiss, "Reflections," 75.

63. Dugard, "Reconciliation and Justice," 298.

64. www.doj.gov.za/tre/report/index.htm.

65. For a critique of the process, see Schey, "Addressing Abuses," 331–32; Dugard, "Reconciliation and Justice," 37.

66. Schey, "Addressing Abuses," 328. But see Omar, "Truth and Reconciliation," 11 (stating that the commission has enjoyed "overwhelming support" in South Africa).

67. Lorna McGregor, "Individual Accountability in South Africa: Cultural Optimum or Political Facade?," *American Journal of International Law* 95 (2001): 32, 37 (criticizing the collective general amnesty of 37 ANC leaders).

68. Andrew Maykuth, "Apartheid Aftermath: Presidential Pardons Ignite Political Firestorm," *Seattle Times,* July 24, 2002.

69. Omar, "Truth and Reconciliation," 13–14 (emphasis added).

70. They argue that the "policies and practices of accommodation in the pursuit of political settlement conflict with legal accountability in the pursuit of retributive and restorative justice." M. Cherif Bassiouni, "Combating Impunity for International Crimes," *University of Colorado Law Review* 71 (2000): 409.

71. See Lomé Peace Agreement between the Government of Sierra Leone and the Revolutionary United Front of Sierra Leone (July 7, 1999), available at www.sierra-leone.org/lomeaccord.html.

72. Milosevic is currently on trial before the International Criminal Tribunal for the Former Yugoslavia. Sankoh has been arraigned for murder before a national court in Freetown and is also a prime candidate for the special war crimes tribunal for Sierra Leone. "Caged but Unlikely to Hang," *Economist,* March 23, 2002.

73. See Payam Akhavan, "Justice in the Hague, Peace in the Former Yugoslavia," *Human Rights Quarterly* 20 (1999): 746; Bassiouni, "Combating Impunity;" Cassese, "Reflections"; Osiel, "Why Prosecute"; Carlos S. Nino, "The Duty to Punish Past Abuses of Human Rights Put into Context: The Case of Argentina," *Yale Law Journal* 100 (1991): 2619; Nino, *Radical Evil;* Orentlicher, "Settling Accounts"; Naomi Roht-Arriaza, "State Responsibility to Investigate and Prosecute Grave Human Rights Violations in International Law," *California Law Review* 78 (1990): 451.

74. Diane Orentlicher, in particular, is identified with this position and has argued eloquently in favor of prosecution as a tool for reestablishing the rule of law. Orentlicher, "Settling Accounts," 2547–49; Cherif M. Bassiouni and Edward M. Wise, *Aut Dedere, Aut Judicare: The Duty to Extradite or Prosecute in International Law* (Dordrecht: M. Nijhoff, 1995), 20–25. The reader should note, however, that Orentlicher advocates a duty to *punish;* the *aut dedere aut judicare* principle set out by Bassiouni is slightly different, being to prosecute *or* extradite. Wise and Bassiouni are not completely in agreement in their treatise on the subject, Bassiouni arguing that the principle is not only customary, but a *jus cogens* norm; Wise was skeptical as regards either proposition.

75. David Wippman, "Atrocities, Deterrence, and the Limits of International Justice," *Fordham International Law Journal* 23 (1999): 473.

76. José Alvarez, "Crimes of State/Crimes of Hate: Lessons from Rwanda," *Yale Journal of International Law* 24 (1999): 385. Alvarez is particularly critical of primacy jurisdiction whereby the ICTR can require defendants to be turned over to it. He suggests that "bottom-up" solutions may be the most appropriate.

77. Farer, "Restraining the Barbarians," 94–98.

78. Bradley, "In Search for Justice."

79. Domb, "Treatment of War Crimes," 256–57.

80. Protocol Additional to the Geneva Conventions of August 12, 1949, and Relating to the Protection of Victims of International Armed Conflicts, June 8, 1977, 1125 U.N.T.S. 3.

81. Domb, "Treatment of War Crimes," 261; Michael Bothe, "War-Crimes in Non-International Armed Conflicts," *Israel Yearbook of Human Rights* 24 (1994): 241.

82. There are two related yet distinct issues raised by the question of amnesties. First, whether states have a duty to punish and prosecute (or extradite) those who commit crimes falling under universal jurisdiction. Second, even if no such duty to punish exists, whether international law recognizes the legality of amnesties for such offenses. The two questions are often conflated, but they are distinct. One can answer the first question in the negative, for example, but still recognize that the absence of an affirmative obligation to prosecute does not permit states carte blanche in their reaction to the commission of mass atrocities. On the other hand, an affirmative duty to prosecute or extradite would appear to rule out the legality of amnesties.

83. Scholars are even divided as to this question, however. For the view that the duty imposed by the Geneva Conventions to prosecute or extradite offenders under the laws of war is part of customary international law, see Domb, "Treatment of War Crimes," 263. Meron argues that every state has a duty to try or extradite those guilty of grave breaches and has "the right, although probably not the duty, to prosecute [other] serious violations of the Geneva Conventions." Meron, "Is International Law Moving towards Criminalization?," 23. On the other hand, states have generally not complied with this obligation, thereby undermining its claim as custom. Cassese, "Current Trends," 5; Bassiouni and Wise, *Aut Dedere*, 44–46. Orentlicher takes no position on whether the Geneva Conventions impose a duty to punish that would prohibit amnesties. Orentlicher, "Settling Accounts," 2562 n. 100.

84. Domb, "Treatment of War Crimes," 266–67.

85. Protocol Additional to the Geneva Conventions of August 12, 1949, and Relating to the Protection of Victims of Non-International Armed Conflicts, June 8, 1977, art. 6(5), 1125 U.N.T.S. 609, 614 (hereinafter Protocol II).

86. Roht-Arriaza, *Impunity and Human Rights*, 340.

87. Case No. 4895/96 (South African Cape Provincial Div. Supreme Ct., May 9, 1996), quoted in Sarkin, "Trials and Tribulations," 626–28.

88. Azanian Peoples Organisation (AZAPO) v. The President of the Republic of South Africa, 1996 (4) S.A.L.R. 671, para. 30 (South African Const. Ct.).

89. Dugard, "Reconciliation and Justice," 302.

90. Bothe, "War-Crimes," 248 (arguing that principles of state responsibility may require prosecution). Nonetheless, while one may argue that the distinction between international and noninternational armed conflict is disappearing, it has not done so yet. Roht-Arriaza, *Impunity and Human Rights*, 339.

91. Orentlicher, "Settling Accounts."

92. Article 3 of the Genocide Convention provides that "genocide . . . is a crime under international law which they undertake to prevent and to punish." The convention is not based on a principle of universal jurisdiction but of territorial jurisdiction—

that is, pursuant to Article 6 of the convention, those charged with genocide or similar acts "shall be tried by a competent tribunal of the State in the territory of which the act was committed, or by [an international penal tribunal]." Convention on the Prevention and Punishment of the Crime of Genocide, adopted December 9, 1948, G.A. Res. 260A (II), 78 U.N.T.S. 227, entered into force January 12, 1951. Similarly, Article 4 of the Torture Convention, supra note 20, requires states parties to "ensure that all acts of torture are offences under [their] criminal law," and Article 7 requires them to either extradite or prosecute alleged torturers. Convention against Torture or Other Cruel, Inhuman, or Degrading Treatment or Punishment, G.A. Res. 39/46, 39 U.N. GAOR Supp. (No. 51) at 197, U.N. Doc. A/39/51 (1984).

93. Naomi Roht-Arrizia, "Sources in International Treaties of an Obligation to Investigate, Prosecute, and Provide Redress," 28.

94. Ibid., 29–32. The leading case is *Velásquez Rodríguez*, Inter-Am. Ct.H.R. (Ser. C) No. 4 (1988) (July 29, 1988). *Velásquez* has been followed by the Inter-American Human Rights commission to find that Chile's amnesty laws violated the right to judicial protection in the convention as well as the state's duty to "prevent, investigate and punish" any violations of the rights found in the convention. Garay Hermosilla et al. v. Chile, Inter-Am.C.H.R., Report No. 36/96, para. 73 (October 15, 1996).

95. In the case of *X and Y v. The Netherlands*, European Court of Human Rights, para. 27 (February 27, 1985) (holding that the Netherlands was required to adopt criminal-law provisions to remedy sexual abuse of a mentally handicapped individual living in a home for mentally handicapped children because "the protection afforded by the civil law in [this] case is . . . insufficient. This is a case where fundamental values and essential aspects of private life are at stake. Effective deterrence is indispensable in this area and it can be achieved only by criminal-law provisions.")

96. But see Orentlicher, "Settling Accounts," 2568–81; Geoffrey Robertson, *Crimes against Humanity: The Struggle for Global Justice* (New York: New Press, 2000), 248–53.

97. Roht-Arriaza notes that although some lower courts have been willing to strike down amnesties, or not to apply them in particular cases, courts in Chile, El Salvador, Guatemala, Peru, and South Africa have all ultimately sustained the validity of national amnesties, under international law, their own constitutions, or some combination of both theories. Roht-Arriaza and Gibson, "Developing Jurisprudence"; Schey, "Addressing Abuses," 341–42.

98. Dugard, "Reconciliation and Justice," 279. While noting several flaws of the South African process, Dugard suggests that it complies with international law by requiring that wrongdoers be held accountable by combining a truth commission, conditional amnesties, and criminal prosecutions that were politically feasible. Ibid., 307.

99. Even if amnesties are not "illegal" under international law per se, continuous objection to them from the international community, some international courts, and the human rights community has tended over time to reduce the scope of the amnesties themselves. One study found that with the exception of one country, "the trend has been from broader to more tailored, from sweeping to qualified, from laws with no reference to international law to those which explicitly try to stay within its strictures." Roht-Arriaza, *Impunity and Human Rights*, 884.

100. *Rome Statute of the International Criminal Court*, art. 24, United Nations Diplomatic Conference of Plenipotentiaries on the Establishment of an International Criminal Court, July 17, 1998, Annex II, U.N. Doc. A/CONF.183/9 (1998) (hereinafter *1998 Rome Statute*).

101. Ibid., art. 27.

102. Ibid., art. 29.

103. For a good discussion of some of the issues raised by the statute, see Scharf, 523–25.

104. 1998 *Rome Statute,* art. 53(1)(c). The delegates were largely unable to achieve consensus on the issues of pardons, commutations, and amnesties. See John T. Holmes, "The Principle of Complementarity," in *The International Criminal Court: The Making of the Rome Statute,* ed. Roy S. Lee (The Hague: Kluwer Law International, 1999).

105. According to the Princeton Principles, terrorism, which is not the subject of this essay, is not a crime of universal jurisdiction. See Principle 2(1) in "The Princeton Principles on Universal Jurisdiction," this volume. However, Security Council Resolution 1373 (September 28, 2001), which "decides" that every state must punish and prevent terrorism, suggests that it is the council's belief that this crime is now a crime for which universal jurisdiction exists and for which a duty to punish is present. Therefore, in the council's view, presumably any amnesties granted to terrorists would be illegal.

106. Compare Thomas M. Franck, *Fairness in International Law and Institutions,* 16 (Oxford: Clarendon Press, 1995).

107. Goldstone, *For Humanity,* 122. Justice Goldstone would leave this to the discretion of the prosecutor. Another alternative would be to formulate principles capable of judicial application.

108. Laurent Bijard, "Can Justice Be Done? Massacred: 1,000,000, Tried: 0," *World Press Review,* June 1996, 7 (quoting Rwandan lawyer Frederic Mutagwera), cited in Bradley, "In Search for Justice," 139.

109. Minow, *Between Vengeance and Forgiveness.*

110. In addition to the constitutional challenges brought against the amnesty laws, the families of many of those who were tortured and killed have objected to amnesty proceedings for the perpetrators of those who victimized their loved ones. Dugard, "Reconciliation and Justice," 301.

111. Others go further and label them as morally unjust. Kent Greenawalt, "Amnesty's Justice," in Rotberg and Thompson, eds., *Truth v. Justice,* 189.

112. Dugard, "Reconciliation and Justice."

113. Belatedly recognizing that fact, Sankoh and his followers are likely to be defendants before a new ad hoc tribunal currently being formed under the aegis of the Security Council. Security Council Resolution 1315, dated August 14, 2000, provides for the establishment of an "independent special court" with jurisdiction over persons who bore the greatest responsibility for the commission of crimes against humanity, war crimes, and other serious violations of international law as well as crimes under relevant Sierra Leonean law committed within the territory of Sierra Leone. The resolution specifically rejects amnesty for the perpetrators of such crimes in spite of the provisions of the Lomé Agreement, negotiated with Sankoh in 1999 to attempt to settle the conflict last year, that provide for amnesty, on the basis that the secretary-general of the United Nations appended to his signature of the agreement a statement that the United Nations holds the understanding that the amnesty provisions of the agreement would not apply to the international crime of genocide, crimes against humanity, war crimes, and other serious violations of international humanitarian law. S.C. Res. 1315 (2000), U.N. Doc. S/Res/1315 (2000), to be issued in U.N. SCOR, 55th Year, Resolutions and Decisions 2000.

114. For a fine discussion of the Dayton negotiations, see Bass, *Stay the Hand,* 237–46. As Bass notes, although it was possibly true that the Dayton accords would not have been possible without Milosevic's assistance, they also "would not have been necessary" in the first place. Ibid., 246.

115. Remarks of Paul Williams, at *The International Criminal Court and American National Security,* given at American University Washington College of Law, Thursday, September 14, 2000. (As further evidence of the play of realpolitik in

the former Yugoslavia, it was recently reported that the United States was offering immunity to Milosevic in return for his relinquishing power in the former Yugoslavia). Steven Erlanger, "U.S. Seeks Way out for Milosevic," *International Herald Tribune,* June 19, 2000, 1.

116. The United States government took this position in the Philippines quite recently.

117. The U.S. Department of State website on counterterrorism sets out the basic policy of the U.S. government with respect to terrorists: "First, make no concessions to terrorists, and strike no deals; Second, bring terrorists to justice for their crimes." www.state.gov/s/ct/.

118. See Dan M. Kahan, "The Secret Ambition of Deterrence," *Harvard Law Review* 113 (1999): 416 and n. 6 (noting that empirically, deterrence claims in the United States are speculative).

119. If they concede that empirical claims for deterrence in national legal systems are also speculative, but do not think that national criminal justice systems should be abandoned, the question is why they perceive the importance of deterrence in justifying the existence of an international system of criminal justice to be different.

120. Farer, "Restraining the Barbarians," 92.

121. Aryeh Neier, "What Should Be Done about the Guilty," *New York Review of Books,* February 1, 1990, 35.

122. Minow, *Between Vengeance and Forgiveness,* 146.

123. Osiel, "Why Prosecute," 123 (quoting Judith Shklar. *Legalism: Law, Morals, and Political Trials* [Cambridge: Harvard University Press, 1964], 167).

124. Ibid., 127–28.

125. A different branch of this critique expresses the view that forgiveness may be more important to healing a society, a view often expressed by feminist writers urging reevaluation of the values underlying the criminal justice system (both domestically and internationally). See Dressler, "Hating Criminals"; Hilary Charlesworth and Christine Chinkin, "The Gender of Jus Cogens," *Human Rights Quarterly* 15 (1993): 63.

126. Ruti Teitel, "Transitional Jurisprudence: The Role of Law in Political Transformation," *Yale Law Journal* 105 (1997): 2028.

127. Meron, "Is International Law Moving towards Criminalization?," 30–31.

128. Dugard, "Reconciliation and Justice," 310.

129. Concerns were noted in the following areas: "location of the ICTY; judicial appointments; criticisms by international organizations of the Bosnian legal system; a misunderstanding of the hybrid nature of ICTY judicial procedures; the inherently political nature of a United Nations-sponsored ad hoc tribunal; and the lack of communication between Bosnian and Tribunal legal professionals." *Justice, Accountability, and Reconstruction: An Interview Study of Bosnian Judges and Prosecutors,* 41 (a joint project of the Human Rights Center; International Human Rights Law Clinic, University of California, Berkeley; and the Centre for Human Rights, University of Sarajevo, May 2000).

130. Ibid., 48–51.

131. Ibid., 47.

132. The question how national and international fora should treat international amnesties negotiated in peace treaties or dictated by Security Council Resolution is beyond the scope of this essay. Although there is some contention on this point, it is currently the practice of the United Nations to reject amnesty for crimes against humanity and genocide (and presumably serious violations of international humanitarian law as well). Moreover, two treaties codified in the Rome Statute, the Genocide Convention, and the Grave Breaches provisions of the Geneva Conventions, arguably prohibit amnesties by their requirement that offenders must be punished.

Thus, presumably this problem will not surface extensively. Nevertheless, particularly if immunity is granted pursuant to a treaty to which the forum state is not a party, it is difficult to see why it should or would apply. If the immunity is granted pursuant to a Security Council Resolution, however, the question becomes more difficult, particularly if the council is acting pursuant to its powers under Chapter 7. With respect to the International Criminal Court, Article 16 of the statute appears to specify the only mechanism by which the council may stop a prosecution from proceeding by requiring an affirmative vote from the council to do so. It is unclear how carefully the ICC would treat an amnesty imposed pursuant to Security Council Resolution, although the ICC would presumably think hard before disregarding it out of hand. See Scharf, "The Amnesty Exception," 522–24. I have alluded to this problem as regards terrorism earlier. See note 102 above.

133. Case Concerning the S.S. Lotus (Fr. v. Tur.), 1927 P.C.I.J., Ser. A, No. 10.

134. William S. Dodge, *Breaking the Public Law Taboo,* 43 Harv. Int'l L.J. 161 (2002), quoting Andreas Lowenfeld, *Public Law in the International Arena: Conflict of Laws, International Law, and Some Suggestions for their Interaction,* 163; *Recueil Des Cours* 311, 322–26 (1979–II).

135. This may be less true, however, in the case of conditional amnesties, where the defendant has voluntarily come forward and placed him or herself in jeopardy of prosecution by confessing the crime. In this case the better rule may be that the forum state should examine the particular proceeding to see if the principle of *ne bis in idem* should attach and immunize the particular defendant from subsequent prosecutions. Again, the issue arises whether the forum uses its own rules or an international rule of *ne bis in idem.* The practical response of most fora will most likely be to use some combination of the two, due to the fact that the international law on the subject is not well codified and the need to balance the competing interests involved.

136. As between the state of nationality and the territorial state, if the two were to differ, it would seem logical to look first to the territorial state, the application of the criminal law generally being territorial in nature.

137. Bassiouni, "The Normative Framework of International Humanitarian Law: Overlaps, Gaps, and Ambiguities," 201–2.

138. 1 U.N. GAOR (Part II) at 188, U.N. Doc. A/61/Add.1 (1946).

139. There are two treaties on the subject, but they have not been widely adopted. United Nations Convention on the Nonapplicability of Statutory Limitations to War Crimes and Crimes against Humanity, November 26, 1968, 754 U.N.T.S. 75. The convention came into force on November 11, 1970, and according to the United Nations's website, currently has only ten signatories and forty-four parties. http:// untreaty.un.org/. Shortly thereafter, the Council of Europe adopted a similar Convention. European Convention on the Nonapplicability of Statutory Limitation to Crimes against Humanity and War Crimes, January 25, 1974, E.T.S. No. 82, reprinted in 13 I.L.M. 540 (1974). The European Convention was ratified by only two states and never entered into force. Interestingly, both conventions were largely a response to German statutes of limitation that would have caused Nazi crimes to prescribe and prevented prosecution. This result, which was apparently perceived as desirable in Germany, was viewed as unacceptable by many other countries. See Leila Sadat Wexler, "The Interpretation of the Nuremberg Principles by the French Court of Cassation: From Touvier to Barbie and Back Again," *Columbia Journal of Transnational Law* 32 (1994): 318–21.

140. *1998 Rome Statute,* art. 29 ("The crimes within the jurisdiction of the Court shall not be subject to any statute of limitations").

141. Case Concerning the Arrest Warrant of April 11, 2000 (Congo v. Belgium), ICJ, February 14, 2002, 41 I.L.M. 536 (2002).

142. Pardons and conditional amnesties may be distinguishable, for both involve the use of judicial or quasi-judicial proceedings and involve particularized consideration of a defendant's guilt or innocence in a particular case. Assuming the proceedings are not a sham, even where amnesties are generally prohibited, pardons and conditional amnesties may be acceptable, or even required by the legality principle, if the defendant has been "put in jeopardy" of criminal proceedings.

143. As Anne-Marie Slaughter notes in her essay in this volume, "pure" cases of universal jurisdiction appear to be quite rare. Rather, there generally appears to be some connection between the defendant and the forum state, in most instances, again suggesting the appropriateness of the forum applying its law to the question.

144. 304 U.S. 64 (1938).

145. Guaranty Trust Co. v. York, 326 U.S. 99 (1945).

146. Byrd v. Blue Ridge Rural Electric Cooperative, 356 U.S. 525 (1958).

147. Hanna v. Plumer, 380 U.S. 460 (1965).

148. Paul Craig and Gráinne de Burca, *EU Law: Text, Cases, and Materials,* 214–15 (Oxford: Oxford University Press, 1998).

149. Farer, "Restraining the Barbarians," 115–16.

Chapter 11. The Future of Universal Jurisdiction in the New Architecture of Transnational Justice

I am grateful to M. Gregg Bloche, John Cerone, Jerry Fowler, Stephen Macedo, and an anonymous reviewer for valuable insights and suggestions. My appreciation of the issues addressed in this essay was also enriched by Martha Minow's insightful commentary on an earlier draft presented at a conference at Princeton University in November 2000. I am indebted to Helen Harnett, Kathlyn Mackovjak, Jason Maddux, William Martin, and J. Richard Hamilton for excellent research assistance, and to Robert Starner for skillful assistance in producing the manuscript.

1. International law sets limits on when a state may apply and enforce its own law in respect of persons and conduct, recognizing five broad types of legitimate jurisdiction. While four of these are based upon the links between a state and the conduct it seeks to regulate, universal jurisdiction allows every state to punish certain conduct, wherever committed and regardless of the nationality of the alleged perpetrator or victim. This notion is captured in Principle 1(1) of the Princeton Principles on Universal Jurisdiction: "For purposes of these Principles, universal jurisdiction is criminal jurisdiction based solely on the nature of the crime, without regard to where the crime was committed, the nationality of the alleged or convicted perpetrator, the nationality of the victim, or any other connection to the state exercising such jurisdiction." "The Princeton Principles on Universal Jurisdiction," this volume.

2. A rare example of U.S. legislation providing for criminal prosecution based upon universal jurisdiction is codified at 18 U.S.C. § 2340A. This statute was enacted to bring United States law into conformity with the Convention against Torture and Other Cruel, Inhuman or Degrading Treatment or Punishment, concluded at New York, Dec. 10, 1984; entered into force, June 26, 1987; 1465 U.N.T.S. 85, which the United States ratified in 1994.

3. Recent years have seen a proliferation of new projects and organizations devoted to these challenges. The Geneva-based International Committee of the Red Cross has been working to identify gaps in domestic law that prevent national courts from prosecuting suspected perpetrators of international crimes and to assist governments in drafting legislation enabling their courts to assert universal jurisdiction. Other projects track potential targets of prosecution, civil suit, exclusion or

deportation. For example, the Center for Justice and Accountability, an international human rights legal services organization launched in 1998 (with initial support from Amnesty International USA and the United Nations Voluntary Fund for Victims of Torture), seeks to close off the United States as a safe haven for torturers and other violators of human rights through prosecution, civil lawsuits, visa revocation, exclusion and removal of human rights violators, and by providing witnesses and evidence to federal officials, international tribunals, and other entities responsible for prosecuting perpetrators of human rights violations.

4. This essay focuses on universal jurisdiction for crimes entailing serious violations of international humanitarian law, notably genocide, other crimes against humanity, and serious war crimes—crimes for which I use the shorthand terms "human rights crimes" and "serious violations of international humanitarian law." A broader approach is reflected in Principle 2(1) of the Princeton Principles on Universal Jurisdiction, which provides: "For purposes of these Principles, serious crimes under international law [subject to universal jurisdiction] include: (1) piracy; (2) slavery; (3) war crimes; (4) crimes against peace; (5) crimes against humanity; (6) genocide; and (7) torture." "The Princeton Principles on Universal Jurisdiction," this volume.

5. For a fuller treatment of this issue, see the contribution to this volume by Leila Nadya Sadat, "Universal Jurisdiction, National Amnesties, and Truth Commissions: Reconciling the Irreconcilable."

6. It is generally thought that universal jurisdiction exists over conduct defined as a crime under customary international law. See The Prosecutor v. Duško Tadić, Decision on the Defence Motion for Interlocutory Appeal on Jurisdiction, para. 62, Case. No. IT-94-1-AR72, October 2, 1995 (observing that universal jurisdiction is "nowadays acknowledged in the case of international crimes"). Since customary international law is established in part by state practice, the trend toward increased prosecution of certain crimes bolsters the claim that those crimes are or may eventually become subject to universal jurisdiction.

7. Charter of the International Military Tribunal, concluded at London, August 8, 1945; entered into force, August 8, 1945; 82 U.N.T.S. 280.

8. Charter of the International Military Tribunal for the Far East, proclaimed at Tokyo, January 19, 1946, and amended April 26, 1946; T.I.A.S. No. 1589, 4 Bevans 20. Although the Tokyo tribunal was established by proclamation of a U.S. commander, its judges were drawn from eleven countries. Also, the American chief prosecutor was assisted by ten associate prosecutors, each possessing the nationality of a different country.

9. S.C. Res. 827 (1993).

10. S.C. Res. 955 (1994).

11. Rome Statute of the International Criminal Court, U.N. Doc. A/CONF.183/9 (1998), as corrected by the *procés-verbaux* of November 10, 1998, and July 12, 1999, reprinted in 39 I.L.M. 999 (1998) (hereinafter Rome Statute).

12. The Rome Statute entered into force in accordance with the terms of Article 126(1), which provides for the statute's entry into force after sixty states have formally adhered to it. As of February 10, 2003, eighty-nine states had become parties to the Rome Statute.

13. See, e.g., Yoram Dinstein, "The Universality Principle and War Crimes," in *The Law of Armed Conflict: Into the Next Millennium,* ed. Michael N. Schmitt and Leslie C. Green (Newport: Naval War College, 1998): 27 (idea of pooled universal jurisdiction is the "best rationalization" for the UN Security Council's establishment of the ICTY).

14. See Madeleine Morris, "High Crimes and Misconceptions: The ICC and Non-Party States," *Law and Contemporary Problems* 64 (2001): 26–52. The basic claim that states can jointly exercise jurisdiction they could have exercised singly finds support

in the judgment of the IMT. The Nuremberg tribunal made plain that its jurisdiction derived at least in part from the combined authority of the four states that signed its charter, which were then operating as occupation powers in Germany:

> The jurisdiction of the Tribunal is defined in the . . . Charter . . .
>
> The making of the Charter was the exercise of the sovereign legislative power by the countries to which the German Reich unconditionally surrendered; and the undoubted right of these countries to legislate for the occupied territories has been recognized by the civilized world.
>
> The Signatory Powers created this Tribunal, defined the law it was to administer, and made regulations for the proper conduct of the trial. *In doing so, they have done together what any one of them might have done singly;* for it is not to be doubted that any nation has the right thus to set up special courts to administer law.

Nazi Conspiracy and Aggression: Opinion and Judgment, at 46 (October 1, 1946), reprinted by United States Government Printing Office (1947) (emphasis added). Somewhat less clear is what basis of jurisdiction the IMT had in mind when it asserted that the Allied Powers could do jointly what each could have done alone. For discussion of various possibilities, see Morris, "High Crimes and Misconceptions"; Diane F. Orentlicher, "Politics by Other Means: The Law of the International Criminal Court," *Cornell Journal of International Law* 32 (1999): 493 n.19; Kenneth C. Randall, "Universal Jurisdiction under International Law," *Texas Law Review* 66 (1988): 806; Demjanjuk v. Petrovsky, 776 F.2d 571, 582 (6th Cir. 1985). Outside the context of international tribunals, states have transferred criminal jurisdiction to other countries. See Ethan A. Nadelmann, "The Role of the United States in the International Enforcement of Criminal Law," *Harvard International Law Journal* 31 (1990): 64, 69.

15. Some commentators have assumed, for example, that the ad hoc tribunals established by the UN Security Council in the 1990s derive their authority from Chapter VII of the UN Charter rather than from general principles of international law delimiting when and how judicial power may be exercised. *Cf.* W. J. Fenrick, "Some International Law Problems Related to Prosecutions before the International Criminal Tribunal for the Former Yugoslavia," *Duke Journal of Comparative and International Law* 6 (1995): 104 (asserting that the ICTY "exercises jurisdiction on the basis of internationality and not universality").

16. Acceptance for these purposes can be expressed either by becoming a party to the Rome Statute or by consenting to the ICC's jurisdiction in respect of the crime in question. See Rome Statute, art. 12. The consent requirements set forth in Article 12 of the Rome Statute do not have to be satisfied if the court's jurisdiction is triggered by a referral from the UN Security Council acting under Chapter VII of the UN Charter. Except as otherwise indicated, my analysis here addresses only situations in which jurisdiction is not triggered by such a referral.

17. Responding to the U.S. claim that the Rome Statute breaches basic tenets of treaty law by allowing the ICC to try nationals of nonparty states, Philippe Kirsch, who served as chairman of the Diplomatic Conference that adopted the Rome Statute, has written: "This does not bind states that are not parties to the Statute. It simply confirms the recognized principle that individuals are subject to the substantive and procedural criminal laws applicable in the territories to which they travel, including laws arising from treaty obligations." Philippe Kirsch, "The Rome Conference on the International Criminal Court: A Comment," *ASIL Newsletter* (Washington, D.C.: American Society of International Law, November–December 1998): 1, 8.

18. Leila Nadya Sadat and S. Richard Carden, "The New International Criminal Court: An Uneasy Revolution," *Georgetown Law Journal* 88 (2000): 407 (emphasis in original; footnotes omitted). See also ibid., 412 (asserting that ICC jurisdiction is premised "[f]irst, and foremost" on the principle of universality).

19. Ibid., 413.

20. Alternatively, the court's jurisdiction may be seen as predicated on a model of "universality minus." That is, when the state-consent regime applies, it serves to cut back the jurisdiction the ICC could otherwise exercise pursuant to the principle of universality.

21. The German proposal would have enabled the ICC to exercise jurisdiction over genocide, crimes against humanity, and war crimes without any preconditions involving state consent. See Jerry Fowler, "Not Fade Away: The International Criminal Court and the State of Sovereignty," *San Diego International Law Journal* 2 (2001): 137. The proposal put forth by South Korea would have enabled the ICC to assert jurisdiction when consent is provided by at least one of four states, including the state where a suspect is apprehended. See Philippe Kirsch and John T. Holmes, "The Rome Conference on an International Criminal Court: The Negotiating Process," *American Journal of International Law* 93 (1999): 9. In the view of some writers, only the German proposal would have given the court universal jurisdiction. See, e.g., Elizabeth Wilmshurst, "Jurisdiction of the Court," in *The International Criminal Court: The Making of the Rome Statute—Issues, Negotiations, Results,* ed. Roy S. Lee (The Hague: Kluwer Law International, 1999): 132. Yet by authorizing the ICC to exercise jurisdiction with the consent of the state that has custody of a suspect, the South Korean proposal also seemed to rely upon the principle of universality. Universal jurisdiction is normally exercised by states whose principal link to the crime in question is the presence of the alleged perpetrator.

22. See note 17 above (quoting views of the chairman of the Rome Conference).

23. This is affirmed in the preamble and Article 1 of the Rome Statute.

24. A state exercises nationality jurisdiction when it applies its law to the conduct of its nationals, even when their conduct occurs abroad.

25. As noted, a proposal put forth by Germany was generally seen as relying upon the principle of universality, while a proposal put forth by South Korea also relied in part on this principle. See note 21 above. Although the German proposal did not gain traction, the South Korean approach had substantial support. During the final week of negotiations in Rome, a majority of states expressed support for the South Korean proposal. That the proposed approach did not materialize in the Rome Statute is therefore likely attributable to the opposition of a small but determined group of countries, led by the United States.

26. This points up an issue that is sure to arise as states increasingly exercise universal jurisdiction. It is by no means unusual for national penal law to adopt a broader definition of international crimes than has been accepted internationally. In Spain, for example, the crime of genocide is apparently defined more broadly than its authoritative definition in the Convention on the Prevention and Punishment of the Crime of Genocide, done at New York, Dec. 9, 1948; entered into force, Jan. 12, 1951; 78 U.N.T.S. 277. This is perfectly appropriate when the conduct at issue occurs on Spanish soil. But when Spanish justice reaches conduct half a world away, Spain cannot rely on the criminalization of genocide *under and as defined in international law* in support of its jurisdiction. For further discussion of this issue, see Diane F. Orentlicher, "The Role of Domestic Courts and Judges in the Implementation and Enforcement of International Humanitarian Law" (United States Institute of Peace, forthcoming).

27. Rome Statute, art. 17(1)(a).

28. Ibid., art. 1.

29. Seth Mydans, "U.N. Ends Cambodia Talks on Trials for Khmer Rouge," *New York Times,* February 9, 2002.

30. G.A. Res. 57/228, para. 1 (2002); "UN News Centre Report: UN, Cambodia Wrap Up Exploratory Talks on Special Court for Khmer Rouge," January 14, 2003.

31. Evelyn Leopold, "Annan Opens Door for Talks on Khmer Rouge Trials," Reuters, August 21, 2002.

32. The model envisaged for Cambodia apparently inspired the hybrid courts now operating in East Timor, which I examine below. See Susannah Linton, "Rising from the Ashes: The Creation of a Viable Criminal Justice System in East Timor," *Melbourne University Law Review* 23 (2001): 138, 146.

33. This action was preceded by the adoption of a resolution by the UN Commission on Human Rights in April 1997, calling on the secretary-general to "examine any request by Cambodia for assistance in responding to past serious violations of Cambodian and international law as a means of addressing the issue of individual accountability." That resolution was apparently adopted in response to the initiative of Ambassador Thomas Hammarberg, then serving as the special representative of the secretary-general on human rights in Cambodia. See Stephen Heder with Brian Tittemore, *Seven Candidates for Prosecution: Accountability for the Crimes of the Khmer Rouge* (Washington, D.C.: War Crimes Research Office of American University and the Coalition for International Justice, 2001).

34. Aware that Canadian legislation provided for universal jurisdiction over crimes against humanity, the U.S. government pressed Canadian authorities to seek Pol Pot's extradition. See Anthony DePalma, "Canadians Surprised by Proposal to Extradite Pol Pot," *New York Times,* June 24, 1997. Canada declined, explaining that its legislation applied only when a suspect was already in Canada. Canadian officials may also have been offended by what they viewed as heavy-handed U.S. pressure. Robert Fife and David Gamble, "Canada Scorns U.S. on Pol Pot," *Toronto Sun,* June 24, 1997. A plan devised by the U.S. government to apprehend Pol Pot was aborted in April 1998 after news of the plan was published in the *New York Times;* Pol Pot died six days after the article ran. See Konstantin Richter, "Losing Pol Pot," *Columbia Journalism Review* (July–August 1998): 48–50.

35. Not long after the letter from Cambodia's two co–prime ministers was sent to the UN secretary-general, then second co–prime minister Hun Sen ousted the first prime minister. The coup fundamentally altered the political environment surrounding the question of prosecutions.

36. The Group of Experts presented its report to Secretary-General Kofi Annan on February 22, 1999. See Report of the Group of Experts for Cambodia established pursuant to General Assembly Resolution 52/135 (1999), U.N. Doc. A/53/850, S/1999/231, Annex (March 16, 1999). The Cambodian government rejected its central recommendations by letter dated March 3, 1999.

37. Hun Sen has been the sole prime minister of Cambodia since ousting his co–prime minister in early July 1997.

38. The compromise formulation was approved by Hun Sen in a meeting in April 2000 with a U.S. intermediary, Sen. John F. Kerry (D–Mass.). See Seth Mydans, "Cambodia Agrees to Tribunal Setup for Khmer Rouge Trials," *New York Times,* April 30, 2000; Colum Lynch, "U.N., Cambodia Agree on Court for Khmer Rouge Trials," *Washington Post,* May 25, 2000.

39. Available in English at www.derechos.org/human-rights/seasia/doc/krlaw.html (hereinafter "Law on Extraordinary Chambers").

40. Law on Extraordinary Chambers, art. 16.

41. Ibid., art. 23.

42. Ibid., art. 3.

43. Ibid., arts. 10–11. But see ibid., art. 46 (providing for appointment of Cambodians

as a last resort "in the event any foreign judges or foreign investigating judges or foreign prosecutors fail or refuse to participate in the Extraordinary Chambers").

44. Ibid., art. 14. See also ibid., art. 23 (imposing similar voting requirements for decisions of pretrial chambers).

45. Ibid., arts. 4–8.

46. Ibid., art. 3

47. Press Briefing by United Nations Legal Counsel, February 8, 2000.

48. Ibid.

49. See ibid.; see also Press Briefing by Under-Secretary-General for Legal Affairs and United Nations Legal Counsel, July 13, 2000.

50. Hans Corell, "No Justice for Victims of the Khmer Rouge," *International Herald Tribune,* June 19, 2002. UN officials also cited specific features of the August 2002 Cambodian legislation, such as the law's failure to ensure that individuals previously granted amnesty could be tried before the Extraordinary Chambers, as a factor in their decision. See Colum Lynch, "U.N. Ends Negotiations on Khmer Rouge Trials; Cambodians Accused of Rejecting Key Points," *Washington Post,* February 9, 2002. The UN's decision to withdraw from negotiations drew mixed responses. Human Rights Watch and Amnesty International and some Cambodian activists supported the organization's decision, arguing that participating in flawed proceedings would tarnish the UN and do a disservice to Cambodians. See Amnesty International, "Cambodia: Flawed Trials in No One's Best Interests," AI Index: ASA 23/001/2002, February 11, 2002; Colum Lynch, "U.N. Ends Negotiations on Khmer Rouge Trials; Cambodians Accused of Rejecting Key Points," *Washington Post,* February 9, 2002 (quoting Human Rights Watch staff member saying, "We strongly support the U.N.'s decision to drop the negotiations"). Others criticized the decision, arguing that Cambodians' best hope for justice lies in UN participation in a court constituted to try those most responsible for Khmer Rouge crimes. See, e.g., Youk Chhang, "Cambodia Won't Easily Find Justice on Its Own," *New York Times,* February 14, 2002. Various governments and the European Union encouraged the UN to resume negotiations. See "EU urges UN rethink on Cambodia," *BBC News,* February 21, 2002; Colum Lynch, "U.N. Ends Negotiations on Khmer Rouge Trials; Cambodians Accused of Rejecting Key Points," *Washington Post,* February 9, 2002 (reporting that U.S. and French officials said they hoped the UN's February 2002 decision would not end negotiations aimed at establishing a court to try Khmer Rouge atrocities).

51. The secretary-general characterized the revised agreement as "a considerable improvement over the draft that had been under discussion during his previous negotiations with the Government of Cambodia." Report of the Secretary-General on Khmer Rouge trials, UN Doc A/57/769, Summary (2003). Specific improvements cited by the secretary-general include explicit recognition of the revised UN-Cambodia agreement as an international treaty (see ibid., para. 25), which means that the agreement would take precedence over any inconsistent Cambodian legislation; streamlining the Extraordinary Chambers from the three-tier system contemplated previously to a two-tier structure (see ibid., paras. 17 and 26); and enhanced provision for compliance with international standards of justice (see ibid., para. 27). The secretary-general failed, however, to convince the Cambodian government that a majority of judges should be international personnel. See ibid., para. 29. He also failed to persuade the Cambodian government to accept proposals relating to the structure and decision-making processes of the co-prosecutors and investigating judges. See ibid., paras. 16, 17, 20, 22, and 23.

52. Ibid., Summary. Six weeks after the UN secretary-general submitted his report, the General Assembly approved the draft agreement. Cambodian authorities indicated that Cambodia would be unable to ratify the new text until after general elections scheduled for late July 2003. Alan Boyd, "Cambodian's Legal System on Trial," *Asia Times Online: Southeast Asia,* May 20, 2003.

53. Letter from Ahmad Tejan Kabbah, president of Sierra Leone, to Sec. Gen. Kofi Annan, U.N. Doc. S/2000/786, Annex.

54. The Hon. Solomon E. Berewa, attorney general and minister of justice for the Republic of Sierra Leone, Remarks for Signing Ceremony for Special Court, January 16, 2002.

55. S.C. Res. 1315, preamble; paras. 1 and 2 (2000).

56. Agreement between the United Nations and the Government of Sierra Leone on the Establishment of a Special Court for Sierra Leone, January 16, 2002 (hereinafter "UN–Sierra Leone Agreement"). The Statute of the Special Court is annexed to the agreement and forms an integral part thereof.

57. The Special Court Agreement, 2002, Ratification Act, 2002, Supplement to the Sierra Leone Gazette Vol. 80, No. 2, dated March 7, 2002.

58. Report of the Secretary-General on the Establishment of a Special Court for Sierra Leone, U.N. Doc. S/2000/915, para. 9 (2000).

59. Articles 2 through 4 of the court's statute establish jurisdiction over crimes against humanity, several specified violations of international humanitarian law, and crimes that involve attacking the personnel or property of peacekeeping and humanitarian assistance operations. Article 5 establishes jurisdiction over certain offenses under Sierra Leonean law. The Special Court has jurisdiction only with respect to offenses committed in Sierra Leone since November 30, 1996. See Statute of the Special Court for Sierra Leone, art. 1(1).

60. The bilateral agreement establishing the Special Court provides that it "shall have its seat in Sierra Leone" but "may meet away from its seat if it considers it necessary for the efficient exercise of its functions." The agreement also contemplates the possibility that the court "may be relocated outside Sierra Leone, if circumstances so require." UN–Sierra Leone Agreement, art. 10.

61. See Statute of the Special Court for Sierra Leone, arts. 12(1), 15(3), and 16(3). In April 2002 the secretary-general appointed David Crane, a U.S. national, as prosecutor, and Robin Vincent, a U.K. national, as registrar. See "Pentagon Lawyer Named Prosecutor in Sierra Leone," *Reuters*, April 19, 2002. The two judges nominated by the secretary-general to sit on the three-member trial chamber were Pierre Boutet, a Canadian, and Benjamin Mutanga Itoe, a Cameroonian Supreme Court judge. The secretary-general's nominees to sit on the five-member appeals chamber were Nigerian supreme court justice Emmanuel Ayoola, Gambian supreme court justice Alhaji Hassan B. Jallow, and Kosovo supreme court justice Renate Winter, an Australian national. UN News Centre, "Annan, Sierra Leone Appoint Experienced Judges for Country's Special War Crimes Court," July 25, 2002.

62. See Statute of the Special Court for Sierra Leone, art. 12(1). The government of Sierra Leone appointed former high court justice Bankole Thompson to serve on the three-member trial chamber. It appointed former Sierra Leonean supreme court justice Gelaga King and British barrister Geoffrey Robertson to sit on the five-judge appeals chamber. UN News Centre, "Annan, Sierra Leone Appoint Experienced Judges for Country's Special War Crimes Court," July 25, 2002.

63. See Statute of the Special Court for Sierra Leone, art. 15(4). A Sri Lankan national was nonetheless appointed to serve as deputy prosecutor. Pursuant to an exchange of letters between the United Nations and Sierra Leone, implementing legislation provided that the deputy registrar need not be a Sierra Leonian national.

64. Report of the Secretary-General on the Establishment of a Special Court for Sierra Leone, U.N. Doc. S/2000/915, para. 9 (2000).

65. The Special Court operates alongside national courts of Sierra Leone. The two court systems have concurrent jurisdiction, with the Special Court enjoying primacy when it formally requests a national court of Sierra Leone "to defer to its competence." Statute of the Special Court for Sierra Leone, art. 8(1, 2). The Special

Court's primacy does not extend to courts of states other than those of Sierra Leone. See Report of the Secretary-General on the Establishment of a Special Court for Sierra Leone, U.N. Doc. S/2000/915, para. 10 (2000).

66. See Barbara Crossette, "Cambodians Will Prosecute Khmer Rouge," *New York Times,* May 25, 2000; Seth Mydans, "Cambodian Deputies Back War Crimes Tribunal to Try Khmer Rouge," *New York Times,* January 3, 2001.

67. See note 50 above.

68. Article 281 of the Ethiopian Penal Code criminalizes genocide and crimes against humanity. Although derived from international law, the offenses are defined in the Ethiopian Penal Code somewhat differently than under international law.

69. See, e.g., Human Rights Watch, "Mengistu Haile Mariam: A Human Rights Watch Background Paper," Press Release, November 24, 1999.

70. S.C. Res. 1244 (1999).

71. For example, the presiding judge in a trial involving genocide charges was Swedish, while other members of the judicial panel were Kosovo Albanians. Carlotta Gall, "UN Court Tries Serb in Mass Killing," *New York Times,* December 7, 2000. UN officials have had trouble recruiting local Serbs to serve on these courts. An international prosecutor has explained that foreign nationals dominate the judicial panels because "[l]ocal judges in war crimes cases, which are highly publicized and politicized, can be and are pressured by their community, both implicitly and explicitly. . . . In [Kosovo], the judicial culture and society are not yet ready to handle the war crimes cases without internationals as neutral participants. . . ." Posting by Michael Hartmann to Justwatch-L@LISTSERV.ACSU.BUFFALO.EDU, March 1, 2002.

72. On September 15, 1999, the UN Security Council authorized a peace enforcement operation to restore order in East Timor. S.C. Res. 1264 (1999). The Australian-led mission, known as INTERFET, entered East Timor on September 20, 1999, and operated there until responsibility for administration of the territory was transferred to UNTAET. The latter was established pursuant to S.C. Res. 1272 (1999), which was adopted on October 25, 1999. INTERFET handed over the command of military operations in East Timor to UNTAET on February 28, 2000. See Susannah Linton, "Rising from the Ashes," 132–33.

73. See UNTAET Regulation No. 2000/11, § 10, entered into force March 6, 2000.

74. UNTAET Regulation No. 2000/15 on the Establishment of Panels with Exclusive Jurisdiction over Serious Criminal Offences, § 1, entered into force June 6, 2000.

75. See ibid., § 3.1. See also Susannah Linton, "Cambodia, East Timor, and Sierra Leone: Experiments in International Justice," *Criminal Law Forum* 12 (2001): 206–7 (hereinafter "Experiments in International Justice").

76. Pursuant to UNTAET Regulation No. 2000/15, § 22.1, each panel must include one East Timorese judge and two international judges. The panel that presided over the first case involving charges of crimes against humanity to come to trial before a special panel comprised jurists from Brazil, Burundi, and East Timor. See "Dili District Court Convicts Ten Men of Crimes against Humanity in the Los Palos Case," *Nizkor English Service,* December 10, 2001. Until January 7, 2000, when the first judges, prosecutors, and public defenders were appointed to the District Court of Dili, no East Timorese had served as a judge or prosecutor. See Susannah Linton, "Rising from the Ashes," 133. The new appointees "received no training beyond a week." Ibid., 134. See also Susannah Linton, "Experiments in International Justice," 203. At least initially, the specially constituted prosecution service for serious crimes was "almost exclusively international in composition, with its own totally international investigation unit." Ibid., 204. The Court of Appeal is "also dominated by internationals." Ibid., 205.

77. S.C. Res. 1410 (2002). This resolution establishes UNMISET for an initial period of twelve months (see ibid., para. 1) but contemplates a two-year period of devolution of responsibility from UNMISET to East Timorese authorities. See ibid., para. 8.

78. See Report of the Secretary-General on the United Nations Transitional Administration in East Timor, April 17, 2002, paras. 76–78, U.N. Doc. S/2002/432 (2002).

79. Carlotta Gall, "Serb on Trial for Genocide of Albanians in Kosovo," *New York Times*, December 5, 2000; Carlotta Gall, "UN Court Tries Serb in Mass Killing," *New York Times*, December 7, 2000.

80. R. Jeffrey Smith, "3 Soldiers Convicted in Kosovo Atrocity; Verdict Is First by Military Court," *Washington Post*, December 21, 2000.

81. Rajiv Chandrasekaran, "Prosecutors Name 19 in East Timor Violence Probe," *Washington Post*, September 2, 2000. Eighteen suspects were indicted in January 2002. International Crisis Group Briefing Paper, "Indonesia: The Implications of the Timor Trials" (May 8, 2002): 5. The first three trials of these suspects began in mid-March 2002. As of mid-January 2003, the Indonesian human rights court had acquitted eleven of the eighteen defendants and convicted three. The first verdict was rendered on August 14, 2002. One defendant, the former governor of East Timor, was found guilty of crimes against humanity and sentenced to three years in prison. Five other defendants were acquitted. See Jane Perlez, "Ex-Governor of East Timor Gets Three Years in Army Killings," *New York Times*, August 14, 2002; Matthew Moore with Sophie Douez, Jill Jolliffe, "World Urged to Act after Court Clears Indonesian Officers," *The Age* (Melbourne), August 17, 2002. In late November 2002, another defendant was convicted of two counts of crimes against humanity, but was given the minimum sentence of ten years and has been allowed to remain free pending appeal; three other defendants were acquitted. Human Rights Watch, "Justice Denied for East Timor; Indonesia's Sham Prosecutions, the Need to Strengthen the Trial Process in East Timor, and the Imperative of U.N. Action," December 20, 2002. On December 28, 2002, the Indonesian human rights court rendered its first conviction of an Indonesian military officer in relation to the violence in East Timor and sentenced the defendant to five years' imprisonment. Ellen Nakashima, "First Officer Convicted for E. Timor; Indonesian Lt. Col. Gets 5 Years for Not Stopping Killings," *Washington Post*, December 28, 2002. On March 12, 2003, Brig. Gen Noer Muis, the highest-ranking Indonesian official to be convicted by the human rights court, was sentenced to five years in prison for failing to prevent two deadly attacks against civilians in the 1999 East Timor violence. "Indonesia Sentences General in East Timor Attacks," *New York Times*, March 13, 2003.

82. Agence France-Presse, "East Timor Violence Requires an Accounting, U.N. Official Says," *New York Times*, November 24, 2000.

83. Rajiv Chandrasekaran, "U.N. Names 11 in E. Timor Violence; More War Crime Charges Expected Against Army, Militia Leaders," *Washington Post*, December 12, 2000. Ten defendants were convicted of crimes against humanity one year later. See Judicial System Monitoring Program, "Dili Court Convicts Ten of Crimes against Humanity," December 11, 2001.

84. More senior UN officials have apparently been disinclined to establish such a tribunal. In May 2002, Secretary-General Kofi Annan expressed support for efforts by the Indonesian government to prosecute officials charged with crimes of violence committed in East Timor. See "Annan Downplays International Tribunal for East Timor Suspects," *Associated Press*, May 18, 2002. After an Indonesian court in August 2002 imposed only a three-year sentence on one defendant and acquitted five others accused of serious crimes in East Timor, the former head of the UN Assistance Mission in East Timor called upon the UN to establish an international tribunal. See Moore, "World Urged to Act," *The Age* (Melbourne), August 17, 2002. The UN high commissioner for human rights, Mary Robinson, also voiced concern about

the verdict. See UN News Centre Report: Robinson Concerned by Indonesia's First Verdict on Crimes Committed in East Timor, August 14, 2002.

85. S.C. Res. 731, para. 3 (1992).

86. S.C. Res. 748 (1992); S.C. Res. 883 (1993).

87. One exception is that the defendants' guilt was determined by a panel comprising three Scottish judges instead of a jury.

88. See Paul Lewis, "Libya Sets Date for Turning over 2 Suspects in Lockerbie Bombing," *New York Times,* March 20, 1999. The proposal put forth by the U.S. and U.K. was a modified version of a proposal previously made by the Libyan government for trial in a third country. See ibid.

89. See Daily Press Briefing of Office of Spokesman for Secretary-General, April 5, 1999.

90. See Martin Fletcher, "Moment Relatives Faced the Accused," *Times* (London), May 4, 2000.

91. See Donald G. McNeil Jr., "Libyan Convicted by Scottish Court in '88 Pan Am Blast; 2nd Defendant Freed—Verdict Is Not Likely to End U.S. Curbs," *New York Times,* February 1, 2001.

92. See Marlise Simons, "Lockerbie Bomber Loses Appeal and Begins Sentence," *New York Times,* March 15, 2002.

93. In respect of the Scottish victims, the court's authority was further supported by the principle of passive personality, pursuant to which states may assert jurisdiction over certain crimes when the victims are their nationals.

94. 28 U.S.C. § 1350. Since 1991 the Torture Victim Protection Act (TVPA), 28 U.S.C. § 1350 note, has provided a second basis for suits in U.S. courts based upon acts committed abroad when the alleged violations entail extrajudicial executions and torture. In contrast to the ATCA, which provides jurisdiction only when the plaintiff is an alien, the TVPA provides a cause of action for both U.S. nationals and aliens.

95. 630 F.2d 876 (2d Cir. 1980).

96. Ibid., 890.

97. Ralph G. Steinhardt, "Fulfilling the Promise of Filartiga: Litigating Human Rights Claims against the Estate of Ferdinand Marcos," *Yale Journal of International Law* 20 (1995): 66–67. If the *Filartiga* line of cases seeks legal authority in the principle of universality, key decisions are vague about the extent to which universal jurisdiction can be transposed to a civil context. Consider, for example, Judge Edwards's observation in his concurring opinion in Tel-Oren v. Libyan Arab Republic, 726 F.2d 774 (D.C. Cir. 1984) (per curiam). Parsing the landmark *Filartiga* decision for its legal lessons, Judge Edwards observed: "Judge Kaufman did not argue that the torturer is like a pirate for criminal prosecution purposes, but only for civil actions. The inference is that persons may be susceptible to civil liability if they commit *either* a crime traditionally warranting universal jurisdiction *or* an offense that comparably violates current norms of international law." Ibid., 781 (Edwards, J., concurring) (emphasis in original).

98. See Clifford Krauss, "High Court Voids Charges for Pinochet; Sets New Date," *New York Times,* December 21, 2000 ("[A] trial would have been unthinkable [in Chile] until General Pinochet was arrested two years ago in London on a Spanish warrant").

99. See Richard A. Falk, "Assessing the Pinochet Litigation: Whither Universal Jurisdiction?" this volume.

100. Numerous charges were in fact pressed against Pinochet following his return to Chile in March 2000 (British authorities allowed the former president to return home on grounds of ill health after keeping him under house arrest for sixteen months). In May 2000 a Chilean court ruled for the first time that Pinochet's immunity

as senator for life was not a bar to his indictment in connection with certain crimes then under investigation by Judge Juan Guzmán. See Clifford Krauss, "Chile Strips Pinochet of Immunity, Lifting One Barrier to Trial," *New York Times,* May 25, 2000. The Chilean supreme court upheld this ruling in August 2000. See Clifford Krauss, "Pinochet Ruled No Longer Immune from Prosecution," *New York Times,* August 9, 2000. Efforts to prosecute Pinochet in Chile came to an end as a result of a ruling by an appeals court in Santiago in July 2001 that the former president, then eighty-five years old, was mentally unfit to stand trial. See Clifford Krauss, "Chile Court Bars Trial of Pinochet; Rules He's Too Ill for Charges of Covering Up '73 Killings," *New York Times,* July 10, 2001. One year later the ruling was reaffirmed by Chile's highest court. "Court Rules Pinochet Unfit to Stand Trial," *Associated Press,* July 2, 2002.

101. As noted earlier, on September 1, 2000, Indonesian prosecutors named nineteen people, including three generals, as potential suspects. Later developments in the Indonesian prosecutions are described above in note 81.

102. See David Bosco, "Dictators in the Dock," *American Prospect* (August 14, 2000): 28–29 (quoting views of John Bolton).

103. See Richard J. Wilson, "Prosecuting Pinochet: International Crimes in Spanish Domestic Law," *Human Rights Quarterly* 21 (1999): 931–932.

104. For further discussion of cross-fertilization among courts belonging to different legal systems, see Amnon Reichman, "'When We Sit to Judge, We Are Being Judged': The Israeli *GSS* Case, *Ex Parte Pinochet* and Domestic/Global Deliberation," *Cardozo Journal of International and Comparative Law* 9 (2001): 41–103; Anne-Marie Slaughter, "Judicial Globalization," *Virginia Journal of International Law* 40 (2000): 1103–24.

105. Regina v. Bartle et al., Opinion of Lord Brown-Wilkinson, [1999] 2 W.L.R. 827, March 24, 1999, quoting Prosecutor v. Anto Furundžija, Case. No. IT-95-17/1-T, Judgment, December 10, 1998.

106. See, e.g., The Prosecutor v. Duško Tadić, Case No. IT-94-1-AR72, Decision on the Defence Motion for Interlocutory Appeal on Jurisdiction, para. 57, October 2, 1995 (citing decision of the Supreme Court of Israel in the *Eichmann* case); Prosecutor v. Anto Furundžija, Case No. IT-95-17/1-T, Judgment, para. 153 n. 170, December 10, 1998 (citing five decisions of United States federal courts).

107. See, e.g., Prosecutor v. Anto Furundžija, Case No. IT-95-17/1-T, Judgment, para. 160 nn.179, 180, December 10, 1998 (citing decisions of European Court of Human Rights and UN Human Rights Committee).

108. Still, "correction" through disagreement by a court in another jurisdiction cannot repair the harm to a defendant's rights if he is prosecuted pursuant to an incorrect interpretation of international law. I consider this issue in Orentlicher, "The Role of Domestic Courts."

109. The action that initiated the investigation of Pinochet was filed by the Association of Progressive Prosecutors of Spain acting as private complainants. After this association set the criminal process in motion, lawyers for the victims took over the private prosecution of the case through a device in Spanish law known as an *acción popular.* Originally, the action named only seven victims of Spanish descent who had been killed or disappeared in Chile. The action later broadened to include hundreds of victims, including Chileans who did not possess dual Spanish citizenship. NGOs in Spain and Chile, as well as international NGOs such as Amnesty International and Human Rights Watch, played a key role in support of the private prosecutors' efforts in Spain and in the legal proceedings in England. See Wilson, "Prosecuting Pinochet," 932–36.

110. For a comprehensive account of these proceedings, see ibid.

111. See Stephen P. Marks, "The *Hissène Habré* Case: The Law and Politics of Universal Jurisdiction," this volume; Bosco, "Dictators in the Dock." After the proceedings against Habré were dismissed in Senegal, more than fifty Chadian victims

filed cases against Habré in Chad itself. Again, the victims acted with the support of both national and international NGOs. See Douglas Farah, "Chad's Torture Victims Pursue Habre in Court; Pinochet Case Leaves Ex-Dictator Vulnerable," *Washington Post,* November 27, 2000. Meanwhile, twenty-one victims, including three Belgian citizens, filed a case against Habré in Belgium. The same transnational coalition of NGOs that instituted proceedings in Senegal and Chad supported these victims' efforts in Belgium. See Human Rights Watch, "The Case Against Hissène Habré, an 'African Pinochet'," available at www.hrw.org/justice/habre/intro_web2.htm. A Belgian investigating judge visited Chad to investigate the charges against Habré in February and March 2002. In October 2002, the government of Chad advised Belgian authorities that it had waived Habré's immunity from prosecution.

112. See note 3 above.

113. On the conceptual link between piracy and crimes punished in the postwar period, see Randall, "Universal Jurisdiction," 803–4. For a careful and exhaustive study of the evolution of piracy law, which highlights common misconceptions about its status in international law, see Alfred P. Rubin, *The Law of Piracy* (Newport: Naval War College Press, 1988).

114. Filartiga v. Pena-Irala, 630 F.2d 876, 890 (2d Cir. 1980); see also Prosecutor v. Anto Furundžija, Case No. IT-95-17/1-T, Judgment, para. 147, December 10, 1998 (quoting Filartiga).

115. United States v. Otto Ohlendorf et al., 4 *Trials of War Criminals before Nuernberg Military Tribunals under Control Council Law No. 10* (1950): 411.

116. Ibid., 497.

117. Ibid., 498.

118. Ibid., 499.

119. Attorney General of Israel v. Eichmann, reprinted in 36 I.L.R. 18, 26 (Isr. Dist. Ct.–Jerusalem 1961), aff'd, 36 I.L.R. 277 (Isr. Sup. Ct. 1962) (hereinafter "Eichmann–District Court Opinion").

120. In re List, 11 *Trials of War Criminals,* at 757 (U.S. Mil. Trib.–Nuremberg 1948). See also Hadamar Trial, 1 *L. Rep. Trials of War Criminals,* at 53 (1949) (U.S. Military Commission claimed jurisdiction regardless of nationality of defendants and victims and "of the place where the offence was committed, particularly where, for some reason, the criminal would otherwise go unpunished").

121. The literature on South Africa's Truth and Reconciliation Commission is large and growing. For a particularly thoughtful assessment, see Martha Minow, *Between Vengeance and Forgiveness: Facing History after Genocide and Mass Violence* (Boston: Beacon Press, 1998).

122. United States v. Otto Ohlendorf et al., 4 *Trials of War Criminals,* 411.

123. As Amy Gutmann has argued, our commitment to universal human rights does not override our membership in other communities. In fact, Gutmann insists, "[W]e need to be citizens of some polity to be free and equal." Amy Gutmann, "Democratic Citizenship," in Martha C. Nussbaum et al., *For Love of Country?,* ed. Joshua Cohen (Boston: Beacon Press, 1996, 2002): 68.

124. These values are reflected in Principle 8 of the Princeton Principles on Universal Jurisdiction, "Resolution of Competing National Jurisdictions." Principle 8(g) cites "the fairness and impartiality of the proceedings in the requesting state" as one of the considerations that should be weighed by a state when deciding whether to exercise universal jurisdiction or, instead, to extradite the suspect to another state. "The Princeton Principles on Universal Jurisdiction," this volume.

125. That the territorial state has a special interest in prosecuting persons suspected of having committed an international crime is implicit in Principle 8(b) of the Princeton Principles, which cites "the place of commission of the crime" as one of the factors to be weighed when a state decides whether to prosecute a suspect

pursuant to universal jurisdiction or extradite him to another state. "The Princeton Principles on Universal Jurisdiction," this volume.

126. This restriction operates even if the state has decided not to prosecute a suspect after undertaking an investigation, provided the decision was not itself a result of the state's inability or unwillingness to prosecute. Rome Statute, art. 17(1)(b).

127. Article 17(1) of the Rome Statute provides in pertinent part that "the Court shall determine that a case is inadmissible where:

(a) The case is being investigated or prosecuted by a State which has jurisdiction over it, unless the State is unwilling or unable genuinely to carry out the investigation or prosecution;

(b) The case has been investigated by a State which has jurisdiction over it and the State has decided not to prosecute the person concerned, unless the decision resulted from the unwillingness or inability of the State genuinely to prosecute;

(c) The person concerned has already been tried for conduct which is the subject of the complaint, and a trial by the Court is not permitted under [the provision in the Rome Statute setting forth its *ne bis in idem* rule]. . . ."

In situations where the ICC seeks custody of a suspect from a state party that has received a request to extradite that same person to another state party, the requested state is supposed to give priority to the court's request, provided the court has determined the case to be admissible. Rome Statute, art. 90(2). This requirement is, however, contingent on the court having determined the case to be admissible after taking account of the investigation or prosecution conducted by the requesting state. Conceivably, the court could determine that the requesting state's proceedings render the case inadmissible in light of Article 17 even when the requesting state is exercising universal jurisdiction. (Article 90(6) specifies somewhat different rules for situations in which the requested state is a party to the Rome Statute but the state requesting extradition is not.)

128. Notably, the Israeli court that convicted Adolf Eichmann justified its exercise of universal jurisdiction as a second-best alternative to trial before an international tribunal: international law is, it asserted, "in the absence of an International Court, in need of the judicial and legislative organs of every country to give effect to its criminal interdictions and to bring the criminals to trial." Eichmann–District Court Opinion, 26. More recently, when the U.S. government tried to persuade Canadian authorities to seek the extradition of Pol Pot, many thought it inappropriate for Canada, which had no direct links to the crimes of the Khmer Rouge in Cambodia, to play a central role in punishing them. This, it seemed, was the work of an international tribunal.

129. Opened for signature in Paris, December 13, 1957; entered into force, April 18, 1960; E.T.S. No. 24.

130. Ibid., art. 17.

131. Rome Statute, art. 90(6). This provision addresses only situations where a state party receives with respect to the same person both a request for surrender from the ICC and an extradition request from another state: (1) that is not a party to the Rome Statute; and (2) with which the requested state has a treaty obligation to extradite the person.

132. Several conventions relevant to the issues addressed in this essay contain analogous provisions. The four Geneva Conventions of 1949 and the 1984 Convention against Torture and Other Cruel, Inhuman or Degrading Treatment or Punishment include provisions requiring states parties to either assert jurisdiction over persons in their territory believed to have committed specified offenses or hand them over to another state for prosecution. In the view of some writers, a duty

to extradite or punish also exists with respect to certain human rights offenses under customary international law.

The Princeton Principles address this subject in Principle 10(2). Since the meaning of this provision turns in part on the content of Principle 10(1), it is helpful to read the two paragraphs together:

PRINCIPLE 10—GROUNDS FOR REFUSAL OF EXTRADITION

1. A state or its judicial organs shall refuse to entertain a request for extradition based on universal jurisdiction if the person sought is likely to face a death penalty sentence or to be subjected to torture or any other cruel, degrading, or inhuman punishment or treatment, or if it is likely that the person sought will be subjected to sham proceedings in which international due process norms will be violated and no satisfactory assurances to the contrary are provided.
2. A state which refuses to extradite on the basis of this Principle shall, when permitted by international law, prosecute the individual accused of a serious crime under international law as specified in Principle 2(1) or extradite such person to another state where this can be done without exposing him or her to the risks referred to in paragraph 1.

"The Princeton Principles on Universal Jurisdiction," this volume.

133. These considerations are elaborated in the commentary to the Princeton Principles explaining the background to Principle 8. Principle 8 advocates that states deciding whether to exercise universal jurisdiction or extradite a suspect to another state should base their determination on an assessment of various criteria. The commentary notes:

Originally, the drafters expressed a preference for ranking the different bases of jurisdiction so as to indicate which should receive priority in the case of a conflict. Almost without exception, the territorial principle was thought to deserve precedence. This was in part because of the longstanding conviction that a criminal defendant should be tried by his "natural judge." Many participants expressed the view that societies that have been victimized by political crimes should have the opportunity to bring the perpetrators to justice, provided their judiciaries are able and willing to do so.

"Commentary on the Principles," this volume.

134. The relevance of such links is reflected in Principle 8(c, d) of the Princeton Principles, which recognize the following as circumstances that should be weighed by a state deciding whether to prosecute a suspect under the principle of universal jurisdiction or extradite him to another state:

(c) the nationality connection of the alleged perpetrator to the requesting state;
(d) the nationality connection of the victim to the requesting state.

"The Princeton Principles on Universal Jurisdiction," this volume.

135. This is because the state of nationality of the perpetrator would generally be able to assert jurisdiction based upon the nationality principle, while the state whose nationality the victim possesses may be able to exercise jurisdiction pursuant to the principle of passive personality.

136. Notably, the Spanish criminal proceedings against both Argentine and Chilean military officials began with complaints filed on behalf of victims of Spanish nationality and were thus supported by the jurisdictional theory of passive

personality. As noted earlier, the Chilean case was instituted by seven victims of Spanish descent who had been killed or disappeared in Chile and later broadened to include petitioners who possessed only Chilean nationality. See note 109 above.

137. See generally Diane F. Orentlicher, "Addressing Gross Human Rights Abuses: Punishment and Victim Compensation," in *Human Rights: An Agenda for the Next Century,* ed. Louis Henkin and John Lawrence Hargrove (Washington, D.C.: American Society of International Law, 1994): 425–75.

138. Prosecutor v. Anto Furundžija, Case No. IT-95-17/1-T, Judgment, para. 155, December 10, 1998.

139. One issue meriting further consideration is whether the answer to this question should be different with respect to civil actions than in respect of criminal prosecutions based on universal jurisdiction.

140. The commentary to the Princeton Principles on Universal Jurisdiction notes that some contributors to the principles believed that certain types of amnesties might be legitimate. See "Commentary on the Principles," this volume.

Chapter 12. Universal Jurisdiction and Judicial Reluctance: A New "Fourteen Points"

1. M. D. Kirby, "The Australian Use of International Human Rights Norms: From Bangalore to Balliol: A View from the Antipodes," *University of New South Wales Law Journal* 16 (1993): 363.

2. E. W. Thomas, "Judging in the Twenty-first Century," *New Zealand Law Journal* 228 (2000): 229.

3. Stephen P. Marks, "The *Hissène Habré* Case: The Law and Politics of Universal Jurisdiction," this volume.

4. Attorney General of Israel v Eichmann (1962) 36 ILR 277. Israel is not strictly a common-law country but, because of the period of the British Mandate, it has retained some features of the common law.

5. Nazi and Nazi Collaborators (Punishment) Law 1950 (Israel).

6. R v Bow Street Stipendiary Magistrate and Ors; ex parte Pinochet Ugarte, No. 3, [2000] IAC 147 at 275–76, 290–92; *cf.* Polyukhovich v The Commonwealth (1991) 172 CLR 501.

7. Nulyarimma v Thompson (1999) 165 ALR 621 at 622 (160), per Merkel J. See D Guilfoyle, "*Nulyarimma v Thompson:* Is Genocide a Crime at Common Law in Australia?" *Federal Law Review* 29 (2001): 1.

8. Wadjularbinna Nulyarimma v Thompson (2000) 21(15) Leg Rep SL1a, High Court of Australia, per Gummow, Kirby, and Hayne JJ (refusing special leave).

9. R. Dworkin, *Law's Empire* (Cambridge: Harvard University Press, 1986), 225–30, 378; E. W. Thomas, "Fairness and Certainty in Adjudication: Formalism v Substantialism, *Otago Law Review* 9 (1999): 459.

10. Bush v Gore 531 U.S. 98 (2000).

11. E. W. Thomas, "Judging in the Twenty-First Century," *New Zealand Law Journal* (2000): 228; J. Steyn, "Does Legal Formalism Hold Sway in England?" 49 (II) *Current Legal Problems* 43 at 46.

12. See, e.g., International Covenant on Civil and Political Rights, art. 14(1).

13. Convention on the Prevention and Punishment of the Crime of Genocide, 1948. See Genocide Convention Act 1949 (Aust); Extradition Act 1988 (Aust), s 5. The definition in the latter act of "political offence" excludes genocide from the political offences exemption from orders for extradition from Australia.

14. Thorpe v The Commonwealth, No. 3 (1997) 71 ALR 767.

15. Mabo v Queensland, No. 2 (1992) 175 CLR 1.

16. R v Sparrow [1990] 1 S.C.R. 1108: see also New Zealand Maori Council v Attorney-General (1987) 1 NZLR 641 referred to in Thomas, note 2 above, 231; *cf.* Mabo v Queensland, No. 2 (1992) 175 CLR 1 at 203–5 per Toohey J; *cf.* at 166–67 per Dawson J. See also Coe v The Commonwealth (1993) 68 ALJR 110 at 1116–18.

17. Australian Constitution, s 75(iii).

18. *Re Limbo* (1989) 64 ALJR 241.

19. Nulyarimma v Thompson, unreported proceedings in the High Court of Australia, note 8 above.

20. Nulyarimma v Thompson (1999) 165 ALR 621.

21. Nulyarimma v Thompson, unreported transcript of the special leave hearing in the High Court of Australia, note 8 above, at 22.

22. Anne-Marie Slaughter, "Defining the Limits: Universal Jurisdiction and National Courts," this volume.

23. In Australia the requirement is expressed in John Pfeiffer Pty Ltd v Rogerson (2000) 203 CLR 503 at 562 (154).

24. M. Cherif Bassiouni, "The History of Universal Jurisdiction and Its Place In International Law," this volume.

25. Ibid.

26. Stephen A. Oxman, "Comment: The Quest for Clarity," this volume.

27. Richard A. Falk, "Assessing the Pinochet Litigation: Whither Universal Jurisdiction?," this volume.

28. A point made by Lord Millett in R v Bow Street Metropolitan Stipendiary Magistrate and Ors; Ex parte Pinochet Ugarte [no 3] [2000] IAC 147 at 275–79, noted Falk, "Assessing the Pinochet Litigation." See also Lipohar v The Queen (1999) 200 CLR 485 at 497 (15), 521 (91), 546 (154).

29. Diane F. Orentlicher, "The Future of Universal Jurisdiction in the New Architecture of Transnational Justice," this volume. *Cf.* Lipohar v The Queen (1999) 200 CLR 485 at 550 (164).

30. Bassiouni, "History of Universal Jurisdiction."

31. E.g., in Australia Dietrich v The Queen (1992) 177 CLR 292 (right to counsel); Theophanous v Herald and Weekly Times Limited (1994) 182 CLR 104 (implied right to free speech); Mabo v Queensland, No. 2 (1992) 175 CLR 1 (right to native title).

32. See, e.g., Alien Torts Act (U.S.) considered in *Filartiga* 630 F 2d 876 (1980). See also 18 USC, para. 2340, explained in Orentlicher, "Future of Universal Jurisdiction." For the Canadian position, see The Queen v Finta [1994] 1 S.C.R. 701, reviewed in Slaughter, "Limits of Universal Jurisdiction."

33. This is the language of the German Federal Constitutional Court. See Bassiouni, "History of Universal Jurisdiction."

34. *Cf.* Lipohar v The Queen (1999) 200 CLR 485 at 561 (194).

35. Bassiouni, "History of Universal Jurisdiction."

36. Slaughter, "Limits of Universal Jurisdiction."

37. *The Chinese Exclusion Case* 130 U.S. 581 at 603 (1889); Hyde v United States 225 U.S. 347 at 391 (1911); J. Treves, "Jurisdictional Aspects of the Eichmann Case" 47 Minnesota Law Review 557 at 591; *cf.* The Commonwealth v Yamirr (1999) 168 CLR 426 at 527 (474).

38. The Queen v Foster; ex parte Eastern and Australian Steamship Co Ltd (1959) 103 CLR 256 at 306 per Windeyer J; *cf.* Morgan v White (1912) 15 CLR 1 at 13 per J. Isaacs.

39. Compania Naviera Vascongado v SS Christina [1938] AC 485 at 496–97 per Lord MacMillan.

40. MacLeod v Attorney-General for New South Wales [1891] AC 455 at 458 (PC).

41. See, e.g., Asbhury v Ellis [1893] AC 339 at 358.

42. The King v Oliphant [1905] 2 KB 61 at 72–73.

43. The Queen v Doot [1973] AC 807 at 817 per Lord Wilberforce.

44. Liangsiriprasert v United States [1991] 1 AC 225 at 251 per Lord Griffiths.

45. Marks, "*Hissséne Habré* Case."

46. Slaughter, "Limits of Universal Jurisdiction."

47. Board of Trade v Owen [1957] AC 602 at 628; Lipohar v The Queen (1999) 200 CLR 485 at 555 (175).

48. E.g., by s 118 of the Australian Constitution requiring that "full faith and credit shall be given, throughout the Commonwealth, to the laws . . . and the judicial process of every State."

49. E.g., in Australia the provision of legislation conferring jurisdiction on interstate courts in certain criminal cases mentioned in Lipohar v The Queen (1999) 200 CLR 485 at 545 (148).

50. Lipohar v The Queen (1999) 200 CLR 485.

51. The statute of the International Criminal Court gives primacy to prosecution before national courts. See Orentlicher, "Future of Universal Jurisdiction." Presumably, such primacy is based ultimately on notions of the predominance of the jurisdiction where the crime occurred.

52. The Queen v Barlow (1997) 188 CLR 1 at 31 (1).

53. Reg v Knuller (Publishing, Printing and Promotions) Ltd [1973] AC 435 (HL); Lipohar v The Queen (1999) 200 CLR 485 at 561 (194).

54. *Cf.* Slaughter, "Limits of Universal Jurisdiction."

55. *Cf.* Polyukhovich v The Queen (1991) 172 CLR 501 at 508–610; Lipohar v The Queen (1999) 200 CLR 485 at 561 (194). See also Slaughter, "Defining the Limits."

56. R. Higgins, "The Role of National Courts in the International Legal Process," in *Problems and Process: International Law and How We Use It* (Oxford: Clarendon Press, 1994), 205.

57. The Queen v Finta [1994] 1 S.C.R. 701 at 872–874 per Cory J; *cf.* Slaughter, "Limits of Universal Jurisdiction."

58. Slaughter, "Limits of Universal Jurisdiction."

59. J. J. Paust, "Universal Jurisdiction, Universal Responsibility, and Related Principles of International Law," unpublished manuscript presented at Princeton Project on Universal Jurisdiction Conference, November 10–11, 2000.

60. G. Triggs, "Australia's War Crimes Trials: A Moral Necessity or Legal Minefield?" (1987) 16 *Melbourne University Law* Review 282 at 389, noted Slaughter, "Limits of Universal Jurisdiction," 30; *cf.* Lipohar v The Queen (1999) 200 CLR 485 at 561 (194).

61. Paust, "Universal Jurisdiction."

62. The United States District Court held that "the fact that the State of Israel was not in existence . . . is no bar to Israel's exercising jurisdiction under the universality principle": Demjanjuk v Petrovsky 681 F Supp 896 at 900–901 (1988) aff'd, 924 F 2F 2d 1086 (DC Cir 1991).

63. The Queen v Finta [1994] 1 S.C.R. 701 at 732–33, La Forest, J dissenting, discussed in Slaughter, "Limits of Universal Jurisdiction."

64. Ibid.

65. Bassiouni, "History of Universal Jurisdiction."

66. Ibid.

67. Ibid. On piracy, see also Slaughter, "Limits of Universal Jurisdiction," and Paust, "Universal Jurisdiction," who draws an analogy to modern crimes of aircraft hijacking and international terrorism.

68. Bassiouni, "History of Universal Jurisdiction."

69. Ibid.

70. Ibid

71. Slaughter, "Limits of Universal Jurisdiction."
72. Ibid.
73. Orentlicher, "Future of Universal Jurisdiction."
74. L. N. Sadat, "Universal Jurisdiction, National Amnesties, and Truth Commissions: Reconciling the Irreconcilable.
75. E.g., the case of Chile: see Falk, "Assessing the Pinochet Litigation."
76. Sadat, "National Amnesties."
77. Ibid.
78. Falk, "Assessing the Pinochet Litigation"; see also Marks, "*Hisséne Habré* Case" (discussing the scope of head of state immunity).
79. Ibid.
80. Ibid.
81. Orentlicher, "Future of Universal Jurisdiction."
82. Pablo De Greiff, "Comment: Universal Jurisdiction and Transitions to Democracy", this volume (hereinafter "Transitions to Democracy").
83. Ibid.
84. Marks, "*Hisséne Habré* Case."
85. Paust, "Universal Jurisdiction."
86. Sadat, "National Amnesties."
87. See the recent decision of the International Court of Justice in *Democratic Republic of the Congo v Belgium* (2002) 14 International Legal Materials 536–653. In that decision the court held that the issue of an international arrest warrant under Belgian law against a person who at the time of the warrant (although not thereafter) was the minister of foreign affairs of the Congo, on the basis of allegations that he was guilty of crimes against humanity and the Geneva Convention of 1949, was a violation of international law.
88. Lori F. Damrosch, "Comment: Connecting the Threads in the Fabric of International Law"; *cf.* Slaughter, "Limits of Universal Jurisdiction."
89. E.g., the seizure by Israel of Eichmann or other extraterritorial seizures by the United States. Damrosch, "Connecting the Threads." See also Bass, "Adolf Eichmann Case."
90. Marks, "*Hisséne Habré* Case."
91. Falk, "Assessing the Pinochet Litigation."
92. Orentlicher, "Future of Universal Jurisdiction."
93. Oxman, "Quest for Clarity."
94. Falk, "Assessing the Pinochet Litigation."
95. Orentlicher, "Future of Universal Jurisdiction."
96. Ibid.
97. Marks, "*Hisséne Habré* Case."
98. Ibid.; Orentlicher, "Future of Universal Jurisdiction."
99. Bassiouni, "History of Universal Jurisdiction."
100. See Joint Statement of Dato' Param Cumaraswamy and Sir Nigel Rodley, special rapporteurs of the United Nations, noted in Marks, "*Hisséne Habré* Case."
101. Orentlicher, "Future of Universal Jurisdiction."
102. Sadat, "National Amneties."
103. Orentlicher, "Future of Universal Jurisdiction."
104. Ibid.
105. Ibid.
106. Gary J. Bass, "The Adolf Eichman Case: Universal and National Jurisdictions"; *cf.* Bassiouni, "History of Universal Jurisdiction."
107. Orentlicher, "Future of Universal Jurisdiction."
108. Ibid.
109. Falk, "Assessing the Pinochet Litigation." For a discussion of the ICC and

universal jurisdiction, see N. Strapatsas, "Universal Jurisdiction and the International Criminal Court" *Manitoba Law Journal* 29 (2001): 1.

110. Ibid.

111. Ibid.

112. Bass, "Adolf Eichman Case."

113. Orentlicher, "Future of Universal Jurisdiction."

114. De Greiff, "Transitions to Democracy."

115. Bassiouni, "History of Universal Jurisdiction."

116. Democratic Republic of the Congo v Belgium, (2002) 14 International Legal Materials 536–653, International Court of Justice, February 14, 2002, considered in Regie National des Usines Renaut SA v Zhang (2002) 76 ALJR 551 at 571 (107–8).

117. Slaughter, "Limits of Universal Jurisdiction," citing The Queen v Finta [1994] 1 S.C.R. 701 at 732–33. The same is true about executive governments, which will often be hesitant to override the territorial principle for fear of endangering relationships or provoking retaliation: ibid.

118. On the importance of recording the stories of victims, see Marks, "*Hisséne Habaré* Case."

119. *Cf.* Orentlicher, "Future of Universal Jurisdiction."

120. Oxman, "Quest for Clarity."

121. Bass, "Adolf Eichmann Case."

122. *Cf.* DeL v Director-General, NSW Department of Community Services (1996) 187 CLR 640, concerning the Family Law (Child Abduction Convention) Regulations 1986 (Aust).

123. (1992) 175 CLR 1.

124. (1992) 175 CLR 1 at 42 (footnote omitted).

125. E.G., Tavita v Minister of Immigration [1994] 2 NZLR at 266; R v Oakes [1986] 1 SCR 103 at 120–21; Claydon, "International Human Rights Law and the Interpretation of the Canadian Charter of Rights and Freedoms," *Supreme Court Law Review* 4 (1982): 287.

126. Atkins v. Virginia 70 USLW 4585 at 4589, fn 21 (2002) per Stevens J., with whom O'Connor, Kennedy, Souter, Ginsburg, and Breyer J. J. joined. That approach produced a strong dissent from Rehnquist C. J. at 4591 and Scalia J. at 4598 (with whom Thomas J. joined). See also Lawrence v. Texas 539 US 1 at 16 per Kennedy J. for the Court referring to decisions of the European Court of Human Rights on rights of homosexuals as "values shared with a wider civilization."

127. Bassiouni, "History of Universal Jurisdiction"; *cf.* Orentlicher, "Future of Universal Jurisdiction."

128. Bassiouni, "History of Universal Jurisdiction."

129. Paust, "Universal Jurisdiction."

130. Ibid.

131. Sadat, "National Amnesties."

132. E.g., Nulyarimma v Thompson (1999) 165 ALR 621.

133. Orentlicher, "Future of Universal Jurisdiction."

Contributors

DR. LLOYD AXWORTHY directs the Liu Institute for Global Issues at the University of British Columbia. He is former Minister of Foreign Affairs of Canada.

GARY J. BASS is Assistant Professor of Politics and International Affairs at Princeton University.

M. CHERIF BASSIOUNI is Professor of Law and President of the International Human Rights Law Institute, DePaul University. He was Chair of the United Nations' Drafting Committee on the International Criminal Court and Chair of the Security Council's Commission on the former Yugoslavia.

A. HAYS BUTLER is Librarian and Associate Professor at Rutgers University School of Law, Camden.

RICHARD A. FALK is Albert G. Milbank Professor of International Law and Practice and Professor of Politics and International Affairs, Emeritus, at Princeton University.

LORI F. DAMROSCH is the Henry L. Moses Professor of Law and International Organization at Columbia Law School, and Editor-in-Chief of the *American Journal of International Law.*

PABLO DE GREIFF is Director of Research at the International Center for Transitional Justice in New York.

THE HONORABLE JUSTICE MICHAEL KIRBY, AC CMG, is Justice of the High Court of Australia.

STEPHEN MACEDO is Laurance S. Rockefeller Professor of Politics and Director of the University Center for Human Values at Princeton University. He chairs the Princeton Project on Universal Jurisdiction.

STEPHEN P. MARKS is François-Xavier Bagnoud Professor of Health and Human Rights Harvard School of Public Health.

DIANE F. ORENTLICHER is Professor of International Law and Faculty Director of the War Crimes Research Office at American University's Washington College of Law.

STEPHEN A. OXMAN is a member of the Board of Directors of the American Association for the International Commission of Jurists. He was Assistant Secretary of State for European and Canadian Affairs during the first Clinton administration. He is currently a Senior Advisor at Morgan Stanley.

LEILA NADYA SADAT is Professor of Law at Washington University School of Law, St. Louis.

ANNE-MARIE SLAUGHTER is Dean of the Woodrow Wilson School of Public and International Affairs, and Professor of Politics and International Affairs at Princeton University.

Project Participants

Adoption of Principles, January 25–27, 2001

Adrian Arena
Acting Secretary-General, International Commission of Jurists

Lloyd Axworthy
Director of the Liu Centre for the Study of Global Issues, University of British Columbia; Former Minister of Foreign Affairs of the Federal Government of Canada

Gary J. Bass
Assistant Professor of Politics and International Affairs, Princeton University

M. Cherif Bassiouni
Professor of Law and President of the International Human Rights Law Institute, DePaul College of Law

Nicolas Browne-Wilkinson *(Did not join in the adoption. See "Commentary," note 20)* Law Lord, House of Lords of the United Kingdom

William J. Butler
Former Chairman of the Executive Committee of the International Commission of Jurists, 1975–90; President of the American Association for the International Commission of Jurists

Hans Corell
Under-Secretary-General for Legal Affairs, United Nations

Param Cumaraswamy
United Nations Special Rapporteur on the Independence of the Judiciary

E. V. O. Dankwa
Professor of Law, University of Ghana; Chair, African Commission on Human and Peoples Rights

Richard A. Falk
Professor of Politics and International Affairs, Emeritus, Princeton University

Tom Farer
Dean of the Graduate School of International Studies, University of Denver

Cees Flinterman
Professor of Human Rights, Utrecht University; Director of the Netherlands Institute of Human Rights and the Netherlands School of Human Rights Research

Mingxuan Gao
Professor of Law, China Law Institute

Menno T. Kamminga
Professor of Public International Law, Maastricht University

Michael Kirby
Justice, High Court of Australia

Bert B. Lockwood
Distinguished Service Professor of Law; Director of the Urban Morgan Institute for Human Rights, University of Cincinnati College of Law

Stephen Macedo
Laurance S. Rockefeller Professor of Politics and the University Center for Human Values of Princeton University; Director of the University Center for Human Values

Stephen P. Marks
François Xavier Bagnoud Professor, Harvard School of Public Health

Michael O'Boyle
Section Registrar, European Court of Human Rights

Diane F. Orentlicher
Law and Public Affairs Fellow, 2000–2001, Princeton University; Professor
of Law and Director of the War Crimes Research Office, American
University

Stephen A. Oxman
Member of the Board of Directors, American Association for the
International Commission of Jurists; former U.S. Assistant Secretary of
State for European and Canadian Affairs

Vesselin Popovski
Professor of Law, University of Exeter

Michael Posner
Executive Director, Lawyers Committee for Human Rights

Yves Sandoz
Former Director of Principles and International Law, International
Committee of the Red Cross

Jerome J. Shestack
Former President, American Bar Association; Member of the Executive
Committee, International Commission of Jurists

Stephen M. Schwebel
Former President, International Court of Justice

Kuniji Shibahara
Professor Emeritus, University of Tokyo

Anne-Marie Slaughter
Dean of the Woodrow Wilson School of Public and International Affairs,
and Professor of Politics and International Affairs at Princeton University

Turgut Tarhanli
Professor of International Law, Istanbul Bilgi University

Wang Xiumei
Senior Researcher, Renmin University of China

Index

Acknowledgments

The Princeton Project began with a visit to Princeton by William J. Butler and Stephen A. Oxman in January 2000. Dean Michael Rothschild of the Woodrow Wilson School of Public and International Affairs asked me to join the meeting in my capacity as Founding Director of Princeton's new Program in Law and Public Affairs. The idea had great appeal as a chance to bring scholars and jurists together to reflect upon an important problem in the law and to address that problem in a thoughtful but practical way. Our hope all along has been to wed theory and practice: to study a set of difficult problems of international justice with the goal of arriving at consensus principles.

The Princeton Project on Universal Jurisdiction is a joint venture of Princeton University's Program in Law and Public Affairs, the Woodrow Wilson School of Public and International Affairs, the International Commission of Jurists (ICJ), the American Association for the ICJ, the Urban Morgan Institute for Human Rights, and the Netherlands Institute of Human Rights. The members of the Steering Committee of the Project are Gary J. Bass, Assistant Professor of Politics and International Affairs, Princeton University; William J. Butler, Former Chairman, Executive Committee of the International Commission of Jurists, 1975–90, President, American Association for the International Commission of Jurists; Richard A. Falk, Professor Politics and International Affairs, Emeritus, Princeton University; Professor Cees Flinterman, Director of the Netherlands Institute of Human Rights; Professor Bert B. Lockwood, Distinguished Service Professor of Law and Director of the Urban Morgan Institute for Human Rights, University of Cincinnati College of Law; Stephen Macedo, Project Chair, Laurance S. Rockefeller Professor of Politics and the University Center for Human Values, Founding Director of the Program in Law and Public Affairs (1999–2001), and currently Director of the University Center for Human Values, Princeton University; and Stephen A. Oxman, Board of Directors, American Association for the International Commission of

Jurists, former U.S. Assistant Secretary of State for European and Canadian Affairs.

The Princeton Principles represent many months of drafting, discussion, and redrafting. The Drafting Committee was chaired by Professor M. Cherif Bassiouni of the DePaul College of Law. Professor Bassiouni's expertise and tireless energy have been essential at every stage. I also served on the Drafting Committee, along with Steve Oxman, Bill Butler, and Diane Orentlicher; we were joined in November by Christopher L. Blakesley, J. Y. Sanders Professor of Law at the Paul M. Hebert Law Center, Louisiana State University, as well as Lloyd L. Weinreb, Dane Professor of Law, Harvard Law School. The Drafting Committee benefited from the assistance of Steven W. Becker (J.D., DePaul University College of Law, 2001), Sullivan Fellow, International Human Rights Law Institute, DePaul College of Law, who served as research assistant to Professor Bassiouni and as rapporteur to the Drafting Committee.

Bill Butler and Steve Oxman brought to Princeton the idea of formulating principles of international law. I proposed adding an academic supplement to this worthy and practical endeavor, and this volume is the result. We commissioned a group of leading scholars to write papers on various aspects of universal jurisdiction. We gathered with these scholars in November 2000 to discuss early drafts of the Principles and the papers that compose this volume. Those who gathered ten weeks later to discuss and endorse the Principles in January 2001 had the benefit of the groundwork laid the previous November. Most of the contributors to this volume attended that November meeting, as did Georges Abi-Saab, Professor of International Law, The Graduate Institute of International Studies; George A. Bermann, Charles Keller Beekman Professor of Law and Director of the European Legal Studies Center, Columbia Law School; Marc Henzelin, Lecturer in International Criminal Law, University of Geneva; Jeffrey Herbst, Professor of Politics and International Affairs, Princeton University; Martha L. Minow, Professor of Law, Harvard Law School; Jordan Paust, Law Foundation Professor, University of Houston Law Center; W. Michael Reisman, Myres S. McDougal Professor of International Law, Yale Law School; and Chandra Sriram, Research Associate of the International Peace Academy. These scholars also contributed in important ways to our deliberations.

My thanks to the scholars who contributed essential intellectual underpinnings to this Project and also to the jurists who assembled from around the world in January—their intellectual and moral seriousness were all that we could have hoped for and more. Special thanks to Bill Butler and Steve Oxman for bringing this idea to Princeton University and to three at Princeton: Professors Gary J. Bass, Richard A. Falk, and Diane Orentlicher (who was here as Fellow, 2000–2001, in the Program in Law and Public Affairs). They furnished me with an unexpected but rewarding inaugural project for the Program in Law and Public Affairs, and their collaboration has increased the quality and enjoyment of every aspect of this enterprise.

Many people at Princeton University, especially in the Program in Law and Public Affairs (LAPA) and the Woodrow Wilson School of Public and International Affairs, helped plan and organize the two meetings of the Princeton Project on short notice. Cynthia Kinelski (of LAPA) went above and beyond the call of duty to pull together all of the practical details without which our meetings would not have run smoothly. She was assisted by Simon Stacey. Chandra Sriram helped us with research on universal jurisdiction in foreign legal sources, and Jonathan H. Marks, a Barrister of the Matrix Chambers in London and Visiting Lecturer at the Woodrow Wilson School, prepared an important analysis of recent developments with respect to universal jurisdiction which, unfortunately, there was not time to include in the current volume. Scott Wayland made essential editorial contributions while the Principles and supporting materials were in preparation. In the final stages of producing this book, Valerie Kanka and Kim Girman, of the University Center for Human Values, and Molly Wade spent many hours getting the various chapters in order. My thanks to Bert Lockwood for including this collection in his excellent series, to Peter Agree and Erica Ginsburg at the University of Pennsylvania Press for their care in preparing and producing the final product, and to Susan McWilliams and Will Gallaher for their proofreading assistance.